KERAMET REITER

23/7

PELICAN BAY PRISON
AND THE RISE OF LONG-TERM
SOLITARY CONFINEMENT

Yale
UNIVERSITY PRESS
NEW HAVEN & LONDON

Published with assistance from the foundation established in memory of
Amasa Stone Mather of the Class of 1907, Yale College.

Yale University Press books may be purchased in quantity for
educational, business, or promotional use. For information, please e-mail
sales.press@yale.edu (U.S. office) or sales@yaleup.co.uk (U.K. office).

Set in Scala and Scala Sans types by Integrated Publishing Solutions.
Printed in the United States of America.

ISBN 978-0-300-21146-7
Library of Congress Control Number: 2016939153

A catalogue record for this book is available from the British Library.

This paper meets the requirements of ANSI/NISO Z39.48-1992
(Permanence of Paper).

10 9 8 7 6 5 4 3 2 1

To anyone who has lived or worked
inside an American prison

CONTENTS

List of Abbreviations   ix

Introduction: When Prison Is Not Enough   1

1 A Supermax Life   10

2 The Most Dangerous Prisoner   34

3 The Most Dangerous Policies   59

4 Constructing the Supermax, One Rule at a Time   87

5 Skeleton Bay   121

6 Snitching or Dying   145

7 "You Can't Even Imagine There's People"   166

8 Another Way Out   194

Afterword   206

Notes   211
Bibliography   253
Acknowledgments   287
Index   293

ABBREVIATIONS

AB	Aryan Brotherhood
AC	Adjustment Center (at San Quentin Prison)
ACLU	American Civil Liberties Union
ADX	Administrative Maximum (a federal prison in Florence, Colorado)
ATF	Bureau of Alcohol, Tobacco, and Firearms
BGF	Black Guerrilla Family
CCPOA	California Correctional Peace Officers Association
CCR	Center for Constitutional Rights
CDC	California Department of Corrections (until 2005)
CDCR	California Department of Corrections and Rehabilitation (after 2005)
DSL	determinate sentencing law
ICC	Internal Classification Committee
IGI	internal gang investigator
JLCPCO	Joint Legislative Committee on Prison Construction and Operations
La Eme	Mexican Mafia
LWOP	life without the possibility of parole
NF	Nuestra Familia
PLO	Prison Law Office

SHU   Security Housing Unit
SMU   Special Management Unit
USP   United States Penitentiary
YACA   Youth and Adult Correctional Authority

Introduction

When Prison Is Not Enough

ON AUGUST 12, 2015, STEVE NOLEN WAS listening to the radio when mention of a melee in a California prison caught his attention. He rarely thought about California prisons anymore. Decades had passed since he spent every Sunday shuttling between visits with his brother Cornel, at San Quentin, and his brother W.L., a founding member of the Black Guerrilla Family, at Soledad State Prison. Cornel served his time and eventually was released. But W.L. had been shot to death on a California prison yard thirty-five years before, when Steve was a junior in college.

In the intervening years, Steve had established a successful career selling medical devices; he had never set foot in prison except to visit his brothers. But as he listened to news of the melee, he heard a name he recognized. The one prisoner killed in the fight was his brother W.L.'s old radical buddy Hugo "Yogi" Pinell.[1]

I asked Steve, "When you heard about Yogi, did it bring back memories of W.L. and—"

"Instant flashback. Instant. I fell off my chair. Literally fell off my chair . . . And I said, 'Yogi, still fighting like a young warrior out there.' Seventy-one years old. Seventy-one. By then they should have had compassion and let him go. But these guys—people don't understand these guys . . . They don't forget."[2]

Prison officials never forgot that Pinell was one of six prisoners accused of slitting the throats of prison guards while allegedly helping George Jackson try to escape from San Quentin Prison in August 1971.[3] Ever since that day, before, during, and after his trial as one of the "San Quentin Six," Pinell had been in solitary confinement: forty-five years, twenty-five of them in California's notorious Pelican Bay Security Housing Unit (SHU). Pinell remained in solitary confinement not because of the San Quentin Six accusation, but because every few years prison officials refiled documents, reestablishing the allegation that he was a leader of the Black Guerrilla Family prison gang. In 2014, he was denied parole for the ninth time, even though the parole board noted he had not been charged with a serious rule violation in thirty years.[4]

In 2015, things changed. Prison officials, who make such decisions freely, transferred Pinell from Pelican Bay into the general prison population at California State Prison, Sacramento, as part of an effort to reduce California's use of long-term solitary confinement. In the Sacramento prison, Pinell hugged his mother for the first time in forty-five years. A few weeks later, two prisoners in their late thirties, both with histories of committing assaults, approached Pinell on the prison yard and stabbed him to death.[5] Pinell's lawyer, Keith Wattley, said he had asked the prison system to take steps to protect his client, who was "a marked man," threatened by prison gangs.[6]

Yogi Pinell lived through the entire story of the supermax, or supermaximum-security prison: he was part of the event that inspired its creation, he spent most of his life in one, and he witnessed the first efforts at reform—efforts that led to his own death.

At the center of this story is California's Pelican Bay State Prison, a windowless concrete bunker with hundreds of cells designed for keeping prisoners in total solitary confinement not for days or weeks, as with previous solitary cells, but for years. The "Bay" opened in 1989. By 2010, more than five hundred prisoners had lived in continuous isolation there for more than ten years—a decade without a handshake or a hug. Not one of those five hundred was held because of a specific crime committed inside or outside prison. Instead, officials alleged that they were all dangerous gang affiliates, based on their tattoos, books, letters, or drawings. No judge or jury ever reviewed the decision to place any of these men in solitary, or the decision to keep them there. How did isolation like this become routine practice in California and across the United States?

First, no one was watching. Prison officials envisioned the first sleek, automated supermaxes and sited them in out-of-the-way places. In the 1980s, rural towns such as Crescent City, California, located on the Oregon border, vied for the chance to become home to one of the many new prisons popping up all over the United States.[7] (Between 1972 and 2007, U.S. incarceration rates quintupled—a phenomenon that has been dubbed "mass incarceration." During these years, California's prison population soared to the largest in the United States.)[8] Even after Pelican Bay opened in Crescent City, neither citizens nor local legislators knew what kind of prison had been built in their backyard. No politician took credit for imposing its harsh conditions of isolation.

This was a surprisingly overlooked political opportunity in the era of "penal populism," the modern heyday of tough-on-crime stances.[9] Super-majorities of California voters approved billions of dollars in public bonds to finance new prisons, and legislators and governors competed to look the toughest on crime. Today, Pelican Bay is an icon of this mentality, but in 1989 it was functionally invisible. This book introduces a prison official you have never heard of, Carl Larson, who told me that he designed Pelican Bay. Administrative discretion, the supermax story reveals, is even more powerful than penal populism.

No one was watching when prison officials opened Pelican Bay in 1989, but everyone had been watching eighteen years earlier. On August 21, 1971, George Jackson, best-selling author and founding member of the Black Guerrilla Family (then a behind-bars affiliate of the Black Panthers), was shot to death on the San Quentin prison yard. Prison officials said Jackson had been trying to escape from the isolation unit where he was housed. Three guards and two white prisoners also died in the alleged escape attempt. Two weeks later, prisoners at New York's Attica Correctional Facility rioted, taking control of the prison for four days. The state police effort to retake the facility killed more than forty people. In the face of this organized, radical violence, prison officials knew that prison was no longer enough. To them, George Jackson proved that new times required new tools of control.

At first, the prisoners alleged to have helped Jackson escape were "locked

4

down": isolated in their cells for months, then years. The last time prisoners in the United States were systematically isolated in this way was in the
mid–nineteenth century, in the first penitentiaries in Pennsylvania and
New York. In 1842, Charles Dickens famously denounced this extended
isolation as "worse than any torture of the body," and in 1890 the U.S. Supreme Court noted that the practice had been abandoned as barbaric.[10]

When George Jackson died in 1971, a few hundred beds designed for
temporary solitary confinement were scattered throughout six of California's twelve prisons. "Temporary" was a flexible concept; in practice, prisoners would spend twenty-nine days in these units, be released for a day to
avoid exceeding the legal limit of thirty days, and then be returned to isolation.[11] Just twenty years later, California had 1,056 cells designed for long-
term solitary at Pelican Bay alone, plus hundreds of cells in overflow units
in other new prisons: concentrated isolation, with no days off, in super-
sized facilities. California is an important site of study because its solitary-
confinement building project was unprecedented in both scale and harshness. In 1995, the state opened yet another 500-bed isolation unit in
Corcoran State Prison.[12] Would there ever be enough?

Prison officials, attempting to distinguish supermax units from the stark
image popularized by Dickens, resisted referring to conditions in these
new facilities as "solitary confinement." But in spite of its picturesque
name, Pelican Bay was tougher than the Quaker penitentiaries that shocked
Dickens. In Pennsylvania's Eastern State Penitentiary in the 1800s, prisoners in solitary confinement had access to personal exercise yards, with
grass, gardens, and natural light, along with "cell work" assignments during
the day to keep their hands (and minds) busy.[13] Prisoners at Pelican Bay
touch no grass, see no sunlight, and have no regular access to activities. And
although Pelican Bay is a modern architectural achievement, with smooth,
poured-concrete walls, centrally controlled, computer-automated doors,
and fluorescent lights that never turn off, life inside can be primal. Abuses
proliferated during its early years of operation. Guards dipped one prisoner
in scalding water until his skin peeled off. Other prisoners were left naked
and shivering in outdoor cages for hours at a time.[14] Dickens would have
been horrified.

Thelton Henderson, the federal judge who started receiving letters from prisoners at Pelican Bay soon after the prison opened, *was* horrified. In 1995, in the case *Madrid v. Gomez*, he ordered sustained independent oversight of the prison. Under judicial scrutiny, Pelican Bay guards stopped freely scalding, caging, beating, and shooting prisoners. Practices were streamlined and sterilized, in a rational and superficially compliant response to the legal oversight. Sociolegal scholars call the resulting pattern of compliance "legal endogeneity": courts impose minimum standards of humane treatment, prison officials redefine minimum standards as establishing prisoners' maximum privileges, and the courts defer.[15]

This redefinition produces a litany of justifications for long-term solitary confinement—necessary for safety and security, practical for managing the "worst of the worst"—that have normalized a practice condemned as torture by international human rights bodies.[16] In one reading, this practice illustrates what Hannah Arendt described as the "banality of evil."[17] The ongoing imposition of solitary confinement is not deliberate or malicious; rather, it is a culmination of everyday bureaucratic functioning and path dependency, in which one day of isolation becomes thirty days, and thirty days become thirty years.[18]

Judge Henderson's oversight of Pelican Bay paved the way for other states, and the federal government, to open more supermaxes, following the minimum standards of "humane" treatment established in the *Madrid* case. In 1995, the federal government opened its first supermax, the Administrative Maximum (ADX) in Florence, Colorado. Like Pelican Bay before it, ADX provided modern infrastructure to maintain the kind of long-term lockdowns that were initiated in the 1970s and 1980s in response to violent altercations between prisoners and guards in other federal prisons. Both California's Pelican Bay SHU and the federal ADX were modeled on the first supermax, opened in Arizona in 1986. American punishment policy may appear uniform and national after the fact, but a closer examination of the origins of the supermax reveals that it was actually a local innovation.[19]

The same administrative elites who invented the supermax continue to maintain significant discretion over its day-to-day operation. Just as no one really knew what kind of prison had been built in Crescent City in 1989, no one really knew what kind of prisoners were there, why they were there, or how long they would be there, even after the initiation of federal oversight in 1995. A "double government" was in operation: judges and juries sentenced criminals to prison through an established constitutional process, but prison officials decided which prisoners were punished most harshly through an opaque administrative process.[20] Gradually, the worst thing that a prison official could do to the worst prisoner—place him in indefinite isolation, usually based on gang status rather than a specific bad act—became standard practice for thousands of prisoners. Extreme punishment became routine.

Solitary confinement becomes routinized at the individual level, too. The French philosopher Michel Foucault argued that Western punishment (like all forms of social control) has focused increasingly on disciplining the mind rather than inflicting overt violence on the body.[21] Especially after Judge Henderson curbed the physical abuses at Pelican Bay, the institution operated primarily to control individual prisoners' minds—making some psychotic, driving others to become government informants. Still others have resisted, if only by asserting their rights to something more than bare existence. Any prisoner who survives months and years inside Pelican Bay develops rigid routines in order to cope.

Prisoners' personal narratives are integral to understanding how solitary confinement becomes routinized as supermax life. Some isolated prisoners are relatively famous, and their stories exist in the public record: Hugo Pinell, George Jackson, and others we will meet, including Todd Ashker, an alleged Aryan Brotherhood member who led a series of large-scale, well-publicized hunger strikes in 2011 and 2013, and Rene Enriquez, an admitted former Mexican Mafia member turned FBI informant. These four are among the handful of prisoners that officials identify as the worst of the worst: the dangerous monsters that Pelican Bay was designed to contain. But a close examination of their lives challenges that label.

Other prisoners have struggled more quietly to plead, earn, and litigate their way out of Pelican Bay. My information about them comes from correspondence and interviews that I conducted. All of them have survived years in isolation by imagining and struggling for some alternative reality. Prison officials wanted more prisons; prisoners wanted something other than prison. For both, prison was not enough.

All of this might sound like a story of unintended consequences—of an

exceptional practice accidentally becoming a long-term routine, or of reformers like Thelton Henderson seeking one thing and getting the opposite. But this interpretation oversimplifies. As the sociologist Robert Merton
famously observed, the paradigm of "unanticipated" consequences often
glosses over the complex interplay of competing interests, rational action,
underlying values, and social context.[22] In California, prison officials sought
one thing—indefinite solitary confinement for some prisoners—and they
got it, swerving past elected officials, banking on public callousness, and
overcoming some judicial resistance.

Supermaxes began as prison officials' response to the radical civil rights
movement of the 1970s. They proliferated during the turn toward mass
incarceration in the 1980s. And litigation in the 1990s confirmed their
constitutionality. Racism against radical black activists, economic interest
in building prisons, a punitive culture of control that provides a sense of
stability in precarious times, and a government that derives legitimacy from
looking "tough on crime": all compose the backdrop of a story whose center
stage is occupied by bureaucrats and their politics.[23]

The supermax story reveals that many reform attempts have failed, at
least in part, because of the opacity of prisons within prisons. As Justice
Anthony Kennedy said in a Supreme Court opinion in 2015 criticizing the
overuse of solitary confinement: "The conditions in which prisoners are
kept simply has not been a matter of sufficient public inquiry or interest."[24]
In the 1980s, California legislators proposing alternatives to constructing
more prisons or making existing ones harsher had no idea what kinds of
prisons officials were already building in their state. Later, when officials
said the prisoners in Pelican Bay were uniformly dangerous and that the
institution was absolutely necessary, judges took them at their word. But
when Pelican Bay's smooth concrete walls have been breached, reform has
been possible. In 2011 and 2013, prisoners in Pelican Bay coordinated a
series of hunger strikes; the last involved thirty thousand prisoners, some
of whom refused food for more than six weeks. These extended strikes
rendered the harsh conditions of confinement at Pelican Bay visible and
inspired international condemnation, which finally exerted reform pressure
on the prison system. California prison officials agreed, for the first time, to
review systematically who was in isolation and why, to limit terms of isola-

tion to five years, and to mitigate the debilitating effects of confinement through programs like education and therapy.[25]

This book aims to amplify such public scrutiny by revealing the deepest corners of our most restrictive and least visible prisons. Administrative discretion and institutional opacity have produced a range of physical and psychological terrors. When prison is not enough, there is no end to these terrors, no limit to punishment. Staring into the supermax forces us to reconsider whether prison is ever enough.

The research for this book took place over the course of ten years. To understand the supermax, I drew on historical and media archives about prison history, legislative archives about prison-building decisions, and legal documents filed during litigation challenging prison conditions in California and across the United States between the 1970s and 2015. I conducted forty-one formal oral history interviews with representatives of key prison constituencies: prison officials (twelve), lawyers and judges (four), prison architects (four), current and former prisoners (twenty), and one deceased prisoner's brother; dozens more informational interviews supplemented these formal oral histories. In addition, I collected publicly available information, made formal requests for unpublished data, and analyzed descriptive statistics about the scale of solitary confinement and the characteristics of prisoners in supermax facilities in California and across the United States.

What is and is not known about supermaxes is a political question, and in many cases, what we do not know is as revealing as what we do know. To understand the supermax as completely as possible, I used a combination of disciplinary approaches. Throughout the book, I describe my approach to each field of inquiry: how I identified research materials and research subjects, and how I attempted to balance, as every social scientist must, the demands of empirical investigation with the demands of my own ethics. Transparency in research methods seemed especially critical for this book, which argues, above all, for transparency in punitive decision making and policy implementation.

Reflecting on his own incarceration, Fyodor Dostoyevsky famously said, "The degree of civilization in a society can be judged by entering its prisons."[26] Today, television pretends to offer such an entrance, from the comedy-drama to the documentary special. But if you have not seen Pelican Bay to its institutional roots, examined its history of deprivation by design, looked into the deepest and quietest of its fluorescent-lit corridors, you have not entered America's prisons in their ultimate form, and seen for yourself.

A Supermax Life

TODD ASHKER IS MUSCULAR AND GHOSTLY pale. He has a thick chevron mustache and close-cropped hair. Intricate tattoos cover his torso and arms: an American eagle, the letter *A*, and more than one swastika.[1] Behind and around the tattoos are plenty of scars—stab wounds, gunshot wounds, and other marks of a hardscrabble life. Most of these marks date to his early twenties; he has had virtually no human contact in the intervening three decades.

In 2015, Todd was fifty-two years old and had been in continuous solitary confinement for almost thirty years. He spends at least twenty-two hours of every day locked in a windowless concrete cell measuring eight by ten feet, roughly the size of a wheelchair-accessible bathroom stall. Fluorescent lights remain on all day, every day. Prison slang for this kind of isolation cell captures the visceral experience of the place: the "box," the "hole," the "SHU" (an acronym for the official correctional label Security Housing Unit, which is pronounced "shoe"), and "*zapato*" (the Spanish word for "shoe"). Todd's box, like the 1,055 other isolation boxes at California's Pelican Bay State Prison, has only three furniture-like components: a concrete ledge with a slim foam pad, which serves as a bed; a solid-steel sink-toilet combination fixture; and two cement cubes jutting from the wall, forming an awkward chair and desk of sorts. As long as he follows prison rules precisely and can afford to buy the items, Todd is permitted a small television or radio, ten books or magazines, and one legal pad. Almost everything else is forbidden. Even clocks are not allowed.[2]

While in this box, Todd has written complaints to initiate fifteen lawsuits, learned of his mother's death, been shot at, and (with ten other prisoners) led multiple hunger strikes—one with thirty thousand prisoner partici- pants. This activity makes life in the box sound more exciting than it is.

The boundless reality is minutes, hours, days, weeks, and months spent sealed inside a concrete cube filled with stale air and fluorescent light. One former prisoner, who had spent just one month in a Pelican Bay cell like the one where Todd has lived for almost three decades, suggested that if I wanted to understand life in the box, I should try staying locked in my bath- room for a week.[3] A correspondent of Todd's, the sociology professor Denis O'Hearn, suggested a similar experiment: "Sit in a closet for an hour. Put a metal screen over the doorway that you can barely see through. Now think about sitting there for twenty-five years, communicating only with strang- ers in nearby closets by shouting out the door . . . This is Todd Ashker's life."[4]

I was disinclined to try it. How could a day or a week compare to three decades? Todd's day-to-day existence is almost impossible to imagine. Eas- ier to imagine: what manner of terrible things must he have done to de- serve being "buried alive" in isolation for so long?[5] Media accounts have described him as "sociopathic," "the worst of the worst," and "a convicted murderer with alleged Aryan Brotherhood ties."[6]

But when Todd first entered the box, in 1986, he was none of those things. He was twenty-three and had been in and out of juvenile detention facilities and foster care for years. He had already served one adult "bid," or prison term, for burglary. In prison at nineteen, he got his first swastika tattoo—"white pride" and "juvenile thrill," he later called it.[7] After he fin- ished that first bid, he stayed out of prison for just four months before being rearrested for burglary and assault in January 1985. Sentenced to six years in prison, he started serving time on this second bid at Folsom State Prison.[8] Meanwhile, Todd's father, Lewis Ashker, murdered a retired police officer in a botched attempt to steal the man's gun collection. Lewis was sentenced to life in prison in South Dakota.[9]

In prison on his second bid, with his father incarcerated for life, Todd seemed bound for a life of crime. Over the next two years, he stabbed a pris- oner to death, was implicated in the stabbing of a civilian, was "validated" by prison officials as a member of a murderous prison gang, earned a life sentence, and was assigned to an indeterminate term in isolation. Each event brought him one step closer to the Pelican Bay SHU.

Blood In, Blood Out

As of 1986, all of Todd's previous crimes were burglaries. His prison record was not especially violent, and he was not (yet) affiliated with the Aryan Brotherhood, a white supremacist gang that was gathering power in the 1980s. The brotherhood had a "blood in, blood out" policy: you had to commit a murder to join, and you had to die or be murdered to leave.[10] Todd had murdered no one. His first bid in isolation was, by prison standards, unremarkable. In September 1986, prison officials charged him with assaulting another prisoner and possessing a homemade weapon. No one died, and the charges were ultimately dismissed. But Todd was sent to the box—formally, the Folsom Security Housing Unit—a prototype of the SHU cell he would later occupy at Pelican Bay.[11]

Todd's first box was arguably the most uncomfortable of all the cells he would experience. The Folsom SHU cell was roughly six by eight feet, about half the size of a Pelican Bay cell. And it was overcrowded; prisoners were housed two to a box. Todd was allowed an hour a day out of his cell, to take a cold shower—there was no hot water on the unit—or to exercise alone. For the remaining twenty-three hours of every day, he was locked in his cell with a cellmate, with little to do from hour to hour. The conditions in the Folsom SHU—the tiny, overcrowded cells, the dilapidated facilities, and the total lack of work or education opportunities—were the subject of ongoing litigation and judicial oversight from 1976 through the late 1980s.[12] In 1989, the Pelican Bay SHU, with its sleek and relatively spacious isolation pods, replaced the decrepit Folsom facility and functionally ended the litigation over conditions there. While Todd was in the Folsom SHU, however, he would not have known—few people did—of the brewing plans to open a new isolation facility.

In May 1987, nine months into his box time, Todd got a brief reprieve when he became the "tier tender" for his unit. He was given the responsibility of mopping the floors, or tiers, in front of the cells, which allowed him to leave his cell for extended periods in the evenings. At twenty-three, could Todd possibly have imagined that those evenings spent mopping floors would be the greatest freedom he would ever again experience?

On May 25, on one of his first nights "out," Todd was mopping the floor in front of "Dirty" Dennis Murphy's cell. Murphy had allegedly murdered a disabled prisoner in a dispute over a shot of heroin. Killing a vulnerable victim for a minor transgression violated an unwritten code of prison ethics, earning Murphy his nickname. But according to prison rumor, Murphy was a high-ranking member of the Aryan Brotherhood gang and therefore was able to violate most rules.[13] The "AB," or the "Brand," had formed in San Quentin Prison in the 1960s during a period of acute racial tension. By the mid-1980s, the Brand's brutality had been well established. Even while housed in isolation units, alleged members had lured enemies into close quarters for fatal stabbings, murdered federal prison guards, and coordinated civilian executions by recently released members.[14] Murphy was allegedly involved in all this; Todd was not.

As Todd mopped in front of the cell, Murphy lounged on the bottom bunk.[15] His cellmate, Robert Tanner, was out for his shower. According to facts established at a later trial, as Tanner returned to the cell from his shower, Todd rushed in past him. (Guards did not see a weapon in Todd's hand.) Tanner followed, pulled a mattress off the top bunk, and shoved it in front of the door, blocking guards' view into the cell. Guards fired three shots into the cell, through the mattress. When Tanner removed the mattress, guards rushed into the cell and escorted Todd and Tanner out, neither noticeably injured. The whole altercation lasted just seconds.

But Dirty Dennis Murphy did not walk out of the cell. He was lying on the floor when guards entered. He had been stabbed between seventeen and twenty-six times, according to varying reports, and shot once in the shoulder. A guard asked him: "What happened?"

Murphy replied: "Fuck you, punk."

He died minutes later.

Inside the cell, guards found a prison-made shank with Todd's bloody fingerprints on it. The California Department of Corrections brought the case to Bill Portanova, the local, Sacramento-based prosecutor; he charged Todd with first-degree, premeditated murder. Portanova planned to argue that Todd had carried out the murder on behalf of the Aryan Brotherhood. Todd faced a sentence of at least thirty years if convicted.

Murphy's murder marked a culmination of violent years in the California prison system. Between 1970 and 1987, more than three hundred prisoners were murdered in California, a disproportionate number of them at Folsom. In a later court filing, Todd alleged that between 1984 and 1986 "there were 19 stabbing and strangulation deaths and hundreds of vicious stabbing assaults" at Folsom alone.[16] By 1988, however, the rate of violent deaths in California prisons had fallen to less than half that of the 1970s. By the time Todd's case went to trial, in 1990, California's in-prison murder rate had fallen to about 1 in every 10,000 prisoners—a significant decrease from the 5–7 per 10,000 prisoners murdered annually throughout the 1970s and early 1980s.[17]

While Todd prepared to represent himself at his trial, prison officials mobilized to establish his status as a member of the Aryan Brotherhood. Immediately following Murphy's murder, they assigned Todd to the "Bedrock" unit (in another box-style cell), where many AB gang members and associates were housed. A year later, in the summer of 1988, prison officials labeled Todd a gang "associate"—considered less dangerous than a full "member"—while continuing to build the case that he was an actual AB member.[18]

According to the California Code of Regulations governing the state prison system at that time, three "independent source items" needed to be identified in order to establish that a prisoner was a member of a gang.[19] "Item" is an all-encompassing term that includes what a prisoner is reading, whom he has been seen socializing with on the prison yard, what kind of tattoos he has, and whom he has sent letters to outside prison.[20] Prison officials reviewed and validated these items at their discretion, outside of any criminal proceeding. Defendants were not permitted to see the evidence against them, and prison officials kept their decision-making processes secret. Until 2015, the gang validation process involved an internal gang investigator (IGI) and an Internal Classification Committee (ICC). First, an IGI compiled a package of three source items. Next, the IGI gave the prisoner being considered for validation twenty-four hours' notice of a scheduled interview. At the interview, the IGI described *only* the non-confidential source items in the package to the prisoner. The prisoner could usually challenge the validity of the items (if he even knew what items were in the file) only on the spot, in the interview. Following this interview, the IGI submitted the gang "validation" package to the prison's ICC. The ICC reviewed the file and determined whether to approve the recommendation for validation as a gang member. If the ICC approved the gang validation, it assigned the prisoner to an *indeterminate* term in a Security Housing Unit.[21]

In the 2010s, California prison officials began evaluating these indeterminate SHU cases. In 828 initial file reviews, all but 40 prisoners (95 percent of all reviewed files) were found eligible either to enter a program to transition out of the SHU or to be returned directly to the general prison population.[22] Either the gang validation procedure had an extraordinarily high error rate, or the underlying validation criteria were flawed.

In 2015, state prison officials committed to review and reconsider every gang validation that resulted in an indeterminate assignment to the Pelican Bay SHU, in an effort to phase out indeterminate SHU assignments.[23] Until recently, however, most prisoners believed there were only three ways to escape an indeterminate SHU term: be paroled (released from prison at the end of a prison sentence), snitch (renounce gang membership and give the IGI information about other gang members in order to prove the renunciation), or die. As of this writing, Todd has not been paroled, has not snitched, and has not died; he remains in isolation in the Pelican Bay SHU, in spite of the recent reforms.

On May 23, 1988, prison officials held an administrative ICC hearing and formally validated Todd as a member of the Aryan Brotherhood, making him eligible for an indeterminate SHU term.[24] Since then, he has filed multiple lawsuits challenging this validation, which is based vaguely on the claims of "inmate confidential informants."[25] The timing of his validation is notable: California prison officials completed the process of labeling Todd an Aryan Brotherhood member one year after he was accused of murdering Dennis Murphy, but nearly two years before he stood trial for the murder. At that trial, the prosecution asserted that Todd had plotted Dennis's murder on behalf of the Aryan Brotherhood, but the defense convincingly disputed this claim.

At first, Todd represented himself. But after he complained that constant searches of his cell (he was still in a box-style unit at Folsom) had thwarted his efforts to prepare for trial, the judge ultimately appointed Philip Cozens as defense counsel, and the case went to trial before a jury. In February and March 1990, Cozens and the Sacramento prosecutor, Bill Portanova, called dozens of witnesses to testify about what had happened on the evening that Dirty Dennis was stabbed to death almost three years earlier.[26]

Portanova argued that Todd had killed Murphy on behalf of the Aryan Brotherhood. Todd argued that he had acted in self-defense. Subsequent federal investigations of the Aryan Brotherhood would identify the claim of self-defense as a classic AB strategy following a murder. And AB members, like other prisoner militants, often preferred to act as their own lawyers, as Todd had attempted to do. AB members representing themselves would oversee subpoenas and witness lists and then coordinate efforts to get other AB members into courthouse holding cells, where they could plan and carry out more violence against witnesses or others who had incurred the gang's wrath.[27]

But Todd's case was different. He ultimately accepted legal representation, and his claim of self-defense turned out to be well substantiated. Before Murphy was murdered, the California Department of Corrections had never labeled Todd an AB member, although officials hastened to do so afterward. Nor did Todd have a prior record of extreme violence. Why would he choose to rush into the cell of a convict known to be "dangerous and underhanded"?

Todd maintained that the whole event was staged: Murphy summoned him to a duel. Todd understood that the duel would be a fistfight, and he carried no weapon into Murphy's cell. But he quickly realized Murphy meant to kill him. Murphy had obtained a piece of metal from a senior Aryan Brotherhood member weeks in advance and filed it into a razor-sharp shank. As Todd entered the cell, he caught sight of Murphy's weapon, wrestled him to the ground, and took hold of the shank. According to Todd, Murphy fought viciously up until he was shot by a guard stationed in a control booth outside the cell. According to court records, Todd emerged unscathed, with no marks of a struggle.

At the trial, witnesses identified the chain of possession of the shank; one prisoner cut a piece of metal from the locker in his cell and smuggled it along a so-called underground railroad to Murphy. The many Aryan Brotherhood members who explained the shank's path asserted that Todd had never been a member of their gang.[28] Todd's lawyer, Philip Cozens, expressed confidence that all these witnesses would at least raise doubts in jurors' minds. His goal: for the jury to find little evidence of premeditation and hesitate to convict Todd of first-degree murder. A lesser conviction, for second-degree murder, would significantly reduce Todd's sentence.[29]

Cozens was an experienced litigator who had practiced for seven years in the Sacramento County District Attorney's Office and then for five years as a private criminal defense lawyer. Apparently, he also had a literary flair. At a lunch break two months into the trial, when asked how it was going, he told a *Sacramento Bee* reporter: "Ask for me tomorrow, and you shall find me a grave man," quoting the line spoken by Mercutio in Shakespeare's *Romeo and Juliet* shortly before he is stabbed.[30] Was Cozens trying to warn his listeners that he had been threatened?

Around three that afternoon, Cozens entered a hallway between holding cells in the courthouse. There he met with John Paul Schneider, a known Aryan Brotherhood member, to prepare him to testify as a defense witness for Todd. Schneider, twenty-eight at the time, was serving a sentence of life plus eleven years for an attempted prison murder: stabbing a guard in the throat. That attack was allegedly what earned him membership in the Aryan Brotherhood.

Cozens later told the press he never saw the weapon in Schneider's hand. But he felt the stab wounds: three in his left arm, one in his right leg. Sheriffs saw Cozens bleeding, ran into the hallway and subdued Schneider. They took from his hand an eight-inch prison-made shank, engraved with a shamrock and covered in blood.[31]

Two weeks later, Cozens filed a motion to recuse himself from Todd's case. Investigators hypothesized that Todd, frustrated with his defense, had coordinated with Schneider to plan the attack. Cozens told the court that he suspected his client of plotting his murder, creating a blatant conflict of interest.

The presiding judge, James Morris, disagreed. He called the evidence against Todd "speculation." Furthermore, he declared, a mistrial (or even a decision to excuse Cozens from the case) would waste the two months already invested in the trial, functionally rewarding the Aryan Brotherhood for its violence.

Fourteen years later, reporting on a federal investigation that led to the indictment and prosecution of twenty-nine of the gang's leading members (including many from California), the *New Yorker* called the Aryan Brotherhood "the most murderous prison gang in America."[32] But in 1990, facing a less notorious enemy, Judge Morris refused to back down. He offered Todd the option of representing himself or of keeping Cozens on as his attorney. Todd opted to keep Cozens.[33]

The jury ultimately found Todd Ashker guilty of second-degree murder. Reasonable doubt haunted the case. The jury was not convinced that Todd was an Aryan Brotherhood member or that the murder of Dennis Murphy had been deliberate and premeditated.

The judge sentenced Todd to sixteen years to life in state prison, to be added to the term he was already serving for his residential burglary conviction. Cozens declared this a victory. The sentence could have been twice as long, had Todd been found guilty of the first-degree murder charge.[34] And the judge agreed that another attorney could be appointed to replace Cozens for the subsequent appeal.

Twenty-five years later, Cozens remembered Todd at that 1990 trial as having "a certain willingness and ruthlessness to execute other people to advance his agenda."[35] Prosecutors, however, never sought to bring charges against Todd in Cozens's stabbing (apparently due to inadequate evidence implicating Todd). Whether he was involved, and whether he was grateful for the significant sentence reduction Cozens achieved, the two seemed happy to wash their hands of each other.

Once the sentence was imposed, Judge Morris, too, washed his hands of the case. He had said during the trial that safety and security issues "frankly" overshadowed his concerns with legal questions, such as whether witnesses were providing relevant testimony. And he expressed anxiety that he had no ability to order security measures beyond the bounds of his courtroom.[36] Just as Judge Morris had no control over how witnesses were managed outside his courtroom, he had no control over Todd's fate once he began to serve his sentence.

California prison officials quickly reinterpreted the evidence in Dirty Dennis Murphy's murder, repeatedly labeling the murder an "Aryan Brother-hood hit" even though the jury had failed to convict Todd of either having a gang affiliation or planning the murder. And the California parole board would later give "Aryan Brotherhood ordered hit" as a reason for denying Todd parole.[37] Once they determined that they were dealing with a danger-ous prisoner who was enmeshed in a murderous prison gang, prison offi-cials had nearly total discretion over how to handle Todd.

The Bay

As it turned out, California prison officials had just the place for Todd—a brand-new prison in Crescent City, in the far northwestern corner of the state. When the "Bay," as prisoners would come to call it, opened in Decem-ber 1989, local media described the place as a prison of the future, "a show-case of corrections technology" built to isolate the "worst of the worst."[38]

In addition to a traditional maximum-security complex with a 2,000-prisoner capacity, the facility features a super-maximum security complex consisting of 1,056 windowless isolation cells, neatly compartmentalized into 132 self-contained pods of 8 cells each. Thanks to an ingenious geo-metric design, guards armed with rifles can sit in central control booths and look out over 6 pods (48 cells) at once. Finely perforated steel doors allow guards to look straight into every cell, but prisoners, up close to the perforated steel, have trouble seeing out. Reaching out is impossible. From a control booth, a guard presses a button to release an air-powered lock to open one cell door at a time, letting each prisoner out for a shower or for recreation time in the "dog run." Each pod of 8 cells has one attached dog run—an eight-by-twenty-foot solitary exercise yard (twice the length of a cell), with walls twenty feet high.

As a validated member of the Aryan Brotherhood gang, with four years of box time already under his belt, Todd was an ideal candidate for Pelican Bay. Judge Morris sentenced Todd on the conviction for second-degree murder of Dirty Dennis Murphy on April 24, 1990. Less than two weeks later, on May 2, Todd was transferred to the Bay, just a few months after the institution opened its doors.[39] He has been there ever since.

In California, prisoners are usually transferred between facilities by bus.

Folsom, where Todd had been housed, is located just outside Sacramento. Pelican Bay is located in Crescent City, just a few miles south of California's border with Oregon, in one of the state's poorest counties.[40] The drive from Sacramento to Crescent City winds through the Shasta-Trinity National Forest and Humboldt County's redwood groves, then up the Pacific Coast Highway, overlooking rocky shores. Todd's ride, some four hundred miles, would have taken about seven hours. Driving up to Pelican Bay, I have occasionally seen the unmarked white vans the corrections department uses to transfer prisoners between facilities. Seven hours in a prison van hardly sounds like a joyride. But when I have asked prisoners about the journey to Pelican Bay, they always talk about the view outside the van.

"Max," another former Pelican Bay prisoner, took the same ride as Todd under similar circumstances: transferred in 1990 to serve an indeterminate term in the SHU as a validated gang member. He said of the journey:

> [I] remember they go up on a bus, and it took forever to get there. I'm like, 'Man.' I'm just looking at trees, birds. And you see it's a beautiful coast out there . . . Man, I'm looking at it . . . the big old pelicans, and I'm trying to get everything I can, because I know that it's over—that I already have a life sentence. Then with another life sentence in the Hole . . . And I was trying to look at everything—the waves, everything.

Max went on to describe his first glimpse of the brand-new prison in Crescent City:

> Then finally, we get to Pelican Bay . . . It feels like . . . the best way I can describe the front of the entrance of the SHU is it's like—remember the old Star Wars movies? . . . Han Solo's ship—the big old glass vessel? It's the first thing that came into my mind right then and there. And they make you get off the bus. At that time, we had to get naked and walk all the way down the hallway.[41]

Getting naked and walking all the way down an enclosed corridor might sound a bit dramatic, but Max's experience was mild compared with those of many other prisoners moving into California's new high-tech box cells. "Barry," another former prisoner, described the process of getting off the bus on the way to a California SHU as inevitably brutal: "Everybody knew when you got off the bus, automatically you had an ass-whuppin' coming. They jump on you."[42] By "they," he meant the guards.

Those first years in the Pelican Bay SHU were surprisingly full of "ass-whuppins." In theory, the Pelican Bay SHU eliminated all physical human contact, separating prisoners from one another with thick concrete walls and sealing the guards in their central control booths. In practice, the newly minted guards were eager to establish power over the "worst of the worst" prisoners in their charge. As a former Pelican Bay warden, Steve Cambra, explained: "Officers had the attitude of, 'We're going to be tougher than the tough.' "[43]

One Pelican Bay SHU prisoner annoyed officers by repeatedly kicking his cell door all day long and into the night. Finally, officers tied him in a "fetal restraint" position, wrists and ankles chained together in one knot, and left him that way, naked, for twenty-four hours.[44] Another SHU prisoner threw a food tray at a prison officer; other officers dragged the prisoner out of his cell and beat him unconscious.[45] Similar events occurred at California's other new SHU facility, Corcoran State Prison, located in the state's Central Valley between Fresno and Bakersfield. Guards killed five prisoners in the Corcoran SHU and injured another forty between 1989 and 1994. Most of these injuries, and all five deaths, stemmed from "gladiator fights" staged by the guards. Guards would choose two prisoners known to be from enemy gangs and release them into the exercise yards attached to the corridors of SHU cells. The two rivals would fight each other, and when the fights got heated, guards would shoot the prisoners—in five instances, fatally.[46]

Although the gladiator fights created a media sensation in the late 1990s, they were overshadowed by the case of SHU brutality involving Vaughn Dortch. In April 1992, Dortch was twenty-eight and housed in the Pelican Bay SHU. He had served six years of a ten-year prison sentence for grand theft, and he had been diagnosed with mental illness before his placement in solitary confinement.[47] After he was placed in the SHU, his mental state deteriorated to the point that he regularly smeared his entire body with his own feces.[48]

The Pelican Bay SHU was designed to be maximally hygienic—a new prison with smooth walls that could be hosed down and lights that stayed on twenty-four hours a day. Dortch was making it filthy. He was already in the most restrictive place in the California prison system; there were no more privileges left to remove. Guards were faced with two options, each equally unpleasant. They could leave Dortch in his cell, smeared in feces, or they could get him out and try to clean him.[49]

Eventually, a group of at least five guards decided to take Dortch from his cell, bring him to the hospital infirmary, and attempt to clean him. They cuffed his hands behind his back and pushed him waist-deep into scalding hot water, holding him there. Dortch is African American; one of the guards bathing him said: "Looks like we're going to have a white boy before this is through." Dortch ultimately suffered third-degree burns over much of his lower torso, and his skin peeled away in chunks.[50]

Todd Ashker did not escape these early, brutal years. On October 24, 1990, in his sixth month at Pelican Bay, he got in a fistfight with another prisoner. Given the history of "gladiator fights" in the Corcoran and Pelican Bay SHUs, the fight may have been set up. After all, Todd should have been sealed off in his own concrete box, alone. Instead, two cell doors opened simultaneously. Regardless, the fight ended quickly when the guard on duty, Officer Steve Brodeur, aimed an assault rifle at Todd and shot him in the right arm at close range.

The first doctor to examine Todd recommended emergency surgery at a nonprison hospital. Instead, doctors at the Pelican Bay infirmary simply placed a cast on Todd's arm.[51] Guards gave him a disciplinary report for "assault on inmates."[52] Over the next two months, Todd repeatedly requested medical attention for the excruciating pain in his arm. He was ignored.

Meanwhile, his cell got dirtier and dirtier as a result of his limited mobility. An aneurysm in his arm expanded for weeks before finally bursting in December 1990. Todd was airlifted out of Pelican Bay to a nonprison hospital capable of completing the emergency surgery he had needed for two months.[53]

More than twenty years later, Todd still suffers constant pain in his right forearm, wrist, hand, and fingers—and he has sued the California Department of Corrections repeatedly for ongoing shortcomings in the medical treatment he received for this injury. His first lawsuit was the most successful; he handwrote his own complaint alleging that guards and doctors had violated his civil rights. A jury awarded him $225,000 in damages, and the

U.S. Court of Appeals for the Ninth Circuit upheld the award.[54] In a later interview, Todd said this case introduced him to the power of the law and motivated him to earn a paralegal certificate. He remains a well-known jailhouse lawyer in California.[55]

Reports of gladiator fights, prisoners chained in fetal positions, scalding water baths, and grossly inadequate medical treatment no longer seep out of Pelican Bay. Media attention (including a *60 Minutes* investigative report on the Vaughn Dortch incident) and lawsuits like Todd's eventually led to improved conditions. In 1995, Thelton Henderson, a federal district court judge in California, ruled that Pelican Bay was being run in an unconstitutional manner, violating the prisoners' Eighth Amendment right to be protected from cruel and unusual punishment. For the next sixteen years, Judge Henderson oversaw regular monitoring of Pelican Bay by prisoners' rights lawyers and court-appointed experts. He even made a number of visits to the institution himself. But he never found that long-term solitary confinement was, itself, unconstitutional.[56] Instead, he focused on improving conditions at the SHU to ensure that the institution met minimum constitutional standards.

Judge Henderson's approach echoed that of the judges overseeing cases challenging the conditions of confinement at Pelican Bay's prototype, the Folsom SHU, where Todd spent his first years in the box. Pelican Bay officials responded to litigation just as Folsom officials had: by creating a superficially compliant set of procedures while simultaneously maintaining—and even expanding—extraordinarily harsh punishment policies like long-term isolation. Today, the box is undoubtedly cleaner, more technologically advanced, and better run than it was in 1990. The drama of the gladiator fights and assault rifle shootings is history. Ongoing are the tedium, the psychological trauma, the existential terror of spending twenty-two or more hours a day, for an undetermined number of days, alone in a featureless eight-by-ten-foot cell.

"Any Complaints?"

Every morning, prisoners in the box awake between five and six. That is, assuming they were able to sleep through the fluorescent lights, the middle-of-the-night cell-front checks by guards, and the rants of fellow prisoners who lost their minds overnight. Most prisoners keep their cells neat. In the morning, they roll up their thin foam mattresses, giving themselves a little more room to move around. Many work out before breakfast arrives. A typical SHU workout consists of five hundred or more "burpees"—an aerobic combination of squats, planks, and push-ups—the perfect exercise for someone with no equipment and a scant eighty square feet of space.[57]

Around seven, an officer comes by with a tray of food that includes packets of instant coffee and artificial sugar; some combination of bread and cereal; occasionally some canned fruit (removed from the can, of course, since any metal is considered a weapon); and a brown-bag lunch, usually a slice of bologna on wheat bread with a packet of mustard.[58] Fresh fruit and real sugar are rationed in prison lest prisoners ferment the combination into "pruno"—homemade alcohol.

The perforated steel doors in the Pelican Bay SHU contain a rectangular slot, about waist high, sealed with a padlocked miniature door. At breakfast, an officer unlocks each slot, in each pod, one by one, and slides a food tray in. This is often a prisoner's only human interaction of the day.

The food tray slot doubles as a cuff port. If a prisoner needs to leave the pod to go to the law library, see a doctor, or visit with a lawyer (all rare events in the SHU), he backs up to the cell door and reaches his hands out through the cuff port. An officer handcuffs him before opening the cell door completely. Once the cell door opens, the officer will cuff the prisoner's ankles together and tether his cuffed hands to a chain around his waist. The officer will grab onto the waist chain, at the prisoner's side, and the two will shuffle slowly down the windowless corridors of the SHU. Usually, one or two additional guards will follow to ensure the prisoner remains under control.

On many days, the prisoners never leave their cells. By eight, officers are back to collect the food trays.

On a bad day, a prisoner might refuse to return a food tray, provoking a fight with the officer collecting the trays. When this happens, the officer calls in backup and then pepper-sprays the prisoner through the cuff port. Then he dons a Plexiglas faceguard, grasps an electrified shield, and leads a charge into the cell. Together, five or six officers will subdue the prisoner, cuffing his hands and legs, and dragging him and his food tray out of the cell. Sometimes the prisoner needs to be taken to the infirmary afterward.

But he may just be put back in his cell, still covered in pepper spray, without a shower.[59] Some prisoners experience this standoff as a rewarding moment of human contact or as a fleeting sensation of control over their environment, having forced their guards to act.

Prisoners who survive more than a few weeks in the SHU with their sanity mostly intact develop rigid, repetitive routines to get through the long days.[60] A day often starts with those five hundred burpees before breakfast, followed by a "birdbath" in the small steel sink. Many prisoners limit their television watching—to a favorite soap opera or a specific evening news show or a particular sports team's playoff game. The bulk of the day might be spent preparing legal work, writing letters, reading. The more resilient prisoners teach themselves new skills. Todd taught himself to practice law. Another prisoner with whom I have corresponded taught himself Spanish. Some learn more unusual languages, such as Gaelic or Nahuatl. Prison officials claim that prisoners learn languages like Nahuatl, an indigenous language of Mexico with up to 2 million native speakers, in order to communicate better with fellow gang members without being understood by the guards; prisoners argue that they want to better understand their cultural heritage and have nothing else to do. Sometimes a friendly guard will pass books between cells, or books can be borrowed from a library cart that rolls through every few days. The luckiest prisoners receive books by mail from someone outside the prison.

Many SHU prisoners teach themselves to draw. Some create strikingly realistic images of animals and people, bringing life back into their barren cells. Others draw their surroundings in order to communicate details of their daily lives to advocates or loved ones. Still others draw sinister scenes that depict their hallucinations, demonize their captors, or convey with unsettling vividness the claustrophobic, destabilizing, infuriating emotional experience of being sealed in a concrete box. Until 2012, only black ballpoint pen refills (without the pen casing) were permitted for writing and drawing.[61]

Even in these sparse conditions, ingenuity abounds. Prisoners describe mixing colored candies such as M&Ms or jellybeans with droplets of water to make paint.[62] Those who have some money in their prisoner trust accounts—from family or friends or, like Todd, from legal settlements—can buy candy like M&Ms once a month by ordering it from the prison canteen. Once a year, prisoners in the SHU can receive a package of perishable goods, ordered by family or friends from an approved vendor. Jellybeans can be sent in this way.

Once a week or so, a "psych tech" (the psychiatric equivalent of a nurse's assistant) might come by and ask each prisoner how he is feeling. I have watched these visits in a women's isolation unit in California. The tech stops at the front of the cell door and says, "How are you today?" to which the prisoner answers, "Fine." An exceptionally proactive tech might follow up with "Any complaints?" to which most prisoners answer, "No."

The tech moves on to the next cell and repeats the exchange, which everyone on the pod can hear. Prisoners see this cell-front psychiatric treatment as a charade. If a prisoner had problems, he would seldom disclose them publicly. And prisoners are afraid of having their depression, anxiety, and hallucinations (all common effects of long-term isolation)[63] treated with medications that might leave them susceptible to chemical dependency or compromise their alertness by putting them to sleep for the indefinite duration of their SHU terms.[64]

Prisoners are permitted three fifteen-minute showers a week. Additionally, prison rules require that they have ninety minutes a day in the dog run, but these exercise periods are often cut short or eliminated.[65]

There is no face-to-face interaction between prisoners. Todd might stop briefly in front of another prisoner's cell, stare through the perforated steel door, say something, and get a reply as he walks out to the dog run or to the shower. But such brief chats are technically forbidden. In 2012, for instance, a correctional officer named T. Brewer wrote up a "gang chrono," or formal disciplinary report, noting that Todd Ashker had shouted from his cell to another validated Aryan Brotherhood gang member passing by on his way to a shower. The chrono was placed in Todd Ashker's file as evidence of his continued association with the gang.[66]

Conversations are rare, and physical contact is rarer still. Max, the prisoner who described the drive up the coast to Pelican Bay, remembered each human touch he experienced during his ten years in the Pelican Bay SHU. Once he was standing at his cell front waiting for a guard in the central control booth to press the button that would pop his door so that he could

Inner hallway connecting multiple pods of cells, Pelican Bay SHU
(Monica Lam, Center for Investigative Reporting)

Exercise yard, Pelican Bay SHU
(Monica Lam, Center for
Investigative Reporting)

take his exercise period in the dog run. But as his door popped, he heard his neighbor's door pop, too. No two cell doors are supposed to be simultaneously open in the SHU. Such an occurrence inspires mortal fear among prisoners, who know they could be left alone on the cellblock, fighting to the death with a rival gang member. Max described his heart racing. Then: "Before you know it, [my neighbor] . . . puts his hand like this [reaching around an imaginary door frame] . . . right into my cell. And I look at it . . . I hadn't touched anybody in such a long time. I just, I grabbed his hand, and I shook his hand. And he squeezed it, and I squeezed it."[67]

Prisoners schedule communication time with each other. They conduct virtual chess games and "phone calls" by shouting through pipes or down corridors to communicate with friends in other pods. During scheduled games or chats, other prisoners stay quiet, out of respect. Real telephone calls are permitted only in emergencies—for instance, to notify a prisoner that a close relative has died.

Family visits are permitted on Saturdays and Sundays, but there is no physical contact (bulletproof glass separates the SHU prisoner from his visitor), and few family members have the means to make the trip to Pelican Bay. Even with ample time and money, getting to Pelican Bay can be arduous. The nearest regional airport is 100 miles away, and the nearest international airport, in San Francisco, is 400 miles away. The drive from Southern California's population centers is 700–800 miles.

Todd Ashker's mother, who was paraplegic, was able to visit Pelican Bay only once, in 1993. Like all Pelican Bay SHU visits, hers took place in a booth; bulletproof glass separated mother and son, who talked to each other through a rudimentary phone system. Todd spoke with his mother only twice more after that: once when his sister died, in 1998, and again when his grandmother died, in 2000. Each call lasted ten minutes. His mother has since died.[68]

Even if they rarely have visitors, prisoners do look forward to one thing on Sunday: dinners often contain a fresh, protein-rich treat—an extra hard-boiled egg.[69] Many prisoners describe being hungry in the SHU. The meals are carefully planned to provide the minimum necessary calories, hardly enough to fuel the thousands of burpees necessary to maintain sanity. Dinner is usually served between four and five. The last prisoner count of the

day is at eight thirty. After that, the lights dim somewhat, and many prisoners unroll their mattresses and try to fall asleep.

Unending Isolation

For a prisoner like Todd, with an indefinite SHU term, there is no end
in sight. He can improve his conditions only if he "debriefs," or snitches, by
providing incriminating information about the Aryan Brotherhood, proving that he is no longer loyal to the gang. But Todd insists that he is not
a gang member and therefore has no information to provide. If he did
debrief, whether or not he provided useful information, he would have a
bounty on his head and would likely be targeted for a prison hit. He would
have to spend the rest of his sentence in protective custody, in conditions
that might differ little from SHU isolation. He might get a cell with a
window.

Todd has not had a serious disciplinary infraction in twenty years. The
few violations in his prison file include possession of homemade wine, communicating with prisoners in other pods, talking in the law library (where
SHU prisoners do their research from inside a wheeled cage, about the size
of a telephone booth), and participating in hunger strikes.[70]

Todd has served twenty-four years of his twenty-one-to-life sentence for
murdering Dennis Murphy. He was theoretically eligible for parole three
years ago, but he has been repeatedly denied because of his alleged gang
affiliation and his inability to participate in any rehabilitative programming
from the SHU. Todd summed up his twenty four years in the SHU in a
recent interview: "If you think too much about the past, or the future, it gets
real depressing. I look at it as, my life has been a waste of space."[71]

Seventy-eight California prisoners, including Todd Ashker, have been in
isolation in the Pelican Bay SHU for more than twenty years. Almost five
hundred have been there for at least ten years, and hundreds more have
been there between three months and five years.[72] That is just in California.
Across the United States, there are at least twenty thousand more prisoners
in supermaxes, living in conditions similar to Todd's at Pelican Bay—not to
mention the tens of thousands of prisoners living in some form of shorter-
term isolation.[73] Almost every state has a supermax, in which hundreds,

sometimes thousands, of prisoners live in long-term solitary confinement.[74] These prisons were built between the mid-1980s and the early 2000s, when incarceration rates were rising and the construction of prison facilities was booming.[75] Like Todd, these other supermax prisoners across the United States have been physically isolated, mostly invisible, and literally untouchable for more than two decades.

In Todd's twenty-first year in the SHU, however, things changed. On July 1, 2011, more than six thousand prisoners throughout the California prison system refused all three of their prison-issued meals. They were fasting in solidarity with prisoners in the California SHUs, protesting the restrictive conditions of confinement and the long durations of isolation experienced by their fellow prisoners. This collective action marked the beginning of a statewide prison hunger strike that quickly attracted national and even international media attention.[76]

Todd Ashker's name appeared in the media again and again. Along with Danny Troxell and nine others, he had signed the April 2011 declaration that set the July hunger strike in motion. In a memorandum forebodingly headed "Final Notice," the men stated that starting on July 1, "several inmates" in the Pelican Bay SHU, in the section known as D-Corridor, were planning to refuse food indefinitely until a list of poignantly simple demands was met. These included provision of a handball and warm clothes for use during the prisoners' few hours of outdoor exercise; permission to make one phone call a week; a supply of adequately nutritious food; and the possibility that indefinite assignment to solitary confinement would be reviewed after some number of years.[77] To draft the memo, the prisoners had shouted at one another through plumbing pipes in their cells and drain pipes in the exercise yards, passed notes under cell doors ("kites"), and communicated through advocates in San Francisco, sending letters back and forth, seeking help in amplifying their demands.

"Several inmates" quickly turned into several thousand who refused food for more than two weeks in July 2011, and again in October 2011. Thirty thousand prisoners refused food in another hunger strike in July 2013. Todd and close to one hundred other prisoners refused food for fifty days in the 2013 strike. Dozens of prisoners were hospitalized. At least one participant died after hanging himself in his cell.

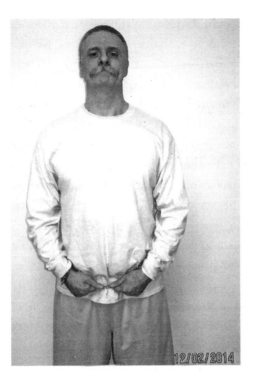

Todd Ashker, 2014
(Courtesy of Todd Ashker)

Throughout the strikes, prison officials argued that Todd and Danny were mischaracterizing the conditions in the SHU by using descriptors like "solitary confinement" and "sensory deprivation." Between the televisions, the "psych tech" visits, time outside in the dog run, and shouting at each other through the pipes, officials argued, prisoners had ample contact with one another and the outside world.[78] Prisoners disagreed. They described time in the SHU as unbroken by visits, holidays, sensations, or human touch.

Opening the Box

Most reporters, and most citizens, did not know the SHU existed until Todd and Danny persuaded several thousand of their fellow prisoners to conduct a sustained nonviolent protest. Public attention had focused on California SHU facilities briefly in the 1990s around the case of Vaughn Dortch's scalding, the Corcoran "gladiator fights," and the *Madrid* lawsuit, in which Judge Henderson ordered changes to isolation policies. But in those days, the Pelican Bay and Corcoran SHUs were still new; no prisoner had been housed in either facility for more than four or five years. No one kept track of who was in the SHU or how long they had stayed there.[79] Until 2011, in fact, there were no recorded data on how many prisoners had been in the Pelican Bay SHU for more than five years, much less twenty years.

Like the California Department of Corrections, state and federal prison systems across the United States have failed to track how many prisoners are in isolation and how long they have been there. Today, calculations of either the scale or duration of solitary confinement use are hardly better than educated guesses. The best estimates consist of voluntary institutional self-reports solicited by private organizations and prisoner self-reports gathered through the National Inmate Survey.[80] Such reports suggest that in 2015, at least one in five prisoners across the United States had spent time in some form of isolated confinement in the prior year.[81] With more than 2 million people incarcerated in the United States, that means that as many as 400,000 prisoners experience some form of isolation every year. Other reports suggest that in some states and in some prison facilities, the *average* lengths of such stays in isolation can be as long as two to three years.[82]

In spite of the supermax data shortage, I knew about the Pelican Bay SHU as well as others like it across the United States. At the time the hunger strikes started in 2011, I had been studying prison history and prison conditions for more than a decade. I did not, however, visit Pelican Bay until after I filed my Ph.D. dissertation, on which this book is based. This was not for lack of trying; I could not get permission to make a formal research visit, talk to prisoners there, or take a tour.

In 2011, I had not met Todd Ashker. My descriptions of his life have been culled from transcripts, court decisions, news stories, and journalists' interviews conducted with Todd in the aftermath of the hunger strike. Prison officials point to prisoners like Todd as archetypes of the "worst of the worst"—the very people who most require housing in the Pelican Bay SHU. But the "worst of the worst" are neither so easy to identify nor so immutable as the stereotypes would suggest.[83]

Todd Ashker may or may not have carried out a gang hit on a fellow prisoner in 1986, but since then he has fought his battles through legitimate legal channels and nonviolent organizing. Even if a few prisoners are so depraved and dangerous that they must be permanently removed from most human contact, there are hardly four thousand such people in California, or tens of thousands across the United States. And if there is no clearly discernible "worst of the worst," if guards and administrators and society sometimes get it wrong, what justifies the scope, duration, and harshness of supermax confinement in the United States? To examine one case out of thousands: should Todd Ashker spend the rest of his life in the Pelican Bay SHU?

I have met Todd once —on a legal monitoring visit in May 2012. We were, of course, separated by bulletproof glass; we communicated over a closed-circuit phone.

Todd was angry with the guard who brought him in and angry with the guard who brought me in, and he threatened both with a complaint and a lawsuit. For a second, noting his anger, I was grateful for the thick pane of shatterproof glass between us. But as we talked, Todd was focused and calm, describing the conditions he lived in, his goals for reform, his hopes that some prisoners might have their lives improved through the hunger strike he had helped organize. He expressed no hope that his own situation would change.

I likewise could not imagine that a prison system that has invested so much in building the case that Todd is one of those "worst of the worst" would ever countenance his release from isolation, let alone from prison. I wondered, too, whether Todd could possibly recover from so many years of solitary confinement. It is impossible to know. America's three-decades-long experiment with this duration and intensity of isolation is unprecedented. The initiation of this experiment long predates Todd's first incarceration in a California prison, as the next chapter reveals, and the repercussions of the experiment seem likely to last long past Todd's life.

Of course, most of these thoughts went unsaid in my brief meeting with Todd. At the end of our conversation, we each pressed our hands against the glass—the SHU equivalent of a handshake, without human touch.

2

The Most Dangerous Prisoner

ALTHOUGH I HAVE BEEN INSIDE THE Pelican Bay SHU only once, in 2012, I have walked across the prison yard at San Quentin State Prison, in Marin County, California, hundreds of times. San Quentin is history, in vivo. It is California's oldest prison, opened in July 1852. In those early days, the "prison" was actually a boat docked off Point San Quentin, which juts into the northern end of San Francisco Bay. Prisoners slept on the boat, named the *Waban*, at night, and went ashore to build the prison during the day.[1]

Approached from the highway, San Quentin looks like a medieval castle, complete with turrets. Up close, it looks just as timeless. The guards carry key rings with three-inch-long tarnished brass skeleton keys. A yellow stucco wall surrounds the prison, and a wrought-iron gate with gold-tipped posts greets visitors at the main entrance. From the prison gates, looking out over the surrounding water on a clear afternoon, you can see both the bright red Golden Gate Bridge leading into San Francisco and the now-empty Alcatraz fortress in the middle of the bay. Although stories from Alcatraz dominate prison lore, it operated as a prison for just three decades (1934–63), one-fifth of San Quentin's fifteen-and-counting decades.

Inside the prison gates, on the path to the prison yard, an American flag perpetually flies at half-staff to commemorate August 21, 1971, the deadliest day in California prison history, when three guards and three prisoners died inside San Quentin. Guards blamed George Jackson, one of the dead prisoners, for causing the carnage in a failed escape attempt; Jackson's supporters blamed guards for setting up the incident in order to justify shooting him in the back. More than forty years later, the debate about exactly what happened persists, and the reverberating memory of the August 21, 1971, carnage at San Quentin has rhetorically justified abuses of prisoners such as the scalding, hog-tying, and gladiator fights that took place in the California SHUs in the 1980s and 1990s, and the now-standard practice of imposing decades in isolation on prisoners like Todd Ashker.

The prison yard I know so well is hard to reconcile with the chaotic San Quentin represented by that flag flying at half-staff. For five years I visited the prison at least once a week to teach math and English in an associate's degree program. I watched twenty-year-old white men and sixty-year-old black men struggling together to learn algebra and Aristotle.[2] I carried a "Brown Card," which gave me permission to shepherd other volunteers across the central prison yard, a vast space made up of baseball fields and basketball courts and surrounded by a wide track of packed dirt. My Brown Card also allowed me to walk alone across the open yard, among hundreds of men dressed in "prison blues"—usually jeans and a white T-shirt—jogging, doing push-ups, sitting around picnic tables, chatting, picking up clean laundry, or negotiating with officers for some privilege or other. As more and more of them took my classes over time, crossing the yard became a reunion of sorts. Guys would wave, stand up, step aside, smile, and say good evening.

I repeatedly confronted the dissonance between the men I came to know through my classes and the dangerous characters whom society imagines congregating on the San Quentin yard. According to my mother and everyone else who expressed concern for my safety, my respectful college students in their prison blues, with their everyday health and work problems and their persistence in the face of educational challenges, were a naive illusion. Mama, I am pretty sure, imagined a prison full of George Jacksons, along with one or two Hannibal Lecters.[3] The fact that San Quentin is home to California's 746 death row prisoners—housed in a separate structure from the general prison population—enhances its image as a home to tiers full of unpredictably violent men. But there has been just one murder at San Quentin in the last ten years, giving the prison a murder rate significantly lower than that of the surrounding, affluent Marin County.[4]

In the 1960s and 1970s, however, San Quentin housed more of California's highest-security prisoners and was a more violent place. For nearly ten years (1962–68 and 1970–71), it was home to George Jackson, called by some the most singularly dangerous prisoner ever housed in California (and by others the most inspiring). Every time I walked along the path from the yellow prison wall to the San Quentin inner yard, past that flag at half-staff, I was reminded that Jackson had died right there.

The events leading up to Jackson's death, and the many conflicting stories re-creating those events, made a supermax prison like Pelican Bay, with cells like Todd Ashker's, seem like a good idea to prison officials. Pelican Bay institutionalized the policies that prison guards developed in direct response to the threat that Jackson and his alleged co-conspirators posed to the prison order. Today, prison officials frequently refer to Jackson's legacy as a dangerous revolutionary in their rationales for the supermax.

George Jackson Politicized

George Jackson's family moved from Chicago to California in 1956. Jackson was fifteen. He was arrested for the first time a year later, for petty theft; he spent seven months locked up in the California Youth Authority. In 1960, at the age of eighteen, he was arrested and charged with second-degree armed robbery. He pleaded guilty to stealing $70 (roughly equivalent to $560 in 2015, adjusted for inflation) from a gas station in Los Angeles.[5] In letters to his family and friends, Jackson repeatedly insisted that he was innocent of this crime.[6] But he pleaded guilty in exchange for the promise of "a short county jail term."[7] The sentencing judge, taking note of his previous convictions, instead sent Jackson to state prison for "one year to life."

Under this indeterminate sentence, Jackson would be eligible for release after one year of incarceration, provided he received good behavioral assessments from prison guards and the Board of Prison Terms (parole officials).[8] At first, Jackson could have reasonably expected to be released within a year or two. After all, his crime was relatively petty; no one had died, and the amount of property taken was small. In his early prison letters, Jackson wrote hopefully about getting out; he said he wanted better shoes so that he could take care of his sore feet before he was released, and he asked his father, a postal worker, to help him to find a job.[9] He even avoided participating in work stoppages, in order to maintain his record of good behavior.[10] But the Board of Prison Terms repeatedly denied him a parole date. In January 1967, after he had already served five years beyond his minimum sentence, and after the Board of Prison Terms had denied his parole for another "14-to-18" months, Jackson acknowledged: "Of course I could do the rest of my life here."[11] His statement was prescient.

Every time he went before the Board of Prison Terms, Jackson experienced the vagaries of the indeterminate sentence, which left the actual length of prison sentences up to guards, who could place favorable or unfavorable disciplinary reviews in a prisoner's file, and parole boards, which decided whether to grant or deny a prisoner's petition for release. Jackson argued that whatever he did, prison guards construed his behavior as revolutionary. If he refused to participate in work stoppages, he was strategically concealing his leadership of those very strikes.[12] He was helpless to dispute the guards' assessments. Because he had pleaded guilty to the original robbery charge against him, he had no right to an appeal of his initial sentence. He also had no right to legal representation at his parole hearings.

Jackson's growing frustration is evident in his letters. He wrote that the prison guards were "pigs," that his sentence was unjust, and that he was being oppressed. He talked increasingly of escape.[13] And he proclaimed his status as a "revolutionary."

Jackson first began studying radical political theorists, including Karl Marx and Frantz Fanon, in 1962, under the supervision of another African American prisoner, W. L. Nolen, who ran a reading group for prisoners. Nolen, Jackson, and other members of the reading group were ultimately affiliated with the Black Guerrilla Family (BGF), which was founded sometime between 1966 and 1971. According to its followers, the BGF is a revolutionary political organization; according to prison officials, it is a prison gang.[14] Many BGF affiliates maintained ties with the revolutionary organization of the Black Panther Party, founded in 1966. Jackson, along with revolutionaries such as Eldridge Cleaver and Huey Newton, who were also imprisoned in California in the 1960s, advocated becoming conscious of racial discrimination, paying close attention to revolutionary theorists, and engaging in violent political activity. As Jackson wrote in one of his letters: "The concept of nonviolence is a false ideal." And later: "Politics is violence."[15] Words would soon become reality.

A Radical and Violent Context

The 1970s were the most violent years in the history of California (and U.S.) prisons. Between 1970 and 1974, there were seventy-one prisoner and eleven guard homicides in California state prisons. Twice as many guards died in the first four years of the 1970s as in the subsequent forty years, and the rate of violent deaths of prisoners between 1970 and 1974 was at least four times as high as in any year since 1974.[16]

This violence followed years of prisoner-initiated work stoppages and guard-initiated lockdowns. Prisoners in the late 1960s, like civil rights activists outside prison, organized to demand certain rights: to be heard in the courts, to freedom of speech and association, and to more just everyday treatment.[17] Many of these demands brought substantive changes in prisoners' lives, especially as federal courts became increasingly open to hearing prisoner-initiated challenges to the conditions of their confinement.[18] By 1975, courts across the United States had found unconstitutional conditions of confinement or operational policies in more than thirty state prison facilities (and had declared the totality of some state prison systems, like Arkansas's, to be unconstitutional).[19]

Sentencing policies faced scrutiny, too. In 1971, the American Friends Service Committee, a progressive Quaker organization, published a provocative report titled *Struggle for Justice,* arguing that indeterminate sentences consistently produced racially biased outcomes and amounted to an extreme form of discrimination. Jackson experienced exactly the kind of discrimination highlighted in the report: he was an African American man who expected to spend one year in prison on a relatively minor robbery conviction, but instead found himself facing a de facto life sentence, at least in part because of his race-based association with the BGF. The California Legislature abolished indeterminate sentencing in 1976, a few years after the publication of *Struggle for Justice,* but the movement against the practice

had hardly coalesced in the 1960s, when Jackson was being repeatedly denied parole.

Although legal rights for minorities and disadvantaged populations expanded throughout the 1960s, Jackson's list of perceived injustices kept
expanding, too. It was not a trivial list. In addition to his parole denials, the
injustices included segregated prison facilities, censorship, rancid food, and
pervasive racial animus; then, murdered friends and, later, being charged
with murder himself. In this political and social environment, Jackson became an increasingly radical, and increasingly vocal, advocate of violent
resistance.

Much of the prisoner organizing in this period took place along racial
lines. The Muslim Brotherhood, for instance, which originated in New
York and organized a significant and successful movement for prisoners'
religious freedom, consisted mainly of African American prisoners.[20] The
line between being a radical political organization or a race-based prison
gang, however, was often blurry, in administrative perception even if not in
practice. The BGF, the Aryan Brotherhood, the Mexican Mafia, and Nuestra
Familia, which all trace their origins to the mid-1960s, are officially moni-
tored as prison gangs and are often blamed for violence in and out of
prison.[21] Even among these groupings, however, prisoners like Jackson
expressed solidarity across racial boundaries. The BGF and Black Panther
Party aligned themselves with the communist parties in China, Cuba, and
North Vietnam, for instance, and these groups had a stated goal of multi-
racial unity among prisoners.[22]

These race-based prison affiliations coalesced as the racial composition
of American prisons, especially those in California, changed drastically. In
1970, whites accounted for 80 percent of California's prison population.
But throughout the 1970s and 1980s, the percentage of whites being admitted to state prison fell to under 30 percent, so that by the 1990s, they
made up less than half of the state's prison population.[23] Today, the proportion of black and Latino prisoners throughout U.S. prisons is grossly disproportionate to their presence in the general population. African Americans make up 38 percent of all U.S. prisoners, but only 13 percent of the
national population; Latinos account for 19 percent of all U.S. prisoners,

but only 15 percent of the national population.[24] In the 1970s, overt racial tensions in prison increased along with these increases in minority incarceration rates.[25]

Carl Larson, who worked as a prison guard and then as a warden during this period, described how the civil rights and social justice movements outside prison aligned with a different, frequently more violent and racially divided rights revolution inside prison: "We had this 'revolution,' and it manifested itself with a lot of rhetoric—in colleges and jails. The manifestation in colleges was mainly peaceful—a lot of rhetoric and thought. [But] in the prisons, it manifested in a lot of violence . . . The Black Guerrilla Family and the Black Panthers, they had a political side . . . but they were mostly gangs, mafia."[26] For Larson, any political radical behind a prison wall (especially a black radical) was a potentially violent criminal, part of an organized gang. Prison officials describe responding as best they could to the increasingly organized populations filling their prisons—identifying cliques of newly established gangs in one facility and dispersing them throughout the prison system.[27] Prison scholars, however, have long argued that prisoners and guards jointly construct the social order of prisons, and that guards reinforce and exploit racial tensions in order to maintain a fragile equilibrium between themselves and the volatile prisoners, who outnumber them.[28] In California in the late 1960s, this equilibrium shattered.

The strategy of dispersing young gang members seemed only to expand their power. Prisoner-on-prisoner assaults increased, as did prisoner-guard altercations. Guards increasingly resorted to lockdowns as a tool of control.[29] During a lockdown, prisoners spent every hour of every day locked in their cells, meals (usually cold) were delivered to the cells, and prisoners were denied any opportunity to congregate in common areas. Lockdowns just escalated the tensions. Reports of confinement in dank hundred-year-old cellblocks, with no hot water or warm food for days, then weeks, and eventually months at a time, fueled the growing prisoners' rights movement. Jackson, the BGF, and their advocates outside prison argued for more public oversight and judicially mandated reform, as well as for revolutionary overthrow. The ongoing lockdowns bolstered their claims.

Jackson thought of himself as a fiercely independent revolutionary, but his radicalism was also the product of complex institutional interactions:

the oppressiveness of the indeterminate prison sentence, the politics of the Black Power movement, the hope of the civil rights movement, and the violence and racism pervading the California prison system.

Eighteen Deaths in Eighteen Months, 1970–71

The first three of the seventy-one prisoner homicides recorded between 1970 and 1974 in California prisons took place in January 1970. Soledad State Prison's O-Wing had been locked down on and off for months. According to prison officials, O-Wing housed some of the biggest security risks in the state, including George Jackson and his mentor, W. L. Nolen. Steve Nolen, the younger brother of W.L., remembered visiting Soledad in those days. Steve was in college at Chico State, so he would drive "two, three hours" to get to Soledad. (Probably longer, in fact: Soledad is about 280 miles south of Chico.) He remembered: "Half the time you get there and they're saying you can't see him" because of the lockdowns.[30]

But sometimes, both W.L. and George Jackson would "try to fix it so they got out at the same time." Steve remembered George Jackson as both "more direct" and bigger than his brother W.L., "by about 30, 35 pounds." Steve knew that W.L. was "George's mentor" and "tried to keep George straight." Steve remembered W.L. as calm and smart: "just the mellowest thing" and "infinitely brighter than I am . . . a really, really sharp guy." The oldest Nolen brother, Cornel, was also in prison at the time, at San Quentin, although Cornel was less politicized. "W.L. and Cornel and the time that they spent—they had nerves of steel. Nerves of steel," Steve said.[31]

On January 13, 1970, guards released the prisoners from Soledad's locked-down O-Wing onto the prison yard. Steve said his brother W.L. "knew that they were setting up something, but he didn't know the moment or the circumstances, how it was going to break out."[32] Nolen had recently circulated a petition among the Soledad prison population, seeking to initiate a lawsuit against prison officials for harassment, abuse, and endangerment of black prisoners.[33] He was not keeping a low profile. On that January day, according to everyone whom Steve asked, W.L. could have chosen not to go out to the exercise yard. "I found that out from everybody I talked to," Steve said.[34] But W.L. had those "nerves of steel," and he went out onto the yard.

There were fifteen prisoners on the yard that day, each "defined as racist by the prison": seven were black nationalists, and the rest were anti-black nationalists (or white racists). All had been locked down, on and off, for months at a time.[35] A fight quickly broke out between white and black prisoners. Officer Opie Miller, watching from a guard tower, shot into the melee with his rifle, hitting three of the black prisoners: Cleveland Edwards, Alvin Miller, and W. L. Nolen.[36] Steve remembered hearing, after the fact, how a fistfight had begun: "So the first guy came, and W.L. knocked him down. Knocked down the second, and the next thing you know, they raised the rifle and they shot him. And then they shot—I know those two guys [Edwards and Miller]—I know their mothers . . . And they killed them, successively . . . it was a grisly day."

Steve said that at first, prison officials told the Nolen family only that W.L. had been shot, but added, "It's not that bad." Steve remembered asking: "I'm saying, 'How is he shot? How did that happen?'" Prison officials responded: "Well, we can't give any explanations right now." Steve said, "You know how that works." The hours dragged on, and then at 3 p.m., "They finally delivered what it was. He's dead. And I just broke down. It was one of the rainiest times ever."[37]

Forty years later, Steve dwelled on the memory: "It was just a terrible, terrible period . . . Shooting W.L. through the heart first and then shooting others. Left his body out for him to bleed out." Steve said the last time he saw his brother was "at [the] funeral home." The experience added to the trauma: "My mother insisted on an open casket. Which is the worst thing she could have possibly done. It was like pieces of parts sewn together."[38]

Soledad prisoners called for murder charges to be brought against Officer Miller, who was white. But three days later, the district attorney in Monterey County, where Soledad prison is located, announced on the local evening news that he considered the deaths "justifiable homicide." Miller had simply fulfilled his duty to keep the prison and the community safe, the prosecutor said.[39] The targeting of W. L. Nolen, and the fact that a sharpshooter in a guard tower had killed three black prisoners (while only injuring one white prisoner), raised questions about Miller's motives and those of the prison administration and prosecutor.[40] Jackson had already declared, nearly two years earlier, that "nonviolence is a false ideal," and his politics were well known to prisoners and officials alike.[41]

On the night that the district attorney indicated he was unlikely to pursue murder charges against Office Miller, Officer John Vincent Mills, another white guard, plummeted off the third tier of Soledad's general population Y-Wing. Witnesses described an explosion of applause among the prisoners as Mills landed on the cement floor.[42] The week's death toll increased to four. A two-week investigation began. Who was responsible for the officer's death? The prison administration fingered George Jackson, along with John Clutchette and Fleeta Drumgo, for the murder. The Soledad Brothers were born.

Jackson was twenty-eight years old. His one-year-to-life sentence was looking more like a death sentence. He was transferred to the Adjustment Center (AC) at San Quentin to await trial for Mills's murder. Prosecutors intended to seek the death penalty. The AC, which had opened in 1960, was a state-of-the-art high-security facility, three stories high with barred windows and doors.[43] Jackson, like the other AC prisoners, was locked into his cell twenty-three hours or more a day with no human contact other than shouting through the bars of his cell to the twenty-seven other prisoners on his tier. Whenever he left the cell, he was handcuffed, his cuffed hands were chained to his waist, and he was leg-cuffed, too. Whenever he returned, he was strip-searched.

The violence continued despite Jackson's near-total isolation. Black prisoners argued that they had avenged only one of the three January deaths.[44] But then another black prisoner died. On February 25, 1970, Fred Billingslea, housed near Jackson in the AC, died in his cell. Prisoner witnesses said he was beaten and teargassed to death; prison officials said Billingslea set a fire in his cell and died of asphyxiation.[45] In March, a white guard at San Quentin sustained stab wounds but survived; James McClain, a black prisoner, was charged. In July, Officer William Schull (a white man) died on duty at Soledad prison, and the local prosecutor indicted seven more black prisoners for his murder. Total prisoner deaths: four. Total officer deaths: two. Total indictments: eleven—all black prisoners.

On August 7, 1970, guards transported James McClain from San Quentin

George Jackson, San Quentin, circa 1970
(From the Freedom Archives collection,
photographer unknown)

to the Marin County courthouse for the first day of his trial. He was the first of the black prisoners to stand trial for charges associated with the recent violence against white officers.

McClain was first part of the growing in-prison movement led by Jackson (and W. L. Nolen before that) and then got swept up in the national wave of support for the Soledad Brothers. Angela Davis, a young assistant professor at the University of California, Los Angeles, and an established member of the Communist Party and the Black Panther Party, together with George Jackson's seventeen-year-old younger brother, Jonathan Jackson, had already drawn national attention by proclaiming the Soledad Brothers' innocence. At least some Californians were watching the McClain trial closely to see how the white guards' accusations against the black prisoner would be resolved.

Shortly after the first witness took the stand, Jonathan Jackson barged into the courtroom, brandishing at least one pistol and a carbine rifle. The guns were later traced to Angela Davis; she had legally purchased them over the past two years.[46] Jonathan Jackson, with the help of McClain and two other prisoners serving as witnesses at his trial, William Christmas and Ruchell Magee, took the judge, the district attorney, and three jurors hostage, demanding safe passage and the release of the Soledad Brothers. The younger Jackson herded the five hostages into a rented van in the courthouse parking lot and began driving out.

Within minutes, the Marin County police arrived on the scene, joining San Quentin guards. They emptied a flurry of bullets into the rented van. When the shooting was over, Jackson, McClain, Christmas, and the judge were all dead. The district attorney was permanently paralyzed. The jurors and Ruchell Magee survived.[47] (A sign over the entry gates of the San Quentin prison yard still proudly asserts the policy that prevailed on August 7, 1970: the prison, like the Marin County police in 1970, maintains a "no hostage policy," meaning that prison staff will not bargain with prisoners who take hostages.) Angela Davis became a fugitive, was caught in October of 1970, jailed, and stood trial in 1972 for the kidnapping and murder of the judge. An all-white jury acquitted her.[48]

As of August 7, 1970, total deaths in and out of prison: ten.

Meanwhile, George Jackson remained in San Quentin's Adjustment Center, awaiting trial. His first book, Soledad Brother, dedicated to his deceased younger brother, Jonathan, came out that fall. It consisted of letters that Jackson had written between 1964 and 1970 to his mother, father, siblings, and lawyers. The book received immediate critical acclaim, and comparisons were made to the best-selling Autobiography of Malcolm X and Soul on Ice, written by Eldridge Cleaver, another black California prisoner and prominent member of the Black Panther Party.

The book's final letter, dated August 9, 1970, is addressed to Joan, a friend and member of the Soledad defense committee. Jackson mourns the death of his little brother: "I can't go any further, it would just be a love story about the baddest brother this world has had the privilege to meet, and it's just not popular or safe—to say I love him."[49] In one sentence, he evokes the tragedy of losing his brother, the politics of mourning a revolutionary, and his own proximity to deadly violence. Tragedy, politics, and violence together encapsulate the ambivalence that the Jackson brothers evoked. On one hand, George Jackson had suffered an extremely harsh punishment for his initial crime of robbery; his writings demonstrate his intelligence and thoughtfulness; he was part of the sweeping 1960s civil rights movement, fighting racism and discrimination. On the other hand, he may have killed a prison guard, he advocated revolutionary violence, and the brother he was so proud of had kidnapped a judge and a prosecutor at gunpoint.

In his published letters, Jackson says more than once that he thought the killing of Officer Mills was justified. But he never admitted to killing him, and no clear evidence linking him to the murder was ever presented in court. The polarized interpretations of Jonathan Jackson's acts at the Marin County courthouse, and George Jackson's role in the events, echoed in the conflicting narratives about what happened next.

In August 1971, as the first anniversary of his brother's death approached, Jackson prepared to face trial for Officer Mills's death. He had completed a second book of letters and essays, *Blood in My Eye,* which would be published early in 1972, to further critical acclaim.[50] By now, Jackson had a substantial team of legal representatives, more than he ever could have hoped for in the early 1960s, when he was an unknown black kid facing a de facto life sentence for robbery. Now, at twenty-nine, as one of the nationally recognized Soledad Brothers, he faced a potential death sentence for murder.

George Jackson's legal team was working hard.[51] In April 1971, they filed a complaint alleging multiple instances of prison officials' interference in preparing Jackson's defense: hiding and paroling prisoner witnesses favorable to Jackson, and abusing and coercing others into testifying against him.[52] Many prisoners filed declarations and depositions about these tactics. But much of the evidence was never formally presented in a court of law because Jackson never got his day in court.

On Saturday, August 21, Stephen Bingham, one of Jackson's lawyers, came into San Quentin for a scheduled attorney-client visit. Bingham, who came from a wealthy Connecticut family, was exactly Jackson's age: twenty-nine. A graduate of Boalt Hall Law School at the University of California, Berkeley, he had participated in the 1964 Freedom Summer in Mississippi, had recently returned from the Peace Corps, and was an avowed member of the New Left, with communist leanings.[53] With him was Vanita Anderson, a defense-team investigator. On that afternoon at the San Quentin prison gate, the two consented to a search of Bingham's papers and Anderson's cassette recorder. A few days later the *Washington Post* reported that Bingham had passed through a metal detector and that a guard inspected the tape recorder's battery case.[54]

Anderson, who had already visited Jackson once that week, was denied entry (because of new rules the prison had instituted in response to the popularity of prisoners like Jackson). According to Bingham, however, the guard on duty encouraged him to take Anderson's tape recorder into the prison, along with the galleys (typeset pages) of Jackson's new book. The guards had already taken the recorder apart to confirm that there was nothing inside it, and Bingham entered the prison without Anderson.[55] In another account of what happened, Daniel P. Scarborough, a guard who was responsible for processing prison visitors that afternoon, said that Bingham also brought in a batch of legal papers, stapled together, carried inside an accordion file folder.[56]

Carl Larson, who was then working as a correctional counselor at the state prison in Chino, in Southern California, remembered talking over the day's events with his friend James Park, the associate warden of San Quentin, who happened to be the administrative officer on duty that afternoon. According to Larson, Park took the call from a lieutenant who wanted to know whether to let Bingham and his tape recorder into the prison: "When Bingham came into the prison, he had a tape recorder, he was going to visit with George Jackson, and the officer at the gate wanted to take the tape recorder apart. The lawyer argued, got offended, resisted, asked for a supervisor. The officer calls a lieutenant, says, 'You can't come in with that.' The officer calls Jim Park, and Jim Park approved it, said, 'Let it go in.' "[57] A day earlier, Park had been less accommodating, issuing a new policy limiting reporter interviewers of prisoners in "lockups" like the Adjustment Center to once every three months.[58] But Bingham was a lawyer, not a reporter, so he entered the prison, allegedly with Park's personal approval. Bingham began his visit with George Jackson, who had just hours to live.

Bingham and Jackson most likely met in the same visiting rooms used for AC and death row prisoners today. In the last twenty-four hours of a death-sentenced prisoner's life, friends and lawyers often maintain a vigil, or a "deathwatch." (Visiting rules for the condemned are traditionally relaxed right before an execution, so multiple visitors can spend up to a full day with the prisoner.) Did Bingham and Jackson know they were keeping a deathwatch, counting the hours until Jackson's death?

Only Bingham can say. He was acquitted in 1986 of all charges relating to the day's events. At the end of the visit, not long before three, he left the prison, tape recorder and briefcase in hand. A guard escorted Jackson back to his cell in the Adjustment Center.

What happened next is another mystery. The historian Eric Cummins says, "According to most versions of the legend . . . Jackson drew a gun on his escorting officer."[59] Johnny Spain, another prisoner, said simply: "There was a gun introduced into the Adjustment Center."[60] At any rate, all the AC prisoners on the first tier, including Spain and Jackson, somehow managed to get out of their cells. Many later testified that Jackson shouted: "The dragon has come!"—a reference to a poem by the North Vietnamese leader Ho Chi Minh about the power of imprisonment to generate revolutionary fervor.

Jackson then dashed from the AC, running toward the middle of the prison yard. Spain followed but ducked under a bush just as gunshots rang out.

Jackson fell down, alone in the open space of the prison yard, dead.

There was a gunshot wound in his back and one in his head.[61] Some autopsy reports said a single bullet had ricocheted from an entry point in his back, up his spine, and out through his head. Others said the bullet traveled in the opposite direction. John Clutchette, one of the other Soledad Brothers, claimed that Jackson was shot in the back by a guard in a gun tower overlooking the yard and was then surrounded by guards from within the prison yard and shot again in the head.[62] However many bullets actually entered his body, he died quickly.

When the prison guards reentered the Adjustment Center, they found more carnage: three guards and two prisoners (all white) stabbed to death, their bodies piled into what had been Jackson's cell. The historian Dan Berger describes the retaliatory violence that followed: guards stripped, handcuffed, and hog-tied twenty-six prisoners from the AC and left them naked in the San Quentin prison yard, where Jackson lay dead, too. That evening, the AC prisoners were systematically interrogated and beaten.[63]

"We Are Investigating"

Within hours, Park, the associate warden, was on-site at the prison, preparing to host a press conference. In an audio recording of that event, a reporter breathlessly describes watching at the prison gates as "an ambulance carrying two bodies, a panel truck carrying two, and that was a station wagon carrying one body" leave the prison in succession. The same reporter describes watching as "reporters and news technicians are given a full-body search."[64]

Park's account of what had just happened was matter-of-fact:

> At 3 p.m., there was an attempted break from our Adjustment Center, which is our maximum-security facility. Apparently a gun was smuggled in . . . in the possession of George Jackson. They captured the officers. They murdered three officers. They murdered white inmates that were tier tenders, who were working in the Adjustment Center. George Jackson was killed as he broke and ran outside of the Adjustment Center. These are the bare facts. We are investigating . . . This apparently was a carefully planned attempt to break out of the institution, a foolish attempt I believe, but an attempt that showed again complete disregard for the lives of officers who did not deserve to die and three inmates who did not deserve to die.[65]

At the end of this statement, a clamor of reporters can be heard, and the questions begin. The first is why the warden mentioned that the dead "tier tender" prisoners were white.

Later in the press conference, Park said: "We can't say who killed who at this point. We're investigating. It'll be a big snarl to unravel."[66] The snarl was never quite unraveled. Even the initial, basic facts that Park presented have been disputed.

Jackson wrote and spoke frequently about his desire to escape. Some claim, however, that he was not trying to escape on August 21, but was set up for assassination by the Criminal Conspiracy Section of the Los Angeles Police Department, which had infiltrated the Black Panther Party in both Los Angeles and the Bay Area in an attempt to track and control the revolutionaries.[67] Others argue that the prison guards set Jackson up, first as a troublemaker, then as the murderer of Officer Mills, and finally as an attempted escapee.[68]

Regarding the causes of death, Park said: "I don't know whether there were any gunshot deaths, other than George Jackson, who was killed from an armed post."[69] Only one other gunshot wound (of one of the guards) was ever established; the five other casualties died of stab wounds.[70] In a pamphlet published in France in November 1971, Michel Foucault, a prominent philosopher of punishment, argued that the news around Jackson's death was plagued with "impossibilities and contradictions," and he called the killing a "masked assassination" in a revolutionary war.[71] So the conspiracy-to-assassinate theory even had international proponents.

A journalist who covered the civil unrest of these years explained that law enforcement officials had "good reason" to fear that the legal system would never sanction or silence Jackson's revolutionary rabble-rousing. Several Black Panther radicals across the United States had been acquitted of conspiracy and murder charges in the two years immediately preceding Jackson's scheduled trial. A jury first convicted Huey Newton, tried for murdering an Oakland police officer, of a reduced charge of manslaughter, and then the conviction was overturned. Charges against Bobby Seale for inciting a riot in Chicago, and later for murder in New Haven, were dismissed, and the related convictions of his codefendants were overturned. And a jury acquitted the Panther 21 defendants, accused of plotting to blow up a New York department store. Karen Wald sums up: "It is no wonder, then, that by the summer of 1971 law enforcement agents—from cops on the beat to guards in prison—had little faith in the reliability of the legal system. If they wanted revolutionary leaders disposed of, they would have to do it themselves, as revelations about the FBI's 'Cointelpro' program have recently revealed. Murder was on the agenda."[72]

Rational justifications aside, prison officials spun a different conspiracy theory. In the days following the six deaths, prison administrators repeatedly retold the conspiracy-to-escape story, claiming that Bingham had smuggled an Astra M-600 nine-millimeter semiautomatic pistol and a wig (in which Jackson could conceal the gun) into the prison inside his tape recorder. As Foucault pointed out in his "masked assassination" pamphlet, the make and model of the gun seemed to change with every telling of the story.[73] Inconsistencies about the kind of gun that Jackson had suggests further ambiguity about what happened on August 21, 1971.

By the time I interviewed Carl Larson, though, forty years later, there was some consistency around the claim that the gun had been a nine-millimeter Astra M-600. Larson told me: "In the tape recorder was an afro and a 9 mm . . . Jim Park had to live with that for the rest of his career. He was a real nice guy; he just made a terrible mistake."[74] Incidentally, an Astra M-600 weighs more than two pounds and is nine inches long (its nickname is the "pipe wrench"), making it difficult to conceal in either a 1970s tape recorder or under a wig, as demonstrated in a simulation by the *San Francisco Chronicle* in 1971 of the alleged events surrounding Jackson's death.[75] One historian called the scenario described by Larson and other guards "implausible in the extreme."[76] Scarborough, the guard who wrote a 2011 memoir about working inside San Quentin in August 1971, tried to clarify. He said Bingham concealed the gun between stapled pieces of paper.[77] The story that Bingham smuggled in a gun, one way or another, lives on, seemingly told and retold by every prison guard who has ever worked at San Quentin or anywhere within the California prison system.

Six prisoners were ultimately charged as accomplices in the murders of the five people found in George Jackson's cell on the day of his alleged escape attempt.[78] One of the six, Fleeta Drumgo, who was also one of the original Soledad Brothers, was acquitted of all the murder charges against him and paroled from prison shortly after the trial. He died in a shootout on the streets of Oakland three years later, in 1979. Luis Talamantez and Willie Tate were acquitted of all charges and paroled in the 1970s. David Johnson was convicted on one count of assault but paroled later in the 1970s. Johnny Spain was convicted on two counts of murder, but the conviction was overturned in 1982, and he was paroled in 1988. Hugo "Yogi" Pinell was convicted on two counts of assault and remained incarcerated—in solitary confinement—for the rest of his life.[79]

In sum, only three of the San Quentin Six were convicted on any of the charges against them, and the single murder conviction was ultimately overturned. We will probably never know the actual circumstances surrounding George Jackson's death: whether the black prisoners who died at Soledad were killed accidentally or were targeted by guards; whether James Park truly believed he was responsible for allowing a nine-millimeter pistol into San Quentin, precipitating the deaths of six people; whether Jackson had plotted to escape that day; or how a gun got into the high-security Adjustment Center in the first place. But the very existence of these questions suggests how much discretion prison administrators had, and continue to have, not just over what happens behind prison walls, but also over what stories get told about what happens there.

A Legacy, Locked Down

Prison officials ultimately controlled the narrative of what happened to George Jackson, and they leveraged this narrative repeatedly to justify harsh, often abusive conditions of confinement.[80] First, they were judicious in collecting—or in failing to collect—evidence surrounding George Jackson's alleged escape attempt and the other violent prisoner deaths in California prisons in 1970 and 1971. Not a single guard or prison official has faced any criminal charges for the deaths of California prisoners in the early 1970s. Of course, none of the San Quentin Six was ultimately convicted of murder, either. But prison officials maintained them all in solitary confinement for the duration of their sentences—up to forty-five years.

Second, prison officials cultivated the image of Jackson as the archetypally dangerous—both physically and ideologically—prisoner. Joshua Page has argued that George Jackson, and everything he represented, was a major impetus in mobilizing the union of California prison guards to become more politically active; thirteen guards resigned in the wake of the Jackson incident.[81] Carl Larson, who would ultimately take credit for Pelican Bay, told me that "the national revolutionary movement that culminated in George Jackson" was pivotal to understanding why California built a supermax.[82] Likewise, when I asked Steve Cambra, who worked as a prison guard in California and later served as the warden of Pelican Bay State Prison, about the origins of supermax prisons, he described to me how just six months after he started working at San Quentin as a correctional officer, three officers were stabbed. He remembered the exact date and the day of the week: Saturday, August 21, 1971. And he described the stabbings in graphic detail—"officers were cut ear to ear."[83] Craig Brown, who served as undersecretary of corrections for the state in the 1980s, also cited "officers killed at the hands of inmates . . . in the '70s" as a justification for the supermax.[84]

None of these prison officials discussed the consistent declines in violence in the California prison system after 1974. (Violence in California prisons has never again risen to pre-1974 levels.)[85] Instead, they spoke of the guards stabbed on the day George Jackson died, nearly forty years before, as if the deaths had taken place last week and as if Jackson's responsibility for them had been conclusively established.

For prison officials, Jackson embodied a genuine fear that they were losing control of the prisons. Carl Larson described to me how officers he was responsible for supervising in the 1970s were threatened, stabbed, or thrown off prison tiers to their deaths. He told me that he felt helpless to protect them, as well as the majority of prisoners—those who wanted only to get through their sentences and had no inclination to murder their cellmates, run gangs, or organize violent resistance. For officials like Larson, the prisons that existed in the 1970s could not control Jackson and his fellow revolutionaries. Permanently isolating George Jackson and his "comrades" seemed like the best possible alternative to revolutionary chaos.

At San Quentin (and also at Folsom, Soledad, and Tehachapi) in the 1970s, guards kept any prisoner who had been active in the Black Guerrilla Family, or who was believed to be associated with George Jackson, in his cell around the clock. These lockdowns were necessary for "management control" of the "race wars" in prison, officials said, based on "an institutional perception" that the prisoners posed "a threat to the safety of other inmates or staff."[86] Lockdowns were not new in California. Soledad's O-Wing had been locked down intermittently for months before the fight that led to the shooting deaths of W. L. Nolen, Cleveland Edwards, and Alvin Miller in January 1970; San Quentin's B-Block had been frequently locked down, too.[87] But after the carnage at San Quentin, the lockdowns became permanent. Some prisoners, like Johnny Spain and Hugo Pinell, were simply never again released from their cells for any kind of group activity.[88] By the mid-1980s, prison officials in California were making plans to turn permanent lockdowns into a physical feature of the system—by building one of the first supermax prisons.

Today, a prisoner's slightest association with Jackson's legacy justifies everything from executions to permanent solitary confinement. For instance, in December 2005, Stanley "Tookie" Williams, a former gang member turned outspoken advocate for nonviolence, sought clemency from Governor Arnold Schwarzenegger. Schwarzenegger denied the petition, noting that Williams's inclusion of George Jackson in the dedication of one of his books "defies reason and is a significant indicator that Williams is not reformed."[89] The governor recast both Williams's and Jackson's radicalism as criminal, and then relied on this criminalization to justify an execution.[90] The State of California executed Williams on December 14, 2005.

Again in 2011, prison officials leveraged Jackson's legacy to resist claims from prisoners that they deserved different, better treatment. During the 2011–13 series of prisoner hunger strikes originating in the Pelican Bay SHU, prison officials "revalidated" Ronnie Sitawa Dewberry, who collaborated with Todd Ashker in leading the strikes, as a Black Guerrilla Family member. By revalidating Dewberry, prison officials further extended his indefinite solitary confinement. Three photographs of George Jackson justified this revalidation; the gang "chrono" reaffirming Dewberry's status as a BGF member explained: "BGF members believe Jackson to be a martyr, and utilize pictures that depict Jackson as a symbol of their dedication to the gang."[91] Jackson may inspire awe in the BGF, but he inspires fear in California prison guards.

Jackson's legacy as the archetypally dangerous prisoner even dominates mainstream cultural interpretations. For instance, in a *New Yorker* article in 2014, Jeffrey Toobin, a well-respected legal journalist, described Jackson's "radical politics, misogyny, and criminality" as the inspiration for the brutality enacted by BGF gang members in Baltimore in 2007.[92] Such an analysis elides Jackson's other legacies as a black intellectual, a best-selling author, and a persecuted revolutionary who maintained his innocence regarding both the initial theft charge that landed him in prison and the later murder charge that saw him presumptively sentenced to death.

Riots Coast to Coast

George Jackson's own guilt might be ambiguous, but his posthumous association with other instances of violence in prison is clear. Just days after he died, on the morning of Thursday, September 9, 1971, a riot broke out at Attica Correctional Facility in upstate New York. Racial tensions were high in the prison; half of the prisoners were black, but all the guards were white. Within hours, prisoners took over the central control facility in the prison, seized forty-two guards and civilians as hostages, and issued a list of demands. Their tactics were dramatic, but the demands were basic (and echoed ones made by prisoners around the country): better medical treatment, cleaner living conditions, decent food, less physical brutality.[93] Prisoners pointed to George Jackson as the inspiration for their revolt.[94] A few days before the riot, Attica prisoners had held a silent fast in observation of Jackson's death.[95]

During the Attica takeover, prisoners beat one guard, who later died, and executed three fellow inmates for failure to participate in the rebellion. But dozens of guards remained safe, and more than 2,200 prisoners survived. Until day four.

At first, the prisoners negotiated peacefully with a group of high-profile public officials, including Russell Oswald (correctional commissioner), Tom Wicker (New York Times editor), John Dunne (state senator), and William Kunstler (noted civil rights lawyer). But seventy-two hours into the standoff, negotiations broke down, and Commissioner Oswald and Governor Rockefeller ordered state police to retake the prison. State National Guard troops joined the police forces.[96] The assault in the prison ended in thirty-nine deaths—twenty-nine prisoners, seven guards, and three civilians. National Guard fire killed all thirty-nine. According to the state commission that later investigated the riot, Attica was "the bloodiest single encounter, Indian massacres aside, between Americans since the Civil War."[97] The death toll rivaled the total of prisoner and guard deaths throughout the California prison system during the entire 1970s.

As with Jackson's death, the events at Attica precipitated years of litigation and unresolved debates over responsibility for the carnage.[98] As recently as 2015, Eric Schneiderman, the New York attorney general, sought the disclosure of documents gathered during the investigation of the incident. These documents revealed that contrary to claims that prisoners caused all the violence, police and guards beat and tortured prisoners after they retook the prison.[99]

Nonetheless, as with George Jackson, Attica itself became iconic in correctional mythology, justifying oppression, abuse, and silence. The "ghosts of Attica" haunt officers, who fear prisoner insubordination, and prisoners, who are still subject to unjustified beatings by unrepentant guards, who face few consequences. A *New York Times* story published on the heels of the riot's fortieth anniversary detailed the near-fatal beating of a black prisoner at Attica by three white guards in 2011. Afterward, the guards falsely charged the victim with possession of a weapon. Each officer ultimately pleaded guilty to a misdemeanor; none served any prison time.[100]

The *Times* explained that the culture of impunity, in which guards beat prisoners, charge the victims with crimes, and face little or no punishment themselves, is directly connected to the ongoing perception among Attica staffers that they must be vigilant against the ever-imminent possibility of a prisoner takeover: "To those who work at the prison, the history of the riot is an everyday reminder of the danger that inmates, who greatly outnumber guards, could take over at any time. Mark Cunningham, an Attica sergeant whose father was killed in the retaking, tells all new recruits about the events of 1971. 'I make sure it gets talked about,' Sergeant Cunningham said."

The summer after Jackson's death and the riot at Attica was particularly violent in prisons across the United States.[101] In April 1972, Brent Miller, a twenty-three-year old white prison guard, was stabbed to death at the infamous Louisiana State Penitentiary in Angola.[102] Albert Woodfox and Herman Wallace, vocal Black Panther members, were charged with the murder. They were placed in solitary confinement immediately, along with a third African American prisoner, Robert King. King remained in isolation for twenty-nine years, Wallace for forty-one years, and Woodfox for forty-three years. Courts overturned all three men's convictions, repeatedly, but Louisiana prosecutors kept appealing every judgment favorable to the "Angola Three." Wallace died of liver cancer three days after he was released from prison, but King and Woodfox have survived to tell their stories.[103]

The pattern was repeated elsewhere in the United States. In June 1972, a prisoner killed a guard at the maximum-security Iowa State Penitentiary. Warner Kelly, the prisoner charged with the murder, was locked down continuously for the next two years (and successfully challenged the conditions of his isolation).[104] In July 1972, in Massachusetts, a prisoner killed a guard, an instructor, and then himself in an escape attempt from the high-security

Norfolk State Prison.[105] In each case, prison officials and prisoners disputed the circumstances of the assaults for decades afterward; meanwhile, prisoners suffered overt abuses and indefinite lockdowns.

This pattern was repeated in federal prisons, too. Between 1972 and the early 1980s, the United States Penitentiary (USP) at Marion, Illinois, saw a series of disturbances. In July 1972, prisoners refused to leave their cells to work. They were protesting conditions such as the CARE (Control and Rehabilitation Effort) program, which subjected prisoners to brainwashing techniques that had been studied and refined by the military in the 1950s and 1960s.[106] The strike continued, on and off, for the next few months. Prisoners were locked down in a newly created "Control Unit" at Marion.[107] A decade later, on October 22, 1983, two prisoners in the USP-Marion Control Unit killed two guards in separate incidents.[108] Following these two deaths, prison officials declared a state of emergency, and all 435 cells at USP-Marion were locked down.[109] Tommy Silverstein, who murdered Officer Merle Clutts at USP-Marion in 1983, remained locked down in 2015, in total isolation, more than thirty years later. Silverstein had been locked down for years before he murdered Clutts, following the 1970s work stoppages at Marion, and he is now one of the longest-isolated prisoners in the United States.[110] He was transferred to the new federal supermax in Florence, Colorado, the Administrative Maximum, when it opened in 1995.

Still, prisoners across the United States continued to organize work stoppages and riots.[111] The Iowa State Penitentiary saw riots in 1981 and 1986.[112] In 1980, 33 prisoners died in a riot at the Penitentiary of New Mexico.[113] One of the most recent incidents took place in Ohio in 1993, when 450 prisoners at Lucasville Penitentiary rioted and took control of the facility for eleven days. Nine prisoners and one officer died; five prisoners were ultimately sentenced to death for their actions.[114] In total, between 1971 and 1986, there were more than three hundred prison riots across the United States.[115]

In each state, the organized and disorganized violence precipitated extended periods of isolation and lockdown. And nearly every state that experienced such riots and lockdowns eventually followed California's lead, building a supermax prison to institutionalize the lockdowns.[116] Prisoners had terrified prison officials; in response, prison officials built new institutions to terrorize prisoners.

The flag at half-staff on the San Quentin yard is a marker of a state of permanent exception: after George Jackson and Attica, chaos demanded an extreme response—an archipelago of concrete boxes.[117]

3

The Most Dangerous Policies

WHEN GEORGE JACKSON DIED IN AUGUST 1971, when Attica rioted in September 1971, and even when Tommy Silverstein murdered Officer Merle Clutts in 1983, prison lockdowns drew frequent public attention and generated significant controversy. As early as 1973, California legislators and federal judges alike criticized long-term lockdowns in places such as San Quentin. Eight members of the California Assembly's Select Committee on Prison Reform and Rehabilitation visited six state prisons in the fall of 1973 in order to inspect, in person, each prison's isolation facilities, including "adjustment centers" like those where Johnny Spain and Hugo Pinell were housed.

In September 1973, the committee issued a report condemning the conditions of confinement that its members had seen; the system the report said, "not only segregates . . . but oppresses and represses."[1] The legislators recommended the immediate closure of some isolation facilities at San Quentin and Folsom and extensive reforms to the remaining facilities, along with reforming the disciplinary-hearing process; establishing rules for when prisoners could be locked up and when they would be released from lockup; providing education, group counseling, and mental and physical health care to prisoners in isolation; maintaining small libraries; providing hot food; and allowing prisoners at least an hour of daily outdoor exercise.[2]

Few of the recommendations were implemented. Instead, prison officials built the Pelican Bay SHU. And for decades, no legislators paid any attention to the place. By 2013, Todd Ashker was complaining—in widely publicized memorandums, through well-organized hunger strikes, and by filing a new federal lawsuit alleging unconstitutional conditions of confinement— about the same lack of due process, education, counseling, health care, food, and exercise that legislators had condemned forty years earlier. And as with Jackson's articulate critiques in *Soledad Brother,* Ashker's critiques forced the prison system to defend its harsh policies to an inquisitive, critical public.

By month two of the 2013 hunger strike, a handful of prisoners (the prison system did not disclose how many) had been hospitalized. Most had signed "do not resuscitate" (DNR) orders. Prisoners' lawyers and state officials, unwilling to stand aside and watch prisoners die, attempted to negotiate an alternative. On August 19, as the strike entered its seventh week, Judge Thelton Henderson, who was then overseeing a statewide class-action case regarding constitutionally inadequate prison health care, signed an order permitting the "re-feeding" of prisoners.[3] The term was unclear. Did it mean prison officials could provide intravenous fluids and nutrients to prisoners who lost consciousness? Or did it authorize forcing a tube down a wide-awake prisoner's nose against his will?[4] With the force-feeding of detainees at the U.S. military base in Guantánamo Bay, Cuba, having already attracted international condemnation, California appeared to be speeding toward a human rights fiasco.

A Bloodless Analysis

On August 30, just over a week after Judge Henderson signed the re-feeding order, state senator Loni Hancock and state assembly member Tom Ammiano, both Democrats representing famously liberal districts in Northern California, held a press conference at which they promised to investigate California's solitary confinement policies and to consider legislative reforms.[5] It was a desperate bid to end the embarrassingly large (thirty thousand prisoners participating) and dangerously long (eight weeks and counting) hunger strike. Given the promise of legislative hearings, the prisoners agreed, to everyone's relief, to resume eating. Judge Henderson and the California Department of Corrections were saved from defining "refeeding."

But hearings alone would not quiet the movement for long: the legislature would need to propose genuine reforms or else risk resumption of the strike. And history suggested that even targeted legislative recommendations for reform could be ignored or at least avoided. The first hearings, in the shadow of this threat, would be tense. I was looking forward to watching them.

A week later, however, Hancock's chief of staff called my office, inviting me to testify. So much for being a bystander. Because I had been researching solitary confinement and California SHUs for more than ten years at that point, I had developed a few theories about what was wrong with California's prison policies. But I also had a few theories about what was wrong with previous reform efforts, such as why the 1973 Select Committee's recommendations had been so thoroughly ignored. Still, one year out of graduate school, I was more accustomed to analyzing archival documents of legislative hearings than to addressing legislators, and thereby becoming part of the archived transcript myself.

I decided that it would be most effective if I wrote my testimony with Carl Larson in mind. If I could convince the former warden, who was still dwelling on George Jackson's legacy of violent revolution, that solitary confinement could be reformed in California, perhaps the politically divided legislature could be convinced, too.

On October 9, I flew from Los Angeles to Sacramento, arriving at eight in the morning. I took a cab directly to the capitol, where Senator Hancock's chief of staff met me and introduced me to Margaret Winter, an ACLU lawyer who would present testimony just before me. "Peggy," as she warmly corrected me, had been litigating prison conditions cases, including the unconstitutional overuse of solitary confinement, across the United States for decades. We spent the morning brainstorming with Senator Hancock's staff about legislation that would improve conditions and policies around solitary confinement—and have a chance of being enacted. After lunch, a staffer walked us over to the legislative hearing room.

I could see the crowds of prisoners' advocates chanting and holding signs on the lawn in front of the capitol. And the hearing room was full. I felt strange not being among the protesters. Over the course of my research, I had found myself drifting away from prison abolitionists, especially as I attempted to communicate more directly with prison officials. This transition seemed to be a prerequisite to gaining access to prisons as sites of research, which in turn created some of the transparency so lacking in correctional practice. Fitting neither outside nor in the hearing, I felt out of place in a staid navy suit, being escorted to the front row by a senator's aide.

At the hearing, when it was my turn to speak, I introduced myself, thanked the legislators, and said: "I would like to make two straightforward points about segregation and solitary confinement. . . . First, segregation is over-used in California today. Second . . . we need more and better information about who is in segregation in this state and why. We need more transparency."[6] I explained my two points carefully, hewing to both the facts that I had gathered through data requests and archival analyses and to the ten-minute time limit the legislators had imposed. The panel of legislators asked a few reasonable questions, especially about the potential benefits and possible alternatives to long-term solitary confinement, which I answered.

Then I stepped away from the microphone and scanned the audience, hoping to see Carl Larson, who lived nearby in Sacramento and was likely to be interested in such a hearing. I sat down in the audience, still wondering what Larson would have to say.

I was followed by Steven Czifra, who had spent eight years in the SHU, and Dolores Canales, the mother of a currently incarcerated SHU prisoner and a formerly incarcerated woman herself.[7] Czifra spoke for barely five minutes: the SHU, he said, was designed to break people, and it had broken him. He concluded: "We don't need to research anything. We already know—we already know without a doubt that long-term solitary confinement is torture."[8]

Canales followed with a detailed description of the terror of solitary confinement. She read from a letter from a young man in the Pelican Bay SHU: "The worst part of solitary confinement is the absolute state of nothingness, and without a vision, the people perish." Then she added: "Sometimes I feel that same despair . . . because nothing really changes."[9] I knew Canales as a Southern California advocate for prisoners' families and a forceful voice in the movement to abolish solitary confinement. I had invited her to speak to my undergraduate students about her passionate advocacy work, which I respected.

As Dolores spoke, I felt a blush of shame. My carefully reasoned, dispassionate testimony suddenly seemed like part of the problem: a bloodless academic analysis that reduced solitary confinement to an administrative problem with administrative solutions in an attempt to find some kind of gentlemanly compromise among diametrically opposed viewpoints. The comfortable hearing room, the well-dressed legislators' polite questions, were a universe apart from the awful reality. I had not identified the SHU as torture, had not called for its abolition. I had said nothing that gave Steven Czifra or Dolores Canales any hope of real change.

I had tried to identify reforms with which a veteran prison warden like Carl Larson might agree. But no one, I realized, was seriously trying to identify reforms (somewhere between transparency and abolition) with which both Larson and a mother like Canales might actually agree. My elation that the legislature was finally paying attention to the SHU gave way to a fear that ill-considered reforms might produce some new form of isolation, something even more hidden and more horrendous than the isolation units that Dolores described so vividly. And the whole debate began to look eerily familiar.

Liberal Intellectuals Attack Discretion

When I testified before the legislature, I focused my analysis on the need to cultivate transparency in prison operations, especially the operation of long-term solitary confinement units. I was thinking of transparency as a stepping-stone toward institutionalizing better oversight of—and restrictions on—which prisoners went to isolation and for how long. So I was making a thinly veiled argument for curbing administrative discretion—an argument that had been made, with only limited success, in the 1970s.

Two of the most trenchant scholarly indictments of the U.S. criminal justice system in the 1970s focused on illustrating the problems inherent in prison officials' discretion: the American Friends Service Committee's *Struggle for Justice,* published in June 1971, and Philip Zimbardo's Stanford

Prison Experiment, conducted in August 1971. The book and the experiment, sandwiched between the release of George Jackson's two best-selling books, changed public perceptions of punishment and provided fuel for reform initiatives.[10]

The American Friends Service Committee, a Quaker organization, commissioned *Struggle for Justice* with the intent of producing a major treatise on the contemporary state of criminal justice in the United States. The seventeen authors who collaborated to write the short volume included some of the greatest—and most radical—sociologists and criminologists of the twentieth century. Four of the authors had served time in prison, and all of them had extensive histories as advocates for the imprisoned.[11] Even with this radical pedigree, the treatise was reviewed in national newspapers such as the *Washington Post* and in elite periodicals such as the *American Scholar*.[12]

The book's authors warned of the "menace of good intentions" evident in the nation's long history of failed attempts at humanitarian prison reforms.[13] Nonetheless, they bravely laid out a new humanitarian plan: reorient criminal law toward punitive responses to specific acts and away from coercive treatment of whole individuals.[14] Redefining "felons" as people first and criminals second would require massive social restructuring. The authors therefore called on society to empower the oppressed, expand prisoners' rights, provide universal access to social services like education and health care, constrain the uses of punishment, reduce sentence lengths, and increase transparency and oversight of the criminal justice system.

Two of these recommendations gained significant traction: prisoners' rights were expanded, and sentencing systems were restructured. These recommendations, in particular, sought to constrain the kind of discretion that had kept George Jackson in prison for ten years on a minor burglary charge (and that later concealed the circumstances leading to his death and protected prison officials from prosecution). The Quakers argued that giving prison officials and parole boards nearly total control to grant or deny a prisoner's release, year after year, permitted abuse and oppression. It forced socially, mentally, or politically nonconforming prisoners to compromise their identities and values in order to earn release. And it created extreme racial disparities; African Americans tended to be denied parole more frequently and to serve longer indeterminate sentences than white prisoners.[15] For instance, in June 1971, when *Struggle for Justice* came out, George Jackson had served eleven years of a one-year-to-life sentence, eight years beyond the median time served for burglary in the California prison system in the 1960s.[16]

Imposing fixed sentences, the Quakers believed, would refocus the criminal law on acts rather than individuals, avoid the forced conformity of rehabilitation (prisoners would get out at the end of their terms, reformed or not), and eliminate racial disparities in sentencing. "It would be far better to tear down all jails," they wrote, "but we recognize this is not a real option."[17] In fact, even though prison abolition was just a dream, the abolition of indeterminate sentences would turn out to be surprisingly attainable.

Other liberal activists joined the chorus condemning the indeterminate prison sentence. Hill and Wang, which published *Struggle for Justice*, released Marvin Frankel's *Criminal Sentences: Law Without Order* the next year. Frankel, a renowned legal scholar and federal district court judge, argued that indeterminate sentencing laws gave judges and parole boards too much unchecked discretion in imposing sentences.[18] In 1974, in the best-selling book *Kind and Usual Punishment: The Prison Business*, the investigative journalist Jessica Mitford condemned both indeterminate sentences and the ideology of rehabilitative treatment, which justified the system. Mitford described a litany of abuses that prisoners suffered in the name of "treatment," including being stripped naked in isolation and being subjected to electric shock therapy and spinal punctures.[19]

Throughout the 1970s, social scientists entered prisons to study them and worked, sometimes collaboratively and sometimes contentiously, with prison administrators to improve systems of confinement and rehabilitation programs.[20] But another national report, released in 1974, critiqued many of these programs, echoing Mitford's analysis. *Effectiveness of Correctional Treatment*, commissioned by the New York governor's office, offered a meta-analysis of 231 local, national, and international studies.[21] At 1,400 closely printed pages, it hardly seemed poised to attract attention. And the governor's office avoided disseminating the report because it suggested that most governmental programs were ineffective.

But one of the report's authors, Robert Martinson, worked hard to publicize the findings. He wrote a series of popular articles, including one in *Public Interest,* in which he famously asked: "Does nothing work?"[22] The answer he gave was nuanced. Prison-based rehabilitation programs failed to reduce recidivism. Therefore, creative alternatives to incarceration deserved consideration and analysis. But a conceptually cruder message resonated with the public: rehabilitation programs did not work. The dry *Effectiveness of Correctional Treatment* report became colloquially known as the *Nothing Works Report.*[23] And *Nothing Works* merged with the larger movement against the rehabilitative ideal.[24]

Philip Zimbardo's Stanford Prison Experiment provided empirical evidence for the claim that prison could not possibly rehabilitate by documenting the abuse that inherently arises when some people have institutional power over others—even without the racial disparities that the *Struggle for Justice* authors highlighted. In August 1971, Zimbardo, a newly tenured psychology professor at Stanford University, began a carefully planned experimental simulation in a university laboratory. (The U.S. Office of Naval Research funded the project, hoping it would provide insights into guard-prisoner conflicts in military prisons.) Zimbardo and his team, including a graduate student named Craig Haney (who later became a nationally recognized prison scholar himself), recruited twenty-four middle-class, psychologically stable, college-age young men to participate in a two-week intensive study. Each man would be paid $15 a day (the equivalent of nearly $100 a day in 2015) for participating.[25] Zimbardo randomly assigned each young man to be either a guard or a prisoner. On August 14, Palo Alto Police assisted in arresting the "prisoners" and bringing them to the lab. There, the young men assigned to be guards, armed with batons, strip-searched the new prisoners, gave them prison uniforms, and locked them into cells, three at a time.

The prisoners quickly began to resist their treatment, first subtly and then more overtly. The guards retaliated. Within thirty-six hours, middle-class, psychologically healthy, randomly assigned guards were torturing middle-class, psychologically healthy, randomly assigned prisoners.

The guards forced the prisoners to strip naked, took away their bedding and blankets, ordered them to do hundreds of push-ups at a time, withheld food, locked some in a broom closet, and threatened them with worse punishments to come. After six days, less than halfway through the planned duration of the experiment, the abuse was so extreme that Zimbardo called off the simulation. That was on August 20, 1971.[26] George Jackson was killed the next day, and the Attica prison riot began nineteen days later. In the span of a few short months, popular conceptions of what was possible inside prison walls changed dramatically. The Stanford Prison Experiment became national news, and Zimbardo became an overnight celebrity in popular psychology.[27]

The participants in the Stanford study experienced "acute emotional disturbances" within two days of participation.[28] Yet their experiences paled in comparison with actual prisoner research experiences described by Jessica Mitford in *Kind and Usual Punishment*: prison administrators had induced scurvy in prisoners, infected them with malaria, and irradiated them, all for research purposes. By 1978, Congress had enacted federal regulations for all research involving human subjects—including the requirement that researchers outline the risks and benefits of any study—and heightened protections for vulnerable populations, including prisoners.[29]

Social distrust of existing imprisonment policies kept growing. By 1976, federal courts in California (and across the United States) were requiring substantial reforms to conditions in isolation units, and the California Legislature had abolished the indeterminate prison sentence, apparently further curbing discretion over the treatment of criminal defendants and prisoners alike.

Federal Judges Refine Prison Conditions

Throughout the 1970s, reformers like the authors of the *Struggle for Justice* report, Jessica Mitford, Robert Martinson, and Philip Zimbardo had good reason to think that courts were attentively limiting prison officials' discretion over the treatment of prisoners, making prisons both more transparent and more humane.[30]

In 1970, W. L. Nolen was shot dead before he could pursue his plan to litigate the constitutionality of prison conditions at Soledad. But the Soledad Brothers, and later the San Quentin Six, pursued the litigation. By early 1971, a group of ambitious young lawyers had persuaded the federal courts to recognize a "class" of all prisoners living in lockup units—like those where Nolen, and then Jackson, and finally Pinell were housed. Three cases stemming from this class-action litigation, collectively known as the *Toussaint* cases, led to a series of rulings requiring greater procedural protections for prisoners and significant ameliorations to the conditions of their confinement.[31]

When the Soledad Brothers first challenged California's practice of indeterminate isolation, they were being held in San Quentin's Adjustment Center, locked into their cells twenty-three or more hours a day, pending adjudication of their murder charges in the death of the Soledad guard John Vincent Mills.[32] Jackson and Clutchette argued that they—along with one hundred others in the AC—had been placed in indeterminate isolation without adequate due process.[33] When Clutchette filed his suit, he had already spent ten months in isolation, ten times the traditional maximum term of thirty days.[34] This indeterminate isolation, potentially lasting for "the duration of his sentence," was what first caught Judge Alfonso Zirpoli's attention.[35]

In June 1971, Judge Zirpoli, a federal judge for the Northern District of California, ordered the California Department of Corrections to halt all disciplinary proceedings at San Quentin. He required prison officials to design, for judicial review, a constitutionally adequate set of rules for disciplinary hearings, including the provision of "counsel or a counsel substitute." This ruling overturned the disciplinary proceedings that had landed Clutchette and Jackson in the San Quentin AC.[36]

But Judge Zirpoli delayed implementation of his order, pending appeal by the state's attorney general, who pursued the case all the way to the U.S. Supreme Court. In April 1976, the Supreme Court ruled that prison disciplinary hearings required some due process: notice of the hearing and presentation of evidence in a prisoner's defense. But the Court overturned earlier decisions requiring counsel for prisoners facing in-prison disciplinary hearings.[37]

Meanwhile, Clutchette had been acquitted of the murder charges in Mills's death—further calling into question the validity of the prison disciplinary hearing that sent him to isolation. Clutchette was released from prison in March 1972, four years before the Supreme Court heard the case that he had initiated with Jackson.[38]

After Clutchette was released from prison, the San Quentin Six (Johnny Spain, Fleeta Drumgo, David Johnson, Hugo Pinell, Luis Talamantez, and Willie Tate), who were divided into six "management cells" on the first floor of the San Quentin AC, kept the litigation about indefinite solitary confinement going.[39] They filed *Spain v. Procunier* in December 1973, again complaining about the lack of due process in their assignment to the AC and the harsh conditions of confinement there. Again, Judge Zirpoli handled the case—this time overseeing a twenty-nine-day trial and interrogating the prisoners' claims. By the time he issued a decision in January 1976, each of the San Quentin Six had spent at least four years in the AC—"with no indication of when they will be released therefrom."[40]

Although Judge Zirpoli chastised the San Quentin Six's lawyers for attempting to "excuse the seriousness" of their clients' crimes, and asserted that the plaintiffs, especially Hugo Pinell, were considered to be among the state's "most dangerous" prisoners, he still found egregious constitutional violations in the San Quentin AC.[41] He ordered that each of the San Quentin Six plaintiffs either be granted a proper disciplinary hearing, with full due process protections, or else be released into the general prison population, as he had ordered for Clutchette. He also condemned the prison system for using tear gas, neck chains, and other non-handcuff mechanical restraints on AC prisoners, and he ordered prison officials to provide prisoners at least five hours a week of outdoor exercise.[42] This time, Judge Zirpoli did not delay implementation of his order pending appeal, but the attorney general appealed even more persistently. Ultimately, appellate courts upheld Judge Zirpoli's limitations on the use of tear gas, abolition of neck chains (but not other mechanical restraints), and requirements for outdoor exercise.[43]

But the litigation continued. In 1976, prisoners in four of California's maximum-security isolation units (San Quentin, Folsom, Soledad, and Tracy) brought suit, reiterating the claims made in *Clutchette* and *Spain* about conditions and durations of confinement in the San Quentin AC. In *Wright v. Enomoto*, hundreds of prisoners across the state alleged that they were spending months—sometimes years—almost continuously locked in cells measuring five by eight feet, with poor ventilation and poor lighting.

None of the *Wright* prisoners had been convicted of in-prison disciplinary violations. Instead, the reasons for their confinement included "institutional convenience," "being a threat," and "believed to have leadership qualities."[44] Many of the hearings in which these assessments were made lasted less than five minutes, and were neither recorded nor transcribed. A three-judge panel found that the hearing and isolation assignment procedures described by the prisoners were egregiously unconstitutional and issued a corrective order before even conducting a formal hearing. The judges ultimately ordered that all prisoners in "administrative segregation" receive the same procedural safeguards that had been upheld for Clutchette, including notice of placement and a hearing.[45] Over the next ten years, courts found that everything about the state's isolation facilities—inadequate lighting and ventilation; the inadequate provision of clean clothing, bedding, and basic medical care; the overcrowding and even double-bunking of locked-down prisoners—was unconstitutional.[46] These cases continued to be litigated until 1986.[47]

Prisoners in other states, and within the federal prison system, also challenged the conditions of lockdown confinement.[48] All of this litigation was part of a national trend of federal courts demonstrating an increased willingness to hear large class-action cases challenging the conditions of confinement in individual prisons and entire state prison systems.[49] In 1981, the U.S. Supreme Court noted that eight thousand prisoner lawsuits challenging conditions of confinement were pending in the United States; by 1981 dozens of suits had already resulted in court orders to remediate unconstitutional conditions of confinement.[50] Reformers counted up win after win in the 1970s battles to establish more humane conditions of isolated confinement and more constraints on administrative discretion over who could be assigned to long-term lockdown.

Yet state prison officials continued to maintain, and even expand, the number of prisoners held in long-term solitary confinement in California. In 1973, when the Assembly's Select Committee on Prison Reform toured lockup units in California state prisons, there were six such units, each with a capacity of roughly a hundred prisoners.[51] Ten years later, California had more than three times as many prisoners—1,780—housed in indeterminate isolation.[52] In other states too, lockdown policies gradually became standard procedure: prisoners' out-of-cell time was severely curtailed, and work programs were abolished.

The litigation of the 1970s—hopeful, progressive, humanely intended—ultimately helped normalize and standardize these conditions.[53] In California, prison officials made plans to construct new lockup units that would be free from the meddling of judges like Zirpoli. In May 1986, the undersecretary of corrections Rodney J. Blonien argued to California legislators that they needed to commit to fund a new high-security prison to replace the long-term lockdown unit at San Quentin. Blonien said that building a new prison was prison officials' only hope of reaching financially sustainable court settlements in the *Toussaint* and *Wilson* cases, in which the judges kept ordering expensive repairs to the San Quentin AC. Blonien projected that funding "a replacement facility [for San Quentin]" would cost "an estimated $250 million."[54]

Steve Fama, the attorney who represented the plaintiffs in the *Toussaint* case, said he thought a Ninth Circuit opinion issued in that case might have helped pave the way for the idea of building new prisons to avoid existing court oversight: "At a particular point there, the department opened New Folsom [later renamed California State Prison–Sacramento], and the Ninth Circuit held that the [*Toussaint*] order did not apply, and this gave the department the idea of a way out of the consent decree [oversight]."[55] In the end, prison officials in California built institutions that were explicitly isolated from public view, in rural locations, with rigid limitations on prisoners' access to mail, telephones, and visitors. In other words, prison officials implemented rules inside these new institutions that, in practice even if not in principle, discouraged prisoners from accessing either the courts or the rest of the outside world.

Prison officials avoided oversight in other ways, too. Intervention by judges like Zirpoli inspired frustration and resistance among prison officials, who responded by tailoring policies to do no more than meet bare minimum standards for constitutional conditions.[56] In a report investigating the lockup facilities at Folsom Prison in 1986, for instance, the state auditor general noted that the *Toussaint* court had not required contact visits for prisoners in lockup units. The report, therefore, recommended eliminating contact visits for these prisoners.[57] In a response to the audit, prison officials agreed that this was a reasonable goal and committed to work toward providing adequate space for noncontact visits, using the court order to justify a reduction in prisoners' privileges.[58] Prison officials exercised a kind of compliant resistance, rejecting the spirit of humane (or at least not cruel and unusual) confinement underlying the court orders.[59] Meanwhile, prison officials faced meddling oversight not only from the courts, but from the legislature as well.

Legislators Make Sentencing Determinate

When *Struggle for Justice* was published, and throughout the early years of the *Clutchette* and *Toussaint* litigation, indeterminate sentences (wide-ranging and vague periods such as George Jackson's "one year to life") seemed well established. In 1970, former U.S. attorney general Ramsey Clark praised California's indeterminate sentencing law as providing "the best of both worlds—long protection for the public yet a fully flexible opportunity for the convict's rehabilitation."[60] Most states had adopted indeterminate sentencing systems (along with parole) between 1876 and 1922; California adopted such a system in 1917. By 1970, thirty-seven states had these systems, and Clark predicted that the indeterminate sentence would only grow in popularity.[61] But the tide was about to turn.

Under indeterminate sentencing, California judges handed out sentences lasting some indefinite period, frequently one year to life.[62] These terms, they believed, encouraged prisoners to work toward rehabilitation in order to keep their prison time as short as possible. In practice, the convicted criminal never knew whether his term would end after a year, or whether, as in George Jackson's case, that year was only the first of tens of years behind bars. After one year, the prisoner would have a parole hearing in front of one member of the Adult Authority, a parole board made up of eight law enforcement and corrections personnel appointed by the governor.[63] Hearings lacked any semblance of due process: they had no written procedural rules, no lawyers were permitted, no cross-examination was allowed, and no transcripts were produced.[64] Hearings were highly individualized, assessing each prisoner's personal situation and progress toward rehabilitation, based on guards' observations about a prisoner's capacity to follow rules and willingness to participate in work or education programs. Until the authority deemed a prisoner ready for parole, and "fixed" his or her sentence, the prisoner was presumptively serving the maximum sentence, usually life.[65] Typical in this regard, George Jackson served eleven years on a one-year-to-life sentence, because the Adult Authority never deemed him eligible for parole and so never "fixed" his sentence at anything less than life.

Originally, the Adult Authority had included some "sympathetic" experts, like educators and social scientists, alongside prison officials. But legislators abandoned this requirement in 1953.[66] By 1971, the authority lacked both sympathetic experts and legitimacy. Critics of the authority complained about exactly the same problems—lack of due process, lack of transparency, and excesses of harshness and discretion—that prisoners and their lawyers had complained about in lockup units like the San Quentin Adjustment Center.

At first, California courts responded to increasing criticism of indeterminate sentencing by tinkering around the edges of the law, case by case. In 1972, for instance, the California State Supreme Court heard John Lynch's appeal of his prison term—five years and counting for the misdemeanor crime of indecent exposure—and summarily ordered his release. The court found fault with the "unreasonably high maximum term" permitted in the law.[67]

Later decisions were less restrained. Over the next three years, California courts identified multiple problems integral to the discretionary authority of parole board members. They overturned dozens of Adult Authority decisions, ordering the release of prisoners who had served sentences grossly disproportionate to the severity of their crimes—in one case, twenty-two years for a single act of lewd and lascivious behavior.[68] Just as they had in overseeing assignments to California's lockup units, courts established new procedural protections for prisoners and parolees appearing before the Adult Authority.[69] State court dockets were suddenly filled with a seemingly endless register of prisoner challenges to individual sentencing decisions. The indefinite-sentencing system looked irreparably broken.

By 1974, California legislators were considering writing an entirely new criminal code. In September of that year, Raymond Parnas, a law professor at the University of California, Davis, and Michael Salerno, a legislative aide, wrote a working paper on sentencing reform at the request of state senator John Nejedly. By December, Parnas and Salerno had drafted Senate Bill 42, a proposal for incremental modifications to the indeterminate sentencing law. The bill responded to judicial and public critics alike—specifying the conditions under which the Adult Authority could deny parole and narrowing slightly the sentence ranges associated with crimes (for example, shifting from one-year-to-life sentences to three-to-ten-year sentences).[70]

At first, determinate sentencing seemed to lack adequate political backing; even Senator Nejedly's supporters could not agree on the provisions of a new sentencing scheme.[71] The American Civil Liberties Union argued that the proposed penalties were too harsh, while the District Attorneys Association found them not harsh enough.[72] The California Peace Officers' Association (later a significant political lobby in its own right) joined with the District Attorneys Association to urge eliminating the judicial power to lower sentences from the proposed law.[73] At least one judge agreed, complaining that SB 42 was much too lenient.[74] The California Association of Judges likewise "consistently opposed" the bill, but only halfheartedly, perhaps not believing until too late that it might actually pass.[75]

The widespread objections to Senator Nejedly's proposal seemed only to encourage debate over what kind of reform would be acceptable. Congress even weighed in. The House Committee on the Judiciary held hearings around the country on "prisons, prison reform, and prisoners' rights," including one in California in October 1971.[76] Much of the testimony centered on indeterminate sentencing.[77] And in an address to the California Legislature in 1975 about rising rates of violent crime, President Gerald Ford urged lawmakers to pass a determinate sentencing law, arguing that indeterminate sentencing produced unpredictably short sentences for some offenders.[78] (That, it turned out, was the argument that finally got legislatures to pass fixed terms: not that people were serving life sentences for misdemeanors, but that criminals were not being put away for long enough).

The U.S. murder rate had begun a steady climb in 1964, doubled by

1974, dropped briefly in 1976, and peaked in 1980 at 10.2 murders per 100,000 people. That was more than twice the 2013 murder rate of 4.5 murders per 100,000.[79] At the time he addressed the California Legislature, President Ford had just acquired a personal interest in knowing that violent criminals in California would not be released early at some parole board's whim. He had survived an assassination attempt that very morning, hours before he addressed the legislature. Lynette "Squeaky" Fromme, a Charles Manson groupie, aimed her gun at the president as he strode across the palm-tree-lined front lawn of the state capitol in Sacramento on his way to meet with Governor Jerry Brown.[80] Secret Service agents wrestled Fromme to the ground before she was able to fire.[81] Ford was already planning to make an advocacy pitch to the legislature to pass determinate sentencing in its harshest possible form, extending Nixon's tough-on-crime agenda.[82] But the experience with Fromme might well have affected his normally bland speaking style, giving it a note of urgency.

Just as George Jackson's death haunted prison officials, these moments of public violence haunted lawmakers. And in both cases, prison officials and lawmakers strategically leveraged the violence in order to advocate for harsher punishments. So while the Quakers and other reformers argued for less discretion and more humanity in punishment, Republicans like Ford argued for less discretion and more severity. Perhaps liberal reformers should have foreseen the symbiotic relationship between fear of violent crime and severity of punishment.[83] But many, evidently, did not.

In fact, there was a growing consensus that sentencing required less discretion and more "certainty and uniformity."[84] Even prison officials called for constraints on discretion. As early as 1971, Raymond Procunier, then the director of the California Department of Corrections, was trumpeting the efforts of prison officials to respond to critics of indeterminate sentences. In testimony before Congress, he noted that from 1970 to 1971, the Adult Authority had gone from granting only 30 percent of the prisoners who came before it a parole date to granting dates to 45–50 percent. This "laudable shift," he said, had been accomplished "without heavy-handed legislation to remove the important administrative ability to make individual case judgments." Still, he argued strongly in favor of maintaining the status quo: "I believe the indeterminate sentence is the best sentencing method."[85]

In 1975, Procunier resigned as director of corrections. He immediately took a new position as chairman of the Adult Authority. There, he continued his campaign of resisting major legislative reform of indeterminate sentencing, by implementing minor administrative tweaks to the existing sentencing and parole processes, such as new procedures to fix prisoners' terms early in their sentences.[86] But Procunier's reforms met with increasing hostility.

Proponents of SB 42 approached the Office of Legislative Counsel requesting an invalidation of Procunier's new procedures, which had been implemented with little public input. A column in the *Sacramento Bee* cautioned that the reforms, even if effective, were inherently vulnerable to revision by later boards.[87] Then, in January 1976, a California appellate court held that Procunier's new parole procedures failed to protect prisoners' rights.[88] The decision criticized the substance of Procunier's reforms, but Senator Nejedly and Governor Brown interpreted it as a denial of Procunier's authority to revise any policy. Nejedly, with Brown's support, issued a press release attacking the authority's procedural reforms, using the appellate court decision to mobilize further support for determinate sentencing.[89] Legislators passed SB 42 a few months later.

The final version of the bill represented a more drastic reform than the authors of the original working paper ever contemplated. The law assigned fixed sentences to specific crimes. This change satisfied the authors of *Struggle for Justice* and other liberal, anti-rehabilitation reformers like Jessica Mitford and Robert Martinson, who hoped for greater equity in sentencing. But SB 42 (along with subsequent legislation) provided for relatively long base terms.[90] This provision satisfied conservative reformers, like President Ford, and the law enforcement lobby. It established the purpose of imprisonment as punitive rather than rehabilitative and abolished the Adult Authority.[91] On paper, prison officials would no longer control individual prisoners' terms of incarceration. Instead, the law charged judges with determining the precise amount of time prisoners would serve. The director of corrections would merely set the requirements for behavior upon release from prison and evaluate parole violators for possible resentencing.[92]

Under SB 42, prison officials maintained control over one important administrative decision, one that would ultimately affect the length of time that prisoners actually served (and the conditions of their confinement) more than anyone could have guessed in 1976: "good time" credits.

Prison officials could assess penalties for rule violations and failures to participate in prison programs, thereby extending or shortening a prisoner's time to parole.[93] Unlike the imposition of indeterminate sentences, however, discretion over awarding good time credits was severely restricted: a prisoner's sentence could be reduced by only one-third, and it could never be extended beyond the fixed term determined by prosecutors and judges— in theory.

But as we will see, Fleeta Drumgo, Hugo Pinell, and Todd Ashker (among thousands of others) stand as examples of prisoners for whom the loss of good time initiated a slide toward significantly longer prison sentences. First, each of these prisoners misbehaved or was identified by prison officials as being part of the wrong crowd, was put in isolation, and lost good time. While in isolation, each was eventually accused of additional crimes, which resulted in more years being added to his sentence. Ultimately, each faced not only a longer overall sentence, but also a new kind of indeterminate sentence, to solitary confinement. Prison officials' discretion was— and is—hard to control.

Even so, when Governor Brown signed SB 42 into law, in September 1976, everyone was hopeful about this bold new reform. It was one of the first determinate sentencing laws (DSLs) in the United States. Three other states (Maine, Indiana, and Illinois) passed DSLs in that same year.[94] And in the two decades that followed, twenty states adopted either DSLs or sentencing guidelines that functioned similarly.[95] All states adopted some form of mandatory minimum sentencing, requiring judges to impose longer sentences for some categories of offenders such as habitual offenders or drunk drivers.[96] In 1984, Congress passed the Sentencing Reform Act, which ultimately resulted in the federal sentencing guidelines, a complex grid of formulas and rules providing for specific sentences for specific crimes and criminal histories, including mandatory life sentences for "career offenders."[97]

Strict scrutiny of the prison system—by advocates and scholars, judges and legislators, and even employees of the system—had produced a major reform of California's criminal code. And the reform spread quickly across the country. Reformers reasonably believed that even though sentences were harsher than they would have liked, at least the unjust arbitrariness of administrative discretion had been conclusively constrained.

Indeed, prison officials like Carl Larson complained about the loss of discretion incurred through determinate sentencing reforms. Flexible prison sentences, Larson told me, had guaranteed prison officials "a back door to the prison system"—allowing well-behaved prisoners to earn favorable recommendations for parole and also providing a "safety valve" to facilitate the covert early release of groups of prisoners as needed to relieve overcrowding. California's shift in 1976 to determinate sentencing was a "deathblow," Larson explained, not only because it exacerbated overcrowding, but also because prison officials could no longer wield the threat of a never-ending sentence against prisoners who "sodomized littler prisoners, had knives, joined a gang."[98] All in all, California prison officials seemed to be losing both their autonomy to run their prisons free from public scrutiny and their discretion over the intensity and severity of prisoners' punishments. Yet they would soon have more control than ever.

A Litany of Unintended Consequences

As soon as Governor Brown signed SB 42, scholars and practitioners set out to analyze the law's provisions and predict its impacts. Three surprising and unintended consequences soon became obvious: the law produced harsh and inconsistent sentencing outcomes; it failed to provide robust procedural protections to criminal defendants and prisoners; and abandoning the rehabilitative ideal did not inspire new alternatives to incarceration.

Under the new DSL, the California Legislature—not the judiciary or the Adult Authority—controlled sentence lengths.[99] In the first few years after the DSL's passage, prisoners' sentences seemed to be shortening; offenders who had received greater-than-average indeterminate sentences became eligible for, and received, sentence reductions under the new law.[100] But the legislature faced increasing political pressures to "enhance" sentences: to lengthen basic terms of incarceration for crimes and pile on additional time in prison based on characteristics of the crime and the criminal, such as using a gun, being affiliated with a gang, or having a prior criminal record. Passage of the DSL politicized sentencing, and the law enforcement lobby grew in power and influence, even promoting state ballot propositions that codified further sentencing enhancements.[101] Perhaps the most famous of these came in 1994 when California voters approved a ballot initiative providing for a "three strikes and you're out" law, which required judges to impose sentences of twenty-five years to life on any defendant found guilty of three consecutive felonies.[102] Throughout the 1970s and 1980s, California legislators—as well as voters—demonstrated their commitment to fighting crime by increasing prison terms.[103]

Although laws like "three strikes" further constrained judicial discretion and allegedly established additional consistency in sentencing, they represented perversions of the *Struggle for Justice* recommendation that criminal sentences be applied both fairly and sparingly. Ultimately, conservative politicians and intellectuals successfully advocated for a wide array of "law and order" reform possibilities, in direct opposition to those suggested by the *Struggle for Justice* authors, Martinson, and Mitford.[104]

Even consistency, the one thing that liberals and conservatives in the 1970s agreed would be good for the criminal justice system, was not achieved. As early as 1990, scholars noted that sentencing practices varied widely among California counties; Los Angeles County, for example, sentenced convicted felons to state prison at a higher rate than other counties.[105] (This trend continues. Today, Southern California counties, including San Diego and Los Angeles, sentence repeat offenders to life in prison at a much higher rate than Northern California counties like Alameda and San Francisco.)[106] Determinate sentencing laws also have failed to eliminate racial disproportionality in sentencing. In fact, these laws exaggerate the racial disparities noted by the *Struggle for Justice* authors.[107] How, under such rigid determinate sentencing laws, could the same crime rates result in different sentencing rates in different counties, or in different average sentences for offenders of different races?

The answer turns out to be painfully simple: prosecutorial discretion.[108] Prosecutors were the clear winners in the power shift precipitated by determinate sentencing. Legislators decide on only the lengths of sentences imposed for categories of crimes; prosecutors decide what charges to bring against a defendant. If the prosecutor charges *simple* manslaughter, and a defendant is found guilty (or, more likely, pleads guilty), the sentence is four years. If the prosecutor charges *negligent* manslaughter, and the defendant is found or pleads guilty, the sentence is ten years.[109] The crime charged—rather than the crime committed—determines the sentence.

Prosecutorial choices vary from individual to individual, and from county to county. The chief prosecutor in every county in California is elected, and so, like legislators, they are subject to popular pressures to impose ever-longer prison sentences.[110] But unlike legislators, who might change a few criminal laws in any given year, prosecutors make thousands of charging decisions each year. Prosecutorial discretion today is as impossible to monitor or constrain as the Adult Authority's discretion was in the 1970s.

Much of this discretion is exercised behind closed doors. The prosecutor can threaten a negligent manslaughter charge if the defendant goes to trial (with a mandatory ten-year sentence if the defendant loses), but offer a simple manslaughter charge if the defendant pleads guilty (with a four-year sentence, perhaps reducible even further with good time credits). Unlike trials, plea deals are negotiated outside the courtroom, and outside public view. Prosecutors can threaten defendants not only with more severe charges, but also with evidence that would be inadmissible in a trial. Defendants have no recourse to a judge or a jury (although a public defender must be present during plea negotiations) and usually no right to appeal.

Plea bargaining is how the vast majority of felony cases are resolved in the United States today. In the 1970s, 1 in every 12 felony cases in the United States went to trial. In 2011, the number was 1 in every 40, or 2.5 percent.[111] In California in the 2000s, even fewer felony cases went to trial: 2.2 percent.[112] Of the almost 98 percent of felony cases that never go to trial in California, 80 percent are resolved through plea bargains (the other 20 percent are acquittals, transfers or dismissals).[113] The *New York Times* recently blamed the toxic combination of prosecutorial discretion and mandatory minimum sentences (that is, DSLs) for this dramatic decrease in felony trials. Having fewer felony trials means fewer procedural protections for defendants.[114]

Two California-based criminologists conducted a statistical analysis and discovered that the way police, prosecutors, and judges used their discretionary powers under the DSL contributed to dramatic growths in imprisonment. Police arrested more people for drug offenses than ever before, sweeping them into courtrooms, where prosecutors sought and judges implemented individual sentencing decisions to send more people with felony convictions to prison (as opposed to probation or jail) than in previous years. Changes to sentence lengths under the DSL did not enlarge the prison population; changes in how district attorneys charged, prosecuted, and imprisoned felons did.[115]

Determinate sentences, combined with tough-on-crime political posturing, contributed significantly to a vast new problem: a skyrocketing prison population. About 20,000 people were in prison in California in 1970, or roughly 100 state prisoners per 100,000 state citizens, a rate that had remained stable throughout the twentieth century.[116] Senator Robert Presley, who oversaw state criminal justice policy in the California Legislature for nearly two decades (1975–94), explained what happened in the mid-1970s: "When we did this shifting from the indeterminate to determinate [sentence] and then we enhanced those penalties, anybody with any brains at all could see the prison population's going to increase because we're getting tougher on crime, and we're going to need more prisons."[117] As Presley predicted, by 1990 more than 90,000 people were in California prisons, and the imprisonment rate had tripled, to 300 per 100,000 citizens.[118] Progressive advocates of determinate sentencing like Martinson and the Struggle for Justice authors watched in horror as prisons grew, and grew ever harsher.[119] These exponential increases continued through the 1990s. California's prison population peaked in 2006 at 163,000: eight times as many prisoners as in the 1970s, and 4.5 times the 1970s rate of incarceration.[120]

National trends followed the same trajectory, and incarceration rates quadrupled over this period. By 2014, California still had 134,000 people in prison, more than any other state except Texas, and the United States had 2.2 million people incarcerated, more than any other country in the world. (In fact, the U.S. prison population is almost equal to the combined prison populations of China and Russia, the countries with the second- and third-highest prisoner totals.)[121] As prison sentences lengthened, the civil consequences of having a criminal record expanded, too, and former prisoners were disenfranchised, precluded from obtaining public benefits like welfare or government loans for education, and often excluded from employment opportunities because of the "mark" of their criminal records.[122] Prison critics had sought less incarceration, but ended up with more.

Reconsidering the Menace of Good Intentions

In the early 1970s reform effort, as in the Pelican Bay hunger strikes of 2013, a critique initiated from deep inside some of the most isolated and restrictive prison cells in California seeped out, finding both sympathy and amplification beyond the prison walls. The words of W. L. Nolen's legal complaints and George Jackson's *Soledad Brother* letters lingered, long after Nolen and Jackson had been shot to death by correctional officers. Even today, for advocates such as Dolores Canales, who testified after me at the 2013 California legislative hearings, George Jackson remains a symbol of the potential for transformation—not just because of the popularity of his critical writings or the galvanizing injustice of his treatment and death in prison, but also because after he died, reform seemed genuinely possible.[123] For prison officials, however, Nolen and Jackson remain a reminder of failures—to secure dangerous criminals and to silence critical voices. For these prison officials, the 1970s (and also the 2010s) were an era not of welcome reform, but of scrutiny and criticism, which ultimately resulted in newly intrusive oversight and broadly constraining regulations.[124]

In a sense, prison officials and reformers shared a disappointment in the outcome of the 1970s reform efforts. The Quakers were disappointed that attempts to apply criminal laws uniformly instead facilitated the imposition of longer prison sentences. According to academic lore, Robert Martinson, of the *Nothing Works* critique, felt personally responsible for the menace of his own good intentions. Instead of envisioning new rehabilitation programs outside prison, as Martinson had hoped, policy makers just got rid of rehabilitation programs entirely, paving the way for the building of new "warehouse" prisons.[125] In 1980, Martinson jumped from the window of his Manhattan apartment, an apparent suicide.[126] Other scholars have recently exacerbated reformers' worst fears, arguing that "liberals" and the "black silent majority" (working-class and middle-class blacks, as described by the urban studies professor Michael Javen Fortner) built the modern prison state.[127]

Carl Larson, who played a pivotal role in designing California's super-maxes, blamed the liberals and the black silent majority, too. At first, he interpreted the reformers' criticisms as being focused on inequality: "People were critical of not treating people equally." Larson acknowledged the inequality, but he had an explanation: "A lot of black inmates are loud and abrasive." It made a degree of sense to him that their indeterminate sentences lasted longer. Larson's comments—stereotyping African Americans as inherently misbehaving—reveal just how racially charged day-to-day life in California prisons was, and how integral racial stereotypes were to prison management.[128] Whether African American prisoners misbehaved more than other prisoners, or whether, instead, they experienced more abuse and were more articulate in their critiques of this abuse, was at the crux of how George Jackson's alleged, failed escape attempt from San Quentin was interpreted.

Had he been in charge of making a new sentencing policy, Larson said, he would have incorporated a wider array of decision makers into the process by including judges and prisoner members on sentencing panels, along with prison officials. He argued that a more diverse "blue ribbon" commission, with control over sentencing, would have insulated the process from the "punishment hysteria," which he noted "swept the nation" in the 1980s. "State legislatures," Larson said, "can't outdo themselves to look tough enough on crime."[129] Larson's suggestion revealed his most fundamental criticism of the DSL: prison officials had been left out of the reform conversation but were later forced to deal with the consequences of the reformers' mistakes.

In particular, Larson and other prison officials noted that California's DSL in 1976 removed the "carrot" of potential early release for good behavior.[130] Without a say in whether prisoners might be released early, prison officials had few ways to manage violence, either in the global sense, by reducing overcrowding, or in the specific sense, by incentivizing good behavior. According to Steve Cambra, who began working as a correctional officer in California prisons in 1970 and later served as warden of Pelican Bay in the 1990s, the philosophy behind the indeterminate sentencing law was "get everyone on the streets we can" (or release prisoners whenever possible). Cambra explained: "Almost everyone was a lifer . . . It was the way the prisons managed their violence."[131]

Prison officials also complained that court interventions in prison management, just like the DSL reform, constrained their ability to manage overcrowding and control dangerous prisoners. In 1985, Gregory Harding, the deputy director for court compliance for the California prison system, noted with frustration that injunctions in the ongoing cases about "administrative segregation," or isolation in places like the San Quentin AC, tied the hands of legislators and prison officials by prescribing "certain procedures by which the Department can lockup inmates and place inmates in segregated housing." When courts prohibited double-celling in older facilities like San Quentin, Harding explained, then the extra prisoners have to go somewhere else, and overcrowding pressures increase at other prisons such as Folsom.[132] Rodney J. Blonien, then undersecretary of the prison system, emphasized that such court orders affected the entire state prison system as well as thirteen county jails. And judicial intervention in county jails, he argued, just encouraged local judges to give prisoners longer sentences, sending them to the increasingly overcrowded state prisons—yet another unintended consequence of reform.[133]

In California, reformers failed to acknowledge prison officials' perceptions that prisons were out of control. Every step toward reform—reforming and shutting down lockdown units, abolishing the indeterminate sentence, eliminating the parole board—just increased prison officials' fears about out-of-control prisons and the loss of management tools on which they relied. Prison officials responded by resisting interventions, grasping for new forms of control, and designing harsher, but less visible, forms of managing the prisoners they perceived to be most dangerous to the prison order—the "George Jacksons."

The reform proposals and compromises made between the liberals, the black silent majority, the Quakers, Martinson, increasingly powerful law enforcement lobbies, and Republican tough-on-crime executives like Nixon and Ford did not themselves produce the unintended consequence of more incarceration and more isolation. Rather, the negotiation and implementation of these reforms inspired prison officials to seek the preservation and expansion of existing institutional norms and power structures.[134] The oft-repeated "unintended consequences" story of popular reform accidentally producing more prisoners masks an equally important story of administrative retrenchment.[135]

While courts and legislators attempted to mitigate the harshness of prison by constraining prison officials' power over conditions of confinement and sentence lengths, prison officials pursued a clear set of competing goals that included maintaining a subset of prisoners, including George Jackson's alleged co-conspirators, in long-term solitary confinement. The "prisons within prisons" were necessary, they felt, to maintain control over the entire imprisoned population. Bad behavior required consequences: however bad prison was, there had to be someplace worse. Prison was not enough.

Prison officials maintained (and expanded) this discretion over prisoners' conditions of confinement and the durations of their assignment to isolation with little public notice or attention. As the next chapters will reveal, prison officials built different prisons and developed new tools of control over prisoners, all explicitly designed to avoid the kind of public oversight that had plagued them in the 1970s. So for four decades, no one knew who was in isolation in California, why, for how long, or with what effects.

But when the Pelican Bay hunger strikes forced public attention on the conditions and scale of isolation in California—revealing how hundreds of people had been in solitary confinement for decades—legislators and reformers again took serious notice of California's isolation policies. It was their first hard, comprehensive look since the Assembly's Select Committee on Prison Reform and Rehabilitation in 1973. In the intervening forty years, the most dangerous policies had governed, especially in isolation units: opacity and broad administrative discretion, maintained in the face of multiple legislative and judicial attempts at constraining this very discretion.

Transparency, here, is not just a stepping-stone toward curbing discretion but also a tool for understanding when and how discretion operates. Transparency ensures that reform attempts do not turn into mere refinements of existing systems, and prison officials do not resist what they perceive to be the systematic elimination of all their tools of control. Without institutionalizing thorough, ongoing oversight of the entire prison system, legislative and public attention risks being as ineffective—and, indeed, as counterproductive—as the attempted reforms of California prisons in the 1970s.

As I headed back to Los Angeles from the 2013 hearings on solitary confinement, in which I had made my pitch for transparency, I realized I had not seen Carl Larson nor heard from him. I was surprised. Larson was my go-to contact in the prison system; I reached out to him whenever I was unclear about some detail of California prison history. He often knew just the Department of Corrections statistician who could help me to find the data I needed, or the retired warden who could explain some decision that was made at some prison twenty or thirty years ago.

Gradually, we grew to be on friendly terms. Just after I finished my doctorate, Larson heard me quoted on National Public Radio and sent me a note saying that he hoped I was well and congratulating me on becoming a University of California professor. Given this, and given his attention to criminal justice in the state, I expected him to notice that I had testified before the California Legislature.

A few days after I testified, a reporter asked me whether I could recommend someone within the prison system who could talk about solitary confinement, someone who might be thoughtfully critical of current policies. I thought again of Larson, and recommended him. The reporter said: "He's dead."

I searched the *Sacramento Bee* for the obituary. Larson had died, at the age of seventy-six, on September 9, just weeks after our last conversation about the importance of George Jackson, and a month before I testified before the legislature.[136]

I thought about Larson's legacy: the Pelican Bay SHU. If reformers like Senator Hancock or Dolores Canales wanted to change—or abolish—that place, they would need to understand just why and how Larson had built it in the first place.

4

Constructing the Supermax,
One Rule at a Time

WHEN I INITIALLY STARTED TRACKING DOWN and reading through all the legislative reports and transcripts described in the previous chapter, I was looking for something very particular: any mention of supermax prisons, especially California's prototypical supermax, Pelican Bay State Prison. The robust legislative debates that preceded California's decision to pass a determinate sentencing law, along with all of the state and federal legislative hearings about abuse and violence in California prisons in the 1970s and 1980s, made me think I would find a comparable public debate about the decision to authorize the building of Pelican Bay. I wanted to understand who thought a massive new supermax would be a good idea, and why. How did legislators and the governor talk about the idea? Was it, like determinate sentencing, an attempt to make the prison system more fair and efficient? Or was it an intentionally punitive bit of political grandstanding, like three strikes? Understanding the motivations behind the supermax, I thought, would shed light on how the harshest punishments get designed, authorized, and implemented, or how the reform efforts of the 1970s resulted in the supermaxes of the 1990s.

The website of the California Department of Corrections states that Pelican Bay State Prison opened in 1989. So I started with that year and worked my way through the legislative archives, back to the 1970s, looking for any mention of supermaxes or Pelican Bay. The first phase of this search was disappointingly easy.

After a few days in the law library at the University of California, Berkeley, intensive conversations with librarians, and a few more days in the state legislative archives up in Sacramento, I was confident that I had found every legislative document that mentioned Pelican Bay in the 1980s. There was exactly one: Senate Bill 1685, passed in 1988.

In June 1988, a handful of California state senators had an animated discussion about a piece of legislation that would have been unremarkable in those years. SB 1685 authorized the construction of a new prison in Del Norte County, on California's border with Oregon. It was one of a dozen prisons built in California in the 1980s. Most were named simply and functionally after the Central Valley towns where they were located—Avenal, Salinas Valley, Corcoran. But the conference committee notes appended to the bill authorizing the one in Del Norte record a lighthearted debate about what to call it.

"Dungeness Dungeon," one senator proposed.

"No, Casa No Pasa," another countered.

Even if those names "lack official dignity," a third senator argued, at least we can reserve the right to refer to the place as the "Slammer by the Sea."

The ultimate name, codified in SB 1685, was refreshingly dignified.[1] Pelican Bay echoes the name of another of California's infamous prisons—Alcatraz, whose name comes from an archaic Spanish word (originally borrowed from Arabic) meaning "pelican." It sounds like a peaceful place where birds flock above waves that break gently on a rocky coastline. If only a name could actually imbue a place with grace.

And that was it. There were no other references to the decision to build Pelican Bay State Prison—or any references to a supermax—anywhere in the legislative archives. (There were a few other references to a generic prison in Del Norte County.) SB 1685, with its absurd naming conversation, answered none of my questions about who designed Pelican Bay and why.

When the place opened, in 1989, national news reporters called it a "prison of the future" designed for a "new breed of inmate": "the worst of the worst."[2] How could California legislators, Governor Jerry Brown, or his successor, Governor George Deukmejian, have resisted taking credit for this technological marvel, the securest prison facility ever constructed? If not they, then who deserved the credit for designing Pelican Bay and getting it built?

Meeting Carl Larson

I first visited the Sacramento archives in 2009, twenty years after Pelican Bay opened. Someone had to be alive who remembered how the decision had been made to build it.

I asked older colleagues who had taught in prisons or who had studied California political history. Eventually, I found my way back to Don Specter, the director of the Prison Law Office, based in Berkeley, California. I had worked in Don's office as a paralegal in my first full-time job after college. Years later, I still thought of him as the busy director who emerged from his office only to hurry over to the courthouse to try to persuade judges to do the right thing. So I was a bit shy about asking him to help me dig up old history he probably already knew.

Don had been one of the most persistent litigators in lawsuits like *Wright* and *Toussaint*, challenging the conditions and duration of solitary confinement in the 1970s and 1980s. And he later oversaw the litigation in the 1990s that challenged the conditions at Pelican Bay. Don suggested a longer list of names than I had dared hope for: lobbyists, corrections officials, judges, lawyers, and others involved in prison building in the 1980s. One of them was Carl Larson.

As I worked my way through Don's list, Larson's name came up again and again. I heard that Larson had been involved in corrections department financial management and prison building in the 1980s, that he had worked in San Quentin and Folsom. He came to seem so central that I grew afraid to contact him: if he was uncooperative, my research project might fail.

Finally, in January 2010, I emailed him. I had been trying for a year to figure out how Pelican Bay came to be built, and I still had no idea.

I composed a simple note, introducing myself, naming all the people who had mentioned him as a critical informant, asking whether he would talk to me. I sent the note from my official berkeley.edu e-mail account and signed it formally: Keramet Reiter, M.A., J.D., doctoral student. And I waited.

An hour later, Larson wrote back. He would meet with me. But first he wanted a list of every question that I planned to ask him.

Sharing that felt like showing my hand. Ordinarily, I would have started with general questions, learned more about an interview subject, and gradually asked in more detail about the specifics of Pelican Bay—a touchy subject in California, where prison conditions were the subject of frequent litigation. But Larson was not one for an indirect approach. And I really wanted to talk to him. I sent him my list.

The next day, he wrote back with an assignment: read *The Black Hand*, by Christopher Blatchford. When I finished, I should call his assistant to make an appointment to meet with him in Sacramento. He would set aside two hours.

I dutifully completed my homework. *The Black Hand: The Bloody Rise and Redemption of "Boxer" Enriquez, a Mexican Mob Killer* was written by a Los Angeles–based Fox TV network reporter, in close collaboration with the book's protagonist, Rene Enriquez. The book chronicles Enriquez's rise to power as a prison-based leader in La Eme, or the Mexican Mafia. It is a page-turner, with gruesome details about murder plots, drug deals, and the utter inability of even the thickest prison walls to thwart the blood-thirsty will of the Mafia. Enriquez spent ten years in the Pelican Bay SHU—managing, in those years, to order Mafia hits, overdose on heroin, and learn origami. (What is the real point of the SHU if its residents can order murders, obtain high-quality narcotics, and even fold paper cranes with impunity?) In 2002 he agreed to come clean to prison officials about his gang activities, known as "debriefing," or colloquially as snitching. Enriquez is still in prison on a twenty-year-to-life sentence for murder, but he works nearly full-time as an FBI informant, testifying for the prosecution as an expert on the Mexican Mafia and training gang investigators in gang culture and tactics.[3]

The Black Hand gives an informative account of Mafia politics and brutality. But Blatchford also weaves in a conspiracy theory, namely, that a California Assembly member named Gloria Romero and a San Francisco lawyer named Charles Carbone, both vocal advocates for prisoners' rights, accepted Mexican Mafia bribes in exchange for their advocacy work. The theory echoes earlier fears about other lawyers, such as Steven Bingham, who advocated for other allegedly dangerous prisoners, like George Jackson.

I do not think Carl Larson asked me to read *The Black Hand* because he bought into this conspiracy theory. Rather, it was the first step in Larson's multiyear effort to educate me about the intensity of the violence in the California prison system, and the fear prison officials experience in that environment. Larson thought Rene Enriquez could become for me what George Jackson was to him: a nightmare prisoner. I was too young to have lived through the Jackson era, and Larson no doubt thought my Berkeley e-mail address predisposed me to a radical interpretation of what had happened to Jackson. And today, many of the most feared California prison gangs claim Latino heritage (or "Hispanic," in prison officials' parlance). Enriquez was supposed to be a modern worst of the worst, the new archetype of the most dangerous prisoner.

In the small world of people obsessed with supermaxes, I eventually found my way from the *Black Hand* to a correspondence with Enriquez. I never mentioned that to Larson, though.

At ten in the morning, on the appointed day in February 2010, I arrived at the California Department of Corrections headquarters in Sacramento. I had been inside most of California's state prisons, but I had never visited the center of operations. I felt a little like a spy who might get kicked out at any moment.

Larson's administrative assistant escorted me through a maze of offices and cubicles to a windowless corner office. Larson walked out—a portly, grandfatherly man, hardly taller than my five and a half feet. He told me right away, proudly, that he had been in corrections for fifty years, since July 1960. A welcome mat in front of his desk said: "You have entered a no-spin zone."

Larson started talking immediately. Only a few minutes into the interview, in response to my question about who had made prison-building decisions in the 1980s, he said: "I designed Pelican Bay State Prison. If you go up to visit, you'll see they have a plaque with my name on it."[4]

Finally, I had found someone who could tell me the why, what, when, where, and how of Pelican Bay. In that first interview and through subsequent conversations, Larson gave me the framework for understanding that Pelican Bay was truly an administrative innovation—designed, built, and operated with hardly any legislative, judicial, or executive oversight.

I still needed to understand the mechanisms of administrative innovation that created the place. How could the legislature, which in 1985 had nitpicked over details of who was in which isolation unit, have nothing to say three years later about the multimillion-dollar, securest prison ever built except to ask: "Can we call it 'Slammer by the Sea'?" But I had a much better sense of where to look and whom to ask.

Building Prisons Fast and Furious

The administrative details of the prison boom, central as they are to this story, are a muddle of bond and budget regulations.[5] Let me therefore say plainly: Pelican Bay came into existence because numerous legislative checkpoints were deliberately removed.

As the California prison population began its steady, exponential climb following the passage of the determinate sentencing law in 1976, legislators and prison officials panicked about uncontrollable overcrowding, and judges criticized the decrepit, overstuffed conditions of confinement in prisons across the state. As Senator Robert Presley said, he knew in 1976 that "we're going to need more prisons."[6]

And Presley led the charge. A conservative Democrat representing Riverside County, he served in the California legislature from 1975 to 1994. Californians know Riverside County, stretching east from Los Angeles and Orange County all the way to Arizona, as the Inland Empire. And Presley was the inland emperor. During the 1980s, bills he proposed averaged an 80 percent passage rate, well above the 50 percent rate typical for his colleagues.[7] He represented a particular brand of California political leadership, in which certain legislators dominated broad political topics for decades at a time.[8] Criminal justice was Presley's topical domain. Over his two decades in the legislature, Presley presided over a range of criminal justice reforms, including legalizing medical marijuana, designing compassionate release programs for aging and ill prisoners, and lengthening criminal sentences. He also oversaw the largest prison-building project ever undertaken by any state: twenty-three new prisons built between 1984 and 1996.[9] Two of these were supermaxes; in the 1980s, California built more than two thousand box cells like Todd Ashker's.

The prison-building program started in 1982. That June, California voters approved a general obligation bond measure in the amount of $495 million to fund three new prison facilities in Riverside, Los Angeles, and San Diego Counties.[10] Next, Presley created the Joint Legislative Committee on Prison Construction and Operations (JLCPCO), which he would chair for the next ten years. In November 1982, California voters approved another general obligation bond measure in the amount of $290 million to fund local jails.

At first, prison building was a popular and public process. Polls showed that crime was voters' highest concern in the 1982 election year.[11] The *Los*

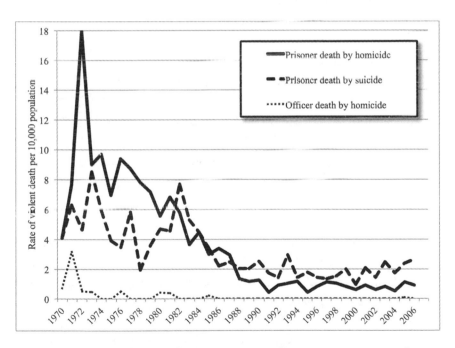

Violent deaths in the California Department of Corrections, 1970–2006
(Statistics compiled by the author from a combination of publicly available documents and archival reports. Raw numbers and specific sources available upon request.)

Angeles Times argued in an editorial that the prison bond measure on the June 1982 ballot was both fiscally responsible and necessary, given prison overcrowding. The *Times* cited 290 violent deaths of prisoners, 15 staff deaths, and 117 prisoner suicides over the preceding twenty years as support for its claim that overcrowding had become excessive.[12] The article did not mention that the number of violent deaths in prisons had decreased every year between 1976 and 1982. And given the increase in the prison population, the *rate* of violent deaths per prisoner had fallen even more dramatically, from a peak rate of 18 per 10,000 prisoners to a low of 3 per 10,000.

Nearly every politician, Democratic and Republican, incumbents and challengers, supported building new prisons. The outgoing Democratic governor, Jerry Brown, supported the prison bond measures, as did the Republican gubernatorial candidate, George Deukmejian. In his campaign, Deukmejian renewed his promises not only to be tough on crime, as he had been in his years as a state senator, but also to build more prisons.[13] He ultimately won by a narrow majority. The June and November prison and jail bond measures passed easily.

But with popularity came a painstaking approval process. The first stages of prison building proceeded haltingly, requiring gubernatorial, legislative, popular, and corrections approval. Presley conceived of the JLCPCO in part to streamline this process.[14] The JLCPCO created a direct bridge between the legislature and the Department of Corrections, completely bypassing the Department of General Services, which usually forced legislative initiatives through a standardized budgeting process.[15]

General obligation bonds, like the two approved in June and November 1982, were another workaround. Presley had wanted to start building prisons in the late 1970s, but he could not persuade the Assembly's Ways and Means Committee to allocate any funding. So he came up with the idea of putting the funding question directly to California voters, who, he suspected, would be more pro-punishment and less tightfisted than the Ways and Means Committee. He was right. Between 1982 and 1986, voters approved $1.5 billion in general obligation bonds to fund prison and jail construction. In addition to the measures approved in 1982, they passed a $300 million bond in 1984, and one for $500 million in 1986.[16] These voter-approved

bonds had the added bonus of being excluded from the state's debt calculation during its annual budget balancing.[17]

With the money in hand, state officials got busy building prisons. Presley
worked especially closely with Craig Brown, the deputy secretary of finance
(1983–85) and then the undersecretary of corrections (1987–96), during
the building years.[18] In his first year as deputy secretary of finance, Brown
worked to exempt the prison system from the usual, complex state budgeting procedures, instead shifting budgeting decisions directly to prison officials like himself. He wanted to make sure prison officials "got to do what
we wanted" with the money allocated for prison building.[19] If he had the
discretion to build prisons fast, he would be better able to please his boss,
George Deukmejian.

Governor Deukmejian (1983–91) was a strong ally in the early stages of
California's prison building. Presley recalled of the governor: "[He] not only
put all these criminals in prison but he wanted to keep them there, and
that's why he wanted us to embark on this prison building effort. . . . And
he was, in a lot of ways, the driving force behind all of that."[20] Brown reiterated this point: "The governor wanted prisons built; we were going to build
prisons. . . . We hired people who knew how to build. . . . Budget and schedule were the only two important commodities."[21]

The state's first new prison-building project was in Solano, not far from
Sacramento. To get the prison built in a year, "proving it could be done,"
Brown had lime added to the muddy soil of the prison's foundation—at
a cost of a quarter-million dollars—so that construction could continue
through the rainy season. And he had temporary wooden doors put in at
the last minute and painted to look like the steel doors that would eventually be installed, in order to make the place look ready before it actually
was.[22] These were the kinds of allocations the Department of General Services, whose reason for being is to prevent expensive political showman-
ship, might have balked at approving.

And Brown achieved his goal: California State Prison, Solano, opened in
August 1984, barely a year into Brown's term as deputy secretary of finance.
But not every prison could be built with limestone infusions and fake doors,
and not every city welcomed a new prison facility. The June 1982 general
obligation bond was supposed to fund three new prisons in the greater Los

Angeles area. Legislators had made prison building in Southern California a priority because the vast majority of the state's prisoners came from that region, and keeping them close to home and better connected with their families and communities seemed like a commonsense policy. But residents of Southern California's relatively wealthy districts fiercely disagreed.[23]

As debates over where to site facilities slowed down construction, state officials continued to plan for a vast new archipelago of prisons, located mostly in the state's Central Valley, an inland corridor of farmland loosely bounded by Interstate 5 and State Route 99. Officials also continued to brainstorm about how to raise money. The twenty-two additional prisons scheduled to be built over the next decade would require much more than the $1.5 billion in bond debt that Presley and Brown had raised.

After the fourth general obligation bond passed in 1986, Elizabeth Whitney, the state treasurer, expressed concern about California's growing bond debt. Although the bonds did not count against the budget deficit in legislative formulas, she was still worried that repaying the debt would harm the state's economy. In 1987, the California Debt Advisory Commission, which Whitney chaired, published the report *The Use of General Obligation Bonds by the State of California*. Whitney's letter introducing the report informed readers that it was prepared in response to "concerns and questions raised by Commission members and others regarding the State's ability to assume additional general obligation debt." The report noted that although California had continued to receive strong municipal credit ratings in 1987, it also had the highest outstanding general obligation debt of any state, $8 billion and rising, and that at some point this debt would jeopardize its municipal credit ratings.[24] The report was prescient. In the 2000s, California's strong municipal credit rating began to fall; the rating fluctuated throughout the early 2000s, sinking to one of the lowest in the United States in 2004.[25]

The treasurer's report must have raised red flags for Presley and Brown. Ruth Gilmore, a historian of California's prison expansion, argued that California legislators were likely also afraid of incurring a tax revolt if they kept asking citizens to approve general obligation bonds. This fear was real: less than a decade earlier, in 1978, voters had passed a state constitutional amendment (Proposition 13) that limited property tax increases and constrained the issuance of general obligation bonds. As Gilmore writes, politicians scrambled to "expand a politically popular program (prisons) without running up against the politically contradictory limit to taxpayers' willingness to use their own money to defend against their own fears."[26]

So Presley and Brown needed a new source of money—one that both avoided reminding voters of the rising costs of incarceration and escaped the bureaucratic oversight of the Ways and Means Committee, the General Services Office, and state treasurer Whitney. Their solution was to privatize the funding process.

Privatization would be efficient (private business is generally assumed to be more efficient than government) and would also avoid scrutiny.[27] To get funding privatization going, Deukmejian and Presley set up a system of lease-revenue bonds. They asked a California investment bank to set up lease-purchase agreements between private funders and the Public Works Board.[28] These agreements, negotiated by a legislative subcommittee in the absence of any general public oversight, provided the initial funds to build state prisons. The full legislature did not need to get involved until after the prisons were built, when it would have to appropriate funds for "lease" payments from the Department of Corrections to the bondholders. The state would take title to the facilities only after private bondholders were fully repaid.[29]

In California, these lease-revenue bonds are not backed by the "full faith, credit, and taxing power" repayment guarantees of general obligation bonds.[30] This means that although the state's Public Works Board issued bonds to private investors, the state was not constitutionally required to repay them. Instead, the state maintained only a moral obligation to repay. Because of this lesser guarantee, the debts required higher interest payments, to compensate investors for the higher risk. Lease-revenue bonds are thus more expensive for the state than general obligation bonds. But they are also faster and simpler to issue, making them a perfect funding source for California's rapid prison construction of the 1980s and 1990s.

While lease-revenue bonds skirted many of the hassles of the budgeting process and legislative oversight, Craig Brown continued to face annoying bureaucratic hurdles. At first, each new prison required an intensive assessment of the environmental impact of the proposed facility, executive approvals of architecture and construction contracts, and legislative hearings to assess individual design plans. Brown worked with Presley and the JLCPCO to design work-arounds for all these requirements.

In a report to the legislature in 1986, *The New Prison Construction Project at Midstream,* the Legislative Analyst's Office (LAO) enumerated the special exemptions that Presley's JLCPCO had granted to the Department of Corrections. The LAO noted that by 1986, legislators were allocating prison-building funds based solely on "general specifications for each proposed prison" that gave the general location, security level, expected bed count, and not much else. The legislature also "provided the Department of Corrections with extraordinary delegations of authority and exemptions from existing law." The department was exempt from requirements for environmental review by independent agencies, from design supervision by the Office of the State Architect, and from the established state process for selecting construction consultants.[31] Unreviewed factors like the allocation of land-use rights, the costs of prison staffing levels, and the correctional management policies underlying design decisions could all have significant economic implications, yet legislators were examining none of them. By 1986, the California Legislature had limited influence over the location of new prisons, and virtually no input into the designs of facilities. At this point, the administrative road to Pelican Bay had been practically built and paved.

As the JLCPCO continued to "oversee" prison construction in the second half of the 1980s, it also continued to increase the procedural exemptions available to the Department of Corrections. In 1986, Presley sponsored a Senate bill that dealt mainly with funding renovations to San Quentin, but also included a provision to prolong the existence of the JLCPCO through 1993. In addition, it made a slight change to the approval process for prison construction plans: if the JLCPCO did not notify prison administrators of any objections within forty-five days after plans had been cursorily reviewed at a legislative hearing, approval would be assumed.[32]

With this change, legislative oversight of prison construction moved from being nominal to almost nonexistent. Presley's JLCPCO occasionally held hearings in which committee members engaged with contractors and architects over questions of cost efficiency, or approved prison officials' building plans.[33] But when it came to design details such as how many cells a prison would have or how secure it would be, prison officials had broad discretion to design and operate prisons as they saw fit. As Presley said, "I certainly didn't feel that I should be trying to beat on some director of Corrections and tell him how to run his shop."[34]

When I asked Craig Brown directly what the debates over building Pelican Bay were like in the 1980s, he summed it up succinctly: "You're not going to find much in the record. It was all negotiated [off the record], and we [corrections] pretty much had our way with the legislature."[35]

After I interviewed Brown, I had a good idea about why I had not found anything in the legislative record or the state archives about the decision to build Pelican Bay. I was beginning to understand how a prison administrator like Brown ended up building "a prison of the future," the securest prison ever built, with more total isolation cells concentrated in one building than had previously existed throughout the state of California, without anyone in the state actually noticing that he was doing it. Prison officials had successfully negotiated a prison-building process that minimized their accountability to legislators—or, for that matter, to anyone else.

In his first term, Governor Deukmejian was a cheerleader for prison construction, and Craig Brown, by finding a way to get the Solano prison built and operational in just a year, worked hard to please him. When he ran for reelection in 1986, Deukmejian made toughness on crime his signature issue; the prison system he was building was strong evidence of his crime-fighting success. But the details were delegated to Craig Brown. No one was checking to see whether the new prison doors were made of wood or steel and California voters were not asked whether they wanted their tax money to pay for the program.

Del Norte County Wants a Prison

At the county level, even if not the state level, Californians were paying close attention to prison building. While Angelenos campaigned to keep prisons out of their backyards, the residents of Del Norte County campaigned to get one built in theirs.

Craig Brown explained: "Every prison in the history of California was built in the boondocks." In the 1980s, he said, "everybody wanted a prison." By which he meant, everyone in an impoverished rural county. "We are a great economic engine. You bring a payroll like that," he added, and "the community is eager for a prison, and the prison serves the community well."[36] In theory, prisons brought jobs: construction jobs to build the facility and guard jobs to run it. And jobs would reinvigorate struggling local economies.

Del Norte was just that kind of rural county, in need of an economic engine and a steady payroll. The county had once thrived on a "wood products economy," boasting seventeen sawmills and twenty-six dairies. But by the mid-1980s, only one sawmill and six dairies remained. Del Norte's unemployment rate had soared to 20 percent, making it one of California's poorest counties.[37] Unsurprisingly, residents lobbied eagerly to get one of California's new prisons.

And state senator Barry Keene, who represented the district that included Del Norte County, obliged. In July 1985, he promoted a bill to require the Department of Corrections to explore the feasibility of building a prison in Del Norte County, hold public hearings, and submit a prison construction plan to the JLCPCO. Keene's bill exemplified the state's newly efficient prison-building procedures; it preauthorized the building of a prison in Del Norte County, subject only to a legislative sign-off on the construction plan, before any site had been officially purchased or even approved. The measure passed both houses unanimously.[38]

One year later, in August 1986, Keene introduced a second bill, this one authorizing the construction of a two-thousand-bed "maximum security complex in Del Norte County." The Del Norte facility would be one of the first prisons funded with those newly privatized, lease-revenue bonds—$325 million worth. The bill appropriated an additional $27 million from the recently approved general obligation bond measures, to fund the initial site studies, land purchase, planning, and construction.

The Assembly Comments on earlier drafts of the bill are revealing: they show how much discretion the JLCPCO had allocated to prison officials by 1986. One commenter noted: "The bill contains no per-cell cost ceilings or staff ratio targets." Another complained that prison officials had not even completed the research mandated a year earlier: "The CDC has not settled upon a site" nor "completed the feasibility study required by last year's leg-islation." A third commentator asked pointedly: "Given that a prison is a major public institution with an expected life span of a century, should there be some independent review of its planning?"[39] Apparently that as-sembly member didn't realize that the JLCPCO had already exempted the Department of Corrections from any independent review.

Keene's bill contained only minimal details about the facility to be built in Del Norte County: it would be a maximum-security prison, half of which *could* be used "for special cases." Assembly members complained about this vagueness, too. They asked: Did "special cases" refer to lockups or to something else? Why only maximum security? Noting the court challenges to high-security conditions at San Quentin and Folsom, commentators sug-gested that rather than having all the high-security prisoners concentrated in one place, each facility should have multiple custody levels, giving pris-oners the opportunity to "work their way through lower custody levels" without incurring high transportation costs between facilities.[40] The very concept of a concentrated maximum-security prison flagrantly contradicted legislative recommendations made a year earlier, when the Assembly in-vestigated conditions at Folsom. The legislative report from that hearing included recommendations that prison officials consider alternatives to in-carceration and reexamine security classification procedures; experts had testified that prisoners were overclassified into unnecessarily high levels of security.[41]

In spite of these concerns, Keene's bill passed both houses unanimously.[42] Del Norte County residents would get the prison that they hoped would fix their economy. As expected, once the decision was made, Del Norte County enjoyed a quick infusion of infrastructure investments. More than one hundred houses were built, along with new shopping centers.[43] An early headline read: "Crescent City Gets Welcome Boom from New Prison; State Institution to Add Millions to Economy."[44] Local business leaders reported that the unemployment rate dropped; property values increased, as did sales tax revenues.[45]

Residents would become less excited over time as they learned more about who would be housed in the prison and as the new institution yielded de-creasing economic benefits. At first, however, they had no more idea of what kind of prison would be built in their backyards than the California legislators did. Prison officials were just beginning to figure that out themselves.

Finding the Supermax

In 1986, Carl Larson had just been promoted to finance director (officially, warden of new prison design and activation) for the California Department of Corrections. He replaced Craig Brown, who was on his way to becoming the undersecretary of corrections, in charge of the state's entire youth and adult correctional system. Larson had started his criminal justice career as a guard in San Quentin State Prison in July 1960, just after he finished high school—the same year that George Jackson went to prison. Over the next two decades, Larson worked at prisons across the state, earned his bachelor's degree, and climbed the ranks of prison management. By 1980, he had returned to San Quentin as chief deputy warden, the same position that Jim Park had held in 1971. Larson had been there a little more than a year when he was asked to take a job in the CDC headquarters, in Sacramento. He accepted the assignment, but felt it to be a poor fit—he had always believed that people got sent to headquarters only if they were too stupid to be trusted in an actual prison. But he found a mentor in Jim Park, who had been reassigned to a staff job shortly after the George Jackson murder. Park told Larson: "Pretend that you were the number two general at Fort Oregon, and now you're being reassigned to Washington at the Pentagon . . . You're just another asshole with a briefcase."[46]

Perhaps because he refused to be an "asshole with a briefcase" and felt that he understood the needs of guards, officials, and prisoners alike, Larson thrived at headquarters. Within five years, he was promoted to finance director, taking over Craig Brown's work of overseeing prison-building plans and policies. At that point, with twenty-six years of correctional experience, Larson knew what the California prison system needed: a unified system of rules, self-contained prisoner units small enough in scale to allow guards to get to know each prisoner, and enough short-term and long-term lockup units to isolate the problem cases so that violence could be controlled. He relied on his own experiences and intuitions, and also looked to national standards to make specific decisions about the size of each prison unit and the number of isolation units needed.

Larson's experience of working in prisons during that peak period of violence in the 1970s, and his brief stint as a deputy warden at San Quentin as the prison struggled with overcrowding in the 1980s, convinced him that the system needed a dedicated set of true maximum-security beds. These would replace the makeshift isolation units (already called SHUs, or Security Housing Units) that had inspired persistent legal challenge at Folsom, San Quentin, and elsewhere. "When we looked at the system," he told me, "the formula we figured we needed was 2 percent SHU inmates."[47] In 1986, when he made these calculations, there were 57,000 prisoners in the state prison system, a number that was projected to rise indefinitely.[48] Based on his 2 percent formula, Larson knew he needed at least 1,100 SHU cells. This was enough for one prison to be designated a single-purpose SHU: "We needed a SHU unit," he explained.[49] The SHU he ultimately built would have 1,056 beds.

Even though Larson referred to formulas, "principles," and coherent "systems," he freely admitted that all these calculations represented imprecise estimates of actual populations and departmental needs. He had a healthy distrust of numbers and formulas. When he was the warden at San Quentin in the 1980s, Ruth Rushen, the director of corrections, "put out all these edicts" demanding information. Larson recalled telling his staff that they should just put new dates on old reports and send them to Rushen. In 2010, when prison experts and a federal judge decided that an acceptable level of overcrowding in California prisons was 137.5 percent of design capacity, Larson said to me, "Do you know how they calculated that number? Well, they picked it out of their noses."

Although he did not describe his own 2 percent formula with such colorful language, he did admit that it turned out to be a bad predictor of how many SHU beds California actually needed. In fact, looking at the reality of California's isolation policies in the mid-1980s, Larson's formula seems downright idealistic. In 1984, the state had 2,600 prisoners, nearly 7 percent of its prison population, housed in "administrative segregation" at Folsom and San Quentin.[50] Based on these numbers alone, Larson was right that the state needed a new high-security unit—or two or three. But he wanted to limit the use of such restrictive confinement. He believed that the vast majority of prisoners could be housed safely in general population units if the prisons were well designed, if guards were well trained and required to maintain frequent interaction with prisoners, and if the true troublemakers were segregated. So he stuck to his principled calculations: he needed one high-security unit to house 2 percent of the state prison population.

By 1986, Larson was under intense pressure to get this prison up and running. Federal courts had ordered the California Department of Corrections either to release prisoners from the San Quentin and Folsom SHUs immediately or move them to other facilities with better conditions of confinement—adequate lighting, outdoor exercise areas, and shower access.[51] While Larson was figuring out what kind of prison to build to meet this need, department officials temporarily transferred prisoners from the San Quentin and Folsom SHUs to a newly constructed maximum-security complex in Tehachapi. This was in 1985 and 1986. When the next maximum-security prison opened in the state in 1988, California State Prison, Corcoran, department officials transferred SHU prisoners there, too.

In the new prisons like New Folsom, Tehachapi, and Corcoran, prisoners in the maximum-security units were locked into cells with solid-steel doors (broken only by a small window at eye level), for at least twenty-three hours a day, every day. But they looked out onto open areas, or "dayrooms," where they theoretically could have sat together at tables to eat meals, play cards, or watch television. The units were divided into pods of sixty-four cells, so prisoners could shout or pass notes to a large number of other prisoners. Because the units were designed to allow prisoners to congregate in groups, there were no solitary exercise yards. If prisoners had time out of their cells, it was often in company with other prisoners. In sum, the new facilities at Tehachapi and Corcoran were designed for the thousands of high-security prisoners deemed capable of interacting with one another in general population facilities, not for the SHU prisoners being temporarily housed there.

In other words, Larson still lacked a dedicated single-purpose facility that would "segregate predatory inmates from the general inmate population" and satisfy constitutional requirements for minimum conditions of confinement.[52] He had the location picked out, in Del Norte County. He just needed the design.

Larson knew that Dan McCarthy, his staff member in charge of architecture for California's new prisons, "had every architect in the world trying to sell him different designs." The Del Norte facility offered an unprecedented opportunity to design the first state-of-the-art single-purpose super-maximum security prison. Larson asked his staff to "identify every maximum security and lockup the U.S. built in the last ten years." He intended to visit each one, learn what the best practices were, and design the perfect facility for California's needs. He invited an architect from the Kitchell Corporation, which the Department of Corrections had chosen to coordinate the construction of the Del Norte prison, to tour the country with him. And they set off.

Larson and the Kitchell architect circled the United States: "Oregon, Washington, Montana, Utah, Michigan, Wisconsin—they were proud of Stillwater, their lockup [that] was fully programmed and real heavily staffed—New York, New Jersey, North Carolina, South Carolina, Georgia, Texas, New Mexico."[53]

"Did any of these states have supermaxes, or SHUs?" I asked.

"None of those states had SHUs. They had lockup units," he answered, no different from all the isolation units that already existed in California—the older SHUs at Folsom and San Quentin, and the new SIIUs at Tehachapi and Corcoran. Larson was looking for something different.[54]

He found it on the last stop on his U.S. prison tour. "The last place we went was Arizona, and what we found . . . They were in the process of construction; it was almost finished. It was the prototype for Pelican Bay."[55] The facility he visited was the Special Management Unit I, or SMU I, just rising out of the desert in Florence, Arizona, a feat of technological innovation designed to impose more restrictive conditions of isolation on more people than any prison ever built.

The prison had been designed by the Phoenix-based architectural firm Arrington Watkins, in close collaboration with Arizona prison officials. Arrington Watkins remains one of the nation's leading "justice architecture" firms, specializing in courts, jails, and prisons. As one of the architects who worked on the project explained, the SMU was "kind of a new breed of unit compared to what everyone called their maximum units, at least as the way it evolved in Arizona."[56] Nearly three decades later, the Arrington Watkins website still proudly outlined the many "design innovations" that made the 768-bed SMU facility uniquely efficient and safe: perforated steel doors with multipurpose slots for passing in food trays and for reaching in to handcuff prisoners; "windowless cells with sky lighted dayrooms"; and "small pods" that allowed one officer to supervise dozens of prisoners at a time.[57] Each cell was made of one solid piece of poured concrete, including a ledge jutting out to form a bed. And each cell had one special bolt, sensitive to the static electricity generated by human touch, by which the prisoner could dim the continuous fluorescent lighting. The lightbulb and electrical outlet were outside the cell, so workers could change bulbs and control the electricity without physically interacting with the prisoner. Indeed, the small pods precluded the need for *any* physical interaction. At the SMU I, pods consisted of three cells on the first floor and three on the second, with a shower at the end of each floor and a solitary exercise yard at the end of each pod.

The empty and pristine SMU I that Larson toured in 1986 must have been a stark contrast with the chaotic San Quentin and Chino prison tiers, where he had spent years patrolling narrow walkways two, three, and four stories above the ground, in front of cell doors made of a few widely spaced steel bars, in dimly lit units where hundreds of prisoners lived, ate, worked, and slept. At the SMU, he would have walked under the central skylights and peered through thick steel doors, perforated with finger-sized holes, into the stark, windowless, fluorescent-lit cells. It would have felt clean, neat, and safe.

The facility had just the effect on Larson that its architects desired. In designing the facility, they had made staff comfort a priority. As one of the facility's architects said in an interview: "In the traditional design, the inmate gets a window in his room. . . . The bad guys get a window, and the staff, the good guys, work inside without a window." But in the SMU, the staffers, working at the intersection of multiple pods, get "the benefit of good natural light, [so] they're not working in a dark natural dungeon." The architect acknowledged that the windowless cells have inspired critics to say that the prisoners are buried alive. But he countered that the pods are "not dark, and . . . not underground . . . just windowless."[58]

For prisoners, though, the windowless cells constitute one of the SMU's harshest innovations. Prisoners describe going years at a time without seeing the sun, the moon, trees, birds, or grasshoppers. In evaluating supermaximum conditions of confinement, federal courts have repeatedly noted the absence of windows, and some courts have specifically required that at least some prisoners, such as the severely mentally ill, be housed in facilities with windows.[59]

At the time, however, the windowless cells seemed like a brilliantly efficient innovation. As one of the facility's architects said: "Windows were always a problem anyway. Inmates always covered them up. They were always a potential for inmates to communicate." And eliminating them made the SMU's unique layout possible. "Because we didn't have windows," an architect told me, "I was able to interlock the buildings like jigsaw puzzles. . . . What would have been an outside wall was a common-use wall for other housing units, so it was a huge savings on construction costs, probably 30 percent. . . . That's why California came and said, 'That's what we want.' "[60]

The interlocking jigsaw of small, self-contained SMU pods can be distinctly seen in aerial views of both Arizona's SMU and the Pelican Bay SHU. From the sky, the tessellated pods look like a game of Tetris or a perfect tangram. From inside, one journalist described walking the halls as like being inside a snowflake: "The hallways radiate from the command center at the hub of the SHU snowflake, and each one has chambers on either side that sprout chambers of their own."[61] Others find the design disorienting. Rich Kirkland, who oversaw the Pelican Bay construction project, explained that the pods were tessellated into a capital T shape, instead of a cross shape, so that officers would have one solid wall at their backs (the top of the T) from which to orient themselves as they looked out over multiple pods.[62] While the prisoners in each pod stare out of their perforated steel doors at a blank wall, the guard overseeing the pods is positioned so that he can see the pods on either side of the prisoners' wall. So in the SMU (and later in the SHU), one guard in a central control booth looks out simultane-

Aerial photograph of the Special Management Unit, Florence, Arizona
(© Christoph Gielen, Untitled Arizona XV, from *Supermax: Structures of Confinement and Rationales of Punishment*, courtesy of Jovis Verlag, Berlin)

ously over six self-contained pods of cells. Through a combination of clear sight lines and well-positioned video cameras, a guard can see into dozens of cells at a time.

The philosopher Jeremy Bentham first proposed the "panopticon" as the ideal structure for a modern prison in the 1780s, arguing that constant surveillance would inspire discipline among the penitent. He envisioned a circle of cells in which prisoners would be completely isolated from one another, separated by high walls, but each would be visible to one guard standing in a central location, who could potentially see into every cell at any given time.[63] The SMU is a modern panopticon except that unlike Bentham's ideal prison, there are no windows in the prisoners' cells. But there are video cameras, and "grating on top of the cells, so the officers can walk on top of the cells and see down into them."[64]

Aerial photograph of the Pelican Bay State Prison. The X-shaped structure toward the top of the image is the SHU; the buildings arranged in semicircles in the foreground are general population units and administrative buildings. (Jelson25/Wikimedia Commons/CC BY 3.0)

The SMU constrained contact between guards and prisoners to the glance of an eye roving over pod upon pod of cells, from the secure vantage point of a central control booth. No need to escort prisoners to showers or exercise yards, to open up an entire cell door just to slide in a tray of food, or to enter a cell to change a lightbulb. The philosopher Michel Foucault predicted in the 1970s that punishment was moving toward a point when "contact between the law, or those who carry it out, and the body of the criminal" would be increasingly reduced until it lasted no more than a "split second."[65] And so it was, hardly ten years later, in the SMU.

Prison officials loved the SMU, flocking to check out the new design. The perforated steel doors became so popular that the architects wished they had thought to patent the design.[66] Arrington Watkins touted the work in an article in *Corrections Today* in 1987, which described the facility's innovations. The scholar Mona Lynch refers to this article as one of "the earliest indicators" of the prison's "avant garde nature."[67] Craig Brown remembered that Arizona's new facility caused a buzz among the old boys' club of prison administrators: "Corrections guys all talk. There's this little secret club of state corrections department directors. They meet and talk." Brown said he visited Arizona about five times in the 1980s to watch as the unique new prison took form.[68]

Prison officials in California seem to have known more about Arizona prison building than the Arizona legislature did. In her history of Arizona corrections, Mona Lynch notes that the SMU I was hardly mentioned in "departmental materials, government papers, or press accounts" as "anything more than a maximum-security prison."[69] Just as in California, Arizona prison officials were largely free from legislative oversight when designing their facilities.

Road Not Taken

While Carl Larson was choosing a design for California's new supermax and implementing it, legislators were discussing alternatives. These two simultaneous dialogues—one legislative subcommittee holding hearings about possible alternatives to long-term lockdown facilities while another subcommittee of that same legislature was approving the building of just such a facility—demonstrate how little control the legislature ultimately had.

In a hearing of the Joint Legislative Committee on Prison Construction and Operations, conducted inside Folsom Prison in 1985, prisoners, experts, and legislators alike reiterated ten-year-old criticisms levied by federal courts against the SHU prototypes. Prisoners at Folsom testified that lockdown conditions imposed in the SHU—being locked in a cell "day in and day out, and week in and month out" with one other person, receiving only two or three hot meals a week—cultivated hatred and violence among prisoners.[70] Craig Haney, a psychologist and professor at the University of California, Santa Cruz, said that the Department of Corrections had avoided major riots only through "a strategy of isolating and segregating inmates and using force and a kind of intimidation to keep them under control." Such practices, he added, came at "a great cost."[71] In a report to the committee, a consultant named Lewis Fudge recommended that the CDC "dispense with the failed notion that the use of weapons [by guards], segregation units and prolonged lockdowns are effective long-term means of control."[72] Fudge argued that extended periods of lockdown were the direct result of cultural shifts in correctional administration: the department's purpose had shifted from rehabilitation to punishment, the correctional officers' union had grown in power, and administrators had adopted "acceptance of violence as a given."[73]

Much as federal courts had done, prisoners, academics, administrators, and legislators suggested myriad ways to avoid the use of isolation and extended lockdowns. In recommendations prepared in response to the Folsom hearings, the Senate Office of Research suggested improving education programs, preparing prisoners to return to their communities, and providing more jobs for prisoners inside.[74] The two prisoners testifying at the hearings emphasized how more humane treatment would help alleviate tensions inside Folsom. "If you start dealing [with] people from a human position, you start eliminating frustration," one said, adding, "If you start providing people with things to do, you start occupying people's time where people don't have to sit up in a cell and focus their attention on a—building up their anger."[75]

Many of the experts who testified suggested that programming was key to reducing violence and improving prison conditions. They proposed a wide array of reforms: increasing work programs, giving prisoners a role in management, better pay and training for officers, more frequent contact between prisoners and staff in order to alleviate grievance complaints, discontinuing double-celling, establishing early-release programs, and building prisoner-designed and prisoner-constructed facilities.[76]

In addition to criticizing the increasingly entrenched practice of controlling violence through long-term lockdowns, experts also suggested that the department's classification system contributed to the perceived need for growing numbers of lockdown units. In the early 1980s, the California Department of Corrections implemented a new prisoner classification system, based primarily on the sentence the incoming prisoner had received.

Prisoners with long prison sentences were treated as dangerous and placed in high-security settings, regardless of their behavior or other risk factors.

The legislature seemed quite interested in encouraging brainstorming around policy alternatives. One year after the hearing at Folsom, it passed a bill establishing the Presley Institute of Corrections Research and Training, near the University of California, Riverside, east of Los Angeles. The institute was to be a "public think tank, structured to study, understand and recommend solutions regarding: (a) Crime. (b) The impact on society after offenders are released for [sic] incarceration. (c) The growing financial burden of prison populations. (d) Prison violence."[77] The institute was named after the inland emperor, Senator Robert Presley, who dominated the state's criminal justice policy during his twenty-year legislative tenure.[78]

It is hard to tell how serious the legislators were about pushing for alternatives to the status quo. They seemed to be invested in gathering information and developing evidence-based policies to both build the best prisons possible and, where feasible, to avoid building prisons in the first place. But they appropriated only $150,000 for their think tank, so perhaps their investment in research was only symbolic. In the same year, they appropriated millions for prison construction, through bond measures and legislative initiatives, while delegating the building process itself entirely to prison administrators. Still, none of the proposed solutions to the administrative challenges facing the California Department of Corrections involved constructing a new high-security, permanent-lockdown facility.

The Final Touches

Carl Larson returned from Arizona in 1986 with a clear vision of exactly what the Del Norte County prison would look like. It would be a bigger, better SMU.

A California architect who worked at Kitchell in the 1980s remembered that when Larson and his team got back from their national prison tour, "they knew what they wanted," and they could point to a model for it: "They had visited the SMU in Arizona, and they said, 'This is the facility we want.' "[79] There was not much design work for Kitchell to do. In fact, Larson hired one of the Arrington Watkins architects who had helped design the SMU to consult on the Del Norte County prison.[80] Larson worked with these architects to implement a few key modifications to the SMU design, to better integrate the new facility into the system of prisons being built in California. Larson noted that Arizona "had some budget constraints . . . and we had a better budget."[81] He had hundreds of millions of dollars of lease-revenue bond funding allocated for the Del Norte prison and plenty of flexibility in how he spent it.

The Arizona SMU, with its 768 high-security isolation beds, was too small for California. Larson needed at least 1,000 beds. He increased the size of each pod from six cells to eight, giving each guard station control over forty eight cells in six pods, and then created a neatly tessellated plan for twenty-two such forty-eight-cell units, for a total of 1,056 isolation cells.[82] At the last minute, he got worried that 1,056 isolation cells might not be enough. By 1988, the department was already operating hundreds of "temporary" SHU beds at both Corcoran and Tehachapi. Before the poured concrete cells were made for the Del Norte prison, Larson ordered a slight alteration to the cell design: the addition of a second concrete ledge, about three feet above the first.[83] This modification left open the possibility of housing two prisoners in each cell. (In addition to the 1,056 SHU cells at Pelican Bay, with the extra ledges to allow for double-bunking, prison officials planned for a 2,000-bed facility, designed for high-security general population prisoners, on the same site.)[84]

To maximize guards' safety, Larson made sure each pod had "lethal gun coverage." The Arizona SMU architect remembered: "That's when we built a quarter of a full-size control room in a warehouse for Carl Larson and those guys to go and stand in and hold their weapons, to make sure they could shoot at everything they wanted. . . . That was their innovation, their model."[85] Larson explained his reasoning by referring to his time as an associate warden at Soledad in the 1970s, "We had eleven staff members murdered. . . . If you had a melee going on, you couldn't get a gun in there."[86] He did not want to have that problem in his new facility, so he ensured that any guard in the prison would be able to see, and aim a deadly weapon, into each cell in his unit.

Prisoner's drawing of a SHU pod
(Drawing by Arturo Mendoza)

Rich Kirkland, who worked under Larson as project manager for the construction of the new prison, argued that the California team also made design tweaks to render the new institution "as light and airy as possible." He
explained: "We made the hallways between the cell and the wall wider. . . .
We put in more skylights at a less sharp angle . . . [and] we used perforated
steel doors . . . letting in more light."[87] In addition to finding the eight-cell
pods "light and airy," Kirkland described the cells themselves as "efficient
and spacious," without all the metal ledges and built-in lockers included in
lower-security cells. And he noted that a deep rust-red paint was used to
color the doors and accents in the pods, adding another layer of comfort.[88]
With the design ready, Larson, Brown, and Kirkland just needed a perfunc-
tory legislative sign-off on the prison plans. Someone would need to make
a brief presentation to the legislature, and as long as no legislators raised

objections within forty-five days (according to the procedural rules that Presley and the JLCPCO passed in 1986), the plans would be automatically approved. As the construction manager for the Del Norte prison, Kirkland had the job of making this presentation.

Kirkland remembered that legislators were initially interested in exactly where the prison would be sited. When he presented the design plans, legislators asked mainly about how much sewage the proposed institution would produce and whether the pollution would damage the local Smith River, "the last wild river in California," according to Kirkland. He was especially proud of the "extra good sewage treatment plant" he ordered built in response to these concerns.[89]

Because no record exists of the hearing that approved the design for the Del Norte prison, I pressed Kirkland for further details about the questions that were asked at the hearing: "Did anyone ask about the high-security design proposed for the facility?" Kirkland said the legislators did ask a bit about the design, but correctional experts readily put the legislators' concerns to rest with clear explanations of the necessity of the facility: "You get someone like Carl, who can sit down and explain . . . [that] we have to have [it]. . . . You've got other jurisdictions that were also using a supermax for their system. . . . We had the credibility of proven experts that could weigh in on why we needed that function."[90]

Larson recalled that he defended the supermax to legislators by saying: "It's not draconian, it's spartan."[91]

In the end, Kirkland said, local politics proved far more important to the legislators than design details. He recalled that legislators asked pointedly: "How many locals are you going to hire?"[92] In sum, he said, the legislators were "engaged, they got credible answers, and made a good decision." Larson's plan for a bigger and better SMU was approved.

Larson insisted that in my earlier writings I had misrepresented the legislature's limited role in the design process.[93] Whether or not there was a legislative record, he personally remembered spending "hundreds and hundreds of hours with Senator Robert Presley's staff—they'd come over to my office, go over the plans."[94] Intrigued, I asked whom he had worked with, imagining that I could conduct further oral history interviews to uncover more unrecorded details of the prison's legislative history. Larson said one of the key players he had worked with to get prison designs approved by the legislature was James Park, whom he described as a "chief staffer" for Senator Robert Presley.

As noted earlier in this chapter, Park was an old friend of Larson's. Unfortunately, Park passed away in 2013, and I was never able to interview him. And there is even less in the California legislative record about James Park than there is about Pelican Bay State Prison. A *Los Angeles Times* article from March 1990 describes him as a consultant to (not a formal staff member of) the JLCPCO, but does not say how long he served in that role.[95] He appears in plenty of other archival sources, however, since he was the associate warden in charge of San Quentin on the day that George Jackson was shot in the prison yard. In other words, James Park was a career prison bureaucrat. He happened to be advising the legislative committee on prison building when the Pelican Bay designs were approved, but his very position confirms the central role that prison bureaucrats, as opposed to legislators, played in innovating and implementing the design of Pelican Bay State Prison.

Larson told me that to call Pelican Bay an administrative innovation is to "play to a liberal audience" that already believes the California Department of Corrections is "renegade." Larson was lumping me together with George Jackson's admirers. That audience is wrong, he insisted. The Department of Corrections was far from renegade. Carl Larson, Craig Brown, and Rich Kirkland conducted thorough research by traveling the country to visit new prisons; consulted prison design standards propagated by professional and federal agencies; followed minimum constitutional standards laid down by the courts; and sought approval for their plans from everyone who mattered, including Senator Robert Presley and the president of the union representing prison guards.[96] Nonetheless, as Larson told me the first time I met him: "I designed Pelican Bay." He found the model in Arizona, oversaw the modification of that prototype to meet California's needs, and secured all the necessary approvals to get the facility built. In that sense, the facility was an administrative innovation.

California legislators, along with Governor Deukmejian, touted their prison-building initiatives throughout the 1980s. They oversaw the passage of hundreds of millions of dollars in general obligation bonds and maintained the Joint Legislative Committee on Prison Construction and Operations. Inland Empire residents elected and reelected Senator Presley, who continued to chair the JLCPCO. And Governor Deukmejian proudly attended the opening of each new prison in California, from the California State Prison at Solano, with its wooden doors painted to look like steel, to Pelican Bay, whose grand opening came in 1990.

Yet neither Deukmejian nor Presley nor any other legislator mentioned that there was anything special about the prison under construction in Del Norte County. When Deukmejian attended the grand opening, more than six months after Pelican Bay first opened its doors, he focused on California's overall prison-building project, not on the details of the Del Norte facility. He used his address to deride efforts at prison reform: "While we were trying to 'understand' these criminals, California's crime rate soared . . . The number of major crimes quadrupled. By 1980, one in every 25 Californians was robbed or beaten, raped or murdered, their homes burglarized or their car stolen." The solution, he urged, was to build even more prisons; Los Angeles residents should be more cooperative and welcoming toward prisons, as the residents of Del Norte had been.[97]

What the governor did not say about Pelican Bay is as interesting as what he did say. Why not celebrate, or at least mention, the technological innovations designed to keep people maximally isolated? When Deukmejian mentioned his problems with "understanding" criminals, why not mention the newly restrictive conditions of confinement at Pelican Bay? One wonders whether Deukmejian actually knew about the design, or the day-to-day conditions, of the new facility.

The residents of Del Norte figured out at least a few details, and many were significantly less excited than Governor Deukmejian. They had not realized that the prison they invited into their backyard would be a maximum-security facility—let alone a supermax. One resident, interviewed for a *Los Angeles Times* story in August 1990, complained: "We were tools in someone else's game. . . . Some people made a lot of money off this prison. . . . And we got something completely different than was promised; we weren't told what was happening until it was too late."[98]

There were many unseen costs. Once the Department of Corrections decided to build the prison, the residents faced a "spiraling county budget and a rising crime rate"; neighboring communities watched the spiral and voted to reject prisons. A *Los Angeles Times* headline suggested that the prison had brought "near bankruptcy" by forcing the town to fund millions of dollars of new infrastructure by constructing roads and utilities, and hiring new teachers, building inspectors, and law enforcement officials. Furthermore, while the new prison had been projected to increase employment opportunities, only 20 percent of the new correctional officers were drawn from local residents.[99]

In the end, Del Norte County got not just any prison, but one of the securest and most punitive in the United States. In interviews, Larson, Brown, and Kirkland stood by their decision to build the facility. Larson asserted the department had "not been renegade."[100] Kirkland called the facility "just beautiful."[101] Brown said, "I think we built the right stuff."[102] All three argued that the prison was a critical tool for controlling violence throughout the California prison system.

The Arizona architect who worked on the design of both the SMU and Pelican Bay, on the other hand, said: "Sometimes I wonder if I ever should've done that."[103] Even Larson complained repeatedly about the expanding use of isolation units beyond the limited facilities that he had designed at Pelican Bay. And he worried that some prisoners—especially gang members sent there on the basis of limited evidence—either did not belong in isolation or had spent too many years there.[104] Brown, too, said: "I don't think we ever conceptualized it as a permanent thing for anyone other than a handful of inmates . . . the assumption [was that prisoners would serve] something like nine months, but no more than eighteen months."[105] By 2011, more than five hundred prisoners had spent more than ten continuous years in total isolation in the Pelican Bay SHU.

Although Rene Enriquez, the star of the book *The Black Hand*, which Carl Larson asked me to read, was no longer in the Pelican Bay SHU in 2011, he had spent ten years there, throughout the 1990s. I suspect that Rene is someone whom Craig Brown would agree belonged in the SHU for ten years—in constant view of guards carefully armed with rifles, just as Larson had planned. But now Enriquez spends most of his time in undisclosed jail cells throughout Southern California, usually with access to his own telephone line, a computer, and decent treatment as a law enforcement collaborator.[106]

I remember vividly one of the first letters Enriquez sent me. It came to my campus mailbox at UC-Berkeley, and I opened it as I was walking to the subway station. Prison letters have a particular feel—the paper is usually very soft, as if it has already been handled repeatedly. (Indeed, it has usually been handled repeatedly, since almost all prison correspondence passes through a rigorous censorship review.) The handwriting—especially of prisoners in isolation—is often precise and compact, meticulously scratched out by someone with infinite time on his hands in a tiny space. And the whole thing always smells institutional—like a stale hospital room. I opened Enriquez's letter and experienced all those familiar sensations. Then something flitted in front of me, and I jumped. A paper crane had floated from the envelope and landed gracefully on the sidewalk in front of me. It was as if Enriquez were there, shaking my hand via the letter.

Learning origami was one of the ways that Enriquez passed the time during his ten years in the SHU. Countless other prisoners over the past twenty-five years have lost their minds inside the confines of the smooth, poured-concrete cells where Enriquez learned to fold origami. Some prisoners were scalded and beaten. Others hanged themselves or beat their heads against the wall until they passed out or cut their wrists or necks. I think of origami as a form of resistance to the experience of these harsh conditions of confinement in the Pelican Bay SHU, the box.

In recent years, the SHU has been roundly criticized. But the question of the impact of the SHU, the box, isolation at Pelican Bay, remains unresolved. Enriquez, like Todd Ashker and George Jackson, puts the question in stark relief. Did the SHU turn Enriquez from a brutal, shot-calling murderer into a docile, origami-folding gentleman? Did it break him—bringing him to the point where he was willing to say anything about anyone in order to escape? Or did he break the SHU, figuring out that the way to a better life was to leverage his insider's knowledge into a coveted role as one of the FBI's leading consultants?

Carl Larson, who worked tirelessly as a public servant for the state of California—first on the front lines of an acutely dangerous prison system and later in the halls of the state capitol, putting his firsthand experiences to work in creating what he hoped would be a better system—built just about the harshest prison anyone had imagined. His goal was to stabilize a system in chaos, creating safe conditions for staff and prisoners alike. But did Pelican Bay do what Carl had hoped? The next three chapters explore the question of the SHU's impact—on institutions and on individuals.

5

Skeleton Bay

THE OPENING OF PELICAN BAY IN DECEMBER 1989 marked both the end of three years of concerted correctional planning and a new chapter in the long aftermath of George Jackson's death. Hugo Pinell, the last of the San Quentin Six still in prison for joining Jackson's alleged takeover of the San Quentin Adjustment Center, was one of the first prisoners transferred to Pelican Bay—along with Todd Ashker. Rene Enriquez was transferred there a few years later. They could hardly have known what to expect. The first statewide news coverage of the institution's opening was in June 1990 in the *Los Angeles Times*; that story said nothing about the conditions of confinement and contained no pictures of the inside of the facility. Not that Pinell, Ashker, or Enriquez would have seen the article. All were transferred to Pelican Bay from older Security Housing Units, where their access to news of the outside world would have been limited, at best. Pinell had spent more than a decade in the San Quentin and Folsom SHUs; Enriquez had spent a few years in the Tehachapi SHU; and Ashker had spent a few years in the Folsom SHU. As discussed in Chapter 3, federal courts had repeatedly condemned both the San Quentin and Folsom facilities for their unconstitutional conditions. Pelican Bay's clean, brightly lit cells, equipped with running water and steel doors that slid silently open, would have at least seemed novel.

The first descriptions of Pelican Bay that trickled out in prisoners' handwritten letters, however, did not dwell on the cleanliness, the lighting, or the miraculously silent doors. Prisoners nicknamed the new institution Skeleton Bay. Their first letters described abuse and conveyed terror.[1]

Judge Thelton Henderson, then the chief justice of the U.S. District Court for the Northern District of California, which encompasses the coastal area from San Francisco north to Del Norte County, recalled how quickly these letters captured his attention: "One of your jobs as chief justice is to notice things that are happening on and to your court. . . . One of the things that started happening is we got a ton of handwritten letters and petitions from this place we had never heard of before—Pelican Bay."[2] California's federal courts receive hundreds of letters and petitions from prisoners annually. Many federal courthouses, especially in districts with large prison populations, have a full-time attorney assigned to handling this barrage of claims—48,000 pro se prisoner petitions were filed in U.S. federal courts in 2010 alone.[3] Among these thousands of petitions, claims of abuse would have had to be consistent and egregious to attract a chief judge's attention.

When I asked Judge Henderson about the first thing he remembered learning about Pelican Bay, no one complaint among the "ton" he was receiving stood out. Instead, he described an overall foreboding that something was very wrong in California's newest prison. He was so worried that he took the unusual step of calling up the warden of Pelican Bay "to talk to him and see what was going on."

I'm not sure I could imagine a more intimidating call, I thought. I was sitting in Henderson's chambers—a vast wood-paneled room at least five times the size of a Pelican Bay box cell, looking at him across the expanse of a long mahogany conference table. Henderson had a full white beard and wire-rimmed spectacles. He wore a button-down blue shirt tucked into dark jeans. Even without his black robes, even confined to a wheelchair and approaching eighty years old, he was an intimidating presence.

Judge Henderson did not want to ask too many questions of the warden over the telephone. Instead, he invited the warden to San Francisco to tell a panel of the court's judges "what was going on" at Pelican Bay. "He kindly agreed to come down," Henderson recalled. I wondered whether any prison warden could refuse a federal judge's invitation to discuss "what's behind the unusual petitions" pouring out of his prison. To a warden, the chief judge's call would have registered as: *I have credible evidence of significant constitutional violations for which I think you may be responsible.*[4]

"It was interesting, and he was forthright," Henderson said of the meeting. Although he did not give the warden's name, it was surely Charles D. Marshall, who ran Pelican Bay from its first months of operation through January 1995.[5] Henderson later described Marshall in court records as displaying a "striking" "lack of concern" for prisoners and as maintaining "complete non-involvement" in critical supervision decisions around excessive (legalese for "brutal" and "fatal") use-of-force incidents.[6] Yet at their first face-to-face meeting, Henderson told me, he found the warden not just personable but reasonable. The warden "proceeded to tell us essentially about the supermax prison . . . that it was patterned after Arizona," that it was "California's attempt to deal with our prisons being run by gangs," that it was "an attempt to put the worst of the worst in one place, to tell us how they [the prisoners] were dangerous," how they "were trying to break the gangs by putting them in isolation, keeping [them] in their cells for twenty-two and a half hours a day."[7]

In Henderson's recollection, the warden constructed a familiar story, one with echoes of the fear George Jackson inspired, of prison officials' pervasive sense that they were losing control and authority to gang leaders, and of Carl Larson's discovery of the first supermax in Arizona.

For the most part, Henderson accepted the story. He said to me of the prisoners in the Pelican Bay SHU: "These are some bad people."

Then he laughed, started to correct himself. Prisoners' rights activists always remind him, he said, that prisoners "are not bad people, but people who have done bad things." Still, he insisted, "These are some bad people." He would come to believe that there was some truth to Marshall's claims about Pelican Bay.

His immediate reaction, however, was not so accepting. The warden "was clueless . . . had not been given any course on constitutional law." Henderson remembered looking around at the other judges in the meeting "and our mouths were open." They said to each other: "You can't do that. That's unconstitutional."[8]

The Most Liberal Judge in America

If any federal judge were going to declare the Pelican Bay Security Housing Unit an affront to the U.S. Constitution, it would be Thelton Henderson, a committed and often controversial civil rights activist. Born in Louisiana in 1933, Henderson moved to California with his mother and grandmother as a toddler, grew up in Watts, in Los Angeles County, and attended college at the University of California, Berkeley, on a football scholarship.[9] He served as a corporal in the U.S. Army from 1956 to 1958 and then returned to UC-Berkeley for law school.[10]

Henderson was one of only two African American men in his law school class. Upon graduation, he became the first African American in the Civil Rights Division of the U.S. Department of Justice in Washington, D.C. This was 1962, and he quickly found himself at the center of the legal battles swirling around the civil rights movement in the Deep South. He traveled to Montgomery, Alabama, to investigate the bombing of the Sixteenth Street Baptist Church in 1963; he attended Medgar Evers's funeral in Washington, D.C.; and he befriended Martin Luther King, Jr. Barely thirty years old, he grappled with the contradictions between representing the federal government and being a black man in the South. He recalled later: "Whether I was going to be Joe Friday and say 'Just give me the facts' or whether I was going to hurl my body against the machine of injustice and make a statement, it was always a personal issue with me that I don't think I ever resolved."[11] In 1963, a federal judgeship would have seemed far-fetched to him.

Local law enforcement officials in Alabama caught him using a federal car to escort Martin Luther King, Jr., to an event in Selma. Henderson was worried about King's safety; this was the same year when the civil rights leader Medgar Evers had been shot in the back, in his own driveway, in Jackson, Mississippi. Byron De La Beckwith, a prominent Ku Klux Klan member, was convicted of the murder—thirty years later.[12] Not lending federal protection to King, Henderson thought, would have been as reckless as lending it. But Alabama police saw a chance to discredit the federal government for assisting the controversial civil rights leader. Henderson left the Justice Department in a swirl of controversy. He returned to Northern California, jobless and "shattered."[13]

Within five years, he was running a legal aid office in East Palo Alto—a high-crime, notoriously gang-dominated low-income neighborhood just east of Stanford University—and serving as an assistant dean at Stanford Law School, charged with recruiting minority law students. His career recovered quickly enough that he was appointed to the federal judiciary by President Jimmy Carter and confirmed in 1980. With no prior work history as either a judge or a prosecutor, he lacked the traditional experience most lawyers bring to the federal bench.[14]

Henderson became embroiled in California prison politics almost as soon as he joined the San Francisco–based federal court, where he was the only African American judge.[15] In June 1982, he overturned Johnny Spain's two murder convictions. A Marin County jury had found Spain guilty in 1976 of two counts of murder in two of the three officer deaths that took place in San Quentin on August 21, 1971. These were the only two murder convictions obtained from the epic prosecution of the San Quentin Six, the prisoners who had allegedly conspired with George Jackson in his "revolt," but the verdicts were tenuous at best.[16] As the *Los Angeles Times* later explained, "The prosecution never contended that Spain stabbed or shot any of the victims."[17] Rather, he was convicted on a theory of "vicarious liability" —"conspiring with Jackson to escape"—and therefore was "held responsible for the two deaths that resulted."[18] The jury deliberated for twenty-four days before agreeing to convict, after which Judge Henry Broderick of the Marin County Superior Court sentenced Spain to two life sentences. The California Court of Appeals upheld Spain's convictions, and the California Supreme Court twice declined to reconsider the case.[19]

Spain filed a petition for habeas corpus—traditionally, a challenge to a custodian's authority to detain a prisoner, often filed in federal court, questioning the legitimacy of state court proceedings. In March 1982, Henderson held a hearing to evaluate Spain's claims that there had been two significant constitutional violations at his 1976 trial. First, Spain alleged, Judge Broderick had twice communicated privately (ex parte) with a juror about the juror's emotionally uncomfortable and potentially disqualifying realization that one of the people mentioned repeatedly in the trial had murdered a close friend of hers.[20] This violated both Spain's right to be present at a critical stage of his trial and his right to be represented by an attorney. Second, Spain was extensively shackled throughout the trial, "in leg irons and belly chains." His hands were bound to his waist, his waist chain shackled to a chair, and the chair bolted to the floor; guards armed with machine guns stood by.[21] This violated his right to be presumed innocent. Henderson found that Spain's first claim alone required "automatic reversal."[22] He granted the habeas petition and ordered that Spain be retried within three months or else be released from prison. The decision attracted national attention.[23]

Letting Spain's conviction stand would have been easy, given the extensive state court record. Overturning it was politically and legally controversial—especially for a relatively inexperienced federal judge. Although Henderson could not—and cannot—be fired from the district court, he ended any chance he might have had of being promoted to an appellate court.[24] Spain was the only San Quentin Six defendant who claimed membership in the Black Panthers. By taking his side in the San Quentin Six case, Henderson was seen as aligning himself with the Black Panther Party against the state prison system.

Moreover, by overturning the multiple state court decisions upholding Spain's conviction, Henderson imposed federal constitutional standards on local judicial decision makers—a decisively federalist stance. In his decision, Henderson pointedly cited the Supreme Court case *Powell v. Alabama,* from 1932, which overturned the rape convictions in Alabama of nine black men (known colloquially as the "Scottsboro Boys"), because they had been inadequately represented at their criminal trial.[25] *Powell* was a landmark civil rights and federalism case that represented the first Supreme Court application of a federal criminal right—the Sixth Amendment right to counsel—to overturn a state conviction. Henderson's decision also had more immediate implications: it was likely to bring the release of a prisoner whom California prison guards held responsible for murdering three of their peers.[26]

Ruth Rushen, the director of the California Department of Corrections, appealed Henderson's decision in the *Spain* case. The Ninth Circuit Court of Appeals upheld the decision. But the U.S. Supreme Court "emphatically disagree[d]," condemning the district court's lack of deference to the comprehensive record of state court decisions, and sent the case back to Judge

Henderson for reconsideration.[27] A *Los Angeles Times* story situated the Supreme Court decision as part of a growing legal trend toward "limiting the ability of prison inmates to challenge their convictions in the federal courts."[28] Neither this legal trend nor the Supreme Court's summary dismissal of his legal reasoning deterred Judge Henderson, though.

Even if Spain's first claim, about his right to be present at his trial with an attorney, did not withstand Supreme Court scrutiny, Henderson reasoned, his second claim certainly should. Spain's right to be presumed innocent had been egregiously violated by the "uninterrupted use of maximum physical restraints on a defendant whose disruptive conduct can best be characterized as minor."[29] Again, Henderson concluded that the state had to retry Spain or release him.[30] Again, the U.S. Court of Appeals for the Ninth Circuit agreed, and this time the Supreme Court declined to reconsider the case.

In 1988, Spain earned parole on his original conviction—for a murder in Los Angeles in 1967. He was seventeen at the time of the crime.[31] By 1990, California prosecutors had given up all hope of prosecuting him for the 1971 prison guard deaths. As then–district attorney Jerry Herman told the *Los Angeles Times:* "Since this case is now 19 years old, and since the defendant Spain has now been out of custody and led a crime-free life for three years, it is impossible to believe that a conviction secured after a retrial would result in the defendant Spain being resentenced to prison."[32]

Spain's case was just one of many controversial decisions Henderson negotiated in the 1980s. He first appeared in the national news in December 1981 when he threatened to hold the state social services director in contempt of court because she had failed to give proper notice to 150,000 residents before cutting their welfare benefits. The state office quickly agreed to pay the money it had refused recipients and to delay cutting the benefits.[33] In April 1985, Henderson found that State Farm Insurance Company had systematically excluded women from lucrative sales agent positions; he ordered the company to pay millions of dollars in damages and to institute hiring quotas.[34] In January 1989, Henderson entered the dolphin-safe-tuna debate and required U.S. tuna boats to carry observers, at a cost of $1 million a year, to ensure that no needless killings of dolphins occurred.[35] In May 1989, he ordered the Veterans Administration to reconsider the eligibility of more than 31,000 Vietnam War veterans for health benefits for a range of skin diseases and cancers associated with exposure to Agent Orange.[36]

In 1999, Berkeley Law (then Boalt Hall) founded the Thelton E. Henderson Center for Social Justice in honor of "a man who embodies the essence of social justice." When I enrolled at Berkeley Law, the film *Soul of Justice*, about Henderson's life, was an unofficial part of the school's curriculum. I saw the film just after I returned to Berkeley from a summer in Atlanta, my birthplace. I had spent June and July working ten-, twelve-, and, in the end, twenty-hour days on behalf of a death-row client in Alabama facing imminent execution. Watching the wheels of justice turn quickly enough to expedite an execution, awaiting the series of prosecutorial motions and judicial orders required to make the process go forward, I became cynical about the legal system I was working so hard to join. I had never considered medical school, because blood made me queasy. But there I was, delivering habeas petition after habeas petition to courts across Alabama, shaking blood-stained hands again and again. Each legal defeat brought my client a week, a day, an hour closer to death. On July 26, 2007, the State of Alabama executed Darryl Grayson. I wondered whether my zealous representation had just legitimized the execution.

But *Soul of Justice* reinspired me—made me feel like there was a possibility of being a lawyer and having clean hands. Thelton Henderson's law was one I could believe in. At the time, Henderson's role in the Pelican Bay litigation, mentioned in the film, registered with me as yet another example of his legal heroism.

Henderson's reputation had been well established by 1990. When he placed his call to Warden Marshall that year, Johnny Spain had been out of prison for just two years. Marshall certainly would have heard of Judge Henderson and would have had notions of the kind of judge he was facing.

Digging Up Skeleton Bay

After that first call, Henderson moved quickly, not only to investigate what was happening at Pelican Bay, but also to appoint counsel on behalf of the prisoners housed there. On October 26, 1990, Alejandro Madrid filed a complaint with the U.S. District Court for the Northern District of California. The complaint became the first entry in the case docket in *Madrid v. Gomez*, which, over the next twenty-one years, would come to include more than 2,200 separate entries. There is little about Madrid in the record—no digitized file of his original complaint, no mention of what specific abuses he suffered.

Instead, the *Madrid* docket reveals an increasingly complex case with an ever growing list of plaintiffs and legal representatives. On May 9, 1991, Judge Henderson issued an order referring Alejandro Madrid to the Federal Pro Bono Project for appointment of counsel. Wilson Sonsini Goodrich & Rosati, a large corporate litigation firm based in Palo Alto, took the case three months later. Barely half a year later, Henderson certified a class action of "all prisoners who are, or will be, incarcerated" at Pelican Bay State Prison.[37] By the fall of 1992, Wilson Sonsini had recruited a team of prisoners' rights advocates to work on the case, including Steve Fama and Don Specter from the Prison Law Office, and Michael Bien from the San Francisco firm of Rosen Bien & Asaro (now Rosen Bien Galvan & Grunfeld), a frequent collaborator with the Prison Law Office. These lawyers, along with Judge Henderson, became some of the first civilians to cross the threshold of the Pelican Bay Security Housing Unit.

Between 1990 and 1993, each of them made the trip from San Francisco up the coast of California to Crescent City (nearly four hundred miles) multiple times.[38] Sometimes they flew into the tiny Del Norte County Regional Airport. Henderson never told the prison when he was planning a visit, but he said the town was so small that if he arrived at the airport or spent the night in a local hotel, everyone working at the prison would know the second he was in town. So he took to making the six-hour drive through the redwoods and along the rocky coastline, to make his arrivals less predictable. (Also, he confessed, he had heard of a case alleging that the Crescent City airport, which had been built as a military facility to test new instruments for navigating in dense fog, was too dangerous for commercial planes.)[39]

He described his initial experiences at the prison: "My first visit to Pelican Bay, I went up with three of my law clerks. The first thing [the officials] did—they were very intent on showing me how bad these people were." Officials ushered him first into a large room, which he estimated was about the size of his judicial chambers. Table after table was covered in weapons: knives, zip guns. "It was a stunning display," he remembered. He thought the prison officials wanted to convey a simple message: "Just leave it to us, and we'll take care of this really bad situation."

I asked him: "What surprised you the most?"

"The inhumanity of the thing. They were treating prisoners like animals." He thought for a minute and recalled a more specific image—of prisoners outside, in the solitary exercise yards. "I said I wanted to see one of their breaks [from the twenty-two hours spent in their cells]. They took one prisoner out and took him into a wired cage, maybe about the size of this"—he gestured down the length of his office. "They put him in there. That was his exercise. I can picture that as clear as when I first saw it. He walked around in a figure eight. I remember so clearly going to the zoo with my kids, seeing a cat walking around like that." This bird's-eye view—looking down at a tableau of human suffering—would characterize much of the *Madrid* case.

Henderson continued, describing his first tour of the Pelican Bay SHU: "It was drizzling rain, and I saw human beings in their underwear, outside in the cold."[40] In the *Madrid* ruling, he would later describe evidence that prisoners had been held in cages, naked, outside, in pouring rain, for hours at a time.[41] At the time, he said, he was surprised that prison administrators "weren't hiding anything."[42] He ultimately concluded that the prison administration enforced a pervasive "code of silence" about much worse abuses.[43]

Henderson was exercising his authority as a judge to visit prison facilities. Few other outsiders, beyond the growing team of lawyers representing the prisoner plaintiffs, set foot inside the institution. Media access was strictly limited, and few families could afford the long trip north to the isolated facility. One-third of all prisoners in California are from Los Angeles (which is twice as far from Pelican Bay as San Francisco), a trip of nearly eight hundred miles.[44]

Most Californians (and Americans more generally) got their first glimpse inside Pelican Bay on September 12, 1993, when *60 Minutes* aired a news story about the "high-tech, silent, grim" facility.[45] Although the glimpse was limited—Pelican Bay prison administrators refused the *60 Minutes* camera crews access to the Security Housing Unit pods—it was haunting. The show relies on pictures provided by the Department of Corrections, along with interviews, to convey the conditions in the pods. (Two more decades would pass before the prison's administrators granted an open media tour of the isolation pods.) In one exchange during the broadcast, a public information officer described the restrictive conditions in the institution: "They can talk, but they have no physical contact."

Mike Wallace, the *60 Minutes* news anchor, responded: "Good God—and this can go on for years in here?"

"Depending on the circumstances of the case, it could go on for years."

"There's an eerie quality here."[46]

James Gomez, then the director of the California Department of Corrections, described the Pelican Bay SHU population as made up not of prisoners who "commit five murders on the outside" but of those who "stab staff and stab other inmates"—the institutionally rather than socially dangerous. Mike Wallace interviewed Todd Ashker, who illustrated Gomez's point by describing how he stabbed another prisoner in self-defense.

The more memorable story, however, was Vaughn Dortch's. The prison's public information officer described Dortch as a mentally disturbed prisoner who believed he was a killer bee and smeared himself with his own feces. Officers ordered him to take a bath. Dortch, interviewed by *60 Minutes* producers, recalled being held in scalding water: "I started hollering . . . You could smell my skin burning. I was cooking, the same way you broil or cook food. You could smell it, my skin burning." The chief doctor examined Dortch and determined that he had not been burned. Then Dortch went into shock. Gomez described the incident in more staid terms: "[Dortch] was put into a bath to remove fecal matter from his body, and the water was too hot. It scalded him." Gomez added that the medical technician who was responsible was fired. The case, however, was far from closed.

The *60 Minutes* team interviewed Stuart Grassian, a Harvard Medical School psychiatrist, who queried why someone like Dortch was in the SHU in the first place. "A lot of people who end up in the Pelican Bay SHU are the last people who ought to go there," Grassian said, explaining that more than a third of the dozens of people he had interviewed in the Pelican Bay SHU were psychotic. "People describe the walls of their cell start[ing] to

move in and out. The lights start to be brighter and duller. . . . People . . .
are smearing themselves with feces, drinking out of their toilet bowl, eating their feces. . . . A good example is a prisoner who hears the faucet drip,
and it starts to get louder and louder. . . . What happens in the Pelican Bay
SHU is a form of punishment that is far more egregious [than the death
penalty]."[47] Additional interviews—with a person who tried to commit suicide by jumping from the second floor of a SHU pod, and another with
brain damage and seizures who had been brutally extracted from his cell—
supported Grassian's point.

Still, Gomez called Pelican Bay "a success story about isolating victimiz-
ers from other inmates who want to [stick to the] program and go back into
society." The prison's public information officer said: "It's safe for our staff
who work here, and it's safe for our inmates who are housed here."[48] Gomez
and the public information officer were planting the first seeds of a public
relations campaign intended to help the prison withstand the legal scrutiny
it was about to get in Judge Henderson's courtroom.

The 60 Minutes story aired two days before the start of the ten-week trial
in Madrid v. Gomez, the first case to assess the constitutionality of supermax incarceration. During that interval, Judge Henderson made one more
trip up to Pelican Bay. "I wanted to see it so I could better run the trial," he
explained.[49] This gave Gomez, Marshall, and their staff one more chance to
bolster their public relations campaign.

At the prison, the officers leading Henderson's tour suggested that he
see the prison yard from above by climbing one of the guard towers. They
were insistent: "We want you to see the yard." Henderson acquiesced. He
and his clerk, Karen Kramer, ascended a narrow spiral stairway, such as one
might find in a lighthouse. Two other law clerks remained below in the
prison yard.

The tower overlooked not the solitary yards attached to the SHU pods
but rather a general-population prison yard in the adjacent high-security
facility. In addition to its 1,056 SHU cells, Pelican Bay State Prison includes
2,000 beds intended for high-security prisoners not deemed to require long-
term isolation; these cells are arranged in two semicircular tiers around
open spaces where prisoners can watch television, play games, exercise,

and eat together during daytime hours. Although much of the *Madrid* case would focus on conditions in the SHU, the class of plaintiffs included prisoners housed anywhere in the Pelican Bay complex, and, as Judge Henderson was about to see, abuses were not confined to the SHU pods.

When he got to the top of the tower and looked down at the yard, Henderson found it in chaos: "Everyone was spread out, including my law clerks, in their suits."[50] In the time it had taken him to ascend the stairs, a riot had apparently broken out. Guards had rushed on to the scene and ordered everyone to lie flat on their stomachs. This was more dramatic than the tables spread with knives and zip guns; here was a federal judge caught in the middle of a brawl—seeing his clerks lying flat on the ground, amid some of the state's most violent prisoners.

As it turned out, the timing was too perfect. A subsequent investigation revealed that two guards, Jose Garcia and Michael Powers, had set up two prisoners convicted of sexual assaults to be attacked in the yard as Judge Henderson watched. The guards knew that other prisoners had shanks—prison-made knives—hidden away and would bring them out into the yard for the attack. Since they expected the attack, Garcia and Powers were able to quiet things down quickly. After a ten-year investigation and prosecution, they were ultimately convicted and sentenced to six and seven years, respectively, for conspiracy to violate prisoners' civil rights.[51]

Meanwhile, Henderson continued his tour. After the near riot, he told me, "they took us to see some of the real crazies."[52] Then he returned to San Francisco to begin the *Madrid* trial. Over the next three months, fifty-seven witnesses testified, and six thousand exhibits were entered into evidence.[53] The most disturbing evidence concerned how prisoners mistreated one another and how guards and the medical staff mistreated prisoners.

Pelican Bay officials testified that in just over three years (between December 1989 and January 1993), there were 683 officially recorded fights between double-bunked prisoners inside their cells in the SHU. How does a cell fight take place under conditions of total solitary confinement? It turns out that by 1993, Pelican Bay's SHU was bursting at the seams. Within one year of its grand opening, the SHU was overcrowded. In 1990, it housed 1,238 prisoners—meaning that 364 of California's "worst of the worst" were housed two to a cell.[54] By 1995, roughly 1,000 prisoners were double-bunked in the SHU.[55] An additional 1,300 prisoners were in the SHU at Corcoran State Prison.[56]

Unsurprisingly, double-bunking the highest-security prisoners caused problems. The 683 officially recorded cell fights at Pelican Bay in the early 1990s resulted in serious injuries, including comas, brain damage, paralysis, and major bone fractures.[57] But who was responsible for this brutality: the prisoners, who would beat each other to the brink of death when left alone, or the prison administrators, who labeled some prisoners as the most dangerous and then forced them to share an eight-by-ten-foot box for twenty-two or more hours a day?

In his 1995 decision, Judge Henderson grappled with this question. But in the trial, stories about what guards were doing to prisoners upstaged stories about what prisoners were doing to one another. As Steve Cambra, who took over as warden in the mid-1990s, said: "Officers had the attitude of 'We're going to be tougher than the tough.' "[58] To prove how much tougher they were, guards beat, shot, scalded, and starved prisoners, and refused them medical treatment.

Between December 1989 and the start of the *Madrid* trial in September 1993, 177 firearms were discharged at Pelican Bay in 129 incidents. At least 13 of these shots caused serious injuries to prisoners. Todd Ashker was shot in the arm during this period.[59] Comparably sized prison systems in states such as Texas and Ohio allowed no firearms in any prison housing units, regardless of the security level.[60]

The practice of having and using firearms inside Pelican Bay's housing units was even more problematic because medical treatment was so inadequate. In the early 1990s, one or two prisoners a year died from lack of medical care. Dozens more survived despite being refused treatment for "symptoms as serious as chest pain, severe abdominal pain, coughing up blood, and seizures." The average wait to see a doctor for a grave symptom like "unresolved bleeding" was almost thirteen days.[61]

Mental health care was even worse. Interviews and document reviews suggested that at least one-third of the prisoners in the SHU were not just mentally ill but in fact acutely psychotic. Many mentally ill prisoners ended up at Pelican Bay because of misconduct histories traceable to mental illness. Such prisoners received virtually no mental health care in Pelican Bay other than the occasional antipsychotic medication.[62] This neglect occurred in spite of the known risks, even to a previously mentally healthy person, of spending even a few days in isolation.[63] In his decision in the case, Judge Henderson observed that the U.S. Supreme Court had condemned the mental health dangers associated with solitary confinement more than a hundred years earlier, in 1890.[64]

While prisoners in the Pelican Bay SHU had minimal contact with other prisoners or family members, and received little medical or mental health care, they had a remarkable amount of physical contact with guards. Much of this contact occurred during assaultive cell extractions, which were conducted if prisoners refused to return food trays, kicked cell doors, or threw excrement at guards. Recall the novel design of the perforated steel doors; guards would come to hate those tiny holes, from which excrement could fly out. Cell extractions—in which several guards would line up at a prisoner's cell behind a single leader armed with a shield (often electrically charged), lob pepper spray canisters into the cell, rush in, and drag the prisoner out—resulted in serious head wounds, broken jaws, and broken arms. In addition, prisoners and staff members testified about the use of hog-tying: between 1991 and 1992, an unknown number of prisoners had their cuffed hands chained to their cuffed legs, with their four limbs locked together into a fetal position, for as long as nine hours at a time.[65] Prison officials stated that this measure was necessary to prevent prisoners from kicking their feet and beating their heads against the steel doors, which were subject to metal fatigue.[66]

National newspapers took notice of the horror stories being told in Judge Henderson's courtroom in late 1993; headlines included "America's Devil's Island" and "A Prison for Cruel and Unusual Criminals."[67] *Dateline*, National Public Radio, and *CNN Investigations* all visited Pelican Bay to report on allegations of unconstitutional treatment.[68]

The *Madrid* trial ended on December 1, 1993. It took Henderson just over a year to issue his final opinion, after assessing the hundreds of hours and thousands of pages of evidence presented at trial.

Triumph or Tragedy: Did Judge Henderson Civilize Hell?

On January 10, 1995, Judge Henderson issued a sweeping 126-page order describing the conditions and condemning the operational practices in the Pelican Bay Security Housing Units. The catalogue of abuses he documented was dizzying. As in earlier cases in which he identified rights violations, Henderson expressed eloquent outrage, condemning the prison administrators for maintaining a code of silence, questioning the necessity of the harsh conditions in the SHU, and ordering the appointment of a special master to oversee reforms.

In the end, he concluded that three aspects of Pelican Bay's operation were unconstitutional and required remedy: the pattern of excessive use of force by guards against prisoners; the grossly inadequate medical and mental health care provided to prisoners; and the housing of prisoners with preexisting mental illnesses in the SHU, where the conditions "press the outer bounds of what most humans can tolerate."[69]

Yet Henderson equivocated about whether double-bunking could be avoided and whether the prison system's procedures for validating "gang affiliates" and giving them indeterminate terms were constitutional. He noted problems with these policies, but stopped short of ordering reforms.[70] When I spoke with him years later, he lamented that the case against the gang validation policy at Pelican Bay was weak. The plaintiffs' lawyers, he said, "were so busy" and "focused on other things." Judge Henderson remembered: "I did everything but call for further briefing on it. . . . That would have been too obvious. . . . They just didn't make the case." But "it could have been made."[71] Since 1995, the gang validation policy has been extensively litigated.[72] Until 2015, it remained substantively similar to what Todd Ashker experienced in the 1980s. In 2015, however, prison officials drastically reformed the policy and ceased sending prisoners to isolation for gang validations alone.[73]

After Judge Henderson issued his order in 1995, *Prison Legal News* proclaimed "a moral victory for prisoners."[74] And the order in the *Madrid* case was only the beginning. Pelican Bay would be under constant scrutiny for the next fifteen years. Monitors would report regularly to Henderson about conditions in the prison.

Only a few months following the *Madrid* order, Judge Lawrence Karlton, of the U.S. District Court for the Eastern District of California, issued an even more sweeping decision in *Coleman v. Wilson*, ordering improvements in the provision of mental health care throughout the California prison system and citing Henderson's *Madrid* decision six times.[75] Both Don Specter and Michael Bien were part of the prisoner plaintiffs' litigation team in *Coleman*. In 2001, Specter filed another lawsuit, *Plata v. Davis*, alleging constitutionally inadequate health care throughout the California prison system. While such a lawsuit would normally have been randomly assigned to a judge in the U.S. District Court for the Northern District of California, where it was filed, Henderson volunteered to oversee the case because of the expertise he had developed during the course of the *Madrid* litigation. Ultimately, Karlton and Henderson combined the *Coleman* and *Plata* cases in 2006 and issued a drastic injunction to reduce overcrowding in the California prison system by tens of thousands of prisoners.[76] Jonathan Simon, a scholar of mass incarceration, has argued that the *Plata* case put "mass incarceration on trial" and injected the long-neglected subject of dignity back into legal analyses of imprisonment.[77] The chain of cases from *Madrid* to *Plata* suggests that *Madrid* was not only a moral victory, but also a catalyst for even greater victories over the next two decades.

But another reading of the *Madrid* decision suggests a civil rights tragedy. Judge Henderson never found—over more than twenty years of investigating, litigating, and monitoring—that conditions in the Pelican Bay SHU were unconstitutional. Some policies and procedures, such as fetal-position restraints, were unconstitutional, as was placing some prisoners such as the psychotic, into the SHU. But the institution itself, in spite of conditions that Henderson acknowledged pressed at the outer bounds of human tolerance, was deemed constitutional. Hence, a correctional trade magazine proclaimed in 1995: "State Wins Pelican Bay Suit."[78]

While *Madrid* upheld the principle that prison officials cannot terrorize prisoners, it also upheld the principle that supermax conditions of confinement do not violate the Eighth Amendment prohibition against cruel and unusual punishment. As *Prison Legal News* put it in 1995: "The court has given the green light for the proliferation of super-max control units, even those as harsh as Pelican Bay, and politicians and prisoncrats throughout the country are already moving forward with efforts to do just that."[79] This was only a slight exaggeration. Although Henderson was critical of the supermax control units, *Madrid* provided a road map for rendering them constitutional, much as 1970s litigation about California's Adjustment Centers and lockdown units had provided a road map for Pelican Bay.

In 1995 there were at least twenty supermaxes in the United States.[80] This number nearly tripled over the next decade as Illinois, Massachusetts, New Mexico, Ohio, Pennsylvania, and Virginia—to name just a few homes of the more infamous facilities—expanded their facilities for long-term solitary confinement by opening supermaxes.[81] In many of these states, as in California, the supermaxes institutionalized existing long-term lockdowns, which had followed violence and riots. In the 1990s, for instance, Massachusetts created the 124-bed Departmental Disciplinary Unit at Walpole, the site of a prisoner takeover in the 1970s, and built a new 224-bed supermax, the Souza-Baranowski Correctional Center, in Shirley, named after two correctional staff members murdered by a would-be escapee.[82] In 1998, five years after an eleven-day prisoner takeover at the Southern Ohio Correctional Facility in Lucasville, Ohio opened a supermax facility at the Ohio State Penitentiary; it went on to become the first and only supermax prison to attract the attention of the U.S. Supreme Court, in a case from 2005 challenging the restrictive conditions of confinement at the facility.[83] By the 2000s, the New Mexico Department of Corrections, which had endured a deadly riot in 1980, had more than 450 prisoners housed in long-term isolation in the newly renovated Special Control Facilities at the Penitentiary of New Mexico and the Southern New Mexico Correctional Facility.[84]

Pelican Bay served as a model for the first federal supermax, the Administrative Maximum (ADX) in Florence, Colorado, as well as for the restrictive isolation units built in 2006 at Camp Delta at the U.S. military prison in Guantánamo Bay, Cuba.[85] As at Pelican Bay and Corcoran, each opening of a supermax was followed by a period of intense violence in which guards tried to prove that they were tougher than the "worst of the worst."[86] Could a different decision in *Madrid* have stopped the spread of the supermax across the United States, and its exportation beyond U.S. borders? The legal analysts at *Prison Legal News* certainly thought so.

Even Judge Henderson, with his willingness to take unpopular judicial positions, hardly slowed the trend toward the increasingly restrictive conditions of confinement institutionalized in supermaxes.[87] Over the past twenty years, *Madrid* has been cited in 292 cases, an impressive total. Although most of these citations refer to the principle that mentally ill prisoners must be excluded from restrictive isolation conditions, at least a dozen decisions have cited *Madrid* in upholding restrictive conditions of confinement in long-term isolation.[88] And no court has found unconstitutional any duration in long-term solitary confinement for any (nominally) mentally healthy prisoner.[89]

The Golden Handcuffs of Prison Law Precedent

About an hour into my interview with Judge Henderson, I finally worked up the courage to ask the question that had bothered me ever since I first read his decision in *Madrid*. It bothered me more as our interview went on, as Judge Henderson described his initial instinct that Pelican Bay was "unconstitutional," as he described his haunting first impression of prisoners pacing in figure eights in the solitary exercise yards like animals in a zoo, as he described his frustration that plaintiffs' lawyers had failed to make the case against the prison's gang validation policy. Finally, I asked: "Why didn't you hold that the conditions in the Pelican Bay SHU were unconstitutional?"

He answered simply: "That case was not made." He offered no suggestion for how a conditions challenge could have been successful, but instead reiterated the distinction between the physical structure of the SHU (constitutional) and its unconstitutional operation in 1995.[90]

At the time of the decision, though, Henderson must have felt constrained by the state of prisoners' rights litigation. Courts across the United States in the 1980s and 1990s were pulling back, limiting their holdings, constraining prisoners' abilities to challenge the conditions of their confinement.[91] Just one year after the *Madrid* decision, Congress passed the Prison Litigation Reform Act and the Anti-Terrorism and Effective Death Penalty Act, both of which severely limited prisoners' rights to bring civil rights lawsuits and to file habeas petitions.[92] But throughout his career, Henderson seems rarely to have been constrained by legal trends; this is the same judge who was comfortable dismissing state court rulings, reconsid-

ering cases overturned by the U.S. Supreme Court, and issuing a wide variety of compliance orders to federal and state agencies. Constraint was not
exactly his judicial style.

I felt almost absurd in asking: "Did you feel constrained by prior case
law?"

"No." He explained: "I looked at it anew . . . Things were evolving all the
time." Since the prison population was "in an upward spiral," he told me,
"I thought things were different, and I didn't feel limited."[93]

Throughout the *Madrid* decision, Henderson applied prior prisoners'
rights case law to support his conclusions. He used the U.S. Supreme
Court case *In re Medley* (1890), for instance, to establish the detrimental
health impacts of long-term isolation. He used more recent and more restrictive case law as well. *Farmer v. Brennan,* a U.S. Supreme Court decision
issued in 1994, between the conclusion of the *Madrid* trial and the issuing
of Henderson's order, set a tough standard for prison officials' liability for
Eighth Amendment violations, but Henderson applied the standard to find
that prison officials were unequivocally liable for violations at Pelican Bay.[94]

But even if he was able to look at the legal claims in *Madrid* "anew," legal
precedents must have colored his vision. Throughout the 1960s and 1970s,
federal courts grappled with an explosion of litigation challenging conditions in U.S. prisons. Many cases concerned punitive isolation—often in
cramped, dark cells that were no more than pits in the ground (explaining
the prison slang term for isolation, the "hole"). No court ever required the
complete elimination of such practices, or held that the hole per se was
unconstitutional. Instead, courts placed limitations on durations of confinement in the hole and ordered changes to conditions, for example, by
requiring a reduction in overcrowding or mandating the provision of basic
necessities such as food, clothing, light, and exercise.[95]

Because supermaxes met the minimum standards for isolation outlined
in prison-conditions lawsuits resolved before *Madrid* (such as the *Toussaint*
litigation), the institutions were hard to challenge later. And Henderson, like
every other judge who would review the constitutionality of modern supermaxes, had to acknowledge that the Pelican Bay SHU just looked nicer—
cleaner, brighter (even "light and airy," as Rich Kirkland described it)[96]—
than older facilities in Alabama, Arkansas, Mississippi, and California's

lockdown units in San Quentin and Folsom. Whether or not prior case law constrained Henderson and other judges, knowledge of worse conditions in these older prison facilities might have.

Constraint played out, too, in strategic avoidance of risky appeals. Unlike his decision in Johnny Spain's habeas case, Henderson's decision in *Madrid v. Gomez* was never appealed. Steve Fama, the attorney who represented plaintiffs in both the *Toussaint* and *Madrid* cases, noted this when I asked him about whether he was satisfied with the case's outcome. Fama acknowledged that the ultimate goal of the initial lawsuit was to challenge the sensory deprivation at Pelican Bay as fundamentally unconstitutional. Henderson dismissed this claim, but as Fama remarked, "We didn't appeal the judge's order, did we?"[97]

Weighing the significant improvements that Judge Henderson ordered in the *Madrid* case against the possibility of reversal on appeal, Fama and his team decided that an appeal would be too risky. A reversal would have left prisoners languishing in the Pelican Bay SHU worse off than if the decision were allowed to stand. Perhaps an initial finding that the entire institution was unconstitutional would likewise have been too risky. Such a finding would have been likely to motivate an appeal, and might have inspired prison officials to develop even more hidden, more litigation-resistant, and perhaps even harsher alternatives to the supermax.

Darkness Under Fluorescent Lights

The more I have learned about both Judge Henderson and the Pelican Bay SHU, the more I have thought that prior case law is only one among many factors that impeded a comprehensive condemnation of supermax conditions. Another major factor: prison administrators. Just as Craig Brown and Carl Larson teamed up to get the Pelican Bay SHU designed and built, administrators like Marshall and Gomez collaborated to keep it running on their terms. Persistent claims that they were guarding the "worst of the worst," flamboyant displays of knives and zip guns, manufactured riots, and even the figures for how many prisoners participated in gangs, got into cell fights, and got shot at, contributed to a counterimage of the SHU not as a brutalizing place but as a place full of brutes.

While Judge Henderson, *60 Minutes'* Mike Wallace, and Steve Fama all questioned the morality and constitutionality of conditions at the SHU, few questioned the claim that it was full of the most dangerous prisoners. Henderson emphasized to me that "these are some bad people." Later in our interview, he said that the prisoners' lawyers had failed to prove that the gang validation policies—by which the "worst of the worst" were identified —violated any constitutional rights. In the *Madrid* decision, he analyzed no specific evidence about the in-prison disciplinary records of any men in the SHU. Instead, he deferred repeatedly to administrators' claims that these records were full of murders and violent altercations.[98] In assessing both the constitutionality of the conditions of confinement in the SHU and the constitutionality of SHU double-bunking (or, less euphemistically, overcrowding), he never questioned prison administrators' claims about the dangerousness of individual prisoners—even though the severe restrictions in the SHU could be justified only if the prisoners were too menacing to be trusted in the general prison population.[99]

This deference defied logic when Judge Henderson applied it while analyzing whether Pelican Bay staffers should be responsible for the hundreds of cell fights and injuries that took place when the "worst of the worst" were double-bunked.[100] How could the administrators know the prisoners were dangerous enough to require housing in the SHU, but not know whether they were dangerous enough to kill one another?

This was just one of many questions about the men housed in the Pelican Bay SHU that was not addressed at the *Madrid* trial. Beyond the percentage of prisoners with mental illness (just under one-third), as established by experts such as Stuart Grassian and Craig Haney, and the percentage validated as gang members (just over one-third), the evidence presented in *Madrid* revealed little about those housed in the Pelican Bay SHU.[101] How long had they been there, and how long would they stay? What exactly had they done wrong? What happened at the administrative hearings in which they were assigned to the SHU? Who were they? What were their ages, races, gang affiliations? These questions remained unanswered until I made a data request to the California Department of Corrections and Rehabilitation in 2008; I published an analysis of that data in 2012.[102]

This lack of information about who is housed in the Pelican Bay SHU, and why, reveals just how little evidence backs up the claims that the prisoners housed there really are the most dangerous. Even if a few prisoners—such as Todd Ashker, Hugo Pinell, and Rene Enriquez—are known to have been involved in violent incidents in prison, no one has any idea how representative these three men are of the more than three thousand people held in conditions of long-term isolation in California's prisons. Since the same names come up again and again in discussions of who constitutes the "worst of the worst," I suspect that Ashker, Pinell, and Enriquez may be outliers—and even they seem less dangerous today than they did as twenty-year-olds. As long as prison officials have the exclusive power to define dangerousness, we will never know.

If most people in the SHU are not the worst of the worst, perhaps the *Madrid* decision will have a second life as a civil rights triumph after all. If the SHU is not functioning to control the most dangerous prisoners, then its sole justification, as defined by *Madrid,* evaporates.

The Bay Revisited

When I interviewed Judge Henderson in May 2012, he had closed the *Madrid* case one year earlier. Twenty years of oversight and surveillance had ended. Ultimately, Henderson said, he was not convinced that the case needed to remain open any longer: "So I closed it. Looking back on it, it was a sense of closure. Things changed. You don't have the killing. There are still 'code of silence' classes going on. They don't have the shootings." Pelican Bay now has cameras installed throughout; this, he noted, made a major difference in the treatment of prisoners.

From his first visits to Pelican Bay, Henderson told me, the mentally ill prisoners lingered as his most disturbing memories. "I would go visit the prisoners—it was chaotic, they were clearly distressed." This, too, changed. After the mentally ill were transferred to a new unit—one with sunlit windows—things improved. Henderson recalled a visit to this new unit: "I remember one of the first guys I visited [in the Pelican Bay SHU]. He was crazy, wild-eyed. [In the new unit,] he could see out of the window, got some sunlight." As the judge passed the sunlit cell, the prisoner said: "Thank you."

"It was just a miracle," Henderson said.

The new unit even improved the culture among the staff; as guards saw that the unit worked to keep people calmer, they became more willing to work there. And of course, Henderson added, the broader problems with medical and mental health care remained under surveillance in the *Plata* case, which Henderson was still overseeing. Pelican Bay "still has the worst of the worst," he said, "but it's a reasonable place now."[103]

In 2010, prisoners whom I interviewed about their experiences in the SHU never once used the slang name "Skeleton Bay." Today, it is simply the "Bay"—a sanitized name to go with the sanitized walls, ostensibly free of the blood and feces that marked those walls' first years. But is a cleaner, physically safer prison a humane prison? And who are the worst of the worst today?

6

Snitching or Dying

ONE WAY TO THINK ABOUT THE PELICAN BAY SHU post-*Madrid* is to ask what, if anything, has been accomplished there. Has the SHU become the smoothly functioning institution that Henderson saw on his last tours: one capable of differentiating the dangerous from the benign, the mad from the bad? Has it protected other prisoners, and the rest of society, from the most dangerous among us?

There is shockingly little data available for systematically analyzing these questions. But there are thousands of prisoners in California, and tens of thousands across the United States, whose individual stories suggest that, as Steven Czifra said at that legislative hearing in 2013, "we already know."

These prisoners' stories reveal a perpetual paradox: an institution premised on the existence of dangerous and bad prisoners has every incentive to make and remake, label and relabel, prisoners to fit this category. To let a prisoner out of the SHU would be to admit a mistake in these categorizations. As a result, prisoners say that there are only three ways out of the SHU, each treacherous: "parole, snitch, or die."

Common sense suggests that the "worst of the worst" are not often finishing up short criminal sentences and being paroled from the SHU; the next chapter debunks this assumption. For those prisoners with life sentences, however, parole is not an option.[1] Two men, with whom I have corresponded extensively, have faced down the decision either to snitch or to die in the SHU: Rene Enriquez and "Johnny."[2]

Enriquez, whom I have already mentioned, was fifty-two years old in 2015. An acknowledged former member of the Mexican Mafia, he was sentenced to two twenty-to-life terms, with the possibility of parole, for two Mafia-related murders committed in 1989, and he received a third life term for a stabbing he committed in jail awaiting trial on the other two charges.[3] He entered the Pelican Bay SHU in 1993 as a validated gang member and spent ten years there.[4]

Johnny, thirty-six years old in 2015, is white. He was sentenced to life without the possibility of parole (LWOP) at the age of sixteen for a murder he committed in 1995 in the course of a robbery while high on methamphetamine. Johnny entered the Pelican Bay SHU for the first time in 1999, following an attempted murder in prison. He was in the SHU for three years on this bid, briefly returned to the general prison population, and then reentered the SHU in 2006 as a validated Aryan Brotherhood gang associate. An academic mentor of mine introduced me to Johnny around this time; my mentor and Johnny's father had been best friends while growing up in the Midwest. As of 2015, Johnny remained in the SHU, on an indeterminate term.

Until 2015, validation as a gang "associate" required only "evidence indicative of association," while validation as a gang member required "a direct link" with a validated member, another associate, or a dropout who positively identified the person as a gang member.[5] In 2015, validation as either a gang member or a gang associate could still bring indeterminate assignment to the SHU, either for the length of the prisoner's sentence or until the prisoner snitched (or "debriefed," in official terms). Rene Enriquez's and Johnny's parallel trajectories—both entered the SHU because of their alleged gang status and had to decide whether to snitch—provide a context for understanding life in the SHU. Snitching was the only way either man could expect to leave the SHU alive.[6]

Rene Enriquez

Rene Enriquez spent ten years in the SHU, 1993–2003. His neck, torso, and arms are covered in Mafia tattoos, including a life-size black hand with an *M* (the symbol of the Mexican Mafia, La Eme) over his heart. By the time

Example of a prisoner drawing that could be used to "validate" a prisoner as a gang member (image reproduced in its entirety as provided)
(Drawing by Arturo Mendoza)

he received his two life sentences in 1993, he was well known as a mobster, nicknamed "Boxer." Enriquez had worked his way up the ranks of the Mexican Mafia during an earlier prison sentence for armed robbery, making shanks—homemade prison knives—hiding them in his rectum or between his legs and, when ordered, carrying out hits on the yards at San Quentin and Folsom. While awaiting trial for a gang hit he had ordered and one he committed in 1989, Enriquez cornered another detainee in the attorney-client visiting room at the Men's Central Jail in Los Angeles and stabbed him twenty-six times. The victim survived, but the incident earned Enriquez a third consecutive life sentence.[7]

When he returned to the California state prison system in 1993 with three life sentences, prison officials wasted no time in getting Enriquez out of the general prison population. His criminal record alone satisfied the criteria for being validated as a gang member; he was sent directly to the Pelican Bay SHU. Enriquez described entering the SHU in 1993: "What impacts me immediately as soon as I walk in, is the smell. I just stepped outside from the bus and you smell the pines, the redwoods, the forest . . . these earthy, loamy smells. But as soon as you step into the SHU, it hits you like a wave. It's the smell of despair, depression, desperation. This is a place where people come to die."[8]

From the bowels of the SHU, he continued to work as a Mexican Mafia leader. The journalist Michael Montgomery describes how Enriquez led the Mafia from his SHU cell, passing messages through visitors and letters labeled as "legal mail"—ostensibly indicating correspondence with a lawyer and thus exempt from the usual censorship of SHU communications. Enriquez's prisoner trust account, through which he could purchase books, toiletries, and food, remained topped off with taxes paid by low-level drug dealers in return for use of the Mexican Mafia name and protection. He opened savings accounts and invested in government bonds. He orchestrated a cease-fire from the SHU, ordering an end to drive-bys and replacing them with better-controlled, more profitable violence like drug dealing. He even nursed a heroin addiction, finding creative ways to get associates to smuggle him drugs inside the two packages a year he was permitted to receive. In the SHU, Enriquez was safe—from rival gang members who wanted to kill him, from investigators and prosecutors looking to arrest gang leaders on the streets, and from further punishment within the prison system. He was already serving three life sentences in the harshest conditions that California had to offer.[9]

But in 2002 he changed allegiances. Enriquez had been in total isolation, without physically touching a family member or friend, or seeing the sun or moon, for more than nine years. He had overdosed on heroin. He had started having anxiety attacks. He expressed frustration with the "arbitrary targeting of families" by gang members, which he heard about from fellow Mexican Mafia members. He described his feelings as "mob fatigue."[10] Although I wonder whether he just got bored—or depressed.

Whatever his motivation, Enriquez contacted the institutional gang investigators (IGIs). The minute a debriefer verbalizes his plans, his life is in jeopardy. Word of the defection is whispered through the plumbing pipes of the SHU, shouted into drains connecting the exercise yards, written on pieces of paper ("kites") slung underneath cell doors. A snitcher expects a bounty to be put on his head immediately. So as soon as a prisoner makes IGI contact, he is moved into a protective custody cell in a special, isolated subsection of the SHU. An intensive interrogation begins; gang investigators assess how serious the prisoner is, how much he knows. With Enriquez, the investigators could barely contain their glee. "For the first time, we had a Mexican Mafia member defect that was really able to lay out for us how the organization works, the organizational structure," said Robert Marquez, a special agent with the California Department of Corrections and Rehabilitation. Within a year, Enriquez's "former enemies, the cops," had become "his protectors, even his friends."[11]

Enriquez became a different kind of leader. He listened in on investigative wiretaps, translated Mafia messages, testified in more than a dozen criminal trials as a witness and an expert, and led conferences and training sessions for law enforcement officials across the United States.[12] For his trouble, he received $200 a week from the FBI and the Bureau of Alcohol, Tobacco and Firearms (ATF).[13] He told his life story to Chris Blatchford (the resulting book, *The Black Hand*, is the one Carl Larson asked me to read before I interviewed him), and coauthored a textbook, *Urban Street Terrorism*, with a University of California adjunct professor. His days were filled with important work.

Father Greg Boyle, the founder of the Los Angeles gang intervention program Homeboy Industries, performed a marriage ceremony for Enriquez and his longtime sweetheart. They could then have "contact" visits, no longer separated by bulletproof glass. Enriquez spent most of his time in the 2000s after he debriefed in undisclosed local jail locations, where his handler, an FBI agent assigned to facilitate his informant work, oversaw fairly permissive communications with family, reporters, and the public. Enriquez had access to a computer, could make phone calls, and appeared in public in a suit and tie.

Then, in September 2014, he had a parole hearing—his first chance to be released from his three life sentences. Most prisoners with a record like his expect such a hearing to be futile. But Enriquez had unusual supporters. Eleven law enforcement agencies wrote to the parole board to outline the many contributions he had made over the past decade and to advocate for his release.[14] Supporters included county prosecutors, police officers, sheriffs, and even California Department of Corrections and Rehabilitation officials.[15] Many of these supporters attended his parole hearing—and heard the board ask tough questions.

> The Board: "Why did you repeatedly participate in criminal activity?"
> Enriquez: "[I] lacked . . . the qualifications to diagnose myself . . . I could sit here and . . . guess as to what I was looking for . . . I don't know what it was."
> The Board: "Why did you commit a forcible rape in 1985?"
> Enriquez [crying]: "[I] had an understanding that what I was doing was wrong at the time . . . I wasn't the man I am today and I lacked that social awareness at that time."
> The Board: "Why did you join a street gang?"
> Enriquez: "[I was] forced."[16]

The board granted parole. Resilient as he seemed, how would Rene manage the transition from isolated jail cells to the streets?

Although Enriquez was somewhat of a public figure by 2014, the parole board's decision was reported nowhere. Within 120 days of a parole hearing, the parole board sets the prisoner's release date. This happened sometime in January 2015, again with no news coverage. In California, the governor may review the parole board's decision and choose whether to reverse a grant of parole. Still there was no news. Enriquez began making plans for his parole. The FBI recommended that he enter the witness protection program.

On January 28, the Los Angeles Police Department hosted a private dinner party for local police chiefs and business executives. Enriquez, touted as a "criminal corporate executive," although still incarcerated, was the keynote speaker and would be giving "first-hand insight to the group about the inner-workings of the criminal enterprise."[17] He appeared, shackled at the waist and legs but with his hands free, and discussed "gang franchising, marketing, sales, merchandising and branding."[18] Just over one hundred people attended.

The event cost $22,000 to put on, and hundreds of hours of police time were required to plan and to escort Enriquez there.[19] From beginning to end, the high-level security operation took more than eight hours. The *Los Angeles Times*, the *Orange County Register,* and NBC News all reported on the event—expressing some incredulity that so much time and energy had been put into a public event featuring a "convicted hit man."[20]

The stories were strange—Enriquez had been working as an informant and speaking before a range of audiences for years. Why all the attention to this particular event? None of the stories mentioned that the convicted hit man had a recommendation for parole in his prison file or that he expected to be released within weeks.

A few days later, two local reporters did their due diligence. On January 31, the *Los Angeles Times* reported that Rene Enriquez had been granted parole and was awaiting a decision from Governor Brown, who would either affirm or reverse the parole decision.[21] Local newspapers began following the case more closely, tracking down the children of one of Enriquez's victims, investigating just how much the LAPD's January event had cost.

Late in the day on February 20, the last date on which he could weigh in, Governor Brown issued his review of the parole board's recommendation. He noted: "Mr. Enriquez presents a shallow understanding of how he came to perpetuate so many violent crimes." Enriquez claimed to have derived meaning from his "career" in law enforcement, Brown noted, but lapsed into drug use when "not being used by law enforcement," and he posed a security risk to himself and his family. Moreover, the fact that Enriquez would be required to register as a sex offender would make it even harder for him to keep a low profile and would further jeopardize his family.[22] Brown's decision on the release recommendation: reverse.

Shortly thereafter, the California prison system's "inmate locator" reported that Enriquez was at Ironwood State Prison, in Blythe, California, due east of Palm Desert on the border with Arizona. Ironwood has a "Sensitive Needs Yard," primarily for prisoners who debriefed and therefore are at perpetual risk of attack. Since Enriquez was no longer being housed in an undisclosed jail location, he was likely no longer working as an informant for the FBI or the ATF. Given his past crimes and current notoriety, his chances for parole looked slim.[23]

Is Enriquez better off for having snitched? He had ten good years of high-level informant work, for which he was paid well beyond the prison standard. (The hourly wage for prison work in California tops out at 95 cents an hour, before deductions.)[24] And he almost earned parole, supported by the very prison staff members who had labeled him the worst of the worst. In a system in which the label "worst of the worst" is applied liberally, and in which few prisoners, even those who commit only nonviolent crimes and have only nonserious disciplinary problems, earn the respect of the staff, Enriquez stands out. At least some prisoners, his story seemed to illustrate, could be redeemed if they played by the rules of the SHU and followed the only administratively sanctioned road out.

But even the recommendation of eleven law enforcement agencies and a stingy parole board could not convince the governor of Enriquez's redemption. Governor Brown has supported law enforcement and prison officials throughout his career—fighting prison reform litigation as attorney general; resisting federal intervention and appealing cases all the way to the U.S. Supreme Court; backing Jeffrey Beard, the secretary of corrections, when he claimed the prisoner hunger strike leaders were advancing an agenda of violence. But Brown did not support the officials' recommendation that Enriquez be paroled. Either Brown was incorrect about Enriquez, or the parole board was incorrect about him. If prison officials' determinations are fallible, might they also be wrong about the thousands of prisoners they insist are *not* redeemed?

Of course, Enriquez's case is not so simple. Political factors were at work; victims' family members spoke out against his parole, and victims have a history of demanding and receiving deference in sentencing decisions.[25] I even wondered whether the media hullaballoo around the fancy dinner event in January 2015 had been orchestrated to make it difficult for Governor Brown to let Enriquez out of prison. Regardless of the intrigue and the intricacies, and extraordinary as it may be, Enriquez's story reveals the ambiguity about just who is the "worst of the worst," who gets to apply the label, and how long it should stick.

Johnny

While Enriquez was awaiting the governor's decision on his parole recommendation, a thirty-five-year-old white man, validated as an Aryan Brotherhood associate, was sitting in another Southern California jail, awaiting a judge's decision on his resentencing petition. Whereas Enriquez was a Mexican Mafia elder by the time he arrived at Pelican Bay, Johnny first entered the SHU as a twenty-year-old, in 1999. Even today, after nearly twenty years in prison, he is slight by prison standards, with thinning light brown hair and intense blue eyes.

When he entered the California prison system in 1998, Johnny had been sentenced to one life term without the possibility of parole. This sentence automatically classified him as a high-security prisoner, and prison officials sent him straight to High Desert State Prison, one of California's highest-security general population prisons. Within a few months, Johnny had acquired a number of tattoos with Aryan Brotherhood connotations: a swastika on his torso, and "SWP" (Supreme White Power) on each leg and on his neck. He eventually collected more than twenty-five tattoos in prison, most *without* white-power overtones.

But in his first few years in prison, Johnny tried to establish a reputation. He fought repeatedly for his life. In February 1999, he brought a shank onto the prison yard and passed it off to someone else, who stabbed a prisoner. That June, he slashed his cellmate with another shank. Following this incident, he received a disciplinary report, was assigned to a three-year SHU term, and was transferred to Pelican Bay.

These actions could be interpreted in a few ways. Maybe Johnny was a skinny, scared teenager trying to keep himself safe. For some context about the myriad dangers prisoners face: an estimated eighty thousand prisoners a year report being sexually abused in prisons, and many more abuses certainly go unreported.[26] Then again, at sixteen Johnny had murdered a fourteen-year-old with three point-blank shots to the head—albeit while high—so maybe he was a violent, out-of-control kid. Maybe he was hell-bent on getting noticed by the Aryan Brotherhood, calculating his actions carefully, getting highly visible tattoos, following orders to carry out hits, and earning his way into the Pelican Bay SHU, where he was likely to meet some AB leaders. Perhaps all three interpretations are right. Either way, Johnny served three years in the SHU, hard time for a nineteen-year-old far from his family in Southern California.

When Johnny's determinate SHU term ended, in 2002, he was transferred to Salinas Valley State Prison. In 2003, he was involved with other prisoners in two more stabbing incidents; again, the incidents looked possibly gang related. In the first incident, Johnny stabbed a man on the prison yard twenty-six times (the man survived). While facing an attempted murder charge for that incident, he stabbed another cellmate. Johnny went to trial on the yard stabbing, was found guilty, and received a concurrent life sentence. He would later challenge the conviction, win a reversal, and plead guilty in exchange for a two-year sentence.

Then things changed. He stopped. No more violent incidents. No more disciplinary violations. No more trouble. It was too late for him to ever hope to get out of prison, but he decided to make the most of the time he had.

Johnny's sister, seven years his elder, remained loyal to him throughout his early, tough years. She thought of him more like a son, and she visited him in High Desert and later in Salinas Valley as often as she could. She believed he could change. In 2003, Johnny requested a transfer to a prison somewhere in Southern California so that he could be closer to her. For the next few years, he bounced around the California prison system, trying to stay out of trouble. In 2006, he received a disciplinary report for having an "inmate-made handcuff key," but he said he had it for self-protection in case he was jumped by other prisoners while being escorted across the yard in handcuffs. Prison officials at Salinas Valley tried to validate him as an

Aryan Brotherhood associate. But he was able to dispute all the evidence in his file, as well as to remind the prison staff that he had had no violent incidents in three years. Finally, a prison classification committee told him that if he accepted a transfer to the Pelican Bay "mainline," he would get a transfer soon after, back to somewhere near his sister. He accepted and returned to Pelican Bay in 2006—this time to live in the general population section rather than the SHU. Or so he thought.

After only a few days on the mainline, guards found a piece of paper in Johnny's possession with the names of other "Nazi soldiers." Under prison rules, this "kite" was direct evidence of gang association. Under the gang validation rules, only two more pieces of evidence were needed, and these were already in his file. Johnny's name had been found in a note in a validated associate's cell, and another prisoner had debriefed and pointed to Johnny as someone who had been ordered to assault staff (although he never assaulted a staff member). He was quickly brought before a classification committee at Pelican Bay; the committee affirmed his validation as an associate of the AB, and he was summarily transferred to the SHU, for an indeterminate term.

Johnny was serving a life-without-parole sentence. He was young and strong enough that death would have seemed far off. And snitching was not exactly on his mind. At this point, he had not had a serious disciplinary violation in three years and had not gotten any new white power tattoos in nearly seven years. He had pledged to behave and was trying to rebuild a relationship with his sister. He had never gotten close to the Aryan Brotherhood leadership, so he had little of value to say about them, but plenty to fear—for himself and his family—if he snitched.

Instead, he focused on what he could improve. He completed more than twenty college courses and maintained regular correspondence with his sister, his adopted mother, and others, including me.

Johnny remained free of disciplinary violations. This achievement probably sounds unimpressive for someone who was locked in an eight-by-ten-foot cell alone for twenty-two or more hours a day, let out only to shower or to exercise by himself. He had no contact with other prisoners and rarely with other guards. How could he possibly violate a rule or commit a violent act?

Rene Enriquez's history suggests one means: Johnny could have remained involved in gang activity, communicating with Aryan Brotherhood leaders or smuggling drugs. But he was never caught doing any of these things. He could have attempted suicide, refused to return his food tray through the slot in his door, or spit on an officer passing by. All of these would have been serious disciplinary violations. He did none of them.

Johnny even had opportunities for violent altercations. There were the "gladiator fights" in which guards set up SHU prisoners from rival gangs to fight on the small exercise yards. True, there were fewer reports of these coerced battles by the early 2000s, when Johnny began his indeterminate SHU term. Still, prisoners described the constant fear that guards might open two cell doors at once—whether purposefully or accidentally—and that two prisoners would have to face off in the empty hallway in front of their cells, with only a bullet from the guards' post to stop the action. Another prisoner I interviewed, who spent three months in the Pelican Bay SHU in the late 1990s, said: "You were always ready for that worse scenario to happen because they let you out to the yard and accidently pop the other cell, too. So you always have that in the back of your mind all the time that that could happen coming out. Or that could happen while you're sitting there sleeping in your bed. Any time—by then anyway, you'll just wake up anyway once you hear that electric sliding [of the door opening]. You'll just kind of pop up anyway."[27] Johnny said he had plenty of opportunities like this to fight. But he never did.

I first learned of Johnny in 2007 when my academic mentor suggested I start up a correspondence with him. I could not imagine what Johnny's life was like or how he maintained hope. I was afraid to exchange letters with someone that young and that isolated. Also, I was teaching at San Quentin in the prison college program already. I had to renew my security clearance each year and sign a pledge that I was not visiting or corresponding with anyone anywhere in the California prison system. I put off writing to Johnny, as year after year of his life passed in the SHU, but I asked about him whenever I saw my mentor.

In February 2012, I accepted a job as an assistant professor in Southern California. I taught my last class at San Quentin in March. And then I wrote Johnny a letter. We began a regular correspondence. I asked him about his life in prison, his life in the SHU, how he passed his time, what he liked to read, what family he kept in touch with. I found him surprisingly articulate. I had read so much about how isolation destroys people's minds, causes hallucinations and obsessions, and I had received so many letters from prisoners in isolation who could barely say why they were writing. Johnny's long, well-organized letters and precise, compact script impressed me.

Johnny had plenty of questions for me, too. I told him about my research, my career goals. I apologized for being slow to answer his letters. He took to starring the questions in his long letters so that I would remember to answer them all when I finally wrote back to him. He asked me to write to his sister. I did, and we had dinner. I invited her to campus events about sentencing and solitary confinement. Johnny asked whether I was writing to him as a pen pal or as a research subject. "A little of both" was my honest answer.

Prisoners with time on their hands who write compelling letters to women, ensnaring them in a web of attention and admiration, even starting love affairs, are a surprisingly common phenomenon.[28] Johnny's pen pals, many of whom I have now met, are different. Instead of focusing obsessively on one individual, he has managed to maintain a community of supporters, including his sister, an adopted mother, more than one professor, a few lawyers, and friends from high school and prison; he puts these people in touch with one another and talks about them one to another. Johnny has constructed an interconnected web of relationships in which people feel that he is present, even though he is locked in a box cell in a remote corner of California and has not physically touched another human being in years. Doing this and knowing this, I suspect, has allowed him to survive nearly a decade in isolation with his mind seemingly intact.

Early in our correspondence, in June 2012, the Supreme Court decided *Miller v. Alabama.* In *Miller,* the Court declared mandatory sentences of life without parole for crimes committed by juveniles—sentences just like Johnny's—unconstitutional.[29] By January 2013, California had passed legislation implementing *Miller* and setting up a mechanism for people like Johnny to petition their original sentencing court for a resentencing hearing, at which a judge might consider imposing a new sentence *with* the possibility of parole.[30] Johnny's sister was instrumental in getting the Fair

Sentencing for Youth Act passed, and Johnny filed one of the first petitions for resentencing. He asked that his sentence be reduced from life without the possibility of parole to life *with* the possibility of parole. The court assigned him a public defender, and he waited.

Johnny had participated in the first hunger strikes in the Pelican Bay SHU in 2011, and he also joined the longer one, in 2013. He refused food for thirty days in July and August of that year. Then prison officials transferred him to the Administrative Segregation unit (still in total isolation) at Folsom State Prison, to monitor his deteriorating health. He had lost fifty pounds. He got daily injections of vitamins. He remembered getting tired of the needles, being stuck every day, but he was weak, and he recalled little of the trip to Folsom.

Late in August, after nearly forty-five days without food, Johnny was transferred to a suicide watch cell: usually, a completely empty cement box. But the cell he entered was not quite empty. It smelled. He looked around and saw that it was smeared from floor to ceiling with feces.

Johnny had nothing in his possession at the time but the boxers and T-shirt he was wearing. He had nothing to clean the cell with, and nothing to sit on. He complained—politely and deferentially, as he described it—to the officer on duty. The officer shrugged. Later, another officer told Johnny that the guards were trying to break him. If he would just end his hunger strike, they would move him out of the filthy cell. He kept refusing food. After a few days, the officers saw that he was not going to budge. He has a way of earning a begrudging respect. Prisoners working the tier snuck him extra T-shirts, soaked in cleaning fluid. He slowly wiped down the walls.

On September 5, 2013, Todd Ashker and the other strike leaders announced they were suspending the strike.[31] Johnny began eating again, and was returned to the Pelican Bay SHU. He received his first disciplinary report in seven years, for participating in the hunger strike.

Still, things were looking up. Stung by the public scrutiny brought on by the hunger strike, prison officials began to review the files of all prisoners validated as gang associates and serving indeterminate SHU terms. Johnny had hope that he might be eligible for a step-down program that would return him to the general prison population. By the late fall, he had more good news: a judge would hear his petition for resentencing. He was transferred to a Southern California jail in January 2014 so that he could attend the resentencing hearing.

Moving to the jail was a drastic change. Johnny had a cellmate for the first time in eight years. He could call his sister at least once a day, and he could see her (sealed off behind glass in a visiting booth) at least once a week. In the previous eight years, they had not had a single telephone conversation. And they had visited only two or three times a year, when his sister could find the time and money to make the eight-hundred-mile drive north to Pelican Bay.

Months passed in the jail as Johnny's resentencing hearing was delayed for a psychological evaluation, postponed for a probation investigation, and put off so that the district attorney could prepare. He maintained his perfect disciplinary record, adjusting remarkably well to the new "freedoms" of jail life—communal television rooms, basketball games, human contact. Prisoners and guards respected him—he had survived a total of eleven years in the SHU.

I was able to visit Johnny in the jail on a few quiet Friday mornings. The visits still took place behind bulletproof glass; we talked through an old "telephone," more like two greasy cans attached by a string. Johnny and I settled into a visiting routine. I would spot him in a visiting booth—often the spacious one at the end of the hallway if the guards were being nice to him, which they often were. I would settle onto the steel stool, press the receiver to my ear, and Johnny would be off, talking about life in the jail, his case, his sister, friends who had been able to visit, his hopes.

I wondered again and again how California prison officials could justify the cost—human and financial—of keeping Johnny in total isolation for eight consecutive years. At $70,000 per year of isolation, California had spent more than half a million dollars isolating Johnny. Anyone capable of behaving perfectly for months in a jail setting—a notoriously tense and unpleasant place designed to meet only the barest of needs—ought to be able to get by in the general prison population. I marveled that whatever happened at his resentencing hearing, Johnny would have many more years to serve in prison (and those years would cost the state hundreds of thousands of dollars). He would return to Pelican Bay, relabeled and reboxed, again one of the "worst of the worst."

I kept in touch with Johnny's sister and followed the legal motions in his resentencing hearing closely. Finally, fifteen months into his jail stay, Johnny had a hearing date. His lawyer said the trial would go forward. He subpoenaed the forensic psychologist who had found Johnny to be mentally stable and no longer the violent teenager he once was. The district attorney made travel arrangements for Johnny's victim's mother so that she could present a victim impact statement and argue against Johnny's resentencing. Johnny's sister dropped off black pants and a grey shirt at the jail for him. She arranged for friends and relatives to attend the hearing. She had blue ribbons made that said "Johnny" and "hope." She wanted Johnny to see a courtroom filled with supporters—to walk in with his head high, even if his hands and feet were shackled.

On the day of the hearing, I got to the courthouse early; passed quickly through the attorney entrance, and sat down in the designated courtroom. I wanted to see the judge and meet Johnny's attorney. When his sister came in and sat down next to me an hour later, she smelled of cigarette smoke. I could feel her quivering anxiety.

The next few hours would determine whether Johnny would ever have the chance to go before a parole board and make the case that he should be free. If the judge denied his petition, that was it. He would be stuck with his juvenile life-without-parole sentence. He would go back to the SHU forever. I looked at the judge, wondering whether he had already made a decision, wondering how it felt to hold someone's life in a bundle of papers.

I looked at Johnny's sister, wondering what it would be like to love a brother she had not physically touched in nine years. When Johnny shuffled into the courtroom, his legs cuffed, and sat down at the defense table, he was almost close enough to touch. If I were his sister, I might have run up to the counsel table and touched Johnny's shoulder. She did not. I guess she had learned restraint in nearly a decade of noncontact prison visits.

Finally, the hearing started. The public defender called the forensic psychologist. She testified about Johnny's troubled childhood, his early prison history of violence, and his dramatic improvement since then. Her testimony suggested that Johnny was the perfect *Miller* candidate, someone who had aged out of violence and discipline problems in his early twenties, exactly when science would suggest that his capacity for decision making was neuronally complete. The district attorney cross-examined her, quizzing her on the details of Johnny's in-prison violence, questioning her claim that Johnny had tried to reach out to other at-risk kids by writing to a Youth for Fair Sentencing organization, implying that his actions had been self-interested and that he was motivated only to get himself out of prison. This struck me as a weak line of questioning. Things were going well, I thought.

Then the judge interrupted and started questioning the psychologist himself. First he asked her about the conditions of confinement in the Pelican Bay SHU. This was the first mention of the SHU. The judge asked the psychologist: "Would you consider the SHU inhumane?" She said: "Yes." I was impressed. This judge had heard of the SHU, and he seemed rather critical of the conditions there.

Then he said: "[The SHU] is almost exclusively limited to prisoners with a history of violence, right?" Next, the judge asked a battery of questions about white power prison gangs: "Have you heard of the Blue Birds? Did you know the Aryan Brotherhood started as the Blue Birds? What do you think about the Aryan Brotherhood? How do you get out of the Aryan Brotherhood? Have you heard of the phrase 'de-brief'?"

The psychologist stumbled through her answers. She was not a gang expert. The judge called a lunch break.

The public defender approached Johnny's sister, explained that he had decided Johnny should testify in order to explain the SHU, the structure of gangs, and the debriefing process. Johnny had the expertise to answer the judge's questions, but he had not expected to take the stand. I shuddered to think how he was feeling, locked in a little room behind the courtroom, waiting for his attorney to prepare him for what was ahead, wondering whether he would be able to explain himself well enough to convince the judge he deserved the possibility of a second chance. I had thought the hearing would be over by lunch. I rushed out to postpone my afternoon meetings.

When I returned to the courtroom in the afternoon, Johnny was on the stand. The public defender was asking him to explain how he had been validated as an Aryan Brotherhood member, what his association with the gang was, what life in the SHU was like. Johnny noted that there were "4,836 dime-sized holes" in the perforated steel door of a Pelican Bay SHU cell—a powerful indication of how well he knew every millimeter of the box in which he had spent eight years.

The judge's questions to the forensic psychologist lingered in the background. If Johnny had really changed his ways, if he really regretted his white power tattoos, if he had really sworn off violence, why hadn't he debriefed, or snitched?

I wished Johnny's lawyer could have called Rene Enriquez to the stand to testify about what happens when you snitch, about the best-case scenario, which still leaves you functionally ineligible for parole, which endangers your life and the lives of your family members, which leaves you used up by the prison system but given little in return. And that was for a high-level gang leader, who actually had valuable information to share. I wondered whether Johnny's decision not to snitch would keep him in prison for the rest of his life, too.

On the day Johnny took the stand, California prison officials were in settlement talks with prisoners' advocates, discussing whether to eliminate the whole gang validation system underlying Johnny's indeterminate SHU term in favor of a system of strictly determinate SHU terms tied to specific disciplinary violations. Between these negotiations and the post-hunger-strike file reviews happening at Pelican Bay, Johnny seemed likely to be eligible for release from the SHU soon. But the judge considering his resentencing petition wanted to know why he was still in the SHU on the day of the hearing, not where he would be in a few years.

At four, Johnny was still on the stand, still trying to explain himself, still making a case for why he deserved a reconsideration of the sentence he had earned as a juvenile. The judge decided to break for the day. He scheduled a continuation of the hearing in two weeks. Johnny would have fourteen days to obsess over what he should have done, whether he could have snitched, whether doing so would have changed the outcome, or whether he would even have been alive to know the difference. In those fourteen days, I wrote the remainder of this book. So it seems especially fitting to save the rest of Johnny's story for the conclusion.

Madness and Suicide

The people I have corresponded with and interviewed, such as Rene Enriquez and Johnny, are survivors, but many prisoners do not survive. Life in isolation is stark, and suicides are common. In general, the California Department of Corrections does not report whether suicides in a particular prison took place in the isolation units or in the general population sections.[32] But snapshot data about the mental health care provided to prisoners suggests that suicide rates in California's isolation units are much higher than those in the general prison population. In 2004, Craig Haney, a leading expert on the psychological effects of solitary confinement, testified in *Coleman v. Schwarzenegger* that 73 percent of all suicides in California prisons that year took place in isolation units.[33] In total, eighteen prisoners committed suicide in 2004 while in isolation in California.[34] Despite almost a decade of litigation about inadequate mental health care in the California prison system, especially for prisoners in isolation, the numbers were no better in 2014. Of the fourteen suicides that had been reported by August of that year, eleven, or 79 percent, took place in isolation.[35] (Short- and long-term isolation units together account for only 10 percent of California's prison population.)

These deaths are often the culmination of years of untreated mental illness. "Untreated" is, perhaps, too neutral a word. More precisely, these suicides often follow years of punishment for being mentally ill.[36] In 2014, a federal judge found that California prison officials had developed a practice of pepper-spraying mentally ill prisoners and putting them in isolation instead of providing them with treatment.[37] One such prisoner, Joseph Duran, died in a "mental health crisis bed"—functionally, a short-term isolation cell—in California's Mule Creek State Prison. Prison officials labeled his death a suicide because he died after he pulled a tracheal tube out of his neck and forced other objects into the hole where the tube had been. But Duran apparently did this because he had been left in his cell, drenched in pepper spray, which likely burned especially intensely in his tracheal hole—and because he had a known mental illness.[38]

Between 1989 and 2006 there were 434 prisoner suicides in California. An additional 5,561 prisoners attempted suicide. No one knows how many of these suicides and attempts took place in some kind of isolation unit. But the estimates provided in 2004 and 2014 in the *Coleman* litigation suggest that some 70 percent—roughly 300 suicides—likely occurred in isolation.[39] Scholars estimate that 50 percent of all prisoner suicides throughout the

United States take place in either short- or long-term solitary confinement, even though, as in California, these prisoners make up only 10 percent of the nation's prison population.[40]

The high rates of suicide in isolation likely relate to the high rates of mental illness in prisons generally, and especially in isolation. Only 4 percent of the U.S. population has a serious mental illness.[41] By contrast, 25 percent of all prisoners have a serious mental illness. And 33 to 50 percent of all prisoners in isolation do.[42]

The overrepresentation of the mentally ill in U.S. prisons resulted from institutional shifts in the mid–twentieth century. In 1963, President Kennedy signed the Community Mental Health Act, which aimed to replace bloated inpatient psychiatric facilities with community mental health centers.[43] Advances in the treatment of mental illness, with drugs like Thorazine (chlorpromazine) and its successors, made this move seem feasible. But the vision was only partially realized. Between 1960 and 1980, 80 percent of long-term psychiatric hospital beds were eliminated, and the population of psychiatric inpatients fell from more than 500,000 people to under 100,000.[44] But the community mental health centers meant to replace these hospitals were barely funded, leaving hundreds of thousands of deinstitutionalized people with nowhere to go.

Rather than thriving outside the asylum walls, many of these people ended up in prisons and jails. James Gilligan and others have called this process "trans-institutionalization": the reforms effectively transferred the seriously mentally ill from locked health care facilities to locked punishment facilities.[45] Today, America's largest jails, in Chicago, Los Angeles, and New York, double as the nation's largest psychiatric hospitals.[46]

Supermaxes such as Arizona's Special Management Unit and California's Pelican Bay Security Housing Unit developed as deinstitutionalization peaked. Litigation such as *Madrid v. Gomez* suggests that since the day supermaxes opened their doors, mentally ill prisoners have landed inside at high rates. Supermaxes quickly became a primary tool for managing the growing mentally ill population in prison; this population has served, in turn, to reinforce the need for supermaxes.[47] The result has been cases like that of Vaughn Dortch—the prisoner who smeared himself in excrement and whom officers forced into a scalding bath until his skin peeled off.[48]

Dortch had a preexisting mental health condition that made him hard to manage in prison and that likely contributed to his placement in solitary confinement. Once in solitary confinement, with presumably even less self-control, he behaved in ways that made him even harder to manage. As Dortch became more disruptive in isolation, prison officials could hardly imagine housing him anywhere *but* in solitary confinement.

So even though Judge Henderson in 1995 ordered prison officials to avoid confining mentally ill prisoners, like Dortch, in the Pelican Bay SHU, these prisoners have simply ended up in other isolation units throughout the state. And Judge Henderson provided few protections for prisoners who developed serious mental illnesses while in isolation in the SHU.

Meanwhile, prison staffers have almost as much trouble distinguishing mad from bad prisoners as dangerous from benign ones. Even psychologists working in SHUs and other isolation units struggle to distinguish everyday misbehavior from real mental illness.[49] Again and again, these mental health professionals ask whether excrement-smearing, self-mutilating, suicidal prisoners are manipulative and in need of tough love, or sick and in need of care.[50] Some observers have argued that prisoners hurt themselves deliberately, to obtain more comfortable quarters. These observers fail to ask: what kind of situation makes a supposedly sane person miserable enough to smear feces all over himself, climb into a noose, or swallow a razorblade?

7

"You Can't Even Imagine There's People"

I WAS EIGHTEEN WHEN I FIRST VISITED AN American prison. In the fall of my freshman year of college, I volunteered for a GED tutoring program in a Boston city jail. I liked teaching, and I liked the idea of trying out my skills in a challenging environment. I also liked the idea of shocking my new friends by saying I was "going to prison."

Instead, I ended up shocked. In that first year of going to prison once a week, I never met a monster. I never even met a prisoner who scared me. Instead, I met respectful kids with tragic histories: drug-addicted mothers, abusive fathers, gunshot wounds, memories of watching their friends and siblings die on the streets.

My own unsettled assumptions left me acutely skeptical of the "prison monster" trope. Years later, living in California, no matter how much I read about riots in prison, gladiator fights, and brutal gang hits, I could never quite shake the suspicion that the guys in the SHUs were not the Hannibal Lecters that prison officials alleged or the public imagined. The very phrase "worst of the worst" rankled me. By the time I started investigating the SHU, I had been fraternizing with criminals for decades. Correspondence with Rene Enriquez and Johnny only confirmed my suspicion that even the "worst" had much to offer. Still, without hard evidence about who was imprisoned in the SHU, I could not entirely rule out the possibility that I was the naive Berkeley liberal that Carl Larson told me I was. What I thought I already knew was upended many times in the course of this research.

I submitted my first request for data about who was in California's SHUs in 2008. The Department of Corrections has a standard form that researchers use to explain what data they want and why. Depending on who is in charge of the department, these forms can be handled thoughtfully and thoroughly or summarily dismissed. The year I made my request was a good year. A real person in the Data Analysis Unit followed up with me and asked questions about what I wanted to know and how he could help me to find answers. We scheduled a telephone call. I tried to mask my skepticism with questions that I hoped sounded harmlessly basic and descriptive: How many people are in Security Housing Units in California? How long have they been there? Why are they there?

"That's complicated," the data analyst explained.

"Complicated" was not exactly the problem I had expected. "Classified," maybe, but not "complicated." Later, another analyst told me exactly what the complication was: the department counts "beds not people."[1] Officials track whether a bed is occupied, not how long one person has occupied a specific kind of bed, such as a SHU cell. On any given day, corrections officials can run a "snapshot" report on the people currently housed in the SHU and assess how long each has been there, but these reports are not regularly run or systematically archived.

The data analyst and I agreed on a workaround. Whenever a prisoner moved between security levels, the data management system registered the change and recorded it. The analyst would look at data about people who had been released from the SHU—either back into the general prison population or on parole. I would just have to wait and see whether enough people were cycling through the SHU to make this data worthwhile.

The catchphrase "parole, snitch, or die," which suggests there are only three ways out of the SHU—none of them easy—made me think that not many people return to the SHU multiple times. But the truth of this catchphrase was belied by the data. The frequent cycling of prisoners in and out of the SHU was the first of many indications that not all of them fulfilled the "worst of the worst" stereotype. The more information I gathered, the harder it was to find evidence of any one prisoner who seemed like the "worst of the worst." Instead, evidence of the misuse and overuse of the label—in data released to me, in data revealed to the public, and in interviews I conducted—piled up.

A First Glimpse of the SHU Population

A few months after my first conversation with that data analyst in 2008, I received twenty-three pages of descriptive tables. To my knowledge, this was the first systematic information anyone had compiled about the SHU population since the *Madrid* case in the early 1990s. The tables showed how many people had been housed in California's two biggest SHU facilities between 1997 and 2007 (2,000–3,000 a year); their average lengths of stay in the SHU before release back into the general prison population (just over two years for prisoners released from Pelican Bay in 2007); the racial breakdown of the population in each year (disproportionately Latino, even relative to the disproportionately Latino general prison population); and the aggregate recidivism rate for SHU prisoners over ten years (slightly higher than the aggregate recidivism rate for all prisoners).[2]

Then I came to an innocuous table on page 16: "Number of Offenders who Paroled Directly from Pelican Bay State Prison SHU Between January 1, 1997 and December 31, 2007." I expected to see very small numbers— if not zeroes—for each month. If these really were the "worst of the worst," they likely would not leave prison at all, and certainly not directly from the SHU.

But I saw double-digit numbers across the page. A dozen prisoners *per month* were paroled directly from the Pelican Bay SHU. Three, four, or five times as many prisoners *per month* were paroled from California's other major SHU, at Corcoran. On average, 100 prisoners per month were paroled directly from the SHUs. Between 1997 and 2007, California sent *more than 10,000 prisoners* from its supermaxes straight onto city streets.[3] Imagine, if you will, spending two years or more in a stark, brightly lit concrete box, about the size of a wheelchair-accessible bathroom stall, in Pelican Bay, and then landing on the bustling streets of San Francisco, full of people, cars, trolleys, and bikes, a day or so and a few long bus rides later.

The hundreds who made that transition from SHU to street were not likely to be the people one thought of as California's scariest criminals. According to both criminal law and standard prison security classifications, the "worst of the worst" should be the guys on death row and those with sentences of life without parole—the ones who would never get out of prison anyway, usually because they repeatedly exhibit seriously violent behavior. Even if someone enters prison with a short sentence for a less serious crime—as both George Jackson and Todd Ashker did—violent behavior in prison can lead to additional criminal charges, new trials, and longer sentences. And people with multiple murder convictions rarely get release dates.

Even the 35,000-plus prisoners serving life sentences *with* the possibility of parole in California rarely get out. Between 2000 and 2008, the California parole board denied 98 percent of the "lifer" parole cases it considered. Of the scant 2 percent of lifers for whom the parole board recommended release in those years, Governor Davis and Governor Schwarzenegger overturned 60 percent of the recommendations.[4] In 2008, because of legal and political changes, the odds of being granted parole improved slightly; the California parole board now recommends release in about 15 percent of lifer cases reviewed, and Governor Brown has overturned fewer than 20 percent of these recommendations during his term.[5] The prisoners with parole-eligible life sentences who do get out tend to be the prison equivalent of college-bound honors students: people with decades of immaculate records who have become community leaders within prison.

How, then, were hundreds of prisoners being released *directly* from California's SHUs every year?[6] As I looked at the table on page 16, I reasoned through two possibilities. The paroled prisoners could be "lifers" with indeterminate sentences who had managed to convince the parole board that they were angels, in spite of being housed in the SHU.[7] But prisoners are often not eligible for parole hearings while detained in the SHU, and even if they are eligible, they often have difficulty presenting compelling cases. SHU prisoners cannot work or participate in programs, so they have trouble proving they have been rehabilitated, and they are not eligible for "good time" credits that might reduce their prison sentences.[8] In court filings, Todd Ashker noted that "from January 1, 1990 to August 31, 2003, the BPT

[Board of Parole Terms] has not granted a parole date to a 'single prisoner' in the Pelican Bay's Security Housing Unit (who is on indeterminate SHU status for administrative reasons), who is eligible for receiving a parole date."[9] As one former prisoner said to me, amending the well-known maxim: "It's you either die or snitch. There's no parole."[10] It is unlikely, then, that even a few hundred, let alone 10,000 prisoners, gained their freedom from the SHU through the parole board.

The other way for a prisoner to go straight from the SHU to the streets is by "terming out" of a fixed sentence. In June 2013, more than two-thirds of California's prisoners were serving fixed sentences.[11] If released, these prisoners would still be categorized as "paroling" from the SHU, since "parole" is used interchangeably with "release" in California. California has a mandatory parole-release system when sentences are completed; with very few exceptions, released prisoners remain subject to supervision by parole agents, who enforce a range of behavioral restrictions, for an average of three years.[12] These people hardly sound like the worst of the worst. A prisoner who terms out of a fixed sentence had a lesser underlying conviction to begin with, and then avoided accruing additional criminal charges in prison. How would such a person end up in the SHU?

There is no publicly available data about the underlying sentences of prisoners in the SHU, and this was not something that the Department of Corrections was willing or able to provide to me in 2008. But in snapshot data presented at a legislative hearing in 2013, Robert Barton, the inspector general, reported that as of that October, only 1,900 of the 4,000 prisoners in the SHU (47.5 percent) were serving life sentences. The other 2,100, more than half of all SHU prisoners, were serving determinate sentences and were therefore potentially eligible to term out. In addition, Barton reported that only 40 percent of the prisoners in the SHU had been assigned for determinate periods of five years or less—the maximum *determinate* SHU term for any single in-prison offense. The remaining 60 percent were serving *indeterminate* terms as validated gang members or associates.[13] These numbers suggest that a minimum of 500 prisoners (12.5 percent), and as many as 2,100 prisoners (52.5 percent), had determinate criminal sentences but indeterminate SHU terms.[14] In other words, they had committed relatively less serious crimes but ended up in the SHU because of a gang validation. When they had served their time on the sentence for the original crime, they popped out of the SHU and straight onto the streets of Oakland, Stockton, Venice—months or years, in some cases, after their last sight of the moon, their last face-to-face conversation, or their last physical contact with another human.

In the 2000s, California's SHU population hovered around 3,000, or about 2 percent of the entire state prison population in any given year.[15] In the 2010s, the SHU population approached 4,000 as the state's overall prison population fell, increasing the rate of SHU incarceration to 3 percent. These percentages understate the actual number of prisoners who experience these conditions of confinement each year. If more than one-quarter of California's SHU population is released to the streets every year, and thousands more prisoners cycle between the SHU and the general prison population, then the number of prisoners who spend time in the SHU each year is much more than 3 percent of the prison population. But the relevant data systems are not set up to provide such figures directly.

The SHU release data reveal that the impact of the SHU ripples into communities, affecting tens of thousands of people a year. And that is just in California. In New York State, the rates of release from supermaxes are double California's: roughly 2,000 New York prisoners are released directly from solitary confinement into the community each year.[16] If the numbers from California and New York are even remotely representative of national trends, thousands of former prisoners in American communities have spent months at a time in long-term solitary confinement right before their release.

Exactly how many prisoners across the country experience solitary confinement in any given year—and how many of these prisoners return to communities near you and me—is a mystery. The most commonly referenced estimate is that 81,622 people are kept in "restricted housing" conditions in state and federal prisons.[17] But this is only a snapshot; it fails to capture the number of people cycling through solitary confinement over months and years. It also fails to capture people in solitary confinement in jails, juvenile detention facilities, immigration detention facilities, and military facilities. Worse, this estimate is more than ten years old; it comes from a Bureau of Justice Statistics report that analyzed data from 2005.[18]

Attempts to update these figures are beset by definitional inconsistencies. The problems are partly structural: because criminal justice decision
making happens largely at the local level, the labels assigned to different
security levels vary widely by jurisdiction.[19] Practically every county, state,
and federal system has a different name for solitary confinement and supermaxes. What California calls a SHU, Arizona calls the SMU (Special
Management Unit), Massachusetts calls the DDU (Department Disciplinary
Unit), Pennsylvania calls the RHU (Restricted Housing Unit), and the federal system calls the CMU (Communications Management Unit).

But the definitional problems are also interpretative. Most prison officials
contest the label "solitary confinement." They enumerate prisoners' many
"privileges" in isolation and thus "prove" that they are not actually in solitary
confinement. During the 2011 prisoner hunger strikes in the Pelican Bay
SHU, for instance, a California Department of Corrections spokeswoman,
Terry Thornton, asked: "Is it really solitary confinement if you can take correspondence courses and watch something like 27 channels on your own
TV? . . . If I went to prison, I wouldn't want to share a cell with anybody."[20]

While not every prison official is so brazen, plenty have echoed Thornton's description of restrictive isolation as "not solitary confinement." Harold W. Clarke, director of the Virginia Department of Corrections, asserted:
"There is no such thing as solitary confinement—nowhere in the country. . . . That went out the window a long time ago."[21] Clarke preferred to
use the word "segregation" for the conditions of confinement at Virginia's
Red Onion State Prison. Human Rights Watch describes Red Onion as a
prototypical supermax, with some of the most restrictive isolation conditions in the United States.[22]

Military commanders have echoed Thornton's and Clarke's arguments.
In a story on the conditions in which an accused military traitor was being
held, the New York Times reported: "Colonel Johnson denied that Private
Manning was in solitary confinement . . . saying that he could talk with
guards and with prisoners in nearby cells, though he could not see them.
He leaves his 6-by-12-foot cell for a daily hour of exercise, and for showers,
phone calls, meetings with his lawyer and weekend visits by friends and
relatives, the colonel said."[23] Such statements systematically minimize the
intensity of isolation. And the persistence with which officials deny having

even one prisoner in solitary provides further evidence that any estimate of the prevalence of the practice relying on data furnished by correctional systems likely undercounts actual isolated populations.

The data I collected in California, in an effort to understand how many people have been in solitary confinement and for how long, is just a first step toward defining the scale of the practice across the United States. Still, the California data, the estimates about supermax populations in other states, and the hints that these estimates understate the real numbers all suggest that the impact of solitary confinement is hardly confined to a few thousand people safely secured for the rest of their lives behind cement blocks and barbed wire. Tens of thousands of people experience solitary confinement annually, and thousands of them leave prison and return, straight from the box, to our communities.

As soon as I saw the SHU release numbers for California, I had some questions: What happens when you leave? What is it like to go from an eight-by-ten-foot box in Pelican Bay to the wide-open California highways, from no human contact to a four-hundred-mile Greyhound bus ride, from fluorescent lights to bright sun, from never having seen a cell phone or interacted with the Internet to iPads and Wikipedia? I wanted to find some of the people tallied up in that data table on page 16.

With so many people experiencing SHU confinement and then being released, how hard could they be to find? I started asking around. I reached out to community organizations in San Francisco, Los Angeles, and New York; identified places that provided reentry services to former prisoners; asked employment counselors, journalists, prison educators, and prison officials if anyone knew any former SHU prisoners. To my surprise, despite networking with parolees' trusted allies, months passed before I identified even one prisoner who had spent time in solitary confinement and was willing to talk to me.

Ray

My first interview, in June 2010, was with "Ray," a forty-seven-year-old Latino man from California's Central Valley. Ray had been out of prison just six months when we met at a Starbucks in Stockton, California. He had served thirty years of a life sentence for a gang murder he committed at age seventeen.

When we met, it happened to be Father's Day weekend. I wished him a happy holiday and immediately realized my faux pas: he said he was not a father. He had been incarcerated all his adult life. Ray faced the parole board twelve times over more than twenty years before he earned his release. He described the repetitive frustration of this process: "It is a devastating experience, especially when you know and you are convinced, like I was, that I have done the necessary work in me to bring myself out of my previous way of thinking, and I don't have those interests in doing the things I used to do. I don't have those interests no more. And especially when you have met every requirement and expectation they have placed on you to have a chance at parole, and when you bring them all this, and they continue to find you unsuitable for insignificant, irrelevant factors."[24]

Early in his incarceration, Ray spent four years in the Pelican Bay SHU, 1993–97. Before that, he had spent three years in the Corcoran SHU. Ray was matter-of-fact about how he got to the SHU: "The administration, because of my gang affiliation, because of my activities, they deemed me as a threat to the security of the institution, so they gave me indefinite SHU term, which meant confined in administrative segregation, and that was what landed me in solitary confinement at Pelican Bay, which was in theory supposed to be designed to keep people like me away from the population, to minimize my accessibility to influence other people." Ray's seven years of SHU confinement in the 1990s hindered his ability to present a compelling case to the parole board. Even though he formally "dissociated" from the gang in the mid-1990s, he looked like a disciplinary problem.

Ray made the decision to dissociate while housed at Pelican Bay in the mid-1990s. He recalled vividly the moment that he "felt empathy" and "hit rock bottom": "Some guards came to my cell and told me: 'We need to escort you to the lieutenant's office.' In Pelican Bay, when they come and get you and tell you they need to escort you to the lieutenant's office, something's not right, something's going on, because they don't pull you out of your cell for nothing, unless they have to. So I walked over there, and they told me to call home, to make a long story short, I got on the phone, and my family, I heard them all disturbed in the background telling me my brother was killed the night before."

Prisoners in the SHU are not permitted telephone calls. The only exception is if someone in their immediate families dies. Then they are permitted to leave their cell, make one call lasting a few minutes, and shuffle back, feet and hands chained, escorted by three or four officers. Back in their cells, they are left alone with the memory of the brief human contact. In the four years that Ray spent at Pelican Bay, his family was able to visit him only once, soon after his brother died. Ray remembered going back to his cell after that call:

I started weeping. But you know what I started weeping for? I didn't realize this then, but it became clearer later, why I started weeping. I didn't start weeping for my brother, I started weeping for that child who was the son of the victim [I killed] that I seen in court in 1980, when I was going for my *in limine*[23] hearing, there was a little child who was jumping up and down in the jury box, and the bailiff had to repeatedly tell him to settle down, because he was distracting the court, and I remember watching that kid, and he was the victim's son, and he [was] no more than about five years [old].

In that moment he decided to dissociate from his gang and debrief—share details about gang life and gang activities with prison officials to prove that he truly was dissociating.

The decision, he explained, was far from easy:

Now all of a sudden you are making a decision to go against the basic principles and values that we live and die for. And you are considering it. That in itself is a psychological stewing up in your head . . . But when you actually make the decision to initiate it [debriefing] . . . you become the person that you despised at one time, and to come to acknowledge and to come to terms with . . . that you are now the piece of shit that everyone else usually despises. When you were up here at one time, and everybody respected you. Those are extreme positions for somebody to go through in life. And that's what a lot of us went through. That's what I went through. And the time that I went through the psychological, uh, conflicting engagement in my head, is the time that I was told about my brother.

After he dissociated and debriefed, Ray spent thirteen more years in prison, shuttling between "sensitive needs yards"—self-contained units for prisoners who need special protections, because of the notoriety or sexual nature of their crimes, because they have a particular infectious disease, or because, like Ray, they snitched on their gang associates to prove that they were no longer part of the gang.

I knew the basics of Ray's story before I met him—he had spent time in the SHU, he had snitched, he had been paroled after thirty years. Although Ray had spent decades in the prison's general population after his release from the SHU—unlike those hundreds of people paroling directly from the SHU every year, whom I was especially curious to meet—I imagined he would still have plenty of insights about transitioning out of the SHU.

"What was the Bay like in the 1990s?" I asked. He gave a vivid description:

> You know one . . . thing about Pelican Bay? It's quiet. . . . See the volume we're talking at right now . . . ? That would be loud. The whole building would be hearing us talk. So when people are in Pelican Bay, they get in the habit of talking like this [whispering] . . . They talk really low . . . You end up realizing that you are talking louder than you realize, and everybody is hearing it, and because of that, everybody gets in the habit, over the years, of talking really low. And it's quiet. Very quiet. And you walk inside the unit, it's so quiet, you can't even imagine there's anybody there. And when you walk in the unit, you don't see bars. All you can see is doors, like that. And you can't even imagine there's people back there. And you even have a sense of, of uh, a sense of isolation, because you don't hear no people, but those people are all around. You don't hear them talking . . . And what's even more creepy, when you go into . . . the little SHU yard they have for us . . . You know what the feeling's like? Someone described it to me once . . . "Imagine yourself walking into a 10-feet empty pool, in the bottom . . . and you stand up, and that's all you see is the all around, the walls." That's what he told me he felt like when he walked onto the yard for the first time, like he was at the bottom of a pool looking up at the top . . . That's what it felt like.

Ray's words captured the dull, hollow creepiness of life in the SHU that photos and architectural descriptions fail to reveal. Talking to him, I started to understand why former prisoners, even if I could find them, might not want to talk to me about their experiences in the SHU. Once out, they never wanted to look back.

Looking over the transcript of my interview with Ray, I see how eager he was to talk with me about the details of his parole hearings, the way he

Cell, Pelican Bay SHU
(Monica Lam, Center for Investigative Reporting)

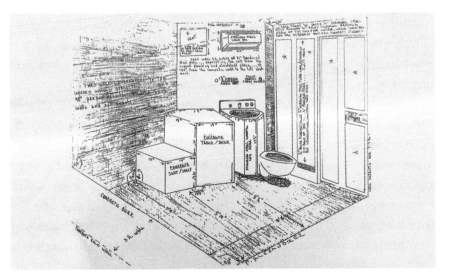

Prisoner's diagram of a SHU cell
(Drawing by Frank Alejandrez)

turned his life around in prison and resisted becoming "hardened," his new life outside of prison, the friends he missed from his years on the sensitive needs yards. And I see how many times I redirected the conversation to life in the SHU and to the process of getting out of the SHU—topics that he clearly wanted to avoid.

Ray recalled little about his transition out of the SHU. He summed up the whole experience as a learning process:

> Because when you are confined in that culture for so many years and you are functioning and operating in that little box and you pull yourself out of that box, you are functioning and carrying yourself in a whole different way that people are not used to, so I literally had to train myself, retrain myself, how to speak, how to conduct myself, how to smile. You understand? And how to greet people. And that was the most difficult thing I ever had to do. But! I was successful at doing it. And Pelican Bay, my stay at Pelican Bay brought me to my knees, but it was also the place that I raised up myself.

When he was validated as a gang member and sent to Pelican Bay, I wondered, had Ray been the worst of the worst? Sitting across from him at a Starbucks, squinting in the sunlight as he sipped a caramel macchiato, noticing his crisp, short-sleeved white button-down, his graying hair, his neat mustache, I could hardly imagine the teenage gangbanger.

I caught a glimpse of the kid he had once been when he said he had never had the chance to have kids. And again when he described a picture that his mom took of him and sent to some of his friends still in prison to give them "a sense of hope" that someday they could "go home" too: "I took a picture of me laying in my bed, and there was a big old comfortable cushion, big old pillows." Former prisoners on parole are forbidden to communicate with anyone currently in prison, but Ray's mom continued to write and visit some of his prison friends after he got out, and she brought back news of the visits: "She told me that [my prisoner buddy] said that when he seen the picture of me in that bed, that he started crying. The reason why he started crying is because he seen me on a bed when we're used to sleeping on metal bunks. And that when she was showing the pictures to all the guys inside, that a lot of them were crying because they were not only seeing somebody out in the world, they were really happy for me."

Regardless of what he had been as a teenager or as a twenty-something earning his way into isolation, Ray had managed, as he put it, to raise himself up. When I interviewed him, only six months out of prison, he said he was no longer as "scared . . . fearful . . . anxious" as when he first got out:

> In certain circumstances, if I'm confined in a little, like inside here [pointing inside the Starbucks], if I go inside here, and it's crowded, I gotta get out . . . But if I go into a big supermarket now, it's OK. But something like that [gesturing inside the small Starbucks], I gotta get out, because I feel bad still. But for the most part, I think that I, the reason why I think that I am reintegrating fairly well and adjusting pretty good is because, uh, I made a point to surround me with people that are going to encourage me and help me and that are generally concerned with me.

He was living with his sister, working for his brother-in-law, and keeping in touch with people in the halfway house where he spent his first few months on parole, encouraging them to change their lives and cut their ties with bad influences. Like many of the people I interviewed, Ray was resilient.

The more difficulty I had in finding people who were willing to talk about the experience of isolation, the more I realized how special was the subset of people who would talk. They were the ones who had learned to speak and smile again; to overcome their fears of booming voices, piercing noises, open spaces, and crowds; to resist the temptation to maintain the rigid routines they had developed to pass the time and maintain a sense of structure over months and years in isolation.

The psychological effects of isolation are well established. Almost two centuries ago, the novelist Charles Dickens and the political historian Alexis de Tocqueville visited the first American prisons, in Pennsylvania and New York. Dickens excoriated the then novel practice of long-term solitary confinement: "I hold this slow and daily tampering with the mysteries of the brain, to be immeasurably worse than any torture of the body: and because its ghastly signs and tokens are not so palpable to the eye and sense of touch as scars upon the flesh; because its wounds are not upon the surface, and it extorts few cries that human ears can hear; therefore I the more denounce it, as a secret punishment which slumbering humanity is not roused up to stay."[26] Tocqueville, although mostly impressed by the American criminal justice system, nonetheless described solitary confinement at New York's Auburn State Prison as an experiment that "proved fatal for the majority of prisoners. . . . It devours the victim incessantly and unmercifully; it does not reform, it kills."[27] A few decades later, in 1890, the U.S. Supreme Court agreed, stating that solitary confinement had been abandoned as a practice because "a considerable number of the prisoners fell, after even a short confinement, into a semi-fatuous condition . . . and others became violently insane; others, still, committed suicide; while those who stood the ordeal better were not generally reformed, and in most cases did not recover sufficient mental activity to be of any subsequent service to the community."[28]

Beginning in the 1950s, psychologists conducted experiments to understand what happens to people under conditions of solitary confinement and sensory deprivation. Donald Hebb, a Canadian psychologist, experimented with the methods and effects of brainwashing, allegedly with funding from the U.S. Central Intelligence Agency. He recruited students to sit for an entire day in silence and darkness, with gloves on to prevent tactile sensation. The students reported being unable to think clearly, performed poorly on basic tasks, and experienced hallucinations. Although Hebb paid participants twenty dollars a day, many quit the studies early; none lasted for more than a week under these conditions.[29] The CIA later developed a military training program dubbed SERE (Survival, Evasion, Resistance, Escape), which was intended to help soldiers withstand sensory deprivation techniques during interrogations.[30]

In the 1960s, these practices were imported directly from military experiments into U.S. prisons. Edgar Schein, a professor of organizational psychology at the Massachusetts Institute of Technology, gave a speech to a group of Federal Bureau of Prisons officials in 1962 in which he argued that brainwashing techniques like those that Hebb pioneered could be used in domestic prisons for "deliberate changing of behavior and attitudes by a group of men who have relatively complete control over the environment in which the captive population lives."[31] In 1968, prison officials at USP-Marion, the high-security federal penitentiary that replaced Alcatraz, implemented a treatment program called Control and Rehabilitation Effort

(CARE). CARE explicitly incorporated Hebb's brainwashing techniques: imposing social isolation on prisoners in order to effect "character invalidation."[32] Prisoners litigated these "experiments," and courts condemned their dangerous psychological effects.[33] Long before the first supermaxes were ever built, then, psychologists, military leaders, and even prison officials were well aware of the dangerous effects of sensory deprivation and isolation.

Over the three decades in which America's supermaxes have flourished, psychologists, psychiatrists, and criminologists have continued to document the extreme mental and physical consequences of even short-term sensory deprivation and isolation. Side effects include problems with concentration; sleep disturbances; hallucinations; paranoid thinking; anxiety; hostility and rage; impulsive behavior; hypersensitivity to light and sound, not unlike the photophobia and phonophobia of a migraine; headaches; and rapid heartbeat.[34]

Only one study of the effects of solitary confinement did *not* find evidence of psychological deterioration, and that study, conducted in a Colorado state supermax, has been criticized for flawed experimental design, biased implementation, and the selective exclusion of data (including a participant suicide) from its analyses.[35] Most researchers studying the effects of supermaxes have found that after even a few days, the majority of prisoners suffer from at least some of the symptoms described above.[36] Terry Kupers, a psychologist specializing in the effects of solitary confinement, has dubbed this constellation of symptoms the "SHU syndrome."[37] While some of these effects recede as prisoners are moved into less restrictive confinement or released from prison, many linger—sometimes for life.

When Steven Czifra testified at the 2013 legislative hearing on solitary confinement, he said: "When I walked into California's torture chamber, I was a whole human being. And when I left there, I was a deeply fractured human being."[38] Just days before he was initially scheduled for release from a general population prison, Czifra got into a fistfight with another prisoner. He was placed in isolation to await a disciplinary hearing. The next day, while in isolation, he spat on a guard. Czifra was charged and convicted in court of felony assault on the guard and sentenced to four more years in prison. He was also assigned to four years in the SHU for violating prison rules against assaulting an officer. Four years later, Czifra was released directly from the SHU to the outside. As Ray told me uneasily at our Starbucks table, when he left the SHU, he had to learn how to smile. Czifra had to relearn human contact: "It took my partner five years before she could touch me without it hurting me."[39]

Ernie

As I continued to investigate supermaxes, and word spread that I was interested in talking to people who had been in isolation and were now on the outside, I gradually collected more stories. I began to correspond with a few people in isolation. I interviewed ten people in California who had experienced isolation at Pelican Bay, at Corcoran, and at federal prisons, and I interviewed eight people in New York who had spent time in that state's isolation units. I met one woman who had spent a total of six months in isolation in two of California's women's prisons. But three years into this work, I still had not interviewed anyone who had been released directly from the Pelican Bay SHU onto the streets of California. I was still trying to imagine what that would be like.

I had read a few prisoners' accounts of what it was like to leave the Pelican Bay SHU for a court hearing or a medical visit. Kijana Tashiri Askari described leaving the SHU for the first time in twenty years to be transferred to a less restrictive facility:

> In hitting the highway, my sensibilities immediately went through the whirlwind cycle of "shock and awe" via the vivid reminder of what freedom used to entail. I mean think about it, we're talking about 20 years of being entombed in Pelikkkan Bay's torture chambers without any environmental stimulation or human contact!! So just imagine how my sense voraciously feasted upon: the sight of cows and horses parlaying in the open fields; the sight of the ocean's waters roaring and brushing up against the elements of Motha Earth; the sight of enormous mountains and trees, along with green grass and birds flying in the clear blue sky—as free as they wanna be!! The sight of social activity, in seeing other human beings exercising, walking, driving their cars, and doing everything they wanted to do—simply because they were free!![40]

Johnny, whose story appears in the previous chapter, described in a letter his temporary respite from the Pelican Bay SHU. He had been housed in the SHU almost continuously for ten years when he was called to testify in a criminal case stemming from a prison incident he had witnessed. He mentioned this in a letter, and I wrote back and asked: "What was it like to leave the SHU?" A few weeks later, I received this reply:

> It was great to leave the SHU. I could tell you about it for pages. We took the route up through Oregon then down so I got to see all the mountains and snow, trees, etc. It was most memorable. But what stuck out the most to me was the ordinary small tasks, things of every day life, watching people get gas, morning coffee, walking the dog, etc. The single memory that stuck out the most was driving next to a car with a dog hanging his/her head out the window, air in his/her face. Made me think how long it's been since I've seen a live dog (20 years). And how much dogs love that. When you've done so much time behind these walls you learn to value and appreciate the small things in life.[41]

He was not complaining about what he could not do, just appreciating what he could see.

Askari and Johnny left the Pelican Bay SHU in cuffs, confined in a prison van with bars on the windows, both of them facing life sentences and knowing they were unlikely to ever walk free. If riding in handcuffs in a prison van was so great, as Johnny said, how much more dramatic would it be to walk free out of the SHU?

In 2012, four years after I learned about the hundreds of people released annually from California SHUs, I was still, somewhat impatiently, searching for someone who could tell me what it was like to leave the SHU without shackles involved. That fall, California voters passed Proposition 36, which revised the state's "three strikes" law. The proposition rolled back the draconian sentencing scheme passed by popular ballot measure two decades earlier. That 1994 law, known colloquially as "three strikes and you're out," represented the apogee of California's determinate sentencing movement, mandating a sentence of twenty-five years to life for any person convicted of three felonies. The 2012 proposition authorized individualized resentencing hearings for anyone serving twenty-five years to life for a nonserious, nonviolent "third strike" felony conviction. As it turned out, and to my surprise, at least some prisoners in the SHU—the exact number is unknown, of course—were in prison for nonviolent, nonserious third-strike offenses. "Ernie" was one of them.

As soon as he learned of the passage of Proposition 36, Ernie filed a petition for a resentencing hearing. If Ernie had nothing else, he had the time to write a careful petition. He was serving a twenty-five-year-to-life sentence for drug possession. The three-strikes law was hardly a month old on the day that Ernie was arrested, in 1994, with heroin in his pocket. He said he had "never dreamed [that law] applied to me."[42] But at the time of his arrest, he had two prior felony convictions. He became one of the first "third-strikers" sentenced under the new law.

When Proposition 36 passed in 2012, Ernie had served eighteen years in prison, including almost ten years in the Pelican Bay SHU as a "validated" associate of the Aryan Brotherhood. Prison officials established Ernie's Aryan Brotherhood association based on a drawing, alleged to include gang symbols—a shamrock, for example, might qualify—found in his cell. So in 2003 they sent him to the Bay.

Validated gang associates not only are housed in the SHU indefinitely, but also face a permanent presumption of guilt, with virtually no opportunity to appeal the validation to a judge or a jury. Ernie would have to follow every rule in the SHU, avoid anything that might be construed as a gang symbol, and be polite to every guard for *six years* just to be eligible to have his gang validation reconsidered. He kept a clean record for five years and looked forward to the hearing that would review the weak evidence supporting his gang validation. He hoped he might at least be returned to the general prison population.

Then, in 2008, guards conducted a search of his cell. They found the book *Matching Wits with Mensa* (a collection of "mind-bender" games); the name of another prisoner, alleged to be an Aryan Brotherhood associate, was inscribed inside the front cover. An unnamed prisoner who was leaving the SHU had given the book to Ernie a few months before, and Ernie knew nothing about the person whose name was inscribed in the book. Regardless, the clock started over; he needed six more years of perfect behavior to be eligible for a gang status review hearing.

This cycle of hope and futility was a primary reason for the hunger strikes that Todd Ashker helped lead. The first two of the hunger strikers' five core demands concerned gang validation: "1. End Group Punishment and Administrative abuse . . . justifying indefinite SHU status" and "2. Abolish the Debriefing Policy, and Modify Active/Inactive Gang Status Criteria . . . Perceived gang membership is one of the leading reasons for placement in solitary confinement."[43]

Although he knew that he risked incurring a disciplinary violation, Ernie refused all food in the first round of hunger strikes in 2011: "I was there for both hunger strikes. We did ten days in my pod. We went ten days in July of 2011. We turned right around in September and did three more days." The strikes brought attention to the conditions of confinement in the SHU, to the long periods prisoners spent there, and to the vague and arbitrary procedures underlying gang validations and indeterminate assignments to isolation.

By 2011, Ernie had little hope that prison officials would ever let him out of the SHU, but maybe a judge would at one of those "Prop 36" resentencing hearings. The critical response to the hunger strikes, in combination with Prop 36's overturn of three strikes, gave prisoners like Ernie hope that a judge's assessment of his risk to *public* safety just might contradict the prison systems' assessment of his risk to *prison* safety. Ernie's nonviolent past and his clean prison disciplinary record—except for possessing that one drawing and that one book—made him a good candidate for resentencing. He hoped.

Ernie learned that a judge had assigned an attorney to his case; this was a good sign. But he said: "Even though I'm getting letters, talking to my attorney, the judge said, 'You're going to be resentenced' . . . I never saw anyone leave . . . I didn't believe it." Ernie was not present at the 2013 hearing at which the judge considered his resentencing petition. He had to wait for his attorney to contact him to learn what had happened.

The judge ordered Ernie's release, with time served. He would be free, not even subject to the restrictions of parole.

I first talked to Ernie on the telephone three months after he left the SHU, and I conducted a formal interview with him six months after his release. We met at a Burger King in Stockton, California, near where he was living.

Ernie, a white man, arrived at the Burger King wearing jeans, a button-down short-sleeved shirt, and Converse-style sneakers—a young-looking style for a sixty-two-year-old. But the last time he was out of prison, Ernie would have been in his forties.

In a sense, time on the outside stands still for former prisoners. When he got out, Ernie saw his first cell phone, opened his first bank account, touched his twenty-four-year-old son, and hugged a woman for the first time in ten years.

We chatted a bit about the daily challenges of his new life. He described things from the utterly mundane—"after nineteen years in prison, you knew the technology in 1994 and the technology now, cell phones are something foreign I'm learning to use"—to the existential: "I have some, like, anxiety attacks being in crowds or around a lot of people . . . You want to get back to your box . . . I kind of miss it." Other former prisoners had told me about similar experiences while transitioning out of prison—getting used to new technology, being afraid of crowds, missing the predictable confinement of four cement walls.

But no former prisoner I had talked to had experienced a transition as abrupt as Ernie's. I finally asked him: "What was it like to leave the SHU? Can you describe that day for me?"

When he heard the news that he was "discharged with time served," he replied, he was still certain he would not leave the SHU, sure the guards would say, "You're not getting out of here. We're going to keep you." But on a spring morning in 2013, barely six months after the passage of Proposition 36, guards came to Ernie's cell. As he must have done dozens of times over the prior ten years, Ernie reached his hands out through the cuff slot in the door. The officers snapped handcuffs on. Then, from the central control booth, a guard pushed a button and Ernie's door slid open. Four guards escorted him to the building where incoming and outgoing prisoners are processed:

> They took me to R and R, which is receiving and release. I had never had handcuffs off of me in front of anybody. They take me to R and R in restraints. When they took them [the handcuffs] off, the cops were looking at me like they almost expected me to do something. I didn't know what to do

with my hands when they took the restraints off. I didn't know what to do, especially with five correction officers—they're looking at me. And I'm like, "Well, what are you guys going to do?" And they're thinking like, "Well, what is he going to do?" And I'm like, "Well, I'm trying to get out of prison."

Ernie's matter-of-fact narrative conveyed more anxiety than excitement. Even the sensation of being free to move his hands was overwhelming—paralyzing.

"But everything worked out fine," he went on. "Now, you got to remember, I am not on parole. I am not under anybody's supervision. I'm a free person." After they uncuffed him, two prison guards led Ernie into the back of a prison van and drove him eighty miles down the Pacific Coast Highway to the nearest bus station, in Arcata. Ernie remembered they arrived at nine in the morning. He had forty-five minutes before his bus left. The guards let him out of the van, escorted him as he bought a bus ticket, and then said: "OK. Take it easy."

But the guards returned to their van. They waited, and watched. So did Ernie. He felt acutely out of place, as if everyone was watching him, not just the guards.

After nineteen years in prison, and almost ten years in the hole, it was really something to walk into that bus station with two big old cops . . . I think people recognized me because I was so white. Everybody else has got luggage. I've got a box. Just a box. Maybe there were apples in it at one time. . . . I'm kind of pacing. I'm white as a ghost. In fact, when I went to the doctor, I had vitamin D deficiency. I'm kind of pacing. It's a very small bus station in Arcata.

Ernie's discomfort in looking so obviously like someone just released from prison was superficial compared with his anxiety about how he would navigate the 333-mile bus journey through Oakland to his home in Stockton. He looked around the bus station for a friendly face. He thought for a second about how to introduce himself, and he decided he would just have to acknowledge the obvious: "It's no secret. Those two cops just walked me in here."

His eyes settled on a young man who reminded him of his twenty-four-year-old son. "I see this kid, and I walk over and introduce myself. I just blurted out, and I said, 'I just got out of prison.'" The passenger's name was Mike.[44] Ernie asked quickly for a big favor: "Look, Mike, I just spent nineteen years in prison, and I've been in that isolation unit at Pelican Bay. I feel like a fish out of water. Is it OK if I—could I just hang out with you— would you walk me through this?"

I tried to imagine standing in that bus station in Arcata, watching a sixty-two-year-old man, covered in tattoos but sickly pale, carrying a repurposed apple carton, eyeing and being eyed by the two guards just outside. What would I say if he approached me?

Ernie's new friend Mike said: "Man, no problem."

"He was just great," Ernie said. "And you know what? Everybody I met was great." Mike and Ernie rode together all the way to Oakland. There, Mike changed for a bus to San Francisco, and Ernie changed for one to Stockton. On the journey, Ernie used a cell phone for the first time.

"This kid, Mike, he walks me through the whole thing. We talk on the bus. He has a cell phone. I'm watching him text. He tells me about Face-book. I'm just full of questions, and he's like a fountain of knowledge to me. And so I tell him, 'Could I use your phone?' He said, 'Yeah.' So I tell him the number, he dials. It's my first time talking on a cell phone. I let my friend Jane know where I am, my estimated ETA."

"And did she know that you were coming out?"

Ernie: "Yeah. Well, she had talked to the attorney. She didn't know what day, you know. There was no way I could write to tell anyone . . . [It] was just like, boom. I called and told her I am on the bus, I'm on my way. Then she picked me up at the bus station that night."

Not long after Ernie called Jane, the bus from Arcata stopped at a Mc-Donald's. Even deciding what to order felt overwhelming, and Ernie was already worried about having enough money to take care of himself: "I was hungry, and I only had two hundred collars cash." This is called "gate money"; in the California prison system, prisoners receive $200 when they are released, to cover the cost of their trip home. Ernie said: "It was a hundred dollars for the bus ticket, so now I'm left with a hundred dollars."

"Oh, [the bus ticket] was a hundred dollars? Wow."

Ernie said, "Actually, I think it was a hundred and one. I saved the bus ticket as a souvenir. So we go in McDonald's, and I remember a Quarter Pounder. So I said, 'I'll have a Quarter Pounder and a soda.' " It was his first McDonald's hamburger in twenty years. But he had ordered in a rush, worried about how little money he had. He had not considered the relatively small size of the burger: "The big problem was I didn't order enough to eat."

Finally, the bus arrived in Oakland. According to the Greyhound website, the trip takes about seven hours. Mike helped Ernie navigate the transfer to the bus to Stockton, another seventy-five miles east. Jane met him at the station late that evening, as promised. With Jane, Ernie experienced the mundane pleasures of good food and human companionship. He was just as happy not to leave her house:

> And then—we probably stayed in the house for the first few days. I didn't even really want to get out much, you know. We stayed in and talked. I ate good food. I ate home cooking. She cooks very well. So that's one of the things you really miss, is the food. And then—not to sound funny, but I'm a man—the presence of a woman. It's different than—talking with Mike, the guy I met, is nice. But talking with an older, old girl that I haven't seen in years, and the presence of a woman and the conversation—and I know her well enough that I can ask, and I did ask—always asking, "How do I look?" I feel sometimes out of place in public.

I asked, "How?"

> "Like people know me, know about me. That's, you know—"
> Me: "Like, someone might know and might be able to tell?"
> Ernie: "Well, you might just guess. You might be able to sit across the room here and say, 'Hey, I bet you that guy—'"
> Me: "And then what?"
> Ernie: "And she would say, 'You look fine. You look okay. You act okay. In fact, I'm a little surprised, that you—you know?' I think she expected chaos."
> Me: "Yeah, well, you hear stories."
> Ernie: "And none of that come to pass. I just discuss with her—she knows what my life was and what I would like my life to be. I would like to live the remainder of my life not incarcerated. With no chaos. I'm sixty-two years old. I just want to be a sixty-two-year-old guy that gets in where he fits in, and go to the meetings that I go to."

I asked Ernie more about this. What surprised him? What was hard about fitting in? What was he still getting used to? He focused in part on the good stuff. Eating was one of the greatest pleasures of being out of the SHU. Everything he tried was the best thing ever. Of his first steak, he said, "I don't think I ever ate a better steak." And "the grilled cheese is the best I ever had." He had looked forward to the food in the SHU: "Because you're hungry. When you're situated in a box like that, eating is a big thing. And we look forward to it, certain meals." But the meals were never warm; Ernie described them as "lukewarm, tepid." And SHU food was bland—punitively so. "They took salt and pepper. Their excuse was: 'There's no nutritional value, so you don't need it.' It's almost a good thing, they took salt out of my diet. It's not something I crave anymore."

"You are remarkably upbeat," I said.

"My attitude is positive. I try to apply discipline."

Ernie described abiding habits he could not quite shake. "One thing about living like that, in isolation, is that you do have control over everything in the box. I'll take the cap off your shampoo and toothpaste and clean the lid. Everything's just got to be, whoa! It's a sickness. I am working on it. I'll try not to be so meticulous." Many prisoners I interviewed talked of their compulsive neatness, attachment to routine, need to control their space and their time.

Leaving the routine of the SHU presented continual challenges for Ernie: "Anything other than being in your box, you go from your box to the yard or from your box to the shower. Anything outside of that is not a daily routine."

My request to meet him was another break in his new routine. He considered not meeting with me because he worried about how he would seem. He gave himself a pep talk: "I said, OK. This is a professional lady. She wants to speak to me. I want to be at my best. I want to at least appear normal and act like I have good sense. So, I have to just dig down and say, 'Man, you can do this. Let's get it done.'"

Leaving Jane's apartment at all was hard at first. Even though he was out of the SHU, Ernie had a lingering fear that he was still at risk of losing his mind.

One of the things was, just, you know, going shopping, going to a Walmart or a Target—any of the stores that are around— to buy clothes. There's a lot of—just being around a lot of people was strange at first. Now I don't worry. I've read a lot of stuff from psychologists, psychiatrists: "You got people locked up in cages, who [psychiatrists] say it's not *if* they come off, they come undone, it's *when*." So in the back of my mind, I wondered when that's going to happen to me . . . I worry about other people's conduct more than mine. How will I react to a situation? In prison, we react one way. In the free world, you're to act like you have good sense. I tell myself often that I don't have real good sense.

"Have there been situations since you got out where you've had to think about reacting?" I asked.

Ernie: "I have. And that's where somebody maybe asks you for something or walks up on you quickly, you know, the people that ask you for money? Do you want to buy CDs? Do you—you know, the people you see in front of stores? Sometimes that's a little—whoa, whoa. I'm getting used to it now."
Me: "So the first few times that happened when—"
Ernie: "The first few times that happened, I felt rigid or stiff, like, whoa."
Me: "So, you . . . ?"
Ernie: "It's too close, you know. Just give me my space. But then I don't want to run my story out and say, 'Hey, you can't do that to me and this is why.' I don't want to say that. I would just rather walk away from it or just say no."

It took Ernie six months to decide he needed mental health care to help him adjust to life out of the SHU. He had mentioned before our interview that he had a doctor's appointment. Later, as we were talking, he said the appointment was actually with a therapist: "I will continue the therapy, the talking—about the therapy I had told you about. When I first went in, that was a very, very hard step for me, to walk in—we'll call it mental health. It's what it is. And you know, I had way too much pride. There was nothing wrong with me."

As I listened to Ernie, I almost agreed that there was "nothing wrong" with him. He survived twenty years in prison, ten of them in the SHU. He filed the petition that initiated the review of his case, and he won. He figured out how to get from Pelican Bay to Stockton. He overcame his fear of technology, of people, of the unpredictable world, and he got on with his life. He was building a relationship with Jane. The fact that he had a welcoming home to move into when he left the SHU was remarkable in the first place. He had navigated the federal bureaucracy, and was getting a "small Social Security check." He was learning to let things go.

I, on the other hand, could not let go of the absurdity. Ernie was so obviously not a threat to public safety that a judge was willing to overturn his life sentence and order the release of someone twice labeled the worst of the worst.

At $70,000 a year, the average annual cost of keeping a prisoner in the SHU at Pelican Bay is $12,000 more than the cost of keeping a prisoner in the general population in a California prison, and $40,000 more than the U.S. average cost per prisoner per year.[45] Meeting Ernie, I could not help thinking again, as I had when talking with other current and former SHU prisoners, like Johnny, that the $700,000 that Californians spent keeping him in the SHU for ten years was a colossal waste of money, of bed space, and, of course, of human life. And I wondered: how many more like Ernie were buried in the SHU?

Then I thought again about all the prisoners being paroled directly from California's SHUs without the hope of applying to get a Social Security check, without a girlfriend to come home to, without the incredible restraint required to just walk away and let things go, over and over. How were they doing?

Very few studies have examined what happens to former supermax prisoners who get out. Many states, like California, do not specifically track them. Even in states that do, monitoring members of this population and predicting the likelihood that they will commit new crimes presents both methodological and ethical challenges. The few studies examining whether released supermax prisoners are more dangerous than other released prisoners are inconclusive.[46]

But two recent events in Colorado and Nebraska suggest that not everyone is as resilient as Ernie in recovering from years in the SHU. In March 2013, Evan Ebel was released directly from an isolation unit in Colorado.

He had been treated for symptoms of mental illness during five continuous years in isolation. Within a few days of being released, Ebel killed a pizza-delivery man, stole his uniform, and drove to the house of Tom Clements, then the director of the Colorado Department of Corrections, who was actively working to reduce the state's reliance on isolation. Ebel knocked on the door and then shot Clements at close range, killing him instantly.[47] A few months later, in July 2013, Nikko Jenkins was released from a Nebraska prison where he had spent nearly two years in continuous solitary confinement. Like Ebel, Jenkins had displayed symptoms of serious mental illness, repeatedly cutting himself and using the blood to write on the walls of his cell. In August 2013, he went on a ten-day killing spree, shooting three strangers and one former prison acquaintance, each at close range, in the head.[48]

These are disturbing reminders that supermaxes do not cure violence. If anything, supermaxes exacerbate both mental illness and violent tendencies. Of the thousands of individuals who experience no human contact for months, years, or decades, and are then returned to communities across the United States every year, some are as harmless as Ernie, but others are not. The prison system that classifies and houses these prisoners seems exceptionally bad at telling the difference.

8

Another Way Out

THE SHU ENSNARES THE MENTALLY ILL, THE nonviolent third-striker, the young kid and the middle-aged man, the one with the wrong drawing, the right tattoo, or too many books. Once ensnared, SHU prisoners find few easy ways out. "Parole, snitch, or die" is not just prison lore; the saying accurately captures how treacherous SHU departures can be. Prisoners struggle to work their way out of the SHU. And then they struggle to survive the sensory overload and chaos outside the box. Their stories reveal how supermaxes have failed to distinguish violent from nonviolent prisoners, failed to distinguish mad from bad, failed to cure violence, and failed to meet a battery of basic human needs.

Supermaxes, however, have succeeded in one thing. They have eliminated the kind of widespread collective resistance characterized by George Jackson and Attica in the 1970s. They have silenced the radicals. Even in cases like *Madrid,* which challenged the constitutionality of the SHU, prison officials successfully leveraged stories about dangerous prisoners to justify the practice. Carl Larson and Craig Brown built the Pelican Bay SHU with minimal legislative oversight, and wardens like Charles Marshall successfully resisted judicial oversight. For more than two decades, from the opening of Pelican Bay in 1989 until 2011, California prison officials controlled not only who was sent to isolation there but also the stories about why, and the details about how. One letter, sent out of the Pelican Bay SHU in April 2011, changed all that.

The Hunger Strikes

On April 3, 2011, eleven prisoners mailed multiple copies of one letter from the Pelican Bay SHU. Todd Ashker was the first signatory. The ten other prisoner signatories were racially diverse—black, Latino, and white, according to correctional classifications. In subsequent months, news outlets uncovered the criminal histories of each signatory; the Department of Corrections identified each as a gang leader hailing from prison gangs traditionally considered to be mortal enemies of one another, including the Black Guerrilla Family, the Mexican Mafia, Nuestra Familia, and the Aryan Brotherhood.[1] Prisoners sent the neatly handwritten proclamations to well-known prisoners' rights advocates in the San Francisco Bay area: California Prison Focus, Critical Resistance, and Legal Services for Prisoners with Children, a list with a strong abolitionist character.

In the letter, the prisoners proclaimed their intention to initiate a hunger strike on July 1, 2011. The letter said the prisoners would refuse food until they died if their demands were not met.[2] The prisoners asked, first, for some alternative way out of the SHU. They did not ask to be released, only to be given hope, to have some possibility other than the parole-snitch-or-die cycle of futility. And they asked, second, for amelioration of the harsh conditions of their confinement: better food, warmer clothes, and something, anything, to occupy their minds during years of isolation.[3]

On July 1, these eleven prisoners, along with hundreds of others in the Pelican Bay SHU, began refusing meals. Over the next few days, more than five thousand prisoners across the California prison system refused meals in solidarity. During the first week of the strike, Terry Thornton, spokesperson for the California Department of Corrections, sought to discredit the strikers' demands: "The department is not going to be coerced or manipulated. . . . That so many inmates in other prisons throughout the state are involved really demonstrates how these gangs can influence other inmates, which is one of the reasons we have security housing units in the first place."[4]

But the strike went on, peacefully. National and international media outlets took notice. The hunger strikers implicitly threatened to synchronize the hundreds of suicides that had taken place in California isolation units over the previous twenty years. A mass suicide, in the form of a well-publicized hunger strike, would be hard to dismiss as either uncontrollable acting out or untreatable mental illness. The threat worked.

On July 20, Scott Kernan, the undersecretary of corrections, flew from Sacramento to Crescent City. He sat down at a table in a Pelican Bay conference room with four of the hunger strike leaders (who wore white jumpsuits and had their hands and legs cuffed). Kernan insisted that he was "not negotiating stuff," but acknowledged that reforms might be necessary: "We're trying to do what we think is right."[5] He agreed to some of the prisoners' demands: allowing prisoners to take one picture of themselves per year and send it home, letting them have colored pencils and wall calendars, allowing warm caps in winter on the solitary exercise yards, installing a pull-up bar for exercise in those yards, allowing prisoners who could afford it to order pickles from the canteen.[6] The simplicity of the concessions spotlighted the restrictiveness of conditions in the SHU.

Kernan also committed to review the procedures by which prisoners were assigned to solitary confinement. He, at least, did not seem to think that the hunger strikers were manipulative gang leaders, strategizing to trick prison officials into mass releases from solitary confinement.

The prisoners agreed to begin eating again. Kernan, however, faced criticism from prison officials, who accused him of having been coerced by gang leaders; he retired a few weeks later. Carl Larson explained the corrections perspective on Kernan to me: "You cannot negotiate under duress."[7]

The California prison system, however, remained under duress as public criticism of the state's isolation policies grew. Immediately following the first hunger strike, the U.N. special rapporteur on torture said that as few as fifteen days in solitary confinement constitutes torture.[8] Prisoners like Todd Ashker had spent five hundred times that long in solitary. During the strike, prison officials, in response to media pressures for more information about who was inside the SHU, provided snapshot data revealing that Ashker was one of 513 prisoners who had been in the Pelican Bay SHU for ten years or more.[9]

Less than a year after the first hunger strike, in May 2012, the Center for Constitutional Rights, a New York–based nonprofit civil rights litigation firm, joined a case that Todd Ashker and Danny Troxell had filed pro se (representing themselves) in 2009. The San Francisco–based Legal Services for Prisoners with Children also joined the case. It alleged that these men's long periods of confinement in the SHU were unconstitutional, in violation of the Eighth Amendment.

Of course, California prison officials had already won the right to maintain prisoners in long-term solitary confinement with Judge Henderson's decision in *Madrid v. Gomez* in 1995. But the prisoners and their lawyers argued that since then, more prisoners had been kept in isolation longer than anyone had known or imagined possible. On June 2, Judge Claudia Wilken of the U.S. District Court for the Northern District of California certified a class of all prisoners at Pelican Bay who had been in solitary confinement for ten years or more. The class certification signaled that Wilken thought the case raised viable questions about the constitutionality of the SHU, and she planned to evaluate them carefully. The case of *Ashker v. Brown* would go forward.

In the face of growing criticism from the U.N. special rapporteur on torture, the media, and the courts, prison officials piloted revisions to the gang validation policy. On August 16, 2012, Terri McDonald, the undersecretary of operations for the prison system, issued a memorandum to "extended executive staff" about a new gang management policy. First, no prisoner validated as a gang associate would be automatically assigned to an indeterminate SHU term anymore unless he was also personally disciplined for a specific rule violation. Second, validation source items, like the drawing and the book that had served as source items for Ernie, or the "kite" that had served as a source item for Johnny, would be assigned point values based on their importance and reliability. The new policy required at least three sources that summed to at least ten points. In addition to outlining these reforms, the memorandum pledged: "In the near future, case-by-case reviews will begin for the existing validated gang population housed in SHU facilities to determine their appropriate placement and/or retention within the SHU."[10]

But reform was slow, and the hunger strikers remained frustrated. They coordinated another strike, in which thirty thousand prisoners participated, in August and September 2013. Ignoring the many concessions that prison officials had already made in response to prisoners' presumably legitimate demands, Jeffrey Beard, the state's newly appointed secretary of corrections, argued that Todd Ashker's leadership of the hunger strike exemplified his ability to coerce other prisoners into doing his bidding, rejustifying his restrictive confinement. "We're talking about convicted murderers who are putting lives at risk to advance their own agenda of violence," Beard said.[11] "They are terrorists," a correctional department spokesperson reiterated.[12] Department of Corrections lawyers filed seven official affidavits in the *Ashker* case by seven prisoners who had debriefed. Each alleged that Todd Ashker and the other strike leaders were active gang members, coercing prisoners into participating in the hunger strike—as well as in the lawsuit.[13]

The strike ended only when state assembly member Ammiano and state senator Hancock agreed to hold the legislative hearings at which I would later testify. At those hearings, prison officials attested that as of September 2013, they had reviewed 528 case files of SHU prisoners; 343 were approved for general population housing, and an additional 150 were placed in step-down programs designed to prepare them to enter the general prison population within a few months. Only 35 prisoners, out of more than 500 cases reviewed, remained in the SHU.[14] Eighteen months later, by June 2014, department officials had reviewed an additional 300 files, released 214 more people into general population, and placed an additional 180 in step-down programs. Only 5 prisoners—less than 2 percent—from this second batch remained in the SHU.[15]

These numbers are remarkable. In less than two years, galvanized by prisoners' refusal of food, journalists' requests, and legislators' interrogations, prison officials determined that nearly one thousand prisoners—one-quarter of the state's entire SHU population—no longer needed to be held in restrictive isolation conditions. Of the files they reviewed, fewer than one in twenty prisoners merited continued SHU confinement. The Department of Corrections appeared to have created another way out of the SHU: parole, snitch, die, or reconsider. Or had it?

Unsettling Solitary Confinement

The movement of a thousand prisoners out of the SHU over the course of 2013–14 happened while prison officials continued to litigate the *Ashker* case. Facing this new legal challenge, prison officials did what they had done for decades: they designed creative workarounds to avoid external oversight. The initial reforms were therefore as preemptive as they were superficial.

First, officials prioritized the *Ashker* class of prisoners for case-by-case reviews of indeterminate SHU status. Rather than reviewing all prisoners being held in the SHU indeterminately, they reviewed only those prisoners who had been there ten years or more. By doing this, they systematically shrank the class of prisoners making up the *Ashker* lawsuit. The class of prisoners bringing the litigation risked becoming a victim of their own re-form efforts; their lawsuit might be dismissed before new policy could be legally established to protect future prisoners from long SHU placements.

Second, in the fall of 2014, prison officials began moving some prisoners who had been in the Pelican Bay SHU for more than ten years to other SHUs around the state. Kijana Askari, for instance, whose description of leaving the SHU for the first time in twenty years appeared in Chapter 7, was neither revalidated as a gang member nor endorsed for a step-down program. Instead, he was simply transferred to a different SHU, at the California Correctional Institution at Tehachapi. By moving him out of Pel-ican Bay, prison officials removed Askari's status as a member of the class of prisoners in Pelican Bay litigating *Ashker*. In total, prison officials trans-ferred eight of the ten named class members in the Pelican Bay case into other SHUs throughout the state—maneuvers difficult not to characterize as a cynical shell game.

Lawyers from the Center for Constitutional Rights, seeing that their cli-ents were disappearing, quickly filed a motion to include any prisoners transferred out of Pelican Bay to other SHUs in the state in the class of prisoners they represented. Judge Wilken granted the motion in March 2015.[16]

As it turned out, even without Judge Wilken's attention, prison officials could not reconsider, transfer out, or hide every member of the *Ashker* class. The very existence of the SHU depended on the official claim that Todd Ashker and some other high-profile class members were the worst of the worst, too dangerous to step-down or to move out of the SHU. Instead of moving these prisoners, prison officials conducted a public relations campaign to discredit them—through Secretary Beard's frequent public comments and through debriefers' affidavits.

Behind closed doors, officials worked to discredit the claims of the prisoners' lawyers and advocates, too. My own research on Pelican Bay was cited in documents filed in the litigation, and the state attorney general's office subpoenaed all my research pursuant to an article cited in the litigation—including all my research notes about everyone I interviewed, every document I consulted in writing that article, all e-mails concerning the research, and all drafts of the article. The University of California objected to the production of the documents: producing such documents would have had a chilling effect on my own research into prison history and policy, and on any future research too. The attorney general's office did not pursue the matter further, though the lawyers might have simply been waiting to see whether the case would settle or go to trial.

Secretary Beard's comments, debriefers' affidavits, and overbroad subpoenas directed at critics of prison policies failed to buttress the SHU's eroded legitimacy. The litigation continued. In March 2015, in preparation for a trial before Judge Wilken on the constitutionality of long durations of confinement in the SHU, lawyers from the Center for Constitutional Rights submitted ten expert reports documenting in harrowing detail the "impact of prolonged solitary confinement" and "severe physical and psychological harm among California SHU prisoners as a result of their isolation."[17] The affidavits were damning, and prison officials backed off their claims about how dangerous and manipulative each and every SHU prisoner was.

Terry Thornton, the same prison spokesperson who had condemned the hunger strikers in 2011 for their manipulative tactics, admitted in 2015 that the prisoners had legitimate claims. In a news story, she described how prisoners had been placed in the SHU for indeterminate periods based only on the word of confidential informants or on one document, such as a drawing. "Unfortunately, they would just keep somebody in the SHU based on this kind of evidence," she said.[18] The system, according to its own spokesperson, had simply been wrong. Thornton even distanced herself from the old policy: the department she called "we" in 2011 had become "they" by 2015. Still, she could not help adding: "We have an obligation to manage these gangs."

Meanwhile, prison officials continued transferring *Ashker* class members out of the SHU and into other isolation units throughout the state or into step-down programs designed to reintegrate them into the general prison population. One of these prisoners was Hugo Pinell, the last of George Jackson's alleged co-conspirators left in the SHU. Pinell had spent twenty years in isolation in California before Pelican Bay ever opened, and he spent twenty-five more years in isolation at Pelican Bay. Sometime in 2015, he was moved to California State Prison, Sacramento, where he remained in isolation. Then, on July 29, prison officials moved Pinell into the general prison population.

To prison officials, Pinell would have seemed like the perfect test case for California's experiment with reforming solitary confinement—an experiment the hunger strikers had forced prison officials to undertake. Pinell was the prisoner in California who had been in isolation the longest, so his move into the general prison population would please reformers or at least mollify some of their complaints about excessive terms of isolation. Pinell was seventy-one years old, so he seemed unlikely to pose a serious threat to any prison guard. But he was infamous among California prisoners, so he seemed likely to attract attention from, as well as to be threatened and controlled by, fellow prisoners from rival gangs. If Pinell were to be injured or killed, that would bolster prison officials' claims that prisoners like Pinell were dangerous to prison order and belonged in isolation after all.

Within two weeks of his transfer into the general prison population, Pinell was stabbed to death by two prisoners. This is the moment that Steve Nolen recalled hearing about on the radio—the moment that snapped him back to the California prison violence of the 1970s, before his own brother was shot by guards.

Pinell's death foreshadows just how difficult solitary reform will be, at individual and institutional levels. Prisoners like Pinell, who have spent decades in isolation, are likely to suffer from at least some mental health problems—anxiety, depression, even hallucinations—and to face challenges adjusting to life in the general prison population, much as Ray and Ernie faced when they left the SHU. And prison officials have few incentives to protect such prisoners. In their own version of Asimov's laws of robotics, officials want to minimize injuries to guards first and to prisoners second. And they want to maximize their repository of tools with which to keep prisons both safe and silent—and full. These goals are fundamentally at odds with humanitarian reforms. The more that corrections officials can demonstrate that some prisoners are uncontrollably dangerous, and the more that long-term solitary confinement is hidden away deep within the prison system, the more readily officials can maintain discretion over prisoners' day-to-day conditions of existence.

Nonetheless, on September 1, 2015, prison officials and prisoners agreed to settle *Ashker v. Brown*. The thirty-three-page agreement prohibited the assignment of prisoners to the SHU based solely on their status as gang members, capped all stays in the SHU at five years, made the provisions retroactive, and required prison officials to provide prisoners' lawyers monthly data reports for two years about the characteristics of the SHU population.[19]

The settlement attracted national attention, and celebration. Since September 2015, other state prison systems, including those in Arizona, Illinois, Nebraska, New York, Ohio, and Wisconsin, have implemented similar reforms, through some combination of legal settlements and legislative initiatives.[20] Settlement agreements and legislative initiatives, however, may not result in the actual reform of prisoners' conditions of confinement, as the history of isolation policies in California has revealed again and again. However limited Judge Henderson's *Madrid* opinion was in its assessments of the constitutionality of the supermax, the *Ashker* settlement is even more limited, since settlements do not create legal precedents that bind future decisions.

And no settlement, nor any legislative initiative, will cure prison officials of the fear they experience daily in managing mentally ill prisoners, negotiating hunger strikes, and fighting the memory of George Jackson. The resistance of both high-level prison officials and frontline prison guards at every step of the recent reform efforts in California suggests that these fears are alive and well, awaiting acknowledgment. As a spokesperson for the California prison guards' union said on the day after the *Ashker* settlement was announced: "The union was disappointed that 'the practitioners who are actually doing the work are just now seeing the settlement.'"[21]

In 2015, however, concerned parties—I, for one—finally were able to form a good idea of who was in the Pelican Bay SHU, and why. The *Ashker* settlement promised to monitor this information carefully for at least two more years. But what about prisoners like Hugo Pinell, Kijana Askari, and the thousands of others being transferred out of the SHU into other, as-yet-unknown isolation units or into general prison populations? What will happen to them, and who will know?

Three factors forged the supermax: fear of uncontrollably violent prisoners, lack of transparency, and bureaucratic discretion. The resulting windowless concrete-and-steel bunkers, as opaque as the process that made them, will not be easily unmade or depopulated.

Reconsidering the Supermax

California is not alone in reconsidering its practice of isolating thousands of prisoners for thousands of days. Public condemnation has forced prison officials, first, to defend the necessity of long-term solitary confinement and, second, to reduce reliance on this practice—or at least to appear to do so.

A recent report by the Vera Institute of Justice, a leading criminal justice policy think tank, identified many of the misconceptions about modern solitary confinement. The authors found that supermaxes across the United States share many of the defects of those in California: they isolate non-violent prisoners, they are used for extended sentences, they have well-documented harmful effects, they boast no real evidence of providing safety or deterrence, and they release prisoners directly from segregation to the streets.[22] The myth that thousands of the "worst of the worst" prisoners exist today, or ever existed, also continues to crumble, eroded by stories like Ernie's and Johnny's, and battered by the growing evidence in the *Ashker* litigation that prison officials have never been able to consistently identify gang leaders or truly isolate them.

Across the United States, the SHU-legitimizing legends about George Jackson and Attica, gang wars and monsters, finally face sustained attack. A few departments of corrections are even preempting legal and legislative interventions, proactively adopting isolation-reduction policies from within: Colorado, New Mexico, Maine, Mississippi, and Washington.[23]

Illinois closed its supermax, Tamms Correctional Center, in 2013 when the governor simply eliminated the facility's funding from the state budget.

Opened in 1998, the prison never operated at more than about 50 percent
of capacity. Close to 200 prisoners from Tamms were moved into other,
theoretically less restrictive facilities across the state.[24] The U.S. Department of Justice issued a report condemning isolation policies throughout
Pennsylvania's state prisons in 2013, especially criticizing the placement
of seriously mentally ill prisoners in isolation and ordering substantial reforms.[25] The New York Civil Liberties Union brought a class action lawsuit
in 2013, *Peoples v. Fischer,* challenging the state's overuse of solitary confinement and alleging that New York placed minors, pregnant women, de-
velopmentally disabled people, and people with serious mental illness in
isolation for average terms of 150 days. The lead plaintiff, LeRoy Peoples,
served more than two years in isolation for "filing false legal documents," a
nonviolent offense. In 2014, state officials agreed to reform the state's isolation practices and promised to remove all individuals under eighteen, all
pregnant women, and all intellectually disabled prisoners from isolation.[26]
New York City's Rikers Island jail implemented similar reforms in 2015.[27]
The Rikers reforms were motivated in part by Kalief Browder, who was
arrested at sixteen and spent two years in isolation in Rikers before being
released with all charges against him dropped. Six months later, he committed suicide.[28]

As of 2015, twelve state legislatures had bills pending to mandate reforms in the use of segregation and isolation.[29] Dozens of states have faced
pressure from prisoners organizing inside, from litigation, from legislators questioning the costs and benefits of supermaxes, and from journalists and human rights advocates condemning the inhumanity of solitary
confinement.

But few reformers argue for abolition of the SHU. Most litigation and
proposed legislation would impose limits on who can be placed there.[30]
Even the U.N. special rapporteur on torture, who has called long-term solitary confinement torture, advocates restrictions—on the means of placement, on the duration of confinement, on the conditions in which prisoners
are kept—but not abolition.[31] Are all these reforms just further refinements
of a fundamentally flawed institution?

I worry that all the prisoners in isolation who are not mentally ill, under
eighteen, or pregnant will be left never to feel a human touch again—even

the ones with no history of violence. At worst, the reforms might represent a superficial shuffling rather than actual reductions in the scale and duration of solitary confinement in U.S. prisons. For instance, although California removed nearly 1,000 prisoners from its SHUs in 2013 and 2014, the state's overall SHU population fell by only a few hundred, from 3,923 in October 2012 to 3,654 in April 2015.[32] SHU beds seemed to be filling almost as fast as they were emptying out. Prison crowding often seems to be as significant a driver of isolation use as prison violence.[33]

In other states that have attempted to reduce reliance on solitary confinement, the problems have been shifted, but have not necessarily been reduced. Famously, for instance, after Mississippi closed a 1,000-bed supermax unit in 2007, all measures of violence within that prison facility fell significantly.[34] But in 2013, a local civil rights organization filed a lawsuit alleging that a new private prison in Mississippi was again isolating mentally ill prisoners in a facility described as a "cesspool."[35] In Illinois, the prisoners from the closed Tamms supermax, transferred into older isolation units in the state, found little amelioration in the restrictive conditions of their new-old confinement.[36]

So far, reforms have failed to confront the fundamental principle underlying the SHU: the assumption that such maximally restrictive institutions are either necessary or useful. The isolation of any subset of allegedly dangerous prisoners, in excessively restrictive and fundamentally invisible institutions, enables a special zone of bureaucratic discretion that is not only hard to see but also impossible to regulate. Real reform must question sweeping claims about dangerous prisoners and render concrete walls transparent—making democratic oversight possible again. When that happens, people might decide whether we ever wanted, or needed, these institutions in the first place.

Afterword

WE LEFT JOHNNY IN CHAPTER 6, WAITING fourteen days for the resentencing decision that might add the possibility of parole to his juvenile murder conviction. I returned to court with Johnny's sister two weeks after the first phase of his sentencing hearing. Johnny spent another three hours answering questions from his attorney, the prosecutor, and the judge about his crime, his prison disciplinary history, his gang tattoos, his knowledge of the Aryan Brotherhood, and life in the SHU. The judge talked to him like the recalcitrant sixteen-year-old he had been when he murdered a fourteen-year-old boy two decades earlier.

The judge homed in on Johnny's tattoos: "The department will help you remove tattoos that identify you as a prison gang member . . . So you could get those swastikas taken off of you . . . And it is painful, but you know you can take tattoos off, right? . . . You ever seen a prison gang force an inmate to take off a tattoo? . . . You have never chosen to do that either, have you?"

Johnny replied, "No, sir. I will, though. I will have these tattoos removed when given the opportunity." Johnny explained that actually, he had formally requested tattoo removal, but the prison system does not provide that service.

Then the judge turned to Johnny's refusal to debrief: "You would rather stay affiliated with the Aryan Brotherhood, leave on the white power ink, and live in the SHU rather than take the chance by debriefing." The judge sounded angry, almost obsessed with those tattoos.

I started imagining how someone in the SHU would remove his own tattoos: a shank made for scraping, not stabbing? Somehow heating contraband metal and then burning them off? I wondered whether the judge knew how common self-injury is in the SHU. There was a prisoner in Illinois who cut his own testicles off.[1] And did he know the history of Vaughn Dortch? Perhaps it was not farfetched to expect Johnny to remove his own tattoos. But I shuddered. This line of questioning showed no belief that Johnny might no longer be the sixteen-year-old kid who murdered his friend, the eighteen-year-old kid who got a few conspicuous white power tattoos when he arrived in a high-security prison, the twenty-two-year-old kid who stabbed his cellmate when he feared for his life.

The questions droned on, and the clock ticked slowly toward four. Was the judge going to make a decision that afternoon? The judge began questioning the lawyers about the intricacies of how the Supreme Court's ruling in *Miller*, and California's new law implementing that ruling, affected Johnny's petition. Could Johnny have waited to file his petition seeking a resentencing? Could he petition the court again in a few years for a resentencing (reading between the lines: after he removed his white power tattoos)?

Each answer was a simple no. Since 1996, strict rules in the United States have required prisoners to file "writs"—petitions to have their punishments reconsidered—within one year of discovering new evidence, such as a change in the law that might retroactively affect the petitioner. "Successive writs" that raise the same legal issues are strictly barred.[2] Certainly, Johnny's judge knew this. He was just looking for an excuse to postpone a decision about resentencing Johnny. But if he let Johnny's life-without-parole sentence stand, that was it. Johnny would go back to the SHU and would never again have any hope of leaving prison.

I was not brazen enough to verbalize it, but I had been hoping that the judge might release Johnny with time served (nineteen years). Johnny had a perfect disciplinary record in eight years in the SHU and sixteen months in the local jail; he had demonstrated resilience through years of hopeless isolation; he accepted responsibility for all the wrong he had done; he was dedicated to education and committed to family; he had applied and been accepted into a reentry program in a well-respected halfway house; and his petition for resentencing had come with twenty-two letters of support from lawyers, academics, mentors, and friends. Ernie's judge had let Ernie go with time served upon reconsideration of the three-strikes sentence. And Ernie was in his forties when he earned his third strike—unlike Johnny, old enough to know better.

By the end of the second day of Johnny's resentencing hearing, I was sure that he was not getting out of prison anytime soon. I was just hoping that this judge would reduce his sentence to anything less than life without parole, any term of years that would give Johnny some hope.

The judge said he wanted to sleep on it; he asked the lawyers to come back at nine the next morning to hear his decision. I really had no idea what he would decide. I worried he would not see beyond Johnny's white power tattoos, beyond the victim's mother's statement that she would feel better if Johnny stayed in prison forever. I wanted to be there with Johnny's sister the next morning to hear the decision.

But my grandfather had died the night before. I was driving straight from the courtroom to the airport, to fly to his burial. I hugged Johnny's sister good-bye and asked her to call me as soon as she had news.

I slept badly that night, waking up anxiously, missing my grandfather one minute, worrying about Johnny's sister the next, wishing I had called my grandfather the day before, thinking about Johnny returning to the SHU in a few days. I had a vague and continual nightmare: I was locked in some kind of container—a casket, an MRI machine, a cell, I wasn't really sure—and I did not know why I was there, but I was consumed by the fear that I would never escape.

The next morning I stood at my grandfather's graveside and watched as the simple wooden casket was lowered into the ground. I cried for Grandpa Bernie—selfish tears, because I had loved him and I would miss him, because he was my last grandparent to die, and the last of his siblings to die. Throwing dirt onto his grave, we buried an entire generation, silenced the stories of crossing borders and oceans from Russia to the United States, of factory work and deli work and never finishing high school but raising three kids with five graduate degrees among them.

As I was driving to the synagogue for the memorial, Johnny's sister's text came in: "I've decided texting is more appropriate." (She knew that I was burying my grandfather). "25 years to life on the murder. 10 years for the enhancement to run consecutive. Specific recommendation for parole not to consider until 35 years."

I could taste the bittersweet. Johnny had been given some little bit of hope to hold on to. This relief mingled with my relief for my grandfather, too, who had lived ninety-four years and died without much suffering. And even if Johnny never left prison, maybe he would at least get out of the SHU. Under the 2013 reforms to the gang validation policy, Johnny is eligible for a file review, to be considered for return to the general prison population. If he had not spent those sixteen months in jail awaiting his resentencing hearing, his case probably would have been reviewed already. And if the California prison system really starts requiring that SHU terms be based on specific disciplinary infractions, there will be no justification for keeping Johnny in the SHU. Maybe he will be able to hug his sister again.

It will be fifteen years before Johnny is eligible for a parole hearing under the terms of the judge's resentencing.[3] He has already served nearly twenty, so he is more than halfway there. He will be fifty-one. But a parole hearing is no guarantee of release.

Still, I hope I will someday be able to invite Johnny to lecture to my classes in person about his experiences with the U.S. prison system. Maybe courts will keep rolling back long sentences; maybe Johnny will be able to petition the parole board for a hearing sooner. Either way, he has hope now. And his case set a good precedent—if a validated Aryan Brotherhood associate deserves a second chance, maybe the prison system got his validation wrong. Maybe other people deserve a second chance, too. Johnny's resentencing will inspire the more than 130 other prisoners in the Pelican Bay Security Housing Unit sentenced to life without parole for crimes they committed as juveniles.[4]

To me, Johnny's case is a triumph. But perhaps that, too, is a tragedy.

NOTES

Introduction. When Prison Is Not Enough

1. "Hugo 'Yogi' Pinell," *Hard Knock Radio*.
2. Steve Nolen, personal interview.
3. Associated Press, "2 suspects charged in slaying of San Quentin 6 inmate."
4. *In the Matter of the Life Term Parole Consideration Hearing of Hugo Pinell*, CDC Number: A 88401, 80.
5. St. John, "Prison Investigators Name Two Suspects in Killing of Hugo Pinell."
6. St. John, "Slain Inmate Hugo Pinell Was a Target of Prison Gangs, His Lawyer Says."
7. For a discussion of prison building in California specifically, see Gilmore, *Golden Gulag*. For a discussion of increasing incarceration rates across the United States in the 1980s, see Zimring and Hawkins, *The Scale of Imprisonment*.
8. Zimring, "The Scale of Imprisonment in the United States," 1228; Reiter, "Parole, Snitch, or Die," 534.
9. For discussions of the idea of penal populism, especially in the late twentieth century, see, for example, Murakawa, *The First Civil Right*; Barker, *The Politics of Imprisonment*; Page, *The Toughest Beat*.
10. Dickens, "Philadelphia and Its Solitary Prison"; *In re Medley*, 134 U.S. 160, 168 (1890); Beaumont and Tocqueville, *On the Penitentiary System in the United States and Its Application to France*, 41.
11. Nolen interview. See also Berger, *Captive Nation*.
12. Reiter, "Parole, Snitch, or Die," 530–63.
13. Meranze, *Laboratories of Virtue*; Rubin, "A Neo-Institutional Account of Prison Diffusion," 379.
14. See *San Francisco Chronicle*, "Former Inmate at Pelican Bay Wins Judgment Against State"; *Madrid v. Gomez*, 889 F. Supp. 1146, 1168, 1213.

15. See Reiter, "The Most Restrictive Alternative," 69–123. In more general, legal endogeneity terms, courts impose legal norms on organizations, which organizations interpret in ways that suit their own interests; courts, in turn, "recognize and legitimate" these organizational interpretations; see Edelman, Uggen, and Erlanger, "The Endogeneity of Legal Regulation."

16. See United Nations General Assembly, *Convention Against Torture, Cruel, Inhuman and Degrading Treatment or Punishment*, art. 16 (identifying solitary confinement inflicted for retributive, or punitive, purposes as a practice of torture, in violation of the treaty); Casella and Ridgeway, "UN Torture Investigator Calls on Nations to End Solitary Confinement."

17. Arendt, *Eichmann in Jerusalem*.

18. For an introduction to the concept of path dependence, see Pierson, "Increasing Returns, Path Dependence, and the Study of Politics." Pierson explains how policy decisions often produce increasing returns over time, thereby rendering alternative policy choices less lucrative or viable as time goes on.

19. Scholars have recently paid increasing attention to the local nature of criminal justice policies and innovations, challenging the assumption that harsh punishments and the broader system of mass incarceration in which these punishments take place can be understood as national phenomena; see, for example, Barker, *The Politics of Imprisonment;* Campbell, "Politics, Prisons, and Law Enforcement"; Gilmore, *Golden Gulag;* Lynch, *Sunbelt Justice;* Page, *The Toughest Beat;* Schoenfeld, "Mass Incarceration and the Paradox of Prison Conditions Litigation."

20. Bagehot, *The English Constitution;* for a description of how double governments operate in the national security context, see Glennon, *National Security and Double Government.*

21. See Foucault, *Discipline and Punish.*

22. Merton, "The Unanticipated Consequences of Purposive Social Action"; Schlanger, "No Reason to Blame Liberals."

23. See Wacquant, *The Place of the Prison in the New Government;* Gilmore, *Golden Gulag;* Garland, *Culture of Control;* Simon, *Governing Through Crime.*

24. *Davis v. Ayala*, 576 U.S. __, J. Kennedy, concurring, at 5.

25. *Ashker v. Brown*, Case No. 4:09-cv-05796-CW, "Settlement Agreement."

26. *Davis v. Ayala*, 576 U.S. __, J. Kennedy, concurring, at 5 (citing F. Shapiro, *The Yale Book of Quotations*, 210).

Chapter 1. A Supermax Life

1. St. John, "Prison Hunger Strike Leaders Are in Solitary but Not Alone."

2. California Department of Corrections and Rehabilitation, "Sec. 54030.20: High Security and Transitional Housing," *Department Operation Manual*, 486–92.

3. "Rashid" (pseudonym, former supermax prisoner), personal telephone interview. I use pseudonyms for all former prisoners I interviewed. These interviews were recorded and transcribed, so quotations are verbatim. For other current and for-

mer prisoners, such as Todd Ashker, whom I describe with reference to public documents, I use their real names.

4. O'Hearn, "My Friend Todd Ashker."

5. Corradini, Huskey, and Fujio, *Buried Alive.*

6. Morain, "The Real Story Behind Hunger Strike"; Newcomb, "California Prison Hunger Strike Leader Is Convicted Murderer with Alleged Aryan Brotherhood Ties."

7. Wallace-Wells, "The Plot from Solitary."

8. *Ashker v. Schwarzenegger,* "Exhibit UU: *In the matter of the Life Term Parole Consideration Hearing of Todd Ashker,"* 16–17.

9. St. John, "Prison Hunger Strike Leaders."

10. Grann, "The Brand," 156–71.

11. *Ashker v. Schwarzenegger,* "Exhibit UU: *In the matter of the Life Term Parole Consideration Hearing of Todd Ashker,"* 17, and "Exhibit UU: *People v. Ashker.*"

12. See especially *Wright v. Enomoto,* 462 F. Supp. at 399; *Toussaint v. McCarthy,* 801 F.2d at 1106–12. The Pelican Bay SHU represented a superficially compliant institution, in which prison officials reinterpreted the minimum standards that courts set out in *Wright* and *Toussaint* as maximum privileges.

13. *Ashker v. Schwarzenegger,* "Exhibit UU: *People v. Ashker*"; St. John, "Prison Hunger Strike Leaders"; Vargas, "Jury Convicts Folsom Inmate of Prison Murder"; Vargas, "Stabbed Lawyer Ordered to Keep Defending Inmate."

14. Grann, "The Brand"; Skarbeck, *The Social Order of the Underworld.*

15. This reconstruction of the events of May 1987 is drawn entirely from court documents and news reports. The facts presented here are not disputed in these documents, unless otherwise noted; see *Ashker v. Schwarzenegger,* "Exhibit UU: *People v. Ashker*"; St. John, "Prison Hunger Strike Leaders"; Vargas, "Jury Convicts Folsom Inmate"; Vargas, "Stabbed Lawyer."

16. *Ashker v. Schwarzenegger,* "Request for Admissions Set. No. 1," para. 170.

17. Violence rates are discussed further in chapters 2 and 3; see also Reiter, "Supermax Administration and the Eighth Amendment."

18. *Ashker v. Schwarzenegger,* "First Amended Complaint with Supplemental State Law Claims," para. 34.

19. California Code of Regulations, Title 15, Division 3, Chapter 1.4, Article 10, 3378(c)(3) (2014). Between 2013 and 2015, the state made numerous changes to this "independent source item" rule, as discussed in greater detail in the final chapters.

20. The vast majority of prisoners in supermaxes in California are men; the state has just under fifty supermax cells for women, compared to more than three thousand allocated for men; see Reiter, "Parole, Snitch, or Die." Gang-validated women are especially rare in California. Therefore, I typically use male pronouns to refer to supermax prisoners.

21. The process described here uses current California Department of Corrections and Rehabilitation terminology. The validation process Todd underwent in the

1980s would have been practically similar, but some of the officials and commit-
tees would have had different names.

22. California Department of Corrections and Rehabilitation, "Fact Sheet: Security
Threat Group Prevention, Identification and Management Strategy," 2; Law, " 'We
Are Not the Worst of the Worst.' "

23. Center for Constitutional Rights, "Summary of *Ashker v. Governor of California*
Settlement Terms."

24. *Ashker v. Schwarzenegger,* "Opinion: Order Granting, in Part, and Denying, in Part,
Defendants Motion for Summary Judgment," 10.

25. *Ashker v. Schwarzenegger,* "Request for Admissions, Set. No. 1," para. 132.

26. *Ashker v. Schwarzenegger,* "Exhibit UU: *People v. Ashker*"; St. John, "Prison Hunger
Strike Leaders"; Vargas, "Jury Convicts Folsom Inmate"; Vargas, "Stabbed
Lawyer."

27. Grann, "The Brand," 156–71.

28. *Ashker v. Schwarzenegger,* "Exhibit UU: *People v. Ashker*" and "First Amended
Complaint with Supplemental State Law Claims."

29. When Ashker was ultimately convicted of second-degree murder, Cozens told
the press this was a "moral victory" won after he "convinced the jury to knock the
charged crime down to second-degree murder"; see W. Wilson, "Prison Killer
Gets 21-Years-to-Life Term."

30. Vargas and Wilson, "Defense Lawyer Stabbed by Witness in Inmate's Trial."

31. Ibid.

32. See Grann, "The Brand."

33. See Vargas, "Stabbed Lawyer."

34. W. Wilson, "Prison Killer Gets 21-Years-to-Life Term."

35. Newcomb, "California Prison Hunger Strike Leader"; see also Morain, "The Real
Story Behind Hunger Strike"; Cozens, "Law Office of Philip Cozens."

36. Vargas, "Stabbed Lawyer."

37. *Ashker v. Schwarzenegger,* "Request for Admissions, Set. No. 1," para. 94.

38. Corwin, "High-Tech Facility Ushers in New Era of State Prisons"; Griffith, "New
Border Prison Spurs Concerns."

39. *Ashker v. Schwarzenegger,* "First Amended Complaint with Supplemental State
Law Claims," para. 32; St. John, "Prison Hunger Strike Leaders."

40. In 1986, Del Norte County had a 25 percent unemployment rate, and the median
income was 57 out of 58, in rank order of the state's counties. Assembly Comments to Senate Bill 1222, June 30, 1986. As of 2012, Del Norte County still had
one of the highest poverty rates in California, according to the Public Policy Institute of California; see its "California Poverty Rates by County."

41. Max, personal interview.

42. Barry, personal interview.

43. Steve Cambra, personal interview. Unless otherwise noted, prison officials, experts, and other nonprisoner interview subjects are identified by their full names.

44. *Madrid v. Gomez,* 899 F. Supp at 1168–69.

45. Ibid., 1165.
46. Heller, "They Shoot Prisoners, Don't They?"
47. *San Francisco Chronicle*, "Former Inmate at Pelican Bay."
48. Smearing, throwing, or eating excrement, whether as a signal of despair or as a tool of manipulation, is associated with long-term solitary confinement. For instance, all twenty-eight "gassing" incidents—when "inmates throw a mixture of urine and feces in officers' faces"—documented in the California Department of Corrections in 1998 and 1999 took place in supermax units (Shalev, *Supermax*, 73). Another scholar of supermax confinement, the anthropologist Lorna Rhodes, notes that in supermaxes, throwing is "chronic, involving prisoners and their keepers in a persistent round of dirtying and cleaning and keeping everyone engaged in this aversive corporeal 'conversation'" (Rhodes, *Total Confinement*, 48); see also Rosenberg, "Waste Wars."
49. While the evidence about Dortch strongly suggests that he was mentally ill, other prisoners have used excrement as a means of control and resistance. For instance, Feldman describes the dirty protests that Northern Irish prisoners (from the Irish Republican Army) engaged in to protest their restrictive conditions of confinement in the 1970s (Feldman, *Formations of State Violence*, 147–217). A report in the *Miami Herald* described a more recent instance of a prisoner using excrement to control his environment—this time in the supermax wing of the U.S. military prison at Guantánamo Bay, Cuba: "The gut-wrenching odor of excrement has for weeks wafted through the air vents of Camp 5, the Pentagon's state of-the-art, 100-cell maximum-security prison, according to smell-witnesses. It amounts to a kind of collective punishment that assaults the senses of compliant captives and captors alike" (Rosenberg, "Waste Wars").
50. *Madrid v. Gomez*, 889 F. Supp. at 1168, 1213.
51. *Ashker v. California Department of Corrections*, 112 F.3d at 393.
52. *Ashker v. Schwarzenegger*, "Exhibit UU: In the matter of the Life Term Parole Consideration," p. 22.
53. *Ashker v. California Department of Corrections*, 112 F.3d at 393.
54. *Ashker v. Cate*, No. 09-2948-CW, 2012 U.S. Dist. LEXIS 45575.
55. Wallace-Wells, "The Plot from Solitary."
56. *Madrid v. Gomez*, 889 F. Supp. at 1168, 1213; Thelton Henderson, personal interview. This case is discussed in much greater detail in Chapter 5.
57. Max, personal interview.
58. See Pina, "Pelican Bay (shu) Photograph, Canteen List and Menu." In other isolation units elsewhere in the United States, the menu is nonexistent. In 2015, the State of New York settled a lawsuit challenging the harsh conditions of confinement in the state's isolation units and promised to stop feeding prisoners in solitary confinement the "disciplinary loaf"—"a misshapen one-pound brick of cuisine" (McKinley, "New York Prisons Take an Unsavory Punishment off the Table").
59. See, for example, Frontline, *Solitary Nation*.

60. In this way, the prisoners resemble what Foucault describes as a "disciplinary subject"—someone who internalizes prison rules and procedures and who has minimal physical contact with the punisher (Foucault, *Discipline and Punish*, 130–31). I have argued elsewhere, however, that supermaxes produce a new kind of "administrative subject," one more thoroughly excluded from society than Foucault's disciplinary subject; see Reiter and Coutin, "Crossing Borders and Criminalizing Identity."

61. Prisoners advocated to be permitted to use colored pastels, and since 2012, these have been on the list of things that Pelican Bay SHU prisoners may purchase from the canteen.

62. Johnny to author, Sept. 25, 2012.

63. See generally Grassian, "Psychiatric Effects of Solitary Confinement"; Haney, "Mental Health Issues in Long-Term Solitary and 'Supermax' Confinement."

64. Ray, personal interview.

65. *Ashker v. Schwarzenegger*, "Declaration of Todd Ashker in Support of Plaintiffs' Motion for Class Certification."

66. Ibid., 5 and Exhibit B.

67. Max, personal interview. Max did not mention either prisoner being punished for this surreptitious moment of contact. To punish them, prison officials would have needed to explain why two cell doors were open at once.

68. St. John, "Prison Hunger Strike Leaders."

69. Max, personal interview.

70. *Ashker v. Schwarzenegger*, "Declaration of Todd Ashker," para. 26.

71. Wallace-Wells, "The Plot from Solitary."

72. Small, "Under Scrutiny, Pelican Bay Prison Officials Say They Target Only Gang Leaders"; Reiter, "Parole, Snitch, or Die."

73. Naday, Freilich, and Mellow, "The Elusive Data on Supermax Confinement," 77.

74. U.S. Department of Justice, National Institute of Corrections, *Supermax Prisons*, by Chase Riveland (hereafter cited as Riveland, *Supermax Prisons*).

75. See generally Gilmore, *Golden Gulag*; Zimring and Hawkins, *The Scale of Imprisonment*.

76. See, for example, Dayan, "Barbarous Confinement"; *Los Angeles Times*, "California's Hidden Hunger Strike"; Fagan, "Most State Prison Hunger Strikers Are Eating Again"; Van Zuylen-Wood, "Pelican Bay Redux."

77. Ashker and Troxell, "Final Notice: PBSP SHU D-Corridor Hunger Strike."

78. See Beard, "Hunger Strike in California Prisons Is a Gang Power Play."

79. See Naday, Freilich, and Mellow, "The Elusive Data on Supermax Confinement"; Reiter, "Parole, Snitch, or Die."

80. See Baumgartel et al., *Time-In-Cell*, and U.S. Department of Justice, Office of Justice Programs, Bureau of Justice Statistics, *Use of Restrictive Housing in U.S. Prisons and Jails, 2011–12*, by Alan J. Beck (hereafter cited as Beck, *Use of Restrictive Housing*). In particular, the *Time-In-Cell* report noted the severe limitations of data collected through voluntary, institutional self-reports from jurisdictions with

widely variable laws and definitions of what constitutes solitary confinement in the first place.

81. Beck, *Use of Restrictive Housing*, 1. The *Time-In-Cell* report found that of forty-one state and federal jurisdictions reporting, 32,000 prisoners were in "administrative segregation"—the kind of indefinite isolation for safety and security (rather than disciplinary) reasons that Todd Ashker experiences, and twice as many prisoners were in some form of isolated confinement—administrative, disciplinary, or other.

82. Baumgartel et al., *Time-In-Cell*, 27; Reiter, "Parole, Snitch, or Die," 548.

83. In *Caught* (165–95), the political scientist Marie Gottschalk elaborates on this point about the wide variety of offenders whom the public and politicians perceive as deserving of the harshest sentences and who are encompassed within the "worst of the worst" categorization; at the other end of the political spectrum of punitiveness lies the highly specified category of nonviolent drug offenders (called "non-non-nons"), who are increasingly perceived as deserving of mercy.

Chapter 2. The Most Dangerous Prisoner

1. California Department of Corrections and Rehabilitation, "San Quentin State Prison (SQ)."

2. Prisons, especially in California, are notoriously, rigidly segregated by race, so white and black prisoners working together like this is especially unusual; see generally Goodman, "'It's Just Black, White, or Hispanic.'" For an analysis of how prison education programs can reshape these racialized prison social norms, see Pass, "Race Relations and the Implications of Education Within Prison."

3. A fictional psychiatrist and cannibalistic, archetypally monstrous serial killer created by Thomas Harris, Hannibal Lecter is best known as portrayed by Anthony Hopkins in *Silence of the Lambs*.

4. San Quentin's prison yard serves a general prison population of 2,300 low- to medium-security prisoners, that is, about double the population of the average public high school in California. The main population at San Quentin is composed of prisoners serving relatively short sentences for relatively minor crimes, along with prisoners serving long sentences for more violent crimes who have had such good behavior in prison that they have earned their way into a lower security level. San Quentin also houses the Northern California Reception Center, with room for close to 1,000 prisoners who are new to the California state prison system and awaiting sorting and assignment to more permanent placements. See California Department of Corrections, *Average Daily Prison Population: Fiscal Year 2012/13*; for data about in-prison deaths, see California Department of Corrections, *Inmate Incidents in Institutions, Calendar Year 1988* and *Calendar Year 2006*.

5. Cummins, *The Rise and Fall of California's Radical Prison Movement*, 155; E. Mann, *Comrade George*, 21. For other sources on Jackson's life and thought, see Arm-

strong, *The Dragon Has Come;* Berger, *Captive Nation;* Collier and Horowitz, *Destructive Generation;* Durden-Smith, *Who Killed George Jackson?;* D. Rodriguez, *Forced Passages;* Yee, *The Melancholy History of Soledad Prison.*

6. See, for example, Jackson, *Soledad Brother,* "Letter from George Lester Jackson to Robert Lester Jackson, December, 1964," 42–44.

7. See E. Mann, *Comrade George,* 21.

8. Chapter 3 discusses the history of this sentencing system in greater detail.

9. Jackson, *Soledad Brother.* The first letters were from 1964, four years into Jackson's prison bid, when he had already been politicized.

10. E. Mann, *Comrade George,* 22–24.

11. Jackson, *Soledad Brother,* "Letter from George Lester Jackson to Georgia Jackson, January 3, 1967," 98.

12. See E. Mann, *Comrade George.*

13. Cummins, *California's Radical Prison Movement,* 208; Armstrong, *The Dragon Has Come;* E. Mann, *Comrade George.*

14. See McCarty, "Blood In, Blood Out"; Bloom and Martin, *Black Against Empire;* Berger, *Captive Nation,* 224.

15. Jackson, *Soledad Brother,* "Letter from George Lester Jackson to Robert Lester Jackson, April 11, 1968," 167–68, and "Letter from George Lester Jackson to Fay Stender, March 22, 1970," 214–28. Jackson's ideas were in conversation with Mao, Fanon, and anti–Vietnam War activists; see D. Rodriguez, *Forced Passages,* 113–44; Gómez, "Resisting Living Death at Marion Federal Penitentiary, 1972," 64–68.

16. See Reiter, "Reclaiming the Power to Punish" and "Supermax Administration and the Eighth Amendment" for further discussions of these statistics, which were compiled from a variety of California Department of Corrections statistical reports.

17. See generally Chase, "We Are Not Slaves"; Cummins, *California's Radical Prison Movement;* Fitzgerald, *Prisoners in Revolt;* Gómez, "Resisting Living Death"; Losier, " '. . . For Strictly Religious Reason[s]' "; Reiter, "The Most Restrictive Alternative"; Thompson, "Rethinking Working-Class Struggle Through the Lens of the Carceral State"; Thuma, "Against the 'Prison/Psychiatric State.' "

18. Three significant legal changes precipitated and facilitated this steep rise in the number of prisoners' rights claims brought in federal courts. First, federal courts expanded the habeas corpus right to include challenges to conditions of confinement (as well as challenges to terms of sentences) in *Miller v. Overholer* (1953), a Washington, D.C., district court case, and in *Brown v. Allen* (1953), a U.S. Supreme Court case. Second, the Supreme Court incorporated the Eighth Amendment, which prohibits cruel and unusual punishment, against the states, meaning that individual state citizens could seek to enforce their Eighth Amendment right against state actors, whereas previously they had been able to enforce these rights only against federal actors; see *Robinson v. California* (1962). Third, the Supreme Court held in *Cooper v. Pate* (1963) that the Civil Rights Act permitted

prisoners to sue prison officials for civil rights violations experienced in prison. For further discussion of these reforms, see Reiter, "Prisoners' Rights," 1419.

19. Feeley and Rubin, *Judicial Policy Making and the Modern State;* see also *Hutto v. Finney,* 437 U.S. 678. This litigation history is discussed in further detail in Chapter 3.

20. Gordon, "Faith as Liberation: The Nation of Islam and Religion in Prison, 1940–75," in *The Spirit of the Law,* 96–132; see also Losier, "For Strictly Religious Reason[s]."

21. See Grann, "The Brand." The Mexican Mafia was allegedly formed inside Deuel Vocational Institution, in Tracy, California, in the late 1950s, gaining strength through the 1960s; Nuestra Familia formed as a rival gang in the mid-1960s; see Blatchford, *The Black Hand.* See also Skarbek, *Social Order of the Underworld,* 47–72.

22. Bloom and Martin, *Black Against Empire,* 2–3.

23. Blacks, Hispanics, and Others (the main racial categorizations in CDC, with "others" encompassing people of Asian heritage), as well as people of mixed or ambiguous race, made up the difference, accounting for well over half of new prison admissions by 1980; see Reyes, *A Portrait of Race and Ethnicity in California,* 155.

24. Nellis, Greene, and Mauer, *Reducing Racial Disparity in the Criminal Justice System,* 6.

25. This phenomenon has been described as "racialized mass incarceration," and scholars throughout the social sciences have explored the political, economic, and social underpinnings of the racially disparate, and oppressive, effects of mass incarceration; see especially Bobo and Thompson, "Racialized Mass Incarceration." See also Alexander, *The New Jim Crow;* Clear, *Imprisoning Communities;* Goodman, "Race in California's Prison Fire Camps for Men"; Pager, *Marked;* Wacquant, *The Place of the Prison;* Wakefield and Uggen, "Incarceration and Stratification"; Walker, "Race Making in a Penal Institution"; Western, *Punishment and Inequality in America.* Institutions played a significant role in amplifying racial tensions, too, whether through implicitly discriminatory policies like those enacted through indeterminate sentences or through explicit policies of segregating prisoners by race and setting up confrontations between people of different races. See, for example, Goodman, "'It's Just Black, White, or Hispanic,'" and Goodman, "Race in California's Prison Camps." Angela Davis has made an argument explicitly connecting race, mass incarceration, and supermaxes: Davis, "From the Convict Lease System to the Super-Max Prison."

26. Carl Larson, personal interview, Feb. 23, 2010.

27. U.S. Department of Justice, Office of Legal Policy, Federal Justice Research Program, *Prison Gangs,* by Camp and Camp, 93–94; Skarbek, *Social Order of the Underworld,* 53.

28. See generally, Clemmer, *The Prison Community;* Sykes, *The Society of Captives.* See also Wald, "The San Quentin Six Case," 59 (describing "race-baiting" as an ele-

ment of control integral to the operation of California prisons in the 1960s and 1970s); Goodman, "'It's Just Black, White, or Hispanic,'" 740 (revisiting the co-construction of racial categories and prison order in the process of categorizing prisoners by race).

29. Cummins, *California's Radical Prison Movement*, 123, 202, 232.

30. Nolen interview.

31. Ibid.; see also E. Mann, *Comrade George*.

32. Nolen interview.

33. See E. Mann, *Comrade George*.

34. Nolen interview.

35. Yee, *Melancholy History of Soledad Prison*, 57–61; Spiegelman, "Review of *The Melancholy History of Soledad Prison*," 132; Berger, *Captive Nation*, 102.

36. See E. Mann, *Comrade George*.

37. Nolen interview.

38. Ibid.

39. E. Mann, *Comrade George*, 29–30.

40. Steve Nolen told me that a few years later, the family sued Officer Miller for wrongful death and won a $50,000 settlement (Nolen interview).

41. Jackson, *Soledad Brother*, 168.

42. E. Mann, *Comrade George*, 29–30.

43. Mullane, "The Adjustment Center."

44. See E. Mann, *Comrade George*.

45. Ibid., 26.

46. Houston, "Court-Battle Guns Registered in the Name of Angela Davis."

47. E. Mann, *Comrade George*, 41–42.

48. More recently, scholars have noted that one of the jurors was Latino. For more about Davis's life and activism, see Berger, *Captive Nation*, 177–222; Davis, *Angela Davis*.

49. Jackson, *Soledad Brother*, "Letter to Joan, Aug. 9, 1970," 329.

50. Berger notes that Jackson intended *Blood in My Eye* to be a manual for guerrilla warfare, in contrast to the more moderate tone of *Soledad Brother* (*Captive Nation*, 158).

51. The group was substantial relative to Jackson's earlier legal teams, and relative to what most prisoners could expect, but it remained small and divided; see Berger, *Captive Nation*, 91–138; Durden-Smith, *Who Killed George Jackson?*

52. E. Mann, *Comrade George*, 47.

53. Ibid., 68–77.

54. Yee, "San Quentin Probes Smuggling of Gun."

55. Yale University, Class of 1964, "Class News: Stephen Bingham Interviewed by *Marin Magazine*"; Hansen and Stein, "Jury Acquits Bingham in Prison Deaths."

56. Scarborough, *Incident at San Quentin;* Marine, "Exit the Dragon."

57. Carl Larson, telephone interview, July 22, 2013.

58. Cummins, *California's Radical Prison Movement*, 208.

59. Ibid., 209.
60. Ibid. Andrews describes Johnny Spain seeing Jackson with a gun in the Adjustment Center, but provides no reference for this account (Andrews, *Black Power, White Blood*, 158).
61. Cummins, *California's Radical Prison Movement*, 209.
62. E. Mann, *Comrade George*, 85.
63. Berger, *Captive Nation*, 140–41.
64. Park, "Associate Warden's Statement to the Press Concerning the Death of George Jackson."
65. Ibid.
66. Ibid.
67. Schwartz, "The Testimony of Louis E. Tackwood," 6.
68. E. Mann, *Comrade George*; Yee, *Melancholy History of Soledad Prison*.
69. Park, "Associate Warden's Statement."
70. Cummins, *California's Radical Prison Movement*, 209.
71. Foucault, Von Bülow, and Defert, "The Masked Assassination." Four years later, Foucault published the definitive historical and theoretical analysis of modern Western prisons and punishment, later translated as *Discipline and Punish: The Birth of the Prison*.
72. Wald, "San Quentin Six Case," 61–62.
73. In "The Masked Assassination," a November 1971 essay challenging the official account of Jackson's death, Foucault and his coauthors show that national newspapers identified six gun types when describing the model that Jackson pulled from under his wig.
74. Larson telephone interview.
75. *San Francisco Chronicle*, "Pistol and Wig Experiment," Aug. 28, 1971, cited in E. Mann, *Comrade George*. Given the dispute over exactly what kind of gun was used, perhaps a different, smaller gun could have fit in the cassette recorder or in the wig.
76. Cummins, *California's Radical Prison Movement*, 210.
77. Scarborough, *Incident at San Quentin*; Marine, "Exit the Dragon."
78. *Time*, "The Law: The Longest Trial," July 19, 1976.
79. As mentioned in the introduction, Pinell was in isolation for forty-five years in all. At the age of seventy-one, he was released into a general population prison yard and was stabbed a few weeks later, in August 2015. (St. John, "Slain inmate Hugo Pinell").
80. For a discussion of the role of "mythologies, collective representations, and totems" in modern punishment, see especially P. Smith, *Punishment and Culture*, 172. For more general discussions of the role of expression in punishment, see Durkheim, *The Division of Labor in Society*, and Dayan, *The Story of Cruel and Unusual*. In a more concrete sense, prison officials were engaging in what sociological scholars of social movements have called a "contested process" of framing claims—in this case, claims about just punishments and effective prisons—in

response to internal and public challenges; see Benford and Snow, "Framing Processes and Social Movements."

81. Page, *The Toughest Beat*, 25–26.
82. Larson telephone interview.
83. Cambra interview.
84. Craig Brown, personal interview.
85. Reiter, "Supermax Administration and the Eighth Amendment."
86. *Toussaint*, 597 F. Supp. 1388, 1393; see also Berger, *Captive Nation*, 102, 141.
87. Berger, *Captive Nation*, 102; *Toussaint*, 597 F. Supp. 1388, 1393.
88. See California Assembly, Select Committee on Prison Reform and Rehabilitation, *Administrative Segregation in California's Prisons; Spain v. Procunier*, 408 F. Supp. 534, 539–40.
89. Berger, "Two Prisoners Named Williams" and "America's Fortress of Blood." Williams, sentenced to death in 1979 for his role in four murders committed while he was a leader of the Los Angeles–based Crips gang, ultimately renounced his gang membership in prison. He wrote multiple books advocating nonviolence and became an educator. His scheduled execution produced a public outcry.
90. For a growing body of recent literature examining the relationship between constructions of black criminality and systematically oppressive and repressive state policies, see especially Berger, *Captive Nation;* Muhammad, *The Condemnation of Blackness;* Gottschalk, *Caught;* Murakawa, *The First Civil Right;* Haney-Lopez, *Dog Whistle Politics;* Wacquant, "Deadly Symbiosis." Nat Turner is probably at the top of the list of black radicals who inspired oppressive backlashes; see Greenberg, *Nat Turner;* Brundage, "Review of *Nat Turner*"; Gates, "What Were the Earliest Rebellions by African Americans?"
91. *Ashker v. Schwarzenegger*, "Exhibit D."
92. Toobin, "Letter from Baltimore"; also cited in Berger, "America's Fortress of Blood."
93. See generally Feeley and Rubin, *Judicial Policymaking;* Berger, *Captive Nation;* Thompson, "Rethinking Working-Class Struggle," 22–25.
94. Freedom Archives, *Prisons on Fire*. For histories of Attica, see also Thompson, *Blood in the Water;* New York State Commission on Attica, *Attica: The Official Report;* Wicker, *A Time to Die.*
95. Berger, *Captive Nation*, 149.
96. Thompson, "The Lingering Injustice of Attica"; New York State Commission on Attica, *Attica.*
97. Robbins, "A Brutal Beating Wakes Attica's Ghosts."
98. See Thompson, "The Lingering Injustice of Attica"; New York State Commission on Attica, *Attica.*
99. Connolly, "Forty Years Later, Report Details Torture of Inmates During Attica Riot." New York's attorney general released volumes 2 and 3 of the "Meyer Report," which had previously been sealed, on May 21, 2015; see Meyer, "Meyer Report," vols. 2–3.

100. Robbins and D'Avolio, "No Jail Time for Attica Guards."

101. Useem and Kimball, "A Theory of Prison Riots."

102. Laura Sullivan, "Doubts Arise About 1972 Angola Prison Murder."

103. Ibid.; Maza, "LA Prisoner Released After 43 Years in Solitary Confinement"; *Herman's House*, dir. Angad Bhalla.

104. *Kelly v. Brewer*, 378 F. Supp. 447, 449.

105. Bissonnette et al., *When the Prisoners Ran Walpole*, 80–81.

106. See Guenther, *Solitary Confinement*, chap. 4; Leiderman, "Man Alone"; Mitford, *Kind and Usual Punishment*, 134–35; Schein, "Man Against Man." CARE and the importation of military brainwashing techniques into federal prisons are discussed further in Chapter 7.

107. *Adams v. Carlson*, 352 F. Supp. 882; Fitzgerald, *Control Units and the Shape of Things to Come*; Ward and Breed, *The United States Penitentiary, Marion, Illinois*.

108. U.S. Department of Justice, Federal Bureau of Prisons, "Merle E. Clutts" and "Robert L. Hoffman"; *Silverstein v. Bureau of Prisons*, 704 F. Supp. 2d 1077. Clayton Fountain, who murdered Officer Robert Hoffman, died in prison in 2004.

109. Ward and Werlich, "Alcatraz and Marion," 57–58. For a discussion of how this process was politically reactive in much the way the lockdowns in California were, see Gómez, "Resisting Living Death at Marion."

110. Prendergast, "The Caged Life." In the 2010s, Tommy Silverstein brought a case alleging that spending more than thirty years in solitary confinement constituted cruel and unusual punishment. The federal district court in Colorado ultimately dismissed the case, and the Tenth Circuit Court of Appeals affirmed the dismissal; see *Silverstein v. Federal Bureau of Prisons*, No. 12-1450, D. Ct. No. 1:07-CV-02471-PAB-KMT.

111. Thompson, "Rethinking Working-Class Struggle," 22–25.

112. *Chicago Tribune*, "Riot Squad Quashes Iowa Prison Uprising."

113. KOAT (Albuquerque), "Riot Survivors Tour Old Santa Fe Penitentiary."

114. Associated Press, "Chronology of 1993 Lucasville Prison Riot."

115. Useem and Kimball, *States of Siege*, 3.

116. Critics and scholars disagree about exactly how many supermaxes exist in the United States, but for attempts to define and count the institutions, see Casella and Ridgeway, "How Many Prisoners Are in Solitary Confinement in the United States?"; Naday, Freilich, and Mellow, "Elusive Data on Supermax Confinement"; Baumgartel et al., *Time-In-Cell*; Riveland, *Supermax Prisons*.

117. Giorgio Agamben popularized the idea of a "state of exception," first defined by Carl Schmitt as the "unlimited authority" of a sovereign to suspend "the entire existing order" by declaring a "state of emergency"; see Agamben, *State of Exception*; Schmitt, *Political Theology*, 12. The supermax ultimately represented just such a space of suspended law, justified by the existence of imminently dangerous circumstances. The analogy of a Schmittian state of exception is imprecise, however, in that prison officials did not have the sovereign authority to declare a national state of emergency, nor was such a state ever formally declared.

Chapter 3. The Most Dangerous Policies

1. California Assembly, *Administrative Segregation in California's Prisons*, 5.
2. Ibid., 6–13.
3. *Plata v. Brown*, Case No. C01-1351-THE, "Joint Request for Order Authorizing Re-Feeding."
4. For a detailed analysis of the hunger strike timeline and negotiations, see Reiter, "The Pelican Bay Hunger Strike." A number of theorists have written about the problem of refeeding, and force-feeding in particular, arguing that the practice further dehumanizes people already living what Giorgio Agamben calls a "bare life," stripped of all citizenship, dignity, and agency; see Agamben, *Homo Sacer;* Guenther, "The Biopolitics of Starvation in California Prisons"; Murray, "The Living from the Dead." For two other works addressing the ethics of solitary confinement more broadly, see Guenther, *Solitary Confinement*, and Jeffreys, *Spirituality in Dark Places*. And for an analysis of the role of hunger strikes in high-security prisons internationally (especially in Turkey), see Bargu, *Starve and Immolate*.
5. Alcalá, "Public Safety Chairs Ammiano, Hancock Announce Hearings on Hunger Strike Issues."
6. Reiter, "Transcript: Testimony of U.C. Irvine Professor Keramet Reiter."
7. Mohan, "From Prison Isolation to a Sense of Doom."
8. Czifra, "Transcript: Testimony of Former SHU Inmate Steven Czifra."
9. Canales, "Transcript: Testimony of Dolores Canales."
10. I do not mean to suggest that these are the only relevant critiques; both were part of a rich academic dialogue, explored throughout this chapter, and a rich social dialogue, explored especially well in Daniel LaChance's *Executing Freedom* (see especially chapter 2, " 'A Country Worthy of Heroes': The Romance of Retribution in a Polarizing Nation"). For another classic and comprehensive critique of 1970s sentencing and punishment policy, see Morris, *The Future of Imprisonment*.
11. American Friends Service Committee, *Struggle for Justice*, 178–79. The authors were G. Richard Bacon, Richard Boardman, Spencer Coxe, Caleb Foote, James V. Giles, David Greenberg, Mike Ingerman, John Irwin, Alex Knopp, Sam Legg, Jan Marinissen, Charlotte Meacham, Edwin C. Morgenroth (chairman), Tom Nelson, George Sawyer, Jane Schulman, and Mark Morris (staff writer). Caleb Foote, for instance, was a Harvard-educated Quaker who served eighteen months in federal prison during World War II for his refusal to comply with the draft. After the war, Foote attended law school, became a professor, and ultimately joined the law faculty at the University of California, Berkeley, where he worked until 1987. During World War II, both Foote and Morgenroth advocated against the extensive internment of Japanese Americans in concentration camps; see D. Martin, "Caleb Foote, Law Professor and Pacifist Organizer, 88, Dies." Another of the authors, John Irwin, served five years in California's Soledad Prison in the 1950s on an armed robbery conviction. While in prison, he began the coursework for a BA in sociology—an educational opportunity that vanished in the aftermath of the anti-rehabilitation criticisms leveled at the California prison system in the 1970s.

Irwin ultimately earned his Ph.D. from the University of California, Berkeley, and became a prolific scholar of prison culture and policy; his works include *The Felon* (1970), *Prisons in Turmoil* (1980), and *The Warehouse Prison* (2004), among dozens of other books and articles.

12. Bagdikian, "Books: Crime, Punishment"; Hallie, "Prisoners, Twaddlers, and the Fire Chief."

13. American Friends Service Committee, *Struggle for Justice*, v; for another iteration of this Quaker argument, see Magnani, *America's First Penitentiary.*

14. American Friends Service Committee, *Struggle for Justice*, 13, 146–47, 151.

15. For a review of racial disparities in incarceration over time, see Mauer, "Addressing Racial Disparities in Incarceration."

16. See Messinger and Johnson, "California's Determinate Sentencing Statute," 16 (describing the median time served in prison on indeterminate sentences for various crimes in California in 1965); U.S. Congress, House, Committee on the Judiciary, Hearing before Subcommittee No. 3, *First Session on Corrections, Part II: Prisons, Prison Reform, and Prisoners' Rights: California*, "Table—Offense, penal code section—Statutory sentence, months to minimum eligible parole as of January 1, 1970—Number and time served in prison before first parole, male felons paroled, 1965 and 1970," 178–83 (the title of the larger work hereafter cited as U.S. House Judiciary Committee, *First Session on Corrections, Part II*). These charts do not provide the median time served for white prisoners for first-degree burglary in these years, but the charts do provide the median time served for all prisoners and for black prisoners for first-degree burglary. The median time served for black prisoners was six months longer than the overall median for all prisoners. George Jackson still served well beyond the median time (of just under four years), even for black prisoners.

17. American Friends Service Committee, *Struggle for Justice*, 23.

18. Frankel, *Criminal Sentences.*

19. Mitford, *Kind and Usual Punishment*, 111.

20. See, for example, Cummins, *California's Radical Prison Movement*, 1–20 (on "the experts pour in"); Simon, *Poor Discipline* (on the clinical period in parole); Jacobs, *Stateville.*

21. Lipton, Martinson, and Wilks, *Effectiveness of Correctional Treatment.*

22. Elliott and Aos, "A Life of Unintended Consequences"; Martinson, "What Works."

23. Miller, "The Debate on Rehabilitating Criminals."

24. Cullen et al., "Deconstructing Farabee's Rethinking Rehabilitation."

25. DollarTimes, Inflation Calculator, www.dollartimes.com/calculators/inflation .htm.

26. Zimbardo, "The Stanford Prison Experiment"; Zimbardo, *The Lucifer Effect; Quiet Rage: The Stanford Prison Experiment*, dir. Ken Musen.

27. See, for example, *Washington Post*, "Prison: In the Mind."

28. Zimbardo, "The Stanford Prison Experiment," "Slide Tour: Grievances: The First Prisoner Released."

29. See Reiter, "Experimentation on Prisoners," 512.

30. For an overview of this litigation, see Feeley and Rubin, *Judicial Policy Making;* Reiter, "The Most Restrictive Alternative." For another account of the relationship between riots, litigation, and reform, see Larry E. Sullivan, *Forlorn Hope.*

31. The *Toussaint* litigation includes *Clutchette v. Procunier, Spain v. Procunier, Wright v. Enomoto, Toussaint v. McCarthy,* and *Toussaint v. Rushen.* (Prisoner plaintiffs and directors of the California Department of Corrections changed over the decade of litigation, which accounts for the changing names.) All of the *Toussaint* cases revolved around how prisoners were being disciplined and assigned to segregation units, and how prisoners were being treated within the confines of those units.

32. *Clutchette v. Procunier,* 328 F. Supp. 767, 769, 776.

33. *Clutchette,* 328 F. Supp. 767, 776; *Spain v. Procunier,* 408 F. Supp. 534, 541 (describing the number of cells in the Adjustment Center).

34. *Clutchette,* 328 F. Supp. 767, 776; Reiter, "The Most Restrictive Alternative."

35. *Clutchette,* 328 F. Supp. 767, 776.

36. Ibid., 785.

37. *Baxter v. Palmigiano,* 425 U.S. 308.

38. Erickson, "Two Soledad Brothers Acquitted of Murder." Clutchette was later arrested for a 1980 murder and remained incarcerated as of 2015. In June 2015, Governor Jerry Brown reversed the parole board's recommendation for release on the basis of his prior association with the San Quentin Six; see Clutchette, "Soledad Brother John Clutchette Asks for Your Help." For more about Clutchette, see generally Berger, *Captive Nation.*

39. Drumgo was another of the Soledad Brothers. Like Clutchette, he was acquitted in the Soledad murder.

40. *Spain v. Procunier,* 408 F. Supp. 534, 539.

41. Ibid., 539–40.

42. Ibid., 547.

43. *Spain v. Procunier,* 600 F.2d 189.

44. *Wright v. Enomoto,* 462 F. Supp. 397, 400–401.

45. Ibid., 405.

46. See, for example, *Toussaint v. Rushen,* 553 F. Supp. 1355, 1371–74.

47. *Toussaint v. McCarthy,* 801 F.2d 1080.

48. For instance, in 1972, prisoners at USP-Marion filed a federal lawsuit challenging their administrative segregation: *Adams v. Carlson,* 352 F. Supp. 882. While the suit was ongoing, Marion prison officials designated two units ("H" and "I") as control units, where prisoners would remain in *indefinite* segregation (*Adams,* 368 F. Supp. 882, 1052). In 1973, Judge James L. Foreman ordered that the thirty-six prisoners in segregation be returned to the prison's general population. In 1978, Judge Foreman ordered officials at USP-Marion to stop using "boxcar cells" for solitary confinement (*Washington Post,* " 'Boxcar' Cells Eliminated"). As at San Quentin, the Marion officials continued to impose indefinite long-term segregation on some prisoners in spite of Judge Foreman's persistent interventions. In

1979, the Federal Bureau of Prisons even added a sixth level of security to the federal prison system and recharacterized USP-Marion as a "Level 6" institution (Ward and Werlich, "Alcatraz and Marion," 57).

49. See generally Reiter, "Prisoners' Rights"; Feeley and Rubin, *Judicial Policy Making*. The case that led to the most sweeping decision began in the mid-1960s. In 1965, three prisoners challenged the egregious abuses in the Arkansas State Penitentiary, where they were subjected to electric shocks, punitive rape, and forced labor. Within five years, their lawsuit, *Talley v. Stevens*, had expanded to include the entire Arkansas state prison system. Officials there, as in California, appealed the case all the way to the Supreme Court. In 1978, just three years after the Court required due process in disciplinary hearings in *Baxter v. Palmigiano*, it ruled that the entire Arkansas state prison system had been operating in violation of the Eighth Amendment's prohibition against cruel and unusual punishment; see *Hutto v. Finney*, 437 U.S. 678; Reiter, "Prisoners' Rights"; Feeley and Rubin, *Judicial Policy Making*. The *Hutto* court required the state to integrate racially segregated housing, improve conditions of confinement, and limit periods of confinement in isolation cells.

50. *Rhodes v. Chapman*, 452 U.S. 337, 354; see also Feeley and Rubin, *Judicial Policy Making*.

51. The estimates provided are based on data in California Assembly, *Administrative Segregation in California's Prisons*, and in *Spain v. Procunier*, 408 F. Supp. 534, 541.

52. *Toussaint v. Rushen*, 553 F. Supp. 1355, 1370.

53. Keve and Alexander, *Prisons and the American Conscience*, 198; see also Ward and Breed, *The United States Penitentiary, Marion, Illinois*; Reiter, "The Most Restrictive Alternative."

54. Rodney J. Blonien to Robert Presley, May 30, 1986.

55. Steve Fama, personal interview. The decision he referred to is *Rowland v. United States Dist. Court for Northern Dist.*, 849 F.2d 380. Assembly comments on drafts of the legislation that ultimately authorized Pelican Bay State Prison reiterate the link between the CDC's decision to build high-security prisons and the consent decree governing San Quentin. Specifically, the Assembly comments note that the "CDC's recently released *Long Range Plan for San Quentin* proposes to build a new maximum security prison on the grounds of San Quentin 'or elsewhere'" and queries whether Pelican Bay will be the "new maximum security prison" referred to in the earlier report (California Senate, Senate Bill 1222 [1986], 5). No responses to this query are recorded, but the very question links Pelican Bay to the department's plans for San Quentin, plans written in response to the *Toussaint* court decrees. Schoenfeld describes a very similar process in Florida, arguing that courts placed the "responsibility of compliance" on prison officials, and this responsibility came with broad discretion. In turn, prison officials leveraged this burden and their discretion to "pry needed resources from the state legislature" (Schoenfeld, "Mass Incarceration and Prison Conditions Litigation," 760). In the case of California, prison officials used the court orders in the *Toussaint* and

Wilson cases to their advantage in two ways. First, as Schoenfeld found in Florida, prison officials in California leveraged the discretion the court left them in handling high-security prisoners to argue for the need to fund new prisons. Second, California prison officials used the minimum constitutional standards for lockdown conditions, as set out by these courts, not as a baseline from which to build more humane institutions, but as an outer limit of privileges and concessions that would be made to maximum-security prisoners in the state.

56. See Reiter, "The Most Restrictive Alternative" (discussing this trend from a national perspective).

57. Hayes, *A Report of an Audit of Security Measures at Two California Prisons*, 155 (containing specific recommendations on isolating and consolidating prisoners in the SHU from Folsom); McCarthy, "Response to: A Report of an Audit of Security Measures at Two California prisons," 44–45 (responding to recommendations on isolating and consolidating prisoners).

58. McCarthy, "Response to: A Report of an Audit," 44–45.

59. See also Guenther, *The Gift of the Other* (discussing how focusing on minimal basic rights can cause stagnation in rights discourses).

60. Quoted in Dershowitz, "Let the Punishment Fit the Crime," 7, 20, 26–27.

61. Cassou and Taugher, "Determinate Sentencing in California," 6; Dershowitz, "Let the Punishment Fit the Crime."

62. Messinger and Johnson, "California's Determinate Sentencing Statute," 15.

63. U.S. House Judiciary Committee, *First Session on Corrections, Part II*, "Statement by Henry W. Kerr," 130.

64. Cummins, *California's Radical Prison Movement*, 17–18.

65. Cassou and Taugher, "Determinate Sentencing in California," 6.

66. Cummins, *California's Radical Prison Movement*, 17–18.

67. *In re Lynch*, 8 Cal. 3d 410, 439.

68. *In re Rodriguez*, 14 Cal. 3d 639.

69. Cassou and Taugher, "Determinate Sentencing in California," 8–9. See also Juarez, "B. Modifying the Indeterminate Sentence." Many of these decisions followed from the U.S. Supreme Court decision in *Morrissey v. Brewer*, 408 U.S. 471 (1972), which mandated due process rights for people facing reincarceration following parole violations. Before *Morrissey*, many parole revocation proceedings, like Adult Authority parole hearings in California, lacked any procedural protections.

70. Cassou and Taugher, "Determinate Sentencing in California," 12.

71. Messinger and Johnson, "California's Determinate Sentencing Statute," 19.

72. Cassou and Taugher, "Determinate Sentencing in California," 14.

73. Campbell, "The Emergence of Penal Extremism in California," 389; see also Page, *The Toughest Beat*.

74. Campbell, "Penal Extremism in California," 392.

75. Messinger and Johnson, "California's Determinate Sentencing Statute," 27.

76. See generally U.S. House Judiciary Committee, *First Session on Corrections, Part II*, serial no. 15.

77. Ibid., "Statement of John Irwin." As mentioned above, Irwin was one of the authors of *Struggle for Justice*.

78. Dershowitz, "Let the Punishment Fit the Crime," 27.

79. Disaster Center, "United States Crime Rates, 1960–2014."

80. Fromme's hero, Charles Manson, was believed to have been responsible for thirty-five murders between 1969 and 1970. Manson is still serving an indeterminate life sentence in long-term isolation in California's Corcoran State Prison SHU; now over eighty, he has been denied parole more than twelve times.

81. Epstein, "Ford Escaped 2 Assassination Attempts."

82. See, for example, Murakawa, *The First Civil Right*.

83. For a comparative historical analysis of the symbiotic relationship between equality, democracy, citizen wariness of state power, and degrading punishments, which James Q. Whitman argues is unique to the United States, see his *Harsh Justice*.

84. In December 1975, Alan Dershowitz, a renowned legal scholar, succinctly summed up in the *New York Times* the possible outcomes of sentencing reform: "greater certainty and uniformity in sentencing" had the power to produce "either harsh or soft sentences" ("Let the Punishment Fit the Crime").

85. U.S. House Judiciary Committee, *First Session on Corrections, Part II*, "Statement of Raymond K. Procunier," 128.

86. Two contemporary analysts of the determinate sentencing negotiations explicitly argued that Procunier's new Adult Authority rules represented "an effort to undermine" the proposed legislative reforms to sentencing; see Messinger and Johnson, "California's Determinate Sentencing Statute," 19.

87. Cassou and Taugher, "Determinate Sentencing in California," 14.

88. *In re Stanley*, 54 Cal. App. 3d; Cassou and Taugher, "Determinate Sentencing in California," 17.

89. Cassou and Taugher, "Determinate Sentencing in California," 16 (citing *In re Stanley*).

90. Ibid., 21.

91. Lipson and Peterson, *California Justice Under Determinate Sentencing*, 2–4.

92. Messinger and Johnson, "California's Determinate Sentencing Statute," 35.

93. Ibid., 3.

94. Zimring, "Sentencing Reform in the States," 101; Brewer, Beckett, and Holt, "Determinate Sentencing in California," 202.

95. For analyses of the trends in the shift to determinate sentencing in California, at the federal level, and across the United States, see Lipson and Peterson, "California Justice Under Determinate Sentencing"; U.S. Sentencing Commission, "An Overview of the United States Sentencing Commission"; Goodstein, *Determinate Sentencing and the Correctional Process*; Knapp and Hauptly, "State and Federal Sentencing Guidelines"; Lowenthal, "Mandatory Sentencing Laws."

96. U.S. Department of Justice, Office of Justice Programs, Bureau of Justice Assistance, *National Assessment of Structured Sentencing*, by Austin et al., xii–xiii.

97. U.S. Sentencing Commission, "Overview of the Sentencing Commission."
98. Larson interview.
99. Lipson and Peterson, *California Justice Under Determinate Sentencing*, v.
100. Zimring and Hawkins, "The Growth of Imprisonment in California," 87 (citing Zimring and Frase, *The Criminal Justice System*). The DSL was applied retroactively, requiring the Community Release Board to set a maximum sentence length for all prisoners serving indeterminate terms under the old sentencing regime; see Lipson and Peterson, *California Justice Under Determinate Sentencing*, 7.
101. See Campbell, "Penal Extremism in California," 399, and, generally, Page, *The Toughest Beat* (discussing of the growing power of the law enforcement lobby in the 1980s and 1990s).
102. For analytic histories of the passage of this tough-on-crime ballot proposition, see Domanick, *Cruel Justice*; Zimring, Hawkins, and Kamin, *Punishment and Democracy*. For an analysis of the racial implications of California's ballot proposition system more generally, see HoSang, *Racial Propositions*.
103. See Lipson and Peterson, *California Justice Under Determinate Sentencing*, table 2, at 5; Campbell, "Penal Extremism in California," 396.
104. For a particularly thorough analysis of the development of this conservative agenda in the 1960s and 1970s, see Beckett and Sasson, *The Politics of Injustice*, 45–72. For some of the more conservative academic arguments that grew increasingly popular in the 1980s, see J. Q. Wilson and G. L. Kelling, "Broken Windows," 29–38; Dilulio, "The Coming of the Super-Predators."
105. See Zimring and Hawkins, "Growth of Imprisonment," 88.
106. California Department of Corrections, *Second and Third Striker Felons in the Adult Institution Population*, table 5, "Third Strikers in the Adult Institution Population"; Bowers, "'The Integrity of the Game Is Everything.'"
107. Kansal, *Racial Disparity in Sentencing*.
108. Lipson and Peterson, *California Justice Under Determinate Sentencing*, vi. This RAND Corporation report from 1980 predicted this precise problem, just three years after the first implementation of DSL in California.
109. *California Penal Code*, sec. 191.5, Manslaughter.
110. See, for example, Zimring and Hawkins, *The Scale of Imprisonment*.
111. Oppel, "Sentencing Shift Gives New Clout to Prosecutors."
112. Brown, Cabral, and Steenhausen, *California's Criminal Justice System*, 34.
113. Ibid.
114. Oppel, "Sentencing Shift Gives New Clout to Prosecutors"; see also Rakoff, "Why Innocent People Plead Guilty."
115. Zimring and Hawkins, *The Scale of Imprisonment*, x.
116. Zimring and Hawkins, "Growth of Imprisonment," 84; Blumstein and Cohen, "A Theory of the Stability of Punishment," 198–207.
117. Presley, "Oral History Interview," 53.
118. Zimring and Hawkins, "Growth of Imprisonment," 84.

119. To be clear, DSLs are not solely responsible for this shift. Many researchers have explored the justifications for the massive expansion of the American criminal justice system, which took place in the 1980s and 1990s. Scholars have proposed a variety of factors to explain the incarceration boom, including an excess of constitutional proceduralism (Stuntz, "The Political Constitution of Criminal Justice," 783), a decline in faith in the rehabilitative ideal (Blumstein, "Prison Populations"; Garland, *Culture of Control;* Blumstein, Cohen, and Gooding, "The Influence of Capacity on Prison Population"), racism (Alexander, *The New Jim Crow*), racial liberalism (Murakawa, *The First Civil Right;* Schept, *Progressive Punishment*), and the advent of mandatory minimum and determinate sentences (Tonry, *Sentencing Reform Impacts*). Franklin Zimring and Gordon Hawkins, arguing that none of these explanations is satisfactory, suggest instead that a sense of accountability to citizen-voters among decision makers throughout the criminal justice system has led to a tendency to err on the side of prosecuting, sentencing, and incarcerating more criminals (*The Scale of Imprisonment*). Others have suggested broader sociological explanations for mass incarceration, explanations rooted in more abstract and comprehensive social theories. For instance, Gilmore has argued, from a neo-Marxist perspective, that economic forces, especially the loss of small-scale farms and industrial plants in rural areas, increased the popular demand for prison building, which was seen as a potential infusion of governmental investment and employment opportunities in impoverished and marginalized areas (*Golden Gulag*). Loïc Wacquant argues for an even broader structural explanation: prisons result from a criminalization of poverty, brought about by neoliberal economic policies, which in turn functions both to control the lowest rungs of the labor market and to oppress racial minorities, reinforcing existing hierarchies of power in the United States (*The Place of the Prison,* "Deadly Symbiosis," and *Urban Outcasts*). Jonathan Simon has argued that changes "in the conditions of the working class and . . . in the mode of rationalizing state power," as seen particularly through the lens of reductions in the use of parole as an alternative to imprisonment, contributed to mass incarceration ("From the Big House to the Warehouse," 214; see also Simon, *Poor Discipline*). More recently, Simon has argued that federal and state governments have become dependent on anti-crime policies as a means of establishing legitimacy; this need for legitimacy, in turn, drives punitive politics (*Governing Through Crime*). Other sociolegal scholars have argued that increasing punitiveness, in California and across the United States, has resulted from a historical identity as a convict nation or from a pervasive culture of politicized fear; see Whitman, *Harsh Justice,* and Gottschalk, *The Prison and the Gallows.* Researchers have also looked at the relationship between the mass incarceration trend and crime rates. Pure quantitative analyses find weak to nonexistent relationships between increased incarceration and decreasing crime rates; see Zimring, *The Great American Crime Decline,* and Levitt, "Understanding Why Crime Fell in the 1990s."

120. Grattet and Hayes, "California's Changing Prison Population."
121. The Sentencing Project, "Total Corrections Populations"; World Prison Brief, "Highest to Lowest Prison Population Total."
122. See Gottschalk, *Caught;* Jacobs, *The Eternal Criminal Record;* Pager, *Marked.* Michelle Alexander argued in her best-selling book *The New Jim Crow* that this uptick in incarceration and the associated, exclusionary civil consequences should be understood as new forms of "Jim Crow laws": legalized segregation of racial minorities. Twenty-first-century American states, Alexander said, deploy mass incarceration as a tool to extend post–Civil War South, Jim Crow–era economic and social oppression of blacks (and now also Latinos) across the United States; see also Forman, "Racial Critiques of Mass Incarceration." If mass incarceration extends the legacy of racial oppression enshrined in American slavery, the supermax extends a subset of that legacy: institutionalizing and legalizing an abusive backlash following a violent revolt, whether by Nat Turner, George Jackson, or the prisoners at Attica—whose ghosts all continue to haunt the American legal system.
123. For recent references to George Jackson's legacy, especially among more radical, prison-abolitionist organizations, see Meronek, "LSPC Attorney Carol Strickman Speaks Out Against Prison Censorship"; Critical Resistance, "Celebrate Black August"; see also Berger, *Captive Nation* and *The Struggle Within.*
124. Goodman, Page, and Phelps have argued that moments of "intense, open conflict" about punishment such as the one in 1971 following Jackson's death and the one in 2013 following the Pelican Bay hunger strikes are more visible moments of constantly simmering antagonism between ideologies and actors, all shaped by the sociolegal landscape in which they operate ("A Long Struggle").
125. For a discussion of this process, see Feeley and Simon, "The New Penology." For arguments that rehabilitative ideologies continued to function in criminal justice institutions throughout this period, see Lynch, "Waste Managers?"; Phelps, "Rehabilitation in the Punitive Era."
126. See Elliott and Aos, "A Life of Unintended Consequences"; Cullen et al., "Deconstructing Farabee's Rethinking Rehabilitation."
127. See, for example, Murakawa, *The First Civil Right;* Fortner, *Black Silent Majority;* Gottschalk, *Caught.*
128. Naomi Murakawa has recently argued that the sentencing shifts and the onset of mass incarceration in the 1970s cannot be extricated from shifts in understandings of racism. In the 1970s, racism, once understood as a structural problem, came to be seen as a problem of irrational individuals who could be eliminated through fair and consistent policies that punished specific individuals (Murakawa, *The First Civil Right*). But as both Murakawa and Larson acknowledged, reforming a culture of racism requires more than procedural changes in sentencing. Indeed, one of the critiques of the changes in both sentencing and prison conditions implemented in California and nationwide in the 1980s is that they focused excessively on procedural justice—especially what rights indi-

vidual prisoners have—over substantive justice, or how prisoners could be treated ethically; see Stuntz, *The Collapse of American Criminal Justice*.

129. Larson interview.

130. Rich Kirkland, personal interview.

131. Cambra interview.

132. California State Legislature, Joint Legislative Committee on Prison Construction and Operations (hereafter JLCPCO), *California's Prisons: Violence at Folsom Prison*, 56–58.

133. Ibid., 49–50. At the same hearing, Assemblyman Larry Stirling expressed intense frustration at the most recent interventions of a federal judge in the administrative segregation cases. Stirling said he thought that using a judicial law clerk to monitor conditions in segregation facilities was "an outrage," and he suggested that the judge should be "impeached" for ordering California to provide programs to prisoners in lockups (57). The 1985 hearing about violence at Folsom was not unique in mentioning ongoing prison litigation; the litigation over conditions in administrative segregation in California's prisons was mentioned frequently in legislative reports and hearings as well as in correctional planning documents; see Hayes, *A Report of an Audit*, 155 (containing specific recommendations on isolating and consolidating prisoners in the SHU from Folsom); McCarthy, "Response to: A Report of an Audit," 44–45 (responding to recommendations for isolating and consolidating prisoners); California State Legislature, Joint Legislative Committee on Prison Construction and Operations, *Anatomy of a Prison, Folsom* (referring to frustrations with prison litigation).

134. Prison officials, reformers, legislators, and judges were all working within a bigger system, one that David Rothman has described as involving perpetual cycles of "conscience and convenience": penal reformers and prison officials design new policies meant to be more fair and humane (conscience), but in practice these policies are modified in the interest of institutional preservation (convenience); see Rothman, *Conscience and Convenience*. Other scholars have argued that there is much more continuity in theories of punishment than the drastic reforms of the 1970s might at first seem to indicate; the politics of fear and oppression has always been a part of punishment decisions, for instance, and elements of rehabilitation and retribution always coexist in the day-to-day operations of prison facilities; see Whitman, *Harsh Justice*; Gottschalk, *The Prison and the Gallows*; Gartner and Kruttschnitt, "A Brief History of Doing Time."

135. For examples of the unintended consequences story, see Alschuler, "Sentencing Reform and Prosecutorial Power" (predicting the outcomes described in the "Litany of Unintended Consequences" section); Remington, "The Decision to Charge, the Decision to Convict on a Plea of Guilty, and the Impact of Sentence Structure on Prosecution Practice"; Campbell, "Penal Extremism in California"; Tonry, *Sentencing Reform Impacts*. For a critique of the "unintended consequences" theme, see Merton, "Unanticipated Consequences of Purposive Social Action"; Schlanger, "No Reason to Blame Liberals." For another narrative of

administrative retrenchment, although one more focused on bureaucratic iner-
tia than innovation, see Calavita, *Inside the State.*

136. *Sacramento Bee,* "Larson, Carl M., Oct. 25, 1936–Sept. 9, 2013."

Chapter 4. Constructing the Supermax, One Rule at a Time

1. California Senate, Senate Bill 1685, Conference Committee Notes.
2. Corwin, "New Era of State Prisons."
3. See Kim and Mather, "Gov. Jerry Brown Denies Parole for Ex-Mexican Mafia Killer Rene 'Boxer' Enriquez."
4. Larson interview.
5. For an especially readable review of the role of bonds and budgets, and the economy more broadly, in late-modern criminal justice policy in California especially, see Aviram, *Cheap on Crime,* 26–47.
6. Presley, "Oral History Interview," 53. Over the course of the 1990s and early 2000s, the California prison system's problems with overcrowding expanded until the prisons were so crowded that adequate care could not possibly be provided to all the prisoners. In the early 2000s, prisoners' lawyers documented that one prisoner a week was dying unnecessarily throughout the state prison system, and the U.S. Supreme Court ordered the state to do whatever it took to reduce the prison population, even releasing prisoners en masse. For a discussion of the history of this litigation, see Simon, *Mass Incarceration on Trial.*
7. Presley, "Oral History Interview," 75–76.
8. Term limits, which became popular in the early 1990s, altered this model of the entrenched and professionalized legislator; see Cain and Levin, "Term Limits"; Kurfirst, "Term-Limit Logic."
9. Presley, "Oral History Interview," 53–54.
10. Gilmore, *Golden Gulag,* 93.
11. Perlman, "Issue Second Only to Crime Among County Residents Surveyed."
12. *Los Angeles Times,* "Prison Construction: Yes on 1."
13. Endicott, "Support of Fight on Crime Seen" and "The Governor's Race."
14. Presley, "Oral History Interview," 53–54.
15. Gilmore, *Golden Gulag,* 94.
16. Alger and Molinari, *The Use of General Obligation Bonds by the State of California.*
17. Presley, "Oral History Interview," 118; Gilmore, *Golden Gulag,* 97.
18. Technically, Brown was undersecretary of the Youth and Adult Correctional Agency (YACA), the administrative agency, located within the executive offices of the governor, which oversaw the California Department of Corrections (CDC) in the 1980s. According to Brown, the YACA functioned as an intermediary between the CDC and politicians in the executive branch. The CDC has since been restructured at least twice, and the YACA no longer exists.
19. Brown interview.
20. Presley, "Oral History Interview," 116.

21. Brown interview.
22. Ibid.
23. Gilmore, *Golden Gulag*, 105; Presley, "Oral History Interview," 73. Many of the administrators interviewed for this research mentioned their frustrations with the prison-siting process, as well as the inevitability of prison after prison ending up in rural locations. Gilmore's *Golden Gulag* covers the politics and economics of this prison-siting process in great detail.
24. Alger and Molinari, *Use of General Obligation Bonds*.
25. Mattera, "Public Finance and Public Debt." California bond ratings recovered substantially in the 2010s.
26. Gilmore, *Golden Gulag*, 97; Mattera, "Public Finance and Public Debt."
27. For analyses of how this logic has played out in privatizing not just prison financing but also the prison industry itself (often creating surprising inefficiencies), see generally U.S. Department of Justice, Office of Justice Programs, Bureau of Justice Assistance, *Emerging Issues on Privatized Prisons*, by Austin and Coventry; Mason, *International Growth Trends in Prison Privatization*; Herivel and Wright, *Prison Profiteers*.
28. Gilmore, *Golden Gulag*, 98.
29. Pranis, "Doing Borrowed Time," 37; Mattera, "Public Finance and Public Debt"; Gilmore, *Golden Gulag*, 100–101.
30. Gilmore, *Golden Gulag*, 98; Alger and Molinari, *Use of General Obligation Bonds*, 6.
31. Keller, *The New Prison Construction Program at Midstream*, v, 10–13. Of particular note for the building of Pelican Bay State Prison: in September 1985, Senate Bill 253 specifically exempted the "proposed prisons in Riverside and Del Norte Counties from the California Environmental Quality Act." The bill provided instead for an alternative environmental assessment study, to be conducted by the California Department of Corrections and approved by a local public works board, before purchase of the land on which the prisons would be sited. The legislature was concerned with assessing environmental impact, but quickly, through expedited administrative procedures within the discretion of the Department of Corrections.
32. California Senate, Senate Bill 2098
33. Presley, "Oral History Interview," 65. In this interview, Presley explained that the exemptions were principled. He argued that he founded the Joint Legislative Committee on Prison Construction and Operations explicitly "to try to contain costs" of prison construction. The committee, he argued, was successful in achieving this cost-containing goal: "And believe me, we saved the taxpayers millions of dollars. You couldn't believe how we'd hold hearings and beat on these contractors and beat on these architects about how 'You reduce costs.' Otherwise it would have been an awful lot of money spent. So it did a lot of good." Of course, the prisons constructed in California in the 1980s cost the taxpayers billions of dollars, despite any cost savings Presley and the committee were able to "beat" out of contractors and architects. And administrators and legislators alike often

prioritized quick prison building over cost-effectiveness, as Brown's story about installing temporary wooden doors illustrates.

34. Ibid.

35. Brown interview.

36. Ibid.

37. Newspaper reports alleged that Oregon residents crossing the border into California in search of more generous welfare benefits further burdened Del Norte County; see Griffith, "New Border Prison Spurs Concerns"; Corwin, "New Era of State Prisons."

38. California Senate, Senate Bill 95 (1985).

39. California Senate, Senate Bill 1222 (1986), Assembly Comments, 2–5.

40. Ibid.

41. California State Legislature, JLCPCO, *California's Prisons: Violence at Folsom Prison.*

42. California Senate, Senate Bill 1222 (1986).

43. Griffith, "New Border Prison Spurs Concerns."

44. Calder, "Crescent City Gets Welcome Boom from New Prison."

45. Corwin, "New Era of State Prisons." The state and the Center for the Continuing Study of the California Economy (in Palo Alto) predicted further employment jumps and population jumps, which would combine to produce an increasingly healthy employment rate; see Anderson, "California & Co."

46. Larson telephone interview.

47. Larson interview. In the ten original prisons that the corrections director Richard McGee built in the 1940s and 1950s, four had "lockup units," where prisoners could be held in short-term isolation. McGee's philosophy, Larson explained, was to have "a small unit in each prison" for lock-up. Larson said that lockups were later added in two additional prisons.

48. Zimring and Hawkins argue that these prison population projections have been consistently inaccurate since the mid-1980s (*Prison Population and Criminal Justice Policy in California*). Whether the estimates were accurate or not, the CDC could not build prisons fast enough to keep up with the growing prison population, and the prisons it did build were designed on the assumption that they would function well above capacity: at "130 percent of capacity for celled institutions and 120 percent of capacity for dormitories" (Larson interview).

49. Larson interview.

50. *See Toussaint v. McCarthy,* 597 F. Supp 1388, 1394. The calculated percentage was based on the 1984 state prison population: forty thousand, as reported in California Department of Corrections, *California Prisoners and Civil Narcotics Addicts: 1983, 1984, 1985.*

51. *See Toussaint v. McCarthy,* 801 F.2d 1080.

52. Larson interview.

53. The lockup Larson referred to was Oak Park Heights in Stillwater, Minnesota (not Wisconsin).

54. Larson interview. Craig Brown reiterated what Larson said about looking to other

states for ideas and best practices: "We tried to visit every new prison that was being constructed" (Brown interview).

55. Larson interview.

56. Justice architect (Arizona), telephone interview. To protect the identities of architects who wished to remain anonymous, I have not provided the names of any of the architects involved in building and designing the first supermaxes.

57. Arrington Watkins, "Project Portfolio: Justice: Prisons: Arizona: ASPC—Eyman—Special Management Unit I." The web page for this project was last available in 2014, but it has since been removed.

58. Justice architect (Arizona), telephone interview.

59. See, for example, the litigation in *Madrid,* 899 F. Supp 1146 (discussed further in Chapter 5).

60. Justice architect (Arizona), telephone interview.

61. Wood, "How Gangs Took Over Prisons."

62. Kirkland interview.

63. Bentham, *The Panopticon Writings.*

64. Justice architect (California), telephone interview with the author.

65. Foucault, *Discipline and Punish,* 13.

66. Justice architect (Arizona), telephone interview.

67. Lynch, *Sunbelt Justice,* 137; see generally Lynch, "Selling 'Securityware'" (discussing the marketing of correctional innovations). There is much debate in the literature about which prison was the first supermax. Some scholars argue that it was Alcatraz, the federal penitentiary that operated from 1934 to 1962; others argue that it was USP Marion, and still others that it was ADX, the highest-security federal prison, in Florence, Colorado, which did not open until 1995, nearly ten years after Arizona's SMU; see, for example, Ward, *Alcatraz;* Kurshan, *Out of Control;* Dowker and Good, "The Proliferation of Control Unit Prisons in the United States"; Richards, *USP Marion.* The *Oxford English Dictionary* dates the first occurrence of "super-maximum" in a prison context to 1954; the reference, appearing in the *Annals of the American Academy of Political and Social Science,* was, appropriately, to a prison in California. This was nearly two decades after Alcatraz opened, so referring to Alcatraz as the first supermax is potentially anachronistic; see Scudder, "The Open Institution." References to "supermax prisons" cropped up only in the 1980s, a full decade after experiments with long-term isolation began at USP-Marion with the institutionalization of a control unit in the 1970s, as discussed at the end of Chapter 2. According to the *OED,* the first reference to "super-max" as a noun meaning type of prison appeared in a local Maryland paper, the *Frederick News,* in 1980, and the first reference to "super-max" as an adjective describing a prison (again in Maryland) appeared in the *National Journal* in 1981; *Frederick News,* "Report Recommends Jessup Be Renovated" ("The penitentiary's 'super max' or 'C-block,' where the state's most dangerous prisoners are housed"); Hagstrom, "Crowded Prisons Pose a Budget Problem For This Law-and-Order Administration," 1821 ("The legislation's cen-

terpiece was $44 million for a new 'super-max' prison"). The first reference to the term "supermax" (nonhyphenated) in relation to a modern, new form of extremely high-security prison seems to be from 1984. In that year, the term "supermax" appeared in *Corrections Today* in an advertisement "for a lighting system dubbed Supermax," in reference to Arizona's SMU; see Lynch, "Selling 'Security-ware,'" 313. In other words, even the first uses of the word "supermax" are closely associated with the Arizona SMU. Finally, as discussed in Chapter 5, federal prison architects explicitly copied the Arizona SMU and Pelican Bay SHU designs in building the federal supermax, ADX, in Florence, Colorado, in 1995, almost a decade after the first supermax opened in Arizona.

68. Brown interview.
69. Lynch, *Sunbelt Justice*, 136–37.
70. California State Legislature, JLCPCO, *California's Prisons: Violence at Folsom Prison*, 5–6.
71. Ibid., 30 (testimony of Craig Haney).
72. Ibid., A-30.
73. Ibid., A-27–29.
74. Ibid., iii–vii.
75. Ibid., 15 (testimony of Paul Redd, prisoner).
76. Ibid., 25, 67–73, 82, 86–88, 90.
77. California Assembly, Assembly Bill 277 (1986). The Presley Institute was later absorbed by the University of California, Riverside, becoming a university research center that exists today; see California Senate, Senate Bill 526 (1993). See also the website of the Robert Presley Center for Crime and Justice Studies, http://presleycenter.ucr.edu.
78. California State Archives, Inventory of the Robert Presley Papers.
79. Justice architect (California), telephone interview.
80. Justice architect (Arizona), telephone interview. The Arizona architect remembered that he ended up having an office in Sacramento for about seven years, since he consulted on other California prison projects, too.
81. Larson interview.
82. Kirkland interview.
83. Carl Larson, e-mail exchange, July 20, 2011.
84. Since the year after the Pelican Bay complex opened, it has functioned above its design capacity, housing at least 3,200 prisoners and up to 4,000 on site. The SHU itself has been overcrowded. During a few peak years of crowding in the mid-1990s, more than half of prisoners in the SHU had a cellmate; since the early 2000s, however, fewer than 10 percent of prisoners in the SHU have been double-celled. See Reiter, "Parole, Snitch, or Die," 544; Reiter "Supermax Administration and the Eighth Amendment," 122-25. The "double-bunking" policy is discussed further in Chapter 5.
85. Justice architect (Arizona), telephone interview.
86. Larson interview.

87. Kirkland interview.
88. Ibid.
89. Ibid.
90. Ibid.
91. Larson interview.
92. Kirkland interview.
93. In July 2013, I sent Larson two earlier articles I had written about the day-to-day operations of Pelican Bay and about the post-1989 history of the institution: Reiter, "Parole, Snitch, or Die" and "The Origins of and Need to Control Supermax Prisons."
94. Larson telephone interview.
95. Morain, "San Quentin Warden Views Grim Duty with Equanimity."
96. By all accounts, the correctional officers' union in California, which had become a powerful political force in the state by the time Pelican Bay opened in 1989, played only a minimal role in the design of the supermax; see generally Page, *The Toughest Beat*. Larson remembered that on his first few prison construction projects, union management would intervene late in the project, requesting expensive, last-minute structural changes. By the time he was working on the Del Norte prison, he had developed a protocol. With every new prison, he said, "I called up Don Novey [president of the union], asked for a union guy to participate in the work" (Larson interview). Craig Brown reiterated that the correctional officers' union (known as the California Correctional Peace Officers Association, or the CCPOA) had a nominal role in signing off on designs before construction began. The union representatives, according to Brown, were mainly interested in technical details relating to security: "sight line issues, locking mechanisms, little details like sectional switches to open doors, where you have guns" (Brown interview). Larson, with his long experience of walking prison tiers, was very careful to resolve exactly these kinds of concerns.
97. Weintraub, "Deukmejian Defends Buildup of Prison System."
98. Corwin, "Residents Rattling Local Prison Bars."
99. Corwin, "New Era of State Prisons."
100. Larson telephone interview.
101. Kirkland interview.
102. Brown interview.
103. Justice architect (Arizona), telephone interview.
104. Larson interview.
105. Brown interview.
106. Montgomery, "Gangster Confidential."

Chapter 5. Skeleton Bay

1. CBS News, "Pelican Bay."
2. Henderson interview.

3. U.S. Courts, "Pro Se Law Clerks." See also Schlanger, "Trends in Prisoner Litigation, as the PLRA Enters Adulthood."
4. Henderson interview.
5. *Madrid,* 899 F. Supp 1146, 1156, n2.
6. Ibid., 1190, 1196.
7. Henderson interview.
8. Ibid.
9. Thelton E. Henderson Center for Social Justice, Berkeley Law, "Honorable Thelton E. Henderson."
10. U.S. District Court, Northern District of California, "Senior District Judge Thelton E. Henderson."
11. Chiang, "East Bay: Film Captures Trials of Judge Henderson."
12. For a comprehensive biography of Evers, see, Williams, *Medgar Evers.*
13. Chiang, "East Bay: Film Captures Trials of Judge Henderson."
14. Goldman, *Picking Federal Judges,* 348, table 9.1. Only about 30 percent of Jimmy Carter's appointees had neither judicial nor prosecutorial work experience.
15. Thelton E. Henderson Center for Social Justice, "Honorable Thelton E. Henderson."
16. *Spain v. Rushen,* 543 F. Supp. 757, 761; Stein, "'San Quentin 6' Defendant Spain Will Not Be Retried"; Morain, "Inmate Convicted in Prison Killing Gets Retrial."
17. Morain, "Inmate Convicted in Prison Killing."
18. *Spain,* 543 F. Supp. 757, 761; Morain, "Inmate Convicted in Prison Killing."
19. *Spain,* 543 F. Supp. 757, 764.
20. Ibid., 761–62.
21. Ibid., 762.
22. Ibid., 777.
23. See, for example, Associated Press, "Judge Upsets Conviction of San Quentin Inmate"; J. Mann, "High Court Restores Panther's Conviction."
24. Henderson was never promoted to an appellate court. He did serve as chief judge of the district court from 1990 through 1997, but the position is awarded on seniority; see Thelton E. Henderson Center for Social Justice, "Honorable Thelton E. Henderson"; U.S. Courts, "Federal Judges."
25. *Powell v. Alabama,* 287 U.S. 45.
26. *Spain* 543 F. Supp. 757, 761.
27. *Rushen v. Spain,* 464 U.S. 114, 117–18.
28. J. Mann, "High Court Restores Panther's Conviction."
29. *Spain* 543 F. Supp. 757, 778.
30. *Spain v. Rushen,* 882 F.2d 712.
31. Ibid.
32. The attorney was incorrect; Spain had been out of custody for just under two years; see Stein, "'San Quentin 6' Defendant Spain."
33. Associated Press, "Counties Told to Restore Welfare Cuts."
34. Associated Press, "State Farm Found Guilty of Sex Bias."

35. Associated Press, "U.S. Observers Must Accompany Tuna Boats."
36. Associated Press, "Rule Overturned on Agent Orange."
37. *Madrid v. Gomez*, Order Granting Motion to Certify Class Action, Docket No. 83.
38. Fama interview; Henderson interview.
39. Henderson interview.
40. Ibid.
41. *Madrid*, 889 F. Supp. 1146, 1171.
42. Henderson interview.
43. *Madrid*, 889 F. Supp. 1146, 1196.
44. See California Department of Corrections, *California Prisoners and Parolees, 2010*, 25, table 14.
45. CBS News, "Pelican Bay."
46. Ibid.
47. Ibid. See Chapter 7 for further discussion of mental health problems in isolation.
48. Ibid.
49. Henderson interview.
50. Ibid.
51. Associated Press, "Guards Convicted of Plotting Attacks"; *U.S. v. Powers*, Case No. 3:00-cr-00105-MJJ-2; U.S. Department of Justice, Executive Office for United States Attorneys, *United States Attorneys' Annual Statistical Report, Fiscal Year 2002*.
52. Henderson interview.
53. *Madrid*, 889 F. Supp. 1146, 1156.
54. Reiter, "Parole, Snitch, or Die," 544.
55. *Madrid*, 889 F. Supp. 1146, 1237.
56. Reiter, "Parole, Snitch, or Die," 544. Prison populations were also increasing at this time, so the SHU population actually remained relatively stable as a proportion of the overall prison population, hovering around 2 percent in these years; see Reiter, "Supermax Administration and the Eighth Amendment."
57. *Madrid*, 889 F. Supp. 1146, 1239.
58. Cambra interview (as quoted in Chapter 1).
59. *Madrid*, 889 F. Supp. 1146, 1179, n52.
60. Ibid.
61. *Madrid*, 889 F. Supp. 1146, 1206, 1210.
62. Ibid., 1215–20.
63. See *Madrid*, 889 F. Supp. 1146, 1231, n167 for a summary of this research as established in 1995.
64. Ibid., 1231 (citing *In re Medley*, 134 U.S. 160, 168).
65. Ibid., 1162–69.
66. Ibid., 1170–71.
67. Hentoff, "America's Devil's Island"; Goldberg, "A Prison for Cruel and Unusual Criminals."
68. Goldberg, "Cruel and Unusual Criminals."
69. *Madrid*, 889 F. Supp. 1146, 1267.

70. Ibid., 1269–70, 1278.
71. Henderson interview.
72. See Reiter, "Origins of and Need to Control Supermax Prisons," 155–56.
73. *Ashker v. Brown*, "Settlement Agreement."
74. *Prison Legal News*, "Pelican Bay Ruling Issued."
75. *Coleman v. Wilson*, 912 F. Supp. 1282.
76. See Reiter and Pifer, "*Plata v. Brown*," 5 (analyzing the history and impacts of the *Plata* case).
77. Simon, *Mass Incarceration on Trial*.
78. *Prison Legal News*, "Pelican Bay Ruling Issued."
79. Ibid.
80. Riveland, *Supermax Prisons*.
81. A preliminary list of supermax institutions can be derived from the American Correctional Association's 2010 *Directory of Adult and Juvenile Correctional Departments, Institutions, Agencies, and Probation and Parole Authorities*. But this directory is based on voluntary, institutionally self-reported data, and exact definitions of supermaxes, as well as counts of supermax institutions, vary. This variability is due in part to the question of what constitutes long-term solitary confinement: indefinite isolation for administrative reasons, fixed isolation for disciplinary reasons, or some combination of the two; see Naday, Freilich, and Mellow, "Elusive Data on Supermax Confinement." See also DeMaio, "If You Build It, They Will Come"; King, "The Rise and Rise of Supermax"; Kurki and Morris, "The Purposes, Practices, and Problems of Supermax Prisons," 390–91; Rhodes, "Supermax as a Technology of Punishment," 549. The fact that each state has a different label for these kinds of institutions—SHU in California, SMU in Arizona, etc.—only further complicates attempts to identify and count such facilities.
82. Naday, Freilich, and Mellow, "Elusive Data on Supermax Confinement," 69; Healy, "A System Strains, and Inmates Die."
83. *Wilkinson v. Austin*, 545 U.S. 209.
84. *Ayers v. Perry*, Case No. 02-1438, Complaint.
85. Justice architect (federal), telephone interview with author, June 22, 2010; Justice architect (federal), telephone interview with author, Mar. 4, 2011; Koenig, *Indefinite Detention/Enduring Freedom*; Koenig, "From Man to Beast," 224. Some works mistakenly identify one of three federal facilities—Alcatraz, USP-Marion, or ADX—as the first supermax; see, for example, Ward, *Alcatraz*; Kurshan, *Out of Control*; Dowker and Good, "Proliferation of Control Unit Prisons"; Richards, *USP Marion*. This book reveals that Arizona and California piloted the lockdown policies that preceded the first supermaxes, as well as the supermaxes themselves.
86. See Reiter, "The Supermax Prison," n14. The following cases document just a few instances of abuse in the early years of supermax operation: *Casey v. Lewis*, 834 F. Supp. 1569, 1580–81, describing guard abuse of a mentally ill prisoner; *Taifa v. Bayh*, Case No. 8:92-CV-429 AS, describing arbitrary and excessive use of

force, physical restraints, and chemical agents; *Ayers v. Perry,* Complaint for Class Based Declaratory and Injunctive Relief and for Individual and Compensatory and Punitive Damages, para. 91, describing the use of excessive force against mentally ill prisoners in the supermax; *Ruiz v. Johnson,* 37 F. Supp. 2d 855, describing sexual abuse between prisoners and the sadistic use of force by guards in segregation units; *Jones'El v. Berge,* 164 F. Supp. 2d 1096, 1112, 1114, describing the excessive use of restraints on mentally ill prisoners in the supermax.

87. For a discussion of the trend toward increasingly restrictive incarceration in the 1980s and 1990s, see especially Feeley and Simon, "The New Penology."

88. Haney and Lynch, "Regulating Prisons of the Future." According to a Lexis-Nexis search for citing decisions ("Sheperdization" in legal terms), a few of the decisions relying on *Madrid* to uphold isolation include the following: *Spencer v. Courtier,* 2011 U.S. Dist. LEXIS 73122, No. 09-124 Erie, n.6 (W.D. Penn. May 23, 2011), which upheld non-severely mentally ill prisoners' placement in restrictive segregation; *Washington-El v. Beard,* 2011 U.S. Dist. LEXIS 24562, No. 08-1688, at 10 (W D. Penn, Mar. 11, 2011), which upheld restrictive conditions of confinement; *Wheeler v. Vaughn,* 2004 U.S. Dist. LEXIS 539, No. 01-428, at 62 (E.D. Penn, Jan. 5, 2004), which upheld the inevitability of prison altercations; *Williams v. Branker,* 2011 U.S. Dist. LEXIS 13402, No. 5:09-CT-3139-D, at 12 (E.D. NC, Feb. 10, 2011), which found conditions less restrictive than those found actionable in *Madrid; Watson v. Quarterman,* 2008 U.S. Dist. LEXIS 15169, No. H-06-3260, at 18 (S.D. Tex., Feb. 27, 2008), which cited the authority of prison officials to take restrictive measures to control and eliminate prison gangs; *Brown v. Timmerman-Cooper,* 2013 U.S. Dist. LEXIS 14777, No. 2:10-cv-283, at 12 (S.D. Ohio, Feb. 4, 2014), which upheld prison officials' right to impose "restrictive and even harsh" conditions; *Crow v. Montgomery,* 2003 U.S. Dist. LEXIS 27708, No. 4:02-CV-00352-WRW, at 21–23 (E.D. Ark., Nov. 14, 2003), which upheld the inevitability of attacks in prison; *Griffin v. Gomez,* 741 F.3d 10, n.7 (9th Cir. 2012), which justified continued restrictive segregation conditions; *Castro v. Terhune,* 712 F.3d 1304, 1308 (9th Cir. 2013), which justified placement in segregation based on gang affiliation; *Bruce v. Ylst,* 351 F.3d 1283, 1289 (9th Cir. 2003), which cited a legitimate penological interest in stopping gang activity; *Jeffers v. Gomez,* 267 F.3d 895, 916 (9th Cir. 2001), which upheld the use of firearms during a prison riot; *Pifer v. Marshall,* 1998 U.S. App. LEXIS 3189 (9th Cir. Cal. Feb. 24, 1998), which remanded for reconsideration a challenge to indefinite isolation terms in light of the *Madrid* decision. For reviews of some of the ongoing legal concerns with supermaxes, see U.S. Department of Justice, National Institute of Corrections, *Supermax Prisons and the Constitution,* by William Collins; Fathi, "Anatomy of the Modern Prisoners' Rights Suit"; Lobel, "Prolonged Solitary Confinement and the Constitution."

89. See *Silverstein,* 704 F. Supp. 2d 1077.

90. This distinction between a legal structure and an illegal application is a civil-rights framing that Murakawa criticizes throughout *The First Civil Right.* Hender-

son elaborated, drawing an analogy to a public nursing home: "If you decided the elderly . . . are entitled to public support, and you're going to build somewhere out there a really big residence for the elderly poor, there's nothing unconstitutional about that. What becomes unconstitutional is if we give them half the money [needed to feed the institutionalized population]" (Henderson interview). This pattern of thinking, focusing on problems in the day-to-day operation of an institution rather than on problems with its conceptual justification, potentially limits the power and sustainability of reform.

91. Feeley and Rubin, *Judicial Policy Making*.

92. See Boston, *The Prison Litigation Reform Act;* Schlanger, "Inmate Litigation." For an analysis of the impact and effect of the Prison Litigation Reform Act on prisoners in California in particular, see Calavita and Jenness, *Appealing to Justice*.

93. Henderson interview.

94. But see Reiter, "Supermax Administration and the Eighth Amendment," which discusses how he expanded deference to prison officials in other applications of the standard.

95. See Reiter, "The Most Restrictive Alternative," 85.

96. Kirkland interview.

97. Fama interview.

98. For analyses of the pervasive (and corrosive) effect of deference to prison officials' claims in the context of prison law, see generally Dolovich, "Cruelty, Prison Conditions, and the Eighth Amendment," 961, n306; Dolovich, "Forms of Deference in Prison Law," 245; Fallon, "Judicially Manageable Standards and Constitutional Meaning"; Resnik, "Detention, the War on Terror, and the Federal Courts"; Shay, "Ad Law Incarcerated"; Raghunath, "A Promise the Nation Cannot Keep," 395; Weidman, "Comment, The Culture of Judicial Deference and the Problem of Supermax Prisons."

99. Reiter, "Supermax Administration and the Eighth Amendment," 100.

100. Ibid., 103.

101. *Madrid*, 889 F. Supp. 1146, 1227.

102. Reiter, "Parole, Snitch, or Die." These data are discussed further in Chapter 7.

103. Henderson interview.

Chapter 6. Snitching or Dying

1. Technically, a prisoner with a life sentence *with* the possibility of parole could be paroled directly from the SHU. In practice, however, such prisoners have great difficulty in convincing a parole board that they have been reformed and no longer represent a danger to society (as seen, for instance, in Hugo Pinell's multiple parole denials during his time in the SHU). This is discussed further in Chapter 7.

2. I use Enriquez's real name because I include here only widely publicly available details about his case. I use a pseudonym for Johnny because I include here

details of his history and case that are not publicly available. I have altered some dates and left out some locations in order to further protect his identity. Johnny has given me permission (processed through my Institutional Review Board) to draw on and quote from letters we have exchanged, and I have reviewed court documents and witnessed court proceedings relevant to his case.

3. Kim and Mather, "Gov. Jerry Brown Denies Parole."

4. Montgomery, "Gangster Reveals Mexican Mafia Secrets."

5. California Department of Corrections, *Operation Manual*, sec. 52070.81.2-.3: "Member" Category and "Associate" Category, in "Gang Identification and Validation" subsection (revised Aug. 9, 2011), 398–99.

6. The process of snitching, formally defined as "police and prosecutors offering deals to criminal offenders in exchange for information," and its effect on the legal system overall, tends to be obscure and secretive. Unsurprisingly, it remains understudied. For a thorough analysis of the practice in the context of criminal law, see Natapoff, *Snitching.*

7. Brown, "Indeterminate Sentence Parole Release Review."

8. Montgomery, "Gangster Reveals Mexican Mafia Secrets."

9. Ibid.

10. Ibid.

11. Ibid.

12. Brown, "Indeterminate Sentence Parole Release Review."

13. Mather and Kim, "Gov. Jerry Brown Weighs Parole for Killer in Controversial LAPD Lecture."

14. Kim and Mather, "Gov. Jerry Brown Denies Parole."

15. Mather and Kim, "Gov. Jerry Brown Weighs Parole."

16. Brown, "Indeterminate Sentence Parole Release Review." The board's questions are imputed from Rene's answers, which were quoted in Governor Brown's review. Note that Michael Montgomery reported that Enriquez grew up in a middle-class home in the Los Angeles suburbs ("Gangster Reveals Mexican Mafia Secrets").

17. Blankstein, "Jailed Mafia Hit Man Gets LAPD Escort to Meet L.A. Business Leaders."

18. Mather, Winton, and Vives, "LAPD Criticized for Arranging Downtown Talk by Mexican Mafia Killer"; Blankstein, "Jailed Mafia Hit Man."

19. Pritchard, "L.A. Police Spent $22,000 to Get Mexican Mafia Killer Rene 'Boxer' Enriquez to Fancy Dinner."

20. Blankstein, "Jailed Mafia Hit Man."

21. Mather and Kim, "Gov. Jerry Brown Weighs Parole."

22. Brown, "Indeterminate Sentence Parole Release Review."

23. Parole officials recommended Enriquez for parole again in February 2016; at the time of this writing, Governor Brown had not evaluated the recommendation; see Thompson, "Parole Recommended for Former Mexican Mafia Chief."

24. California Prison Industry Authority, "About CALPIA."

25. Page, *The Toughest Beat*, 81–110; see also Zimring , Hawkins, and Kamin, *Punishment and Democracy.*

26. See Mariner, *No Escape;* Bozelko, "Why We Let Prison Rape Go On"; U.S. Department of Justice, Office of Justice Programs, Bureau of Justice Statistics, "PREA Data Collection Activities, 2015."

27. "Derrick," personal interview with the author.

28. See, for example, Maynard, "The One Good Man."

29. *Miller v. Alabama*, 567 U.S. __.

30. California Senate, Senate Bill 9.

31. Ashker et al. 2013. "Statement Suspending the Third Hunger Strike."

32. Reiter, "Supermax Administration and the Eighth Amendment."

33. *Coleman v. Schwarzenegger*, Case No. Civ S 90-0520 LKKJFM, 2008 WL 8697735: "Expert Report of Professor Craig Haney," 45–46, n119.

34. Reiter, "Supermax Administration and the Eighth Amendment."

35. St. John, "California Proposes Isolation Units for Mentally Ill Prison Inmates."

36. Fellner, *Callous and Cruel.*

37. *Coleman v. Brown*, "Order," Apr. 10, 2014.

38. This case is described in further detail in Reiter and Blair, "Punishing Mental Illness"; see also Stanton and Walsh, "Was It Suicide?"

39. Reiter, "Supermax Administration and the Eighth Amendment."

40. Kupers, "What to Do with Survivors?"; Mears, *Evaluating the Effectiveness of Supermax Prisons.* In New York City's Rikers Island, for instance, suicide is seven times more common in isolation units than in general prison populations. In Indiana, suicide is three times more common in isolation units than in general prison populations; see Kaba et al., "Solitary Confinement and Risk of Self-Harm Among Jail Inmates"; *Indiana Protection and Advocacy Services Com'n v. Commissioner, Indiana Dept. of Correction*, *16. See generally American Civil Liberties Union, *Briefing Paper: The Dangerous Overuse of Solitary Confinement in the United States.*

41. National Institute of Mental Health, "Serious Mental Illness (SMI) Among U.S. Adults."

42. Correctional Association of New York, "States That Provide Mental Health Alternatives to Solitary Confinement."

43. Grob, "The Forging of Mental Health Policy in America."

44. Earley, *Crazy.*

45. Gilligan, "The Last Mental Hospital"; see also Harcourt, "Reducing Mass Incarceration."

46. Torrey, *Care of the Seriously Mentally Ill*; Earley, *Crazy.*

47. For a more thorough discussion of this process, see Reiter and Blair, "Punishing Mental Illness."

48. The Vaughn Dortch incident was not an isolated fluke. Prisoners across the United States have smeared themselves in excrement and then been badly scalded when prison officials tried to clean them off. Most recently, such a case was reported in

Florida. The prisoner subsequently died, and the death inspired a federal investigation; see Brown, "Scalding-Shower Death in Dade Prison Prompts Federal Probe."

49. Reiter and Blair, "Punishing Mental Illness, 249.

50. For an analysis of the difficulty of distinguishing the "mad" from the "bad," especially in supermaxes, see generally Rhodes, *Total Confinement*, and Lovell, "Patterns of Disturbed Behavior in a Supermax Population."

Chapter 7. "You Can't Even Imagine There's People"

1. Reiter, "Parole, Snitch, or Die," 537.

2. See generally, Reiter, "Parole, Snitch, or Die."

3. Ibid., 531, 552–53.

4. Herdt, "Record Numbers of Life-Term Inmates Granted Parole in California"; Weisberg, Mukamal, and Segall, *Life in Limbo.*

5. Ibid.

6. In the first of a series of legislative hearings about solitary confinement in October 2013, Robert Barton, the inspector general, testified that between September 2012 and September 2013, approximately 273 prisoners were paroled directly from SHUs. He gave no context or explanation for the steep drop from the much higher figures I documented in the period 1997–2007; see Barton, "Transcript: Testimony of Inspector General Robert Barton."

7. Following passage of the determinate sentencing law in California in 1976 (as discussed in Chapter 3), California maintained indeterminate life sentences for some serious crimes.

8. For a relatively straightforward analysis of the arcane and complicated rules about parole eligibility in California as of 2014, see Prison Law Office, "California's Prison Crowding Reduction Plans and Credit Laws."

9. *Ashker v. Schwarzenegger*, "Exhibit I: Request for Admissions, Set. No. 1," para. 71.

10. Ernie, personal interview with the author.

11. As Chapter 3 suggested, California's sentencing system, which was already convoluted in the 1970s, has become only more so over the last few decades. The more than two-thirds of California prisoners serving fixed sentences include prisoners with determinate sentences (44 percent, or 59,719) and "second strikers" (25 percent, or 34,699) serving double the usual determinate sentence for a second felony conviction, under California's infamous three-strikes law. In total, 94,418 prisoners, 69 percent of the prison population, have some form of fixed sentence. An additional 25 percent of prisoners (34,070) are serving theoretically parole-eligible life sentences. This number includes 26,095 prisoners (19.5 percent of the total prison population) serving life sentences and 7,975 prisoners (5.9 percent of the total) who are "third strikers," prisoners serving terms of twenty-five years to life for a third felony conviction under three strikes. The release of any lifer requires a parole board recommendation and gubernatorial

approval. Fewer than 5 percent of California prisoners are serving sentences of life without the possibility of parole (4,687 prisoners). Those under sentence of death (734 prisoners) constitute less than 1 percent of the prison population; see California Department of Corrections, *Prison Census Data as of June 30, 2013*, table 10. Throughout the United States, 97 percent of prisoners will eventually be released from prison. This figure is based on adding the number of people sentenced to death in the United States (3,305) to the number of people sentenced to life without the possibility of parole (41,095), and dividing by the number of sentenced people currently in state or federal prison (1,540,805), providing a percentage of people who will never be released: 2.88 percent; see Nellis and King, *No Exit;* U.S. Department of Justice, Office of Justice Programs, Bureau of Justice Statistics, *Sourcebook of Criminal Justice Statistics Online*, table 6.80.2009; U.S. Department of Justice, Office of Justice Programs, Bureau of Justice Statistics, *Prison Inmates at Midyear 2008*, by West and Sabol. Petersilia uses a similar calculation in her book *When Prisoners Come Home.*

12. Grattet et al., "Parole Violations and Revocations in California," 2–11.

13. Barton, "Transcript: Testimony of Inspector General Robert Barton."

14. The minimum overlap between the independent categories of indeterminate SHU terms and determinate criminal sentences is equal to the percentage of prisoners serving indeterminate SHU terms (60 percent) minus the percentage of prisoners with life criminal sentences (47.5 percent): 12 percent, or 500 prisoners. The maximum overlap between these independent categories is equal to the percentage of prisoners serving determinate criminal sentences: 52.5 percent, or 2,100 prisoners.

15. Reiter, "Supermax Administration and the Eighth Amendment," app. A, table 1 (updated data cited here is on file with the author).

16. Kim, Pendergrass, and Zelon, *Boxed In.*

17. U.S. Department of Justice, Office of Justice Programs, Bureau of Justice Statistics, *Census of State and Federal Correctional Facilities, 2005*, study no. 24,642. For further discussions of the derivation of and problems with this number, see Cassella and Ridgeway, "How Many Prisoners Are in Solitary?"; Reiter, "Parole, Snitch, or Die," 532–33.

18. Two reports have recently provided updated estimates (rather than actual counts) of the number of prisoners in any form of short- or long-term solitary confinement in the United States: Baumgartel et al., *Time-In-Cell*, and U.S. Department of Justice, Office of Justice Programs, Bureau of Justice Statistics, *Use of Restrictive Housing in U.S. Prisons and Jails, 2011–12*, by Beck.

19. As noted in the introduction, a growing body of scholarship is attending to the local (rather than federal, or national) sources of punishment innovations in the United States. See, for example, Barker, *The Politics of Imprisonment;* Campbell, "Politics, Prisons, and Law Enforcement"; Gilmore, *Golden Gulag;* Lynch, *Sunbelt Justice;* Page, *The Toughest Beat;* Schoenfeld, "Mass Incarceration and Prison Conditions Litigation." The supermax innovation is yet another example of a punish-

ment phenomenon initiated at the local level. In fact, the very localness of the innovation, and its subtle variations across jurisdictions, is part of what has made it hard to define and analyze.

20. Quoted in Dolan, "Indefinite Solitary Confinement Persists in California Prisons."
21. Kumar, "Virginia Plans Changes in Prisoner Isolation Process."
22. Fellner, *Red Onion State Prison.*
23. Shane, "Accused Soldier in Brig as Wikileaks Link is Sought." Colin Dayan also talks about this phenomenon of using language to conceal the conditions of confinement; see *The Story of Cruel and Unusual,* 79.
24. Ray interview. All subsequent quotations in this section are from this interview.
25. An *in limine* hearing is one that takes place outside the presence of a jury, usually to make a decision about the admissibility of evidence.
26. Dickens, "Philadelphia and Its Solitary Prison."
27. Beaumont and Tocqueville, *The Penitentiary System in the United Sates,* 41
28. *In re Medley,* 134 U.S. 160, 168.
29. Brown and Milner, "The Legacy of Donald O. Hebb"; Heron, "The Pathology of Boredom"; McCoy, "Science in Dachau's Shadow."
30. Koenig, Stover, and Fletcher, "The Cumulative Effect."
31. Quoted in Chorover, *From Genesis to Genocide,* 200.
32. Mitford, *Kind and Usual Punishment,* 134–35; Griffin, "Breaking Men's Minds," 7. For further discussions of this history, see Reiter, "The Most Restrictive Alternative," 81–83; Guenther, *Solitary Confinement,* 65–100.
33. *Adams v. Carlson,* 352 F. Supp. 882.
34. Haney and Lynch, "Regulating Prisons of the Future"; King, "The Effects of Supermax Custody". See also Grassian "Psychiatric Effects of Solitary Confinement"; Kupers, *Prison Madness;* Kupers, "What to Do with Survivors?"; Lovell, "Patterns of Disturbed Behavior"; Scharff-Smith, "The Effects of Solitary Confinement on Prison Inmates."
35. Haney, "The Major Methodological Flaws in the 'Colorado Study'"; O'Keefe et al., *One Year Longitudinal Study of the Psychological Effects of Administrative Segregation;* Grassian, "'Fatal Flaws' in the Colorado Solitary Confinement Study." For further discussion, see Reiter and Blair, "Punishing Mental Illness."
36. Haney and Lynch, "Regulating Prisons of the Future."
37. Grassian, "Psychiatric Effects of Solitary Confinement"; Haney, "Mental Health Issues."
38. Czifra, "Transcript: Testimony of Former SHU Inmate Steven Czifra."
39. Quoted in Law, "One Month After Historic Hunger Strike Ends, Legislators Hold Hearings About Solitary Confinement."
40. Askari, "Voices from Solitary."
41. Johnny, personal letters to the author, July 21, 2013.
42. Ernie interview. All subsequent quotations from Ernie and details of his story are from this interview, with the exception of some supplemental details I noted from our initial telephone conversation on July 5, 2013.

43. *Prisoner Hunger Strike Solidarity,* "Prisoners' Demands."

44. This is a pseudonym, as are the other names that Ernie mentions.

45. California Department of Corrections, "Pelican Bay State Prison"; Henrichson and Delaney, *The Price of Prisons,* 9. California's high costs of solitary confinement are nationally representative. See also American Civil Liberties Union, "Paying the Price for Solitary Confinement."

46. One study compared recidivism rates of prisoners released from Florida supermaxes to those of matched groups of prisoners who had not spent time in a supermax; it found no evidence that supermax prisoners were any more likely than other prisoners to be violent recidivists; see Mears and Bales, "Supermax Incarceration and Recidivism." A second study compared the recidivism rates of prisoners released from a Washington State supermax to those of matched groups of non-supermax prisoners and found that prisoners released directly from supermaxes had the highest felony recidivism rates; see Lovell, Johnson, and Cain, "Recidivism of Supermax Prisoners in Washington State."

47. Ebel died shortly thereafter in a police shootout; see Banda, "Tom Clements Dead"; Ford, "Colorado Governor"; Greene; "Evan Ebel Suicide Note Shows Parolee Was 'Ruined' by Solitary, Bent on Revenge"; Gurman, "Evan Ebel Forced Pizza Driver to Make Recording Before His Murder."

48. Jenkins was arrested at the beginning of September 2013 and pleaded guilty to all four murders. He was eligible for the death penalty, but sentencing proceedings were stayed while Jenkins received psychiatric treatment; see Hammel, "Audit Recommends That State Review Use of Solitary Confinement"; Fuchs, "Robber Who Got Out of Prison Early Allegedly Went on a Killing Spree in Nebraska."

Chapter 8. Another Way Out

1. Uncovering past criminal histories is a timeless tactic for discrediting victims of abuse, incarcerated or not, but especially the marginalized, such as African American victims of police violence or female victims of rape. For two especially good examples, see Eligon, "Michael Brown Spent Last Weeks Grappling with Problems and Promise" (a story infamous for calling the victim of a police shooting "no angel") and Suarez and Gadalla, "Stop Blaming the Victim" (examining the prevalence and understanding of false beliefs about how victims cause their own rapes).

2. *Prisoner Hunger Strike Solidarity,* "Prisoners' Demands."

3. The question of exactly why the prisoners decided to strike in 2011, and why the strike was so successful in garnering public attention, deserves further study. I suggest a number of reasons in Reiter, "The Pelican Bay Hunger Strike," including the fact that Judge Henderson had closed the *Madrid* case, the attention that California was already receiving for prison-overcrowding litigation throughout the state, and the simple power of the prisoners' claims and the ways they refocused attention on bodily suffering. In addition, Hadar Aviram explores possible

economic explanations for the broader critique of prisons of which the hunger strikes were a part, and Jonathan Simon explores human-rights-oriented explanations; See Aviram, *Cheap on Crime*, and Simon, *Mass Incarceration on Trial*.

4. Quoted in Lovett, "California Inmates Fast to Protest Isolation Cells."
5. California Department of Corrections, *Strike Summit*.
6. Reiter, "The Pelican Bay Hunger Strike."
7. Larson telephone interview.
8. United Nations, "Solitary Confinement Should Be Banned in Most Cases, UN Expert Says."
9. Small, "Under Scrutiny, Pelican Bay Officials."
10. California Department of Corrections, "Memorandum from Terri McDonald."
11. Beard, "Hunger Strike in California Prisons."
12. St. John, "Prison Hunger Strike Leaders."
13. See, for example, *Ashker v. Brown*, "Declaration of J. Bryan Elrod."
14. California Department of Corrections "Fact Sheet," 2.
15. Law, "'We Are Not the Worst of the Worst.'"
16. *Ashker v. Brown*, "Order Granting Motion for Leave to file a Supplemental Complaint."
17. Center for Constitutional Rights, "*Ashker v. Governor of California* Case Timeline."
18. Quoted in Lau, "Incarceration to Convocation—Life After Solitary Confinement."
19. *Ashker v. Brown*, "Settlement Agreement."
20. Quandt, "Legal Settlement Demands Better Mental Health Care, Less Solitary Confinement in Illinois Prisons"; Hager and Rich, "Shifting Away from Solitary"; Pearson, "New York, Prodded by Lawsuit, Becomes Latest State to Reform Solitary Confinement in Prison."
21. St. John, "California Agrees to Move Thousands of Inmates Out of Solitary Confinement."
22. Shames, Wilcox, and Subramanian, *Solitary Confinement*.
23. Tapley, "Whistleblower Returns"; J. Martin, "State Prisons Rethink Solitary Confinement."
24. Illinois Department of Corrections, "Tamms Correctional Center Closing," 142; Briggs, Sundt, and Castellano, "The Effect of Supermaximum Security Prisons on Aggregate Levels of Institutional Violence."
25. T. E. Perez and D. J. Hickton to Governor Tom Corbett, May 31, 2013.
26. *Peoples v. Fischer*, Docket No. 11-CV-2694-SAS, "Stipulation for a Stay with Conditions"; New York Civil Liberties Union, "NYCLU Lawsuit Secures Historic Reforms to Solitary Confinement."
27. Weinrip and Schwirz, "Rikers Setting Stricter Limits for Isolation."
28. Gonnerman, "Kalief Browder, 1993–2015."
29. For a list of current and pending solitary reforms, see American Civil Liberties Union, "Solitary Confinement: Resource Materials," 14–16. See also American Civil Liberties Union, "State Reforms to Limit the Use of Solitary Confinement"; Brush, "Senate Law Passes Moriarty Data Bill."

30. American Civil Liberties Union, "Solitary Confinement: Resource Materials," 14–16.
31. United Nations, "Solitary Confinement Should Be Banned."
32. S. Rodriguez, "How Many People are in Solitary Confinement in California's Prisons." According to the most recently available Compstat population report, the California Department of Corrections and Rehabilitation operates four SHU units: one at the California Correctional Institute (1,217 prisoners), one at California State Prison, Corcoran (1,214 prisoners), one at Pelican Bay State Prison (1,171 prisoners), and one at the California State Prison, Sacramento (52 prisoners); see California Department of Corrections, *Compstat DAI [Division of Adult Institutions] Statistical Report—13 Month, High Security.*
33. Reiter, "Supermax Administration and the Eighth Amendment."
34. Kupers et al, "Beyond Supermax Administrative Segregation," 2–14.
35. Cassella and Ridgeway, "In States That 'Reduce' Their Use of Solitary Confinement, Suffering Continues for Those Left Behind."
36. Dunn, "DOC Still Working Out Policy for Former Tamms Prisoners."

Afterword

1. Pittendrigh, "Making Visible Invisible Suffering."
2. Antiterrorism and Effective Death Penalty Act of 1996, Pub. L. No. 104-132, 110 Stat. 1214.
3. Under further reforms in California for the sentencing rules for juveniles, however, Johnny may be eligible for a preliminary parole hearing as early as 2019.
4. W. Smith, "Holding On to Humanity."

BIBLIOGRAPHY

Interviews and Correspondence

Barry [pseud.]. Former supermax prisoner. Personal interview with the author, San Francisco, Calif., Dec. 10, 2010. Transcript on file with the author.

Brown, Craig. Former undersecretary of the Youth and Adult Correctional Authority, California. Personal interview with the author, Sacramento, Calif., Jan. 22, 2010. Notes on file with the author.

Cambra, Steve. Former warden of Pelican Bay State Prison. Personal interview with the author, Sacramento, Calif., Apr. 14, 2010. Notes on file with the author.

Derrick [pseud.]. Former supermax prisoner. Personal interview with the author, Berkeley, Calif., July 25, 2010. Transcript on file with the author.

Ernie [pseud.]. Former supermax prisoner. Personal interview with the author, Stockton, Calif., Sept. 5, 2013. Transcript on file with the author.

Fama, Steve. Attorney with the Prison Law Office and co-counsel in *Madrid v. Gomez*. Personal interview with the author, Berkeley, Calif., Oct. 13, 2010. Notes on file with the author.

Henderson, Thelton. Former chief judge, U.S. District Court for the Northern District of California. Personal interview with the author, San Francisco, Calif., May 24, 2011. Notes on file with the author.

Johnny [pseud.]. Current supermax prisoner. Personal letters to the author, stamped "Pelican Bay Security Housing Unit, July 21, 2013." On file with the author.

———. Personal letters to the author, stamped "Pelican Bay Security Housing Unit, Sept. 25, 2012." On file with the author.

Justice architect (Arizona). Telephone interview with the author, Feb. 10, 2011. Notes on file with the author.

Justice architect (California). Telephone interview with the author, Sept. 1, 2010. Notes on file with the author.

Justice architect (federal). Telephone interview with the author, June 22, 2010. Notes on file with the author.

Justice architect (federal). Telephone interview with the author, Mar. 4, 2011. Notes on file with the author.

Kirkland, Rich. Former project director, Pelican Bay State Prison construction project. Personal interview with the author, Sacramento, Calif., Sept. 9, 2010. Notes on file with the author.

Larson, Carl. Former finance director, warden of New Prison Design and Activation, California Department of Corrections. Personal interview with the author, Sacramento, Calif., Feb. 23, 2010. Notes on file with the author.

———. E-mail exchange, July 20, 2011. On file with the author.

———. Telephone interview with the author, July 22, 2013.

Max [pseud.]. Former supermax prisoner. Personal interview with the author, San Mateo, Calif., July 20, 2010. Transcript on file with the author.

Nolen, Steve. Brother of BGF founder W. L. Nolen. Personal interview with the author, Berkeley, Calif., Dec. 5, 2015. Transcript on file with the author.

Rashid [pseud.]. Former supermax prisoner. Telephone interviews with author, Feb. 18 and 27, 2011. Transcripts on file with the author.

Ray [pseud.]. Former supermax prisoner. Personal interview with the author, Stockton, Calif., June 20, 2010. Transcript on file with the author.

Court Cases

Adams v. Carlson, 352 F. Supp. 882 (E.D. Ill. 1973).

———. 368 F. Supp. 1050 (E.D. Ill. 1973).

Ashker v. California Department of Corrections, 112 F.3d 392 (9th Cir. 1997).

Ashker v. Cate, No. 09-2948-CW, 2012 U.S. Dist. LEXIS 45575 (N.D. Cal., Mar. 30, 2012).

Ashker v. Schwarzenegger, Case No. C05-3286 CW, U.S. Dist. LEXIS 25092 (N.D. Cal., Oakland Div., filed Jan. 30, 2006), later renamed *Ashker v. Brown*, Case No. 4:09-cv-05796-CW (N.D. Cal., Oakland Div.).

———. "Declaration of J. Bryan Elrod in Support of Defendants' Opposition to Plaintiffs' Motion for Class Certification," July 11, 2013. Copy on file with the author.

———. "Declaration of Todd Ashker in Support of Plaintiffs' Motion for Class Certification," with attached "Exhibit B: Gang Chrono," May 2, 2013. On file with the author.

———. "Exhibit D." Attached to "Declaration of Ronnie Dewberry, in Support of Plaintiffs' Motion for Class Certification," Doc. 195-1, May 2, 2013. On file with the author.

———. "Exhibit I: Request for Admissions, Set. No. 1," May 18, 2006. On file with the author.

———. "Exhibit UU: *In the matter of the Life Term Parole Consideration Hearing of Todd Ashker*, CDC No. C-58191, Initial Parole Consideration Hearing, State of California

Board of Prison Terms, Pelican Bay State Prison, Crescent City, CA, Aug. 7, 2003."
Attached to "Request for Admissions, Set. No. 1," May 18, 2006. On file with the
author.

———. "Exhibit UU: *People v. Ashker,* Sup. C. No. 86886 (C008758), Appeal in Ct.
App. 3d App. Dist. Ca., filed Apr. 30 1992." Attached to "Request for Admissions,
Set. No. 1," May 18, 2006. On file with the author.

———. "First Amended Complaint with Supplemental State Law Claims." Jan. 30,
2006. On file with the author.

———. "Opinion: Order Granting, in Part, and Denying, in Part, Defendants' Motion
for Summary Judgment and Denying Plaintiffs' Cross Motion for Summary Judgment and Plaintiffs' Motion for Preliminary Injunction." Mar. 25, 2009. On file
with the author.

———. "Order Granting Motion for Leave to File a Supplemental Complaint." Mar. 9,
2015. Available at https://ccrjustice.org/sites/default/files/attach/2015/06/Order
%20on%20Motion%20to%20Supplement%20Complaint.pdf.

———. "Request for Admissions, Set. No. 1," May 18, 2006. On file with the author.

———. "Settlement Agreement," Aug. 31, 2015. On file with the author.

Ayers v. Perry, Case No. 02-1438 (Dist. N.M., Santa Fe Co., Oct. 2002), Complaint for
Class Based Declaratory and Injunctive Relief and for Individual and Compensatory and Punitive Damages, Nov. 2, 2002. On file with the author.

Baxter v. Palmigiano, 425 U.S. 308 (1976).

Brown v. Timmerman-Cooper, 2013 U.S. Dist. LEXIS 14777. No 2:10 cv 283 (S.D.
Ohio, Feb. 4, 2014).

Bruce v. Ylst, 351 F.3d 1283 (9th Cir. 2003).

Casey v. Lewis, 834 F. Supp. 1569 (D. Ariz. 1993).

Castro v. Terhune, 712 F.3d 1304 (9th Cir. 2013).

Clutchette v. Procunier, 328 F. Supp. 767 (N.D. Cal. 1971).

Coleman v. Wilson, 912 F. Supp. 1282 (E.D. Cal. 1995), later *Coleman v. Schwarzenegger,* then *Coleman v. Brown,* Case No. Civ S 90-0520 LKKJFM, 2008 WL 8697735
(E.D. Cal).

———. "Expert Report of Professor Craig Haney."

———. "Order" April 10, 2014

Crow v. Montgomery, 2003 U.S. Dist. LEXIS 27708, No. 4:02-CV-00352-WRW (E.D.
Ark., Nov. 14, 2003).

Davis v. Ayala, 576 U.S. ___ (2015), No. 13-1428.

Griffin v. Gomez, 741 F.3d 10 (9th Cir. 2012).

Hutto v. Finney, 437 U.S. 678 (1978).

In re Lynch, 8 Cal. 3d 410 (Cal. S. Ct. 1972).

In re Medley, 134 U.S. 160 (1890).

In re Rodriguez, 14 Cal 3d 639 (Cal. S. Ct. 1975).

In re Stanley, 54 Cal. App. 3d 1030 (App. Ct. Cal. 1976).

In the Matter of the Life Term Parole Consideration Hearing of Hugo Pinell, CDC Number: A-88401. May 2, 2014. Transcript on file with author.

Indiana Protection and Advocacy Services Com'n v. Commissioner, Indiana Dept. of Correction, Case No. 1:08-CV-01317 TWPMJD, 2012 WL 6738517 (S.D. Ind. Dec. 31, 2012).

Jeffers v. Gomez, 267 F.3d 895, 916 (9th Cir. 2001).

Jones'El v. Berge, 164 F. Supp. 2d 1096 (W.D. Wisc. 2001).

Kelly v. Brewer, 378 F. Supp. 447 (S.D. Iowa 1974).

Madrid v. Gomez, Case No. 90-3094, 899 F. Supp 1146 (N.D. Cal. 1995).

———. "Order Granting Motion to Certify Class Action." Docket No. 83. Mar. 13, 1992.

Miller v. Alabama, 567 U.S. __, 132 S. Ct. 2455 (2012)

Morissey v. Brewer, 408 U.S. 471 (1972).

Peoples v. Fischer, Docket No. 11-CV-2694-SAS (S.D.N.Y., Feb. 19, 2014). "Stipulation for a Stay with Conditions."

Pifer v. Marshall, 1998 U.S. App. LEXIS 3189 (9th Cir. Cal. Feb. 24, 1998).

Plata v. Brown, No. 09-1233, 563 U.S. ___ (2011).

———. "Joint Request for Order Authorizing Re-Feeding Under Specified Conditions of Hunger-Striking Inmate Patients and Order Thereon." *Plata v. Brown,* Case No. C01-1351-THE (N.D. Cal., Aug. 19, 2013). Order on file with the author.

Powell v. Alabama, 287 U.S. 45 (1932).

Rhodes v. Chapman, 452 U.S. 337 (1981).

Rowland v. United States Dist. Court for Northern Dist., 849 F.2d 380 (9th Cir. 1988).

Ruiz v. Johnson, 37 F. Supp. 2d 855 (S.D. Tex. 1999).

Rushen v. Spain, 464 U.S. 114 (1983).

Silverstein v. Federal Bureau of Prisons, No. 12-1450, D.Ct. No. 1:07-CV-02471-PAB-KMT (10th Cir. May 22, 2014). Document on file with the author.

———. 704 F. Supp. 2d 1077 (D. Col. 2010).

Spain v. Procunier, 408 F. Supp. 534 (N.D. Cal. 1976), *aff'd in part* 600 F.2d 189 (9th Cir. 1979).

Spain v. Rushen, 543 F. Supp. 757 (N.D. Cal. 1982), *overturned by* 464 U.S. 114, 117–18 (1983), *reconsidered at* 882 F.2d 712 (9th Cir. 1989).

Spencer v. Courtier, 2011 U.S. Dist. LEXIS 73122, No. 09-124 Erie (W.D. Penn. May 23, 2011).

Taifa v. Bayh, Case No. 8:92-CV-429 AS (N. Dist. Ind. 1995).

Toussaint v. McCarthy, 597 F. Supp. 1388 (N.D. Cal. 1984), *aff'd in part, rev'd in part,* 801 F.2d 1080 (9th Cir. 1986), *cert. denied,* 481 U.S. 1069 (1987).

Toussaint v. Rushen, 553 F. Supp. 1355 (N.D. Cal. 1983).

U.S. v. Powers, Case No. 3:00-cr-00105-MJJ-2 (N.D. Cal., Feb. 6, 2003).

Washington-El v. Beard, 2011 U.S. Dist. LEXIS 24562, No. 08-1688 (W.D. Penn, Mar. 11, 2011).

Watson v. Quarterman, 2008 U.S. Dist. LEXIS 15169, No. H-06-3260 (S.D. Tex., Feb. 27, 2008).

Wheeler v. Vaughn, 2004 U.S. Dist. LEXIS 539, No. 01-428 (E.D. Penn, Jan. 5, 2004).

Wilkinson v. Austin, 545 U.S. 209 (2005).

Williams v. Branker, 2011 U.S. Dist. LEXIS 13402, No. 5:09-CT-3139-D (E.D. NC, Feb. 10, 2011).

Wright v. Enomoto, 462 F. Supp. 397 (N.D. Cal. 1976).

All Other Sources

Agamben, Giorgio. *Homo Sacer: Sovereign Power and Bare Life.* Palo Alto, Calif.: Stanford University Press, 1998.

———. *State of Exception.* Chicago: University of Chicago Press, 2005.

Alcalá, Carlos. "Public Safety Chairs Ammiano, Hancock Announce Hearings on Hunger Strike Issues." *San Francisco Bay View,* Aug. 30, 2013. http://sfbayview.com/ 2013/08/public-safety-chairs-ammiano-hancock-announce-hearings-on-hunger-strike -issues.

Alexander, Michelle. *The New Jim Crow: Mass Incarceration in the Age of Colorblindness.* New York: New Press, 2012.

Alger, Paula, and Theresa Molinari. *The Use of General Obligation Bonds by the State of California.* Sacramento: California Debt Advisory Commission, Sept. 9, 1987. www .treasurer.ca.gov/cdiac/reports/go_use.pdf.

Alschuler, Albert W. "Sentencing Reform and Prosecutorial Power: A Critique of Recent Proposals for 'Fixed' and 'Presumptive' Sentencing." *University of Pennsylvania Law Review* 126, no. 3 (Jan. 1978): 550–77.

American Civil Liberties Union. *ACLU Briefing Paper: The Dangerous Overuse of Solitary Confinement in the United States.* Aug. 2014. https://www.aclu.org/sites/default/ files/field_document/stop_solitary_briefing paper_updated_august_2014.pdf.

———. "Paying the Price for Solitary Confinement: ACLU Fact Sheet." 2015. https:// www.prisonlegalnews.org/news/publications/paying-price-solitary-confinement -aclu-factsheet-2015.

———. "Solitary Confinement: Resource Materials." https://www.aclu.org/files/as sets/Solitary%20Confinement%20Resource%20Materials%2012%2017%2013.pdf.

———. "State Reforms to Limit the Use of Solitary Confinement." https://www.aclu .org/files/assets/state_reforms_to_limit_the_use_of_solitary_confinement.pdf.

American Correctional Association. *Directory of Adult and Juvenile Correctional Departments, Institutions, Agencies, and Probation and Parole Authorities.* 71st ed. Alexandria, Va.: American Correctional Association, 2010.

American Friends Service Committee. *Struggle for Justice: A Report on Crime and Punishment in America.* New York: Hill & Wang, 1971.

Anderson, Harry. "California & Co.; Prisons: Economic Tonic for Rural Areas." *Los Angeles Times,* Oct. 9, 1990.

Andrews, Lori. *Black Power, White Blood: The Life and Times of Johnny Spain.* New York: Pantheon, 1996.

Arendt, Hannah. *Eichmann in Jerusalem: A Report on the Banality of Evil.* New York: Penguin, 2006; orig. pub. 1963.

Armstrong, Gregory. *The Dragon Has Come*. New York: Harper & Row, 1970.

Arrington Watkins. "Project Portfolio: Justice: Prisons: Arizona: ASPC—Eyman— Special Management Unit I." www.awarch.com/projects/categorylist.php?id=2 (accessed Aug. 28, 2014, but no longer available).

Ashker, Todd, and Danny Troxell. "Final Notice: PBSP SHU D-Corridor Hunger Strike." Apr. 3, 2011. Available on the website of Kersplebedeb, www.kersplebedeb .com/mystuff/july1/finalnotice.php. Copy on file with author.

Ashker, Todd, Arturo Castellanos, Shawn Nantambu Jamas (Dewberry), Antonio Guillen, Danny Troxell, George Franco, Ronnie Yardell, et al. "Statement Suspending the Third Hunger Strike." *Prisoner Hunger Strike Solidarity* (blog), Sept. 5, 2013. https://prisonerhungerstrikesolidarity.wordpress.com/2013/09/05/statement -suspending-the-third-hunger-strike. Copy on file with author.

Askari, Kijana Tashiri. "Voices from Solitary: The Safari from Pelikkan Bay." *Solitary Watch*, Apr. 16, 2015. http://solitarywatch.com/2015/04/16/voices-from-solitary-the -safari-from-pelikkan-bay/.

Associated Press. "Chronology of 1993 Lucasville Prison Riot." Apr. 8, 2013. Available from the *Alliance (Ohio) Review.* www.the-review.com/editors%20pick/2013/04/08/ chronology-of-1993-lucasville-ohio-prison-riot.

———. "Counties Told to Restore Welfare Cuts: Officials Plan to Send Supplemental Checks Later This Month." *Los Angeles Times*, Dec. 2, 1981.

———. "Guards Convicted of Plotting Attacks." *San Diego Union Tribune*, May 16, 2002.

———. "Judge Upsets Conviction of San Quentin Inmate." *New York Times*, July 2, 1982.

———. "Rule Overturned on Agent Orange: Judge Orders VA to Review More than 31,000 Claims." *New York Times*, May 9, 1989.

———. "State Farm Found Guilty of Sex Bias: Insurer Excluded Women from Agent Training, Court Holds." *Los Angeles Times*, Apr. 30, 1985.

———. "Two Suspects Charged in Slaying of San Quentin 6 Inmate." Dec. 8, 2015.

———. "U.S. Observers Must Accompany Tuna Boats." *Los Angeles Times*, Jan. 18, 1989.

Aviram, Hadar. *Cheap on Crime: Recession-Era Politics and the Transformation of American Punishment*. Berkeley: University of California Press, 2015.

Bagdikian, Ben H. "Books: Crime, Punishment." *Washington Post*, Jan. 11, 1972.

Bagehot, Walter. *The English Constitution*. 2nd ed. London: Chapman & Hall, 1873. Available from the Department of Economics, McMaster University, http://socserv2 .socsci.mcmaster.ca/econ/ugcm/3ll3/bagehot/constitution.pdf.

Banda, P. Solomon. "Tom Clements Dead: Colorado Department of Corrections Chief Shot at Home, Gunman on the Road." Associated Press, Mar. 20 2013. Available from the *Huffington Post*, www.huffingtonpost.com/2013/03/20/tom-clements -deadcolorado_n_2914314.html.

Bargu, Banu. *Starve and Immolate: The Politics of Human Weapons*. New York: Columbia University Press, 2014.

Barker, Vanessa. *The Politics of Imprisonment: How the Democratic Process Shapes the Way America Punishes Offenders.* New York: Oxford University Press, 2009.

Barton, Robert. "Transcript: Testimony of Inspector General Robert Barton at the joint legislative hearing on solitary confinement in California–October 9, 2013." Partial transcript available at What the Folly, Oct. 22, 2013, www.whatthefolly .com/2013/10/22/transcript-testimony-of-inspector-general-robert-barton-at-the -joint-legislative-hearing-on-solitary-confinement-in-california-oct-9-2013.

Baumgartel, Sarah, Corey Guilmette, Johanna Kalb, Diana Li, Josh Nuni, Devon Por-ter, Judith Resnik, Camille Camp, and George Camp. *Time-In-Cell: The ASCA-Liman 2014 National Survey of Administrative Segregation in Prison.* New Haven, Conn.: Arthur Liman Public Interest Program, Yale Law School, with the Associa-tion of State Correctional Administrators, Aug. 2015. https://www.law.yale.edu/ system/files/area/center/liman/document/asca-liman_administrativesegregation report.pdf.

Beard, Jeffrey. "Hunger Strike in California Prisons Is a Gang Power Play." Editorial, *Los Angeles Times,* Aug. 6. 2013. http://articles.latimes.com/2013/aug/06/opinion/ la-oe-beard-prison-hunger-strike-20130806.

Beaumont, Gustave de, and Alexis de Tocqueville. *On the Penitentiary System in the United Sates and Its Application to France.* Translated by Francis Lieber. Philadelphia: Casey, Lea & Blanchard, 1833. Available from the Internet Archive, www.archive .org/details/onpenitentiarysyoobeauuoft.

Beckett, Katherine, and Theodore Sasson. *The Politics of Injustice: Crime and Punish-ment in America.* 2nd ed. New York: Sage, 2004.

Benford, R. D, and Snow, D. A. "Framing Processes and Social Movements: An Overview and Assessment." *Annual Review of Sociology* 26, no. 1 (2000): 611–39.

Bentham, Jeremy. *The Panopticon Writings.* Edited by Miran Bozovic. London: Verso, 1995; orig. pub. 1787.

Berger, Dan. "America's Fortress of Blood: The Death of George Jackson and the Birth of the Prison-Industrial Complex." *Salon,* Sept. 7, 2014. www.salon.com/ 2014/09/07/americas_fortress_of_blood_the_death_of_george_jackson_and_the _birth_of_the_prison_industrial_complex.

———. *Captive Nation: Black Prison Organizing in the Radical Civil Rights Era.* Chapel Hill: University of North Carolina Press, 2014.

———. *The Struggle Within: Prisons, Political Prisoners, and Mass Movements in the United States.* Oakland: PM Press, 2014.

———. "Two Prisoners Named Williams." *Nation,* Dec. 26, 2005. www.thenation .com/article/two-prisoners-named-williams#.

Bissonnette, Jamie. *When the Prisoners Ran Walpole: A True Story in the Movement for Prison Abolition.* With Ralph Hamm, Robert Dellelo, and Edward Rodman. Cam-bridge, Mass.: South End, 2008.

Blankstein, Andrew. "Jailed Mafia Hit Man Gets LAPD Escort to Meet L.A. Business Leaders." NBCNews.com, Jan. 29, 2015. www.nbcnews.com/news/us-news/jailed -mafia-hit-man-gets-lapd-escort-meet-l-business-n295841.

Blatchford, Chris. *The Black Hand: The Story of Rene "Boxer" Enriquez and His Life in the Mexican Mafia*. New York: HarperCollins, 2008.

Blonien, Rodney J. Letter to Robert Presley, May 30, 1986. Presley's Bill File on SB-2098, 1986. Sacramento, California State Archives, Loc: LP347: 367—Robert Presley Papers—Subject Files—Corrections. Copy on file with the author.

Bloom, Joshua, and Waldo E. Martin. *Black Against Empire: The History and Politics of the Black Panther Party*. Berkeley: University of California Press, 2013.

Blumstein, Alfred. "Prison Populations: A System Out of Control." In *Crime and Justice: A Review of Research*, edited by Michael Tonry and Norval Morris, vol. 10. Chicago: University of Chicago Press, 1988.

Blumstein, Alfred, and Jacqueline Cohen. "A Theory of the Stability of Punishment." *Journal of Criminal Law and Criminology* 64, no. 2 (June 1973): 198–207.

Blumstein, Alfred, Jacqueline Cohen, and William Gooding. "The Influence of Capacity on Prison Population: A Critical Review of Some Recent Evidence." *Crime and Delinquency* 29 (1983): 1–51.

Bobo, Lawrence D., and Victor Thompson. "Racialized Mass Incarceration: Poverty, Prejudice, and Punishment." *Doing Race* 21 (2010): 322–55.

Boston, John. *The Prison Litigation Reform Act*. New York: Legal Aid Society, Prisoners' Rights Project, 2004. www.wnylc.net/pb/docs/plra2cir04.pdf.

Bowers, Joshua E. "'The Integrity of the Game Is Everything': The Problem of Geographic Disparity in Three Strikes." *New York University Law Review* 76 (Oct. 2001): 1164–1202.

Bozelko, Chandra. "Why We Let Prison Rape Go On." *New York Times*, Apr 17, 2015. www.nytimes.com/2015/04/18/opinion/why-we-let-prison-rape-go-on.html.

Brewer, David, Gerald E. Beckett, and Norman Holt. "Determinate Sentencing in California: The First Year's Experience." *Journal of Research in Crime and Delinquency* 18 (1981): 200–231.

Briggs, Chad S., Jody L. Sundt, and Thomas C. Castellano. "The Effect of Supermaximum Security Prisons on Aggregate Levels of Institutional Violence." *Criminology* 41 (2003): 1341–76.

Brown, Brian, Edgar Cabral, and Paul Steenhausen. *California's Criminal Justice System: A Primer*. Sacramento: Legislative Analyst's Office, Jan. 31, 2007. www.lao.ca.gov/2007/cj_primer/cj_primer_013107.pdf.

Brown, Edmund G., Jr. "Indeterminate Sentence Parole Release Review: Penal Code Section 3041.2: Rene Enriquez, H-69471." Feb. 20, 2015. Document on file with the author.

Brown, Julie K. "Scalding-Shower Death in Dade Prison Prompts Federal Probe." *Miami Herald*, May 19, 2015. www.miamiherald.com/news/special-reports/florida-prisons/article21429693.html.

Brown, Richard E., and Peter M. Milner. "The Legacy of Donald O. Hebb: More Than the Hebb Synapse." *Nature Reviews: Neuroscience* 4 (Dec. 2003): 1013–19.

Brundage, W. Fitzhugh. "Review of *Nat Turner: A Slave Rebellion in History and Memory*." *Journal of Southern History* 70, no. 2 (May 2004): 424–26.

Brush, Chase. "Senate Law Passes Moriarty Data Bill, Debates the Use of Solitary Confinement in NJ." PolitickerNJ, Feb. 12, 2015. http://politickernj.com/2015/02/ senate-law-passes-moriarty-data-bill-debates-the-use-of-solitary-confinement-in-nj.

Cain, Bruce E., and Marc A. Levin. "Term Limits." *Annual Review of Political Science* 2 (1999): 163–88.

Calavita, Kitty. *Inside the State: The Bracero Program, Immigration, and the INS.* New Orleans: Quid Pro Quo, 1992/2010.

Calavita, Kitty, and Valerie Jenness. *Appealing to Justice: Prisoner Grievances, Rights, and Carceral Logic.* Berkeley: University of California Press, 2015.

Calder, Bill. "Crescent City Gets Welcome Boom from New Prison; State Institution to Add Millions to Economy." *Oregonian,* Feb. 9, 1988.

California Assembly. Assembly Bill 277 (Stirling, 1986). Enacted, as amended Aug. 25.

———. Select Committee on Prison Reform and Rehabilitation. Chairman, Walter Karabian. *Administrative Segregation in California's Prisons; Alias: The Hole, Lockup, Solitary Confinement, and the Adjustment Center; Report.* Government Publications, Sept. 1973.

California Department of Corrections [and Rehabilitation]. *Average Daily Prison Population: Fiscal Year 2012/13.* Sacramento: Offender Information Services Branch, July 2013. www.cdcr.ca.gov/Reports_Research/Offender_Information_Services_Branch/ Annual/IPOP2/Ipop2d1306.pdf

———. *California Prisoners and Civil Narcotics Addicts: 1983, 1984, 1985.* Sacramento: Youth and Adult Correctional Agency, Department of Corrections Administrative Services Division, Offender Information Services Branch, 1986. www.cdcr.ca.gov/ reports_research/offender_information services_branch/Annual/CalPris/CALP RISd1983_84_85.pdf.

———. *California Prisoners and Parolees, 2010.* Sacramento: Offender Information Services Branch, Estimates and Statistical Analysis Section, Data Analysis Unit, 2011. www.cdcr.ca.gov/Reports_Research/Offender_Information_Services_Branch/ Annual/CalPris/CALPRISd2010.pdf.

———. *Compstat DAI Statistical Report—13 Month, High Security.* Apr. 13, 2015. www .cdcr.ca.gov/COMPSTAT

———. *Department Operation Manual.* Adult Institutions, Programs, and Parole. Jan. 1, 2015. www.cdcr.ca.gov/Regulations/Adult_Operations/docs/DOM/DOM%20 2015/DOM%202015.pdf. Copy on file with the author.

———. "Fact Sheet: Security Threat Group Prevention, Identification and Management Strategy," Oct. 2013. Copy on file with the author.

———. Inmate Incidents in Institution Report Archive. www.cdcr.ca.gov/Reports_ Research/Offender_Information_Services_Branch/Annual/Beh1Archive.html.

———. *Inmate Incidents in Institutions, Calendar Year 1988.* Sacramento: Offender Information Services Branch, May 1999. www.cdcr.ca.gov/Reports_Research/Offender _Information_Services_Branch/Annual/BEH1/BEH1d1998.pdf.

———. *Inmate Incidents in Institutions, Calendar Year 2006.* Sacramento: Offender Information Services Branch, Sept. 2007. www.cdcr.ca.gov/Reports_Research/Offender _Information_Services_Branch/Annual/BEH1/BEH1d2006.pdf.

———. "Memorandum from Terri McDonald, Under Secretary of Operations, California Department of Corrections and Rehabilitation, to CDCR Extended Staff." August 16, 2012. On file with the author.

———. *Operation Manual.* Jan. 1, 2015. Copy on file with the author.

———. Population Reports. www.cdcr.ca.gov/Reports_Research/Offender_Information _Services_Branch/Population_Reports.html.

———. *Prison Census Data as of June 30, 2013.* Sacramento: Offender Information Services Branch, Estimates and Statistical Analysis Section, Data Analysis Unit, Sept. 2013). www.cdcr.ca.gov/Reports_Research/Offender_Information_Services _Branch/Annual/Census/CENSUSd1306.pdf.

———. "Pelican Bay State Prison." http://www.cdcr.ca.gov/COMIO/Uploadfile/pdfs/ Pelican_Bay.pdf.

———. "San Quentin State Prison (SQ)." www.cdcr.ca.gov/Facilities_Locator/SQ.html.

———. *Second and Third Striker Felons in the Adult Institution Population.* Sacramento: Data Analysis Unit, Estimates and Statistical Analysis Section, Offender Information Services Branch, Mar. 31, 2011.

———. *Strike Summit.* DVD Recording. July 20, 2011. Transcript on file with the author.

California Prison Industry Authority. "About CALPIA." http://pia.ca.gov/About_PIA/ AboutPIA.aspx.

California Senate. Senate Bill 9 ("California Fair Sentencing for Youth") (Yee, 2010). Chaptered at 828 (2012).

———. Senate Bill 95 (Keene, California, 1985) (enacted).

———. Senate Bill 526 (1993). Chaptered at Sec. 2, Ch. 3.5 (commencing at Sec. 5085), Title 7, Part 3 of the Penal Code, Oct. 4, 1993.

———. Senate Bill 1222 (Keene, California, 1986) (enacted). Assembly Comments to Senate Bill 1222 to the Third Reading Comments, June 30, 1986. Enacted Aug. 13, 1986.

———. Senate Bill 1685 (1988). Conference Committee Notes to Senate Bill 1685.

———. Senate Bill 2098 (Presley, California, 1986). California State Archives. Loc: LP220: 30–79; LP228:57–114; LP347:1–347—Robert Presley Papers—Bill File on SB-2098.

California State Archives. Inventory of the Robert Presley Papers. Online Archive of California, www.oac.cdlib.org/view?docId=kt4d5nc7nn;query=;style=oac4;view =admin#bioghist-1.3.3.

California State Legislature. Joint Legislative Committee on Prison Construction and Operations. *Anatomy of a Prison, Folsom: Examination of Selected Operational, Policy, and Fiscal Questions Affecting California's Prisons Today.* Special Report, 1990. California State Archives, AN: 2003-029, Joint Committee on Prison Construction and Operation: Subject Files, Hearing Files 1981–1999, Loc: B4181-2907 (box 1 of 2). Copy on file with the author.

————. *California's Prisons: Vacaville Expansion.* A Hearing held by the Joint Legislative Committee on Prison Construction and Operations, Jan. 5, 1984. Sacramento: Joint Publications Office, 1984. Available at Golden Gate University School of Law, http://digitalcommons.law.ggu.edu/caldocs_joint_committees/57.

————. *Summary of 1986–88 Prison Related Legislation.* Sacramento: Joint Publications, 1989.

————. *California's Prisons: Violence at Folsom Prison; Causes, Possible Solutions.* Transcript of hearing held June 19, 1985, Folsom Prison, Folsom, California. Available at Golden Gate University School of Law, http://digitalcommons.law.ggu.edu/caldocs_joint_committees/60.

Campbell, Michael. "The Emergence of Penal Extremism in California: A Dynamic View of Institutional Structures and Political Processes." *Law and Society Review* 48, no. 2 (June 2014): 377–409.

————. "Politics, Prisons, and Law Enforcement: An Examination of the Emergence of 'Law and Order' Politics in Texas." *Law and Society Review* 45 (2011): 631–61.

Canales, Dolores. "Transcript: Testimony of Dolores Canales, Mother of Current Pelican Bay SHU Inmate, at the Joint Legislative Hearing on Solitary Confinement in California—October 9, 2013." Partial transcript available at What the Folly, Oct. 22, 2013, www.whatthefolly.com/2013/10/22/transcript-testimony-of-dolores-canales-mother-of-current-pelican-bay-shu-inmate-at-the-joint-legislative-hearing-on-solitary-confinement-in-california-oct-9-2013.

Casella, Jean, and James Ridgeway. "How Many Prisoners Are in Solitary Confinement in the United States?" *Solitary Watch*, Feb. 1, 2012. http://solitarywatch.com/2012/02/01/how-many-prisoners-are-in-solitary-confinement-in-the-united-states.

————. "In States That 'Reduce' Their Use of Solitary Confinement, Suffering Continues for Those Left Behind." *Solitary Watch*, Nov. 13, 2013. http://solitarywatch.com/2013/11/13/states-reduced-use-solitary-confinement-suffering-continues-left-behind.

————. "UN Torture Investigator Calls on Nations to End Solitary Confinement." *Solitary Watch*, Oct. 19, 2011. http://solitarywatch.com/2011/10/19/un-torture-investigator-calls-on-nations-to-end-solitary-confinement.

Cassou, April K., and Brian Taugher. "Determinate Sentencing in California: The New Numbers Game." *Pacific Law Journal* 9 (1978): 5–106.

CBS News. "Pelican Bay." *60 Minutes*, Sept. 12, 1993.

Center for Constitutional Rights. "*Ashker v. Governor of California* Case Timeline." https://ccrjustice.org/home/what-we-do/our-cases/ashker-v-brown.

————. "Summary of *Ashker v. Governor of California* Settlement Terms." https://ccrjustice.org/sites/default/files/attach/2015/08/2015-09-01-Ashker-settlement-summary.pdf.

Chase, Robert T. "We Are Not Slaves: Rethinking the Rise of Carceral States Through the Lens of the Prisoners' Rights Movement." *Journal of American History* 102, no. 1 (June 2015): 73–86.

Chiang, Harriet. "East Bay: Film Captures Trials of Judge Henderson." *San Francisco*

Chronicle, Oct. 7, 2005. www.sfgate.com/bayarea/article/East-Bay-Film-captures -trials-of-Judge-Henderson-2604142.php.

Chicago Tribune. "Riot Squad Quashes Iowa Prison Uprising." Jan. 7, 1986.

Chorover, Stephan L. *From Genesis to Genocide: The Meaning of Human Nature and the Power of Behavior Control.* Cambridge, Mass.: MIT Press, 1979.

Clear, Todd. *Imprisoning Communities: How Mass Incarceration Makes Disadvantaged Neighborhoods Worse.* New York: Oxford University Press, 2007.

Clemmer, Donald. *The Prison Community.* New York: Rinehart, 1958.

Clutchette, John. "Soledad Brother John Clutchette Asks for Your Help." *San Francisco Bay View,* June 26, 2015. http://sfbayview.com/2015/06/soledad-brother-john -clutchette-asks-for-your-help.

Collier, Peter, and David Horowitz. *Destructive Generation: Second Thoughts About the Sixties.* New York: Encounter Books, 1989.

Connolly, Amy R. "Forty Years Later, Report Details Torture of Inmates During Attica Riot." United Press International, May 22, 2015. www.upi.com/Top_News/US/ 2015/05/22/40-years-later-report-details-torture-of-inmates-during-Attica-riot/ 7891432286090.

Corradini, Mike, Kristine Huskey, and Christy Fujio. *Buried Alive: Solitary Confinement in the U.S. Detention System.* Washington, D.C.: Physicians for Human Rights, April 2013. https://s3.amazonaws.com/PHR_Reports/Solitary-Confinement-April -2013-full.pdf.

Correctional Association of New York. "States That Provide Mental Health Alternatives to Solitary Confinement." New York: Correctional Association of New York, 2008. www.correctionalassociation.org/wp-content/uploads/2012/05/Out_of_State _Models.pdf.

Corwin, Miles. "High-Tech Facility Ushers in New Era of State Prisons." *Los Angeles Times,* May 1, 1990.

———. "Residents Rattling Local Prison Bars." *Los Angeles Times,* Aug. 6, 1990.

Council of State Governments. *Definite Sentencing: An Examination of Proposals in Four States.* Lexington, Ky.: Council of State Governments, 1976.

Cozens, Phil. "Law Office of Philip Cozens," NOLO, www.nolo.com/lawyers/profile/ law-office-of-philip-cozens.

Critical Resistance. "Celebrate Black August." http://criticalresistance.org/resources/ current-analysis/celebrate-black-august.

Cullen, Francis T., Paula Smith, Christopher T. Lowenkamp, and Edward J. Latessa. "Deconstructing Farabee's Rethinking Rehabilitation: Nothing Works Revisited." *Victims and Offenders* 4 (2009): 101–23.

Cummins, Eric. *The Rise and Fall of California's Radical Prison Movement.* Stanford, Calif.: Stanford University Press, 1994.

Czifra, Steven. "Transcript: Testimony of Former SHU Inmate Steven Czifra at the Joint Legislative Hearing on Solitary Confinement in California—October 9, 2013." Partial transcript available at What the Folly, Oct. 22, 2013, www.whatthefolly.com/ 2013/10/22/transcript-testimony-of-former-shu-inmate-steven-czifra-at-the-joint -legislative-hearing-on-solitary-confinement-in-california-oct-9-2013.

Davis, Angela. *Angela Davis: An Autobiography*. New York: International Publishers, 2013.

———. "From the Convict Lease System to the Super-Max Prison." In *States of Confinement: Policing, Detention and Prisons*, edited by Joy James, 60–73. New York: St. Martin's, 2000.

Dayan, Colin. "Barbarous Confinement." Editorial. *New York Times*, July 17, 2011.

———. *Law Is a White Dog: How Legal Rituals Make and Unmake Persons*. Princeton, N.J.: Princeton University Press, 2012.

———. *The Story of Cruel and Unusual*. Cambridge, Mass.: MIT Press, 2007.

DeMaio, Jerry R. "If You Build It, They Will Come: The Threat of Overclassification in Wisconsin's Supermax Prison." *Wisconsin Law Review* (2001): 207–47.

Dershowitz, Alan. "Let the Punishment Fit the Crime: Indeterminate Prison Sentences, a Major Reform Until Recently, Are Now Considered a Mess, by Liberals and Conservatives Alike." *New York Times*, Dec. 28, 1975.

Dickens, Charles. "Philadelphia and Its Solitary Prison." *American Notes for General Circulation*. London: Penguin, 1985; orig. pub. 1842. Available from the Literature Network, www.online-literature.com/dickens/americannotes/8.

Dilulio, John. "The Coming of the Super-Predators." *Weekly Standard*, Nov. 27, 1995. www.weeklystandard.com/the-coming-of-the-super-predators/article/8160.

Disaster Center. "United States Crime Rates, 1960–2014." www.disastercenter.com/crime/uscrime.htm.

Dolan, Jack. "Indefinite Solitary Confinement Persists in California Prisons." *Los Angeles Times*, Sept. 5, 2011.

Dolovich, Sharon. "Cruelty, Prison Conditions, and the Eighth Amendment." *New York University Law Review* 84 (2009): 881–979.

———. "Forms of Deference in Prison Law." *Federal Sentencing Reporter* 24 (2012): 245.

Domanick, Joe. *Cruel Justice: Three Strikes and the Politics of Crime in America's Golden State*. Berkeley: University of California Press, 2005.

Dowker, Fay, and Glenn Good. "The Proliferation of Control Unit Prisons in the United States." In *Prison Crisis: Critical Readings*, edited by Edward Sbarbaro and Robert Keller, 34–46. Albany, N.Y.: Harrow and Heston, 1995.

Dunn, Jamey. "DOC Still Working Out Policy for Former Tamms Prisoners." *Illinois Issues Blog*, Apr. 1, 2013. http://illinoisissuesblog.blogspot.com/2013/04/doc-still-working-out-policy-for-former.html.

Durden-Smith, Jo. *Who Killed George Jackson? Fantasies, Paranoia, and the Revolution*. New York: Knopf, 1976.

Durkheim, Émile. *The Division of Labor in Society*. Translated by W. D. Hall. New York: Free Press, 2013; orig. pub. 1893.

Earley, Pete. *Crazy: A Father's Search Through America's Mental Health Madness*. New York: Putnam Sons, 2006.

Edelman, Lauren B., Christopher Uggen, and Howard S. Erlanger. "The Endogeneity of Legal Regulation: Grievance Procedure as Rational Myth." *American Journal of Sociology* 105, no. 2 (1999): 406–54.

Eligon, John. "Michael Brown Spent Last Weeks Grappling with Problems and Promise." *New York Times,* Aug. 24, 2014. www.nytimes.com/2014/08/25/us/michael-
brown-spent-last-weeks-grappling-with-lifes-mysteries.html.

Elliott, Delbert, and Steve Aos. "A Life of Unintended Consequences." *Prevention Action,* July 8, 2010. www.preventionaction.org/people/life-unintended-consequences/
5378.

Endicott, William. "The Governor's Race." *Los Angeles Times,* June 6, 1982.

———. "Support of Fight on Crime Seen." *Los Angeles Times,* Apr. 8, 1981.

Epstein, Edward. "Ford Escaped 2 Assassination Attempts: Both Happened in California—One in Capital, Other in S.F." *San Francisco Chronicle,* Dec. 27, 2006.
www.sfgate.com/news/article/Ford-escaped-2-assassination-attempts-Both-2481771
.php.

Erickson, Leif. "Two Soledad Brothers Acquitted of Murder." Associated Press, Mar.
27, 1972. Available from the Harold Weisberg Archive, Hood College, http://jfk
.hood.edu/Collection/Weisberg%20Subject%20Index%20Files/S%20Disk/Soledad
%20Brothers/Item%2011.pdf.

Fagan, Kevin. "Most State Prison Hunger Strikers Are Eating Again." *San Francisco
Chronicle,* Oct. 15, 2011.

Fallon, Richard H. "Judicially Manageable Standards and Constitutional Meaning."
Harvard Law Review 119 (2006): 1274–1332.

Fathi, David. "Anatomy of the Modern Prisoners' Rights Suit: The Common Law of
Supermax Litigation." *Pace Law Review* 24 (Spring 2004): 675–90.

Feeley, Malcolm M., and Edward L. Rubin. *Judicial Policy Making and the Modern
State: How the Courts Reformed America's Prisons.* New York: Cambridge University
Press, 1998.

Feeley, Malcolm M., and Jonathan Simon. "The New Penology: Notes on the Emerging
Strategy of Corrections and Its Implications." *Criminology* 30, no. 4 (1992): 449–74.

Feldman, Allen. *Formations of State Violence: The Narrative of the Body and Political
Terror in Northern Ireland.* Chicago: University of Chicago Press, 1991.

Fellner, Jamie. *Callous and Cruel: Use of Force Against Inmates with Mental Disabilities
in U.S. Jails and Prisons.* New York: Human Rights Watch, 2015.

———. *Red Onion State Prison: Super-Maximum Security Confinement in Virginia.*
New York: Human Rights Watch, April 1999. https://www.hrw.org/legacy/reports/
1999/redonion/index.htm.

Fellner, Jamie, and Joanne Mariner. *Cold Storage: Supermaximum Security Confinement in Indiana.* New York: Human Rights Watch, 1997.

Fitzgerald, Mike. *Control Units and the Shape of Things to Come.* London: Radical Alternatives to Prison, 1975.

———. *Prisoners in Revolt.* New York: Penguin, 1977.

Ford, D. "Colorado Governor: Shooting Suspect Evan Ebel Had Bad Streak." CNN.
com, Mar. 27, 2013. www.cnn.com/2013/03/26/us/evan-ebel-profile.

Forman, James. "Racial Critiques of Mass Incarceration: Beyond the New Jim Crow."
New York University Law Review 87 (2012): 101–46.

Fortner, Michael Javen. *Black Silent Majority: The Rockefeller Drug Laws and the Politics of Punishment*. Cambridge, Mass.: Harvard University Press, 2015.

Foucault, Michel. *Discipline and Punish: The Birth of the Prison*. Translated by Alan Sheridan. New York: Random House, 1995; orig. pub. 1977.

Foucualt, Michel, Catharine Von Bülow, and Daniel Defert. "The Masked Assassination." Translated by Sirène Harb. In *Warfare and the American Homeland: Policing and Prison in a Penal Democracy*, edited by Joy James, 140–60. Durham, N.C.: Duke University Press, 2007.

Frankel, Marvin E. *Criminal Sentences: Law Without Order*. New York: Hill & Wang, 1972.

Frederick (Md.) News. "Report Recommends Jessup Be Renovated." Nov. 3, 1980.

Freedom Archives. *Prisons on Fire: George Jackson, Attica, and Black Liberation*. Audio recording. Oakland: AK Press, 2002.

Frontline. *Solitary Nation*. Documentary. PBS, Apr. 22, 2014. http://video.pbs.org/video/2365229709.

Fuchs, Erin. "Robber Who Got Out of Prison Early Allegedly Went on a Killing Spree in Nebraska." *Business Insider*, Sept. 5, 2013. www.businessinsider.com/nikko-jenkins-alleged-murders-in-omaha-2013-9.

Garland, David. *Culture of Control: Crime and Social Order in Contemporary Society*. Chicago: University of Chicago Press, 2001.

———. *Peculiar Institution: America's Death Penalty in an Age of Abolition*. Cambridge, Mass.: Harvard University Press, 2010.

———. *Punishment and Modern Society: A Study in Social Theory*. Chicago: University of Chicago Press, 1990.

Gartner, Rosemary, and Candace Kruttschnitt. "A Brief History of Doing Time: The California Institution for Women in the 1960s and the 1990s." *Law and Society Review* 38, no. 2 (2004): 267–304.

Gates, Henry Louis, Jr. "What Were the Earliest Rebellions by African Americans?" *Root*, Apr. 22, 2013. www.theroot.com/articles/history/2013/04/did_africanamerican_slaves_rebel.html.

Gilligan, James. "The Last Mental Hospital." *Psychiatric Quarterly* 72, no. 1 (2001): 45–61.

Gilmore, Ruth Wilson. *Golden Gulag: Prisons, Surplus, Crisis, and Opposition in Globalizing California*. Berkeley: University of California Press, 2007.

Glennon, Michael J. *National Security and Double Government*. New York: Oxford University Press, 2014.

Goldberg, Jonah. "A Prison for Cruel and Unusual Criminals." *Wall Street Journal*, Apr. 5, 1994.

Goldman, Sheldon. *Picking Federal Judges: Lower Court Selection from Roosevelt Through Reagan*. New Haven, Conn.: Yale University Press, 1997.

Gómez, Alan Eladio. "Resisting Living Death at Marion Federal Penitentiary, 1972." *Radical History Review* 96 (Fall 2006): 58–86.

Gonnerman, Jennifer. "Kalief Browder, 1993–2015." *New Yorker*, June 7, 2015. www.newyorker.com/news/news-desk/kalief-browder-1993-2015.

Goodman, Philip. "'It's Just Black, White, or Hispanic': An Observational Study of Racializing Moves in California's Segregated Prison Reception Centers." *Law and Society Review* 42, no. 4 (2008): 735–70.

———. "Race in California's Prison Fire Camps for Men: Prison Politics, Space, and the Racialization of Everyday Life." *American Journal of Sociology* 120, no. 2 (Sept. 2014): 352–94.

Goodman, Philip, Joshua Page, and Michelle Phelps. "A Long Struggle: The Agonistic Perspective on Penal Development." *Theoretical Criminology* (2014): 1–21.

Goodstein, Lynne. *Determinate Sentencing and the Correctional Process: A Study of the Implementation and Impact of Sentencing Reform in Three States.* With John R. Hepburn, John H. Kramer, and Doris L. MacKenzie. Washington, D.C.: National Institute of Justice, Oct. 1984. https://www.ncjrs.gov/pdffiles1/Digitization/96333NCJRS.pdf.

Gordon, Sarah Barringer. *The Spirit of the Law: Religious Voices and the Constitution in Modern America.* Cambridge, Mass.: Harvard University Press, 2010.

Gottschalk, Marie. *Caught: The Prison State and the Lockdown of American Politics.* Princeton, N.J.: Princeton University Press, 2015.

———. *The Prison and the Gallows: The Politics of Mass Incarceration in America.* Cambridge: Cambridge University Press, 2006.

Grann, David. "The Brand." *New Yorker,* Feb. 16, 2004, 156–71.

Grassian, Stuart. "'Fatal Flaws' in the Colorado Solitary Confinement Study." *Solitary Watch,* Nov. 15, 2010. http://solitarywatch.com/2010/11/15/fatal-flaws-in-the-colorado-solitary-confinement-study/.

———. "Psychiatric Effects of Solitary Confinement." *Washington Journal of Law and Social Policy* 22 (2006): 325–83.

———. "Psychiatric Effects of Solitary Confinement." Redacted declaration submitted pursuant to *Madrid v. Gomez* litigation, Sept. 1993.

Grattet, Ryken, and Joseph Hayes. "California's Changing Prison Population." Public Policy Institute of California, April 2015. www.ppic.org/main/publication_show.asp?i=702.

Grattet, Ryken, Joan Petersilia, Jeffrey Lin, and Marlene Beckman. "Parole Violations and Revocations in California: Analysis and Suggestions for Action." *Federal Probation* 73, no. 1 (2009): 2–11.

Greenberg, Kenneth S. *Nat Turner: A Slave Rebellion in History and Memory.* New York: Oxford University Press, 2004.

Greene, S. "Evan Ebel Suicide Note Shows Parolee Was 'Ruined' by Solitary, Bent on Revenge: Troy Anderson, Friend of Ebel." *Colorado Independent,* www.coloradoindependent.com/127520/ebel-friend-suicide-note-shows-parolee-ruined-by-solitary-bent-on-revenge.

Griffin, Eddie. "Breaking Men's Minds: Behavior Control and Human Experimentation at the Federal Prison in Marion." *Journal of Prisoners on Prison* 4, no. 2 (1993). Formatted online version, 2006, www.jpp.org/backIssuePages/volume4Number2.html.

Griffith, John. "New Border Prison Spurs Concerns." *Oregonian*, Dec. 1, 1989.

Grob, Gerald N. "The Forging of Mental Health Policy in America: World War II to New Frontier." *Journal of the History of Medicine and Allied Sciences* 42 (1987): 410–46.

Guenther, Lisa. "The Biopolitics of Starvation in California Prisons." *Society and Space*, Aug. 2, 2013. http://societyandspace.com/material/commentaries/lisa-guenther-the-biopolitics-of-starvation-in-california-prisons/.

———. *The Gift of the Other: Lévinas and the Politics of Reproduction*. Albany, N.Y.: SUNY Press, 2006.

———. *Solitary Confinement: Social Death and Its Afterlives*. Minneapolis: University of Minnesota Press, 2013.

Gurman, Sadie. "Evan Ebel Forced Pizza Driver to Make Recording Before His Murder." *Denver Post*, Feb. 10, 2014. www.denverpost.com/news/ci_25106855/evanebel-forced-pizza-driver-make-recording-before.

Hager, Eli, and Gerald Rich. "Shifting Away from Solitary: More States Have Passed Solitary Confinement Reforms This Year than in the Past 16 Years." *Marshall Project*, Dec. 23, 2014, www.themarshallproject.org/2014/12/23/shifting-away-from-solitary#.qdl8F1VcK.

Hagstrom, Jerry. "Crowded Prisons Pose a Budget Problem for This Law-and-Order Administration." *National Journal*, Oct. 10, 1981.

Hallie, Philip P. "Prisoners, Twaddlers, and the Fire Chief." *American Scholar* 41, no. 4 (Autumn 1972): 674–77.

Hammel, Paul. "Audit Recommends That State Review Use of Solitary Confinement, Update Data Systems." *Omaha World Herald Bureau*, Nov. 18, 2014, www.omaha.com/news/crime/audit-recommends-that-state-review-use-of-solitary-confinement-update/article_52ca8254-6e85-11e4-989b-ef67f24c236c.html.

Haney, Craig. "The Major Methodological Flaws in the 'Colorado Study.'" Memorandum on file with the author.

———. "Mental Health Issues in Long-Term Solitary and 'Supermax' Confinement." *Crime and Delinquency* 49, no. 1 (Jan. 2003): 124–56.

Haney, Craig, and Mona Lynch. "Regulating Prisons of the Future: A Psychological Analysis of Supermax and Solitary Confinement." *New York University Review of Law and Social Change* 23, no. 4 (1997): 477–570.

Haney-Lopez, Ian. *Dog Whistle Politics: How Coded Racial Appeals Have Reinvented Racism and Wrecked the Middle Class*. New York: Oxford University Press, 2014.

Hansen, Mariann, and Mark A. Stein. "Jury Acquits Bingham in Prison Deaths: Rejects Charge He Smuggled Gun in '71 San Quentin Riot." *Los Angeles Times*, June 28, 1986. http://articles.latimes.com/1986-06-28/news/mn-25506_1_san-quentin/2.

Harcourt, Bernard D. "Reducing Mass Incarceration: Lessons from the Deinstitutionalization of Mental Hospitals in the 1960s." *Ohio State Journal of Criminal Law* 9 (2011): 53–88.

Hayes, Thomas W. *A Report of an Audit of Security Measures at Two California Prisons*. State of California, Office of the Auditor General, Mar. 14, 1986. Sacramento, California State Archives, AN: 2003-029, Joint Committee on Prison Construction and

Operation Subject Files, Hearing Files 1981–1999, Loc: B4181-2907 (box 1 of 2). Copy on file with the author.

Healy, Beth. "A System Strains, and Inmates Die." *Boston Globe,* Dec. 9, 2007.

Heller, Matthew. "They Shoot Prisoners, Don't They?" *Independent,* Jan. 28, 2001.

Henrichson, Christian, and Ruth Delaney. *The Price of Prisons: What Incarceration Costs Taxpayers.* New York: Vera Institute of Justice, 2012. www.vera.org/sites/default/files/resources/downloads/price-of-prisons-updated-version-021914.pdf.

Hentoff, Nat. "America's Devil's Island." *Washington Post,* Dec. 4, 1993.

Herdt, Timm. "Record Numbers of Life-Term Inmates Granted Parole in California." *Ventura County Star,* Dec. 15, 2013. Available from the *Huffington Post,* www.huffingtonpost.com/2013/12/15/california-parole_n_4447448.html.

Herivel, Tara, and Paul Wright, eds. *Prison Profiteers: Who Makes Money from Mass Incarceration.* New York: New Press, 2007.

Herman's House. Directed by Angad Bhalla. Storyline Entertainment, 2012.

Heron, W. "The Pathology of Boredom." *Scientific American* 196 (1957): 52–56.

HoSang, Daniel Martinez. *Racial Propositions: Ballot Initiatives and the Making of Postwar California.* Berkeley: University of California Press, 2010.

Houston, Paul. "Court-Battle Guns Registered in the Name of Angela Davis." *Los Angeles Times,* Aug. 12, 1970.

"Hugo 'Yogi' Pinell." *Hard Knock Radio,* Aug. 13, 2015, 4 p.m. The episode was available at https://kpfa.org/episode/hard-knock-radio-august-13-2015 (accessed Jan. 15, 2016).

Illinois Department of Corrections. "Tamms Correctional Center Closing: Fact Sheet." http://cgfa.ilga.gov/upload/TammsMeetingTestimonyDocuments.pdf. Page 142 of 698.

Iowa Department of Corrections. *Iowa State Penitentiary Final Operational and Architectural Program.* Lido Beach, N.Y.: Pulitzer/Bogard and Associates, LLC, June 30, 2009. Copy on file with the author.

Irwin, John. *The Felon.* Berkeley: University of California Press, 1987; orig. pub. 1970.

———. *Prisons in Turmoil.* Boston: Little, Brown, 1980.

———. *The Warehouse Prison: Disposal of the New Dangerous Class.* Los Angeles: Roxbury, 2005.

Jackson, George. *Blood in My Eye.* New York: Random House 1972. Reprint, Baltimore: Black Classics, 1990.

———. *Soledad Brother: The Prison Letters of George Jackson.* Chicago: Lawrence Hill, 1969.

Jacobs, James B. *The Eternal Criminal Record.* Cambridge, Mass.: Harvard University Press, 2014.

———. *Stateville: The Penitentiary in Mass Society.* Chicago: University of Chicago Press, 1977.

Jeffreys, Derek. *Spirituality in Dark Places: The Ethics of Solitary Confinement.* New York: Palgrave Macmillan, 2013.

Johnston, Norman. *Forms of Constraint: A History of Prison Architecture.* Urbana: University of Illinois Press, 2000.

Juarez, George A. "B. Modifying the Indeterminate Sentence: The Changing Emphasis in Criminal Punishment." In "The Supreme Court of California, 1974–75," *California Law Review* 64 no. 2 (Mar. 1976): 405–17.

Kaba, Fatos, Andrea Lewis, Sarah Glowa-Kollisch, James Hadler, David Lee, Howard Alper, Daniel Selling, et al. "Solitary Confinement and Risk of Self-Harm Among Jail Inmates." *American Journal of Public Health* 104, no. 3 (2014): 442–47.

Kansal, Tushar. *Racial Disparity in Sentencing: A Review of the Literature.* Washington, D.C.: Sentencing Project, 2005. www.sentencingproject.org/doc/publications/rd _sentencing_review.pdf.

Keller, Richard. *The New Prison Construction Program at Midstream.* Sacramento: Legislative Analyst's Office, 1986. www.lao.ca.gov/reports/1986/386_0486_the_new _prison_construction_program_at_midstream.pdf.

Keve, Paul W., and Merle E. Alexander. *Prisons and the American Conscience: A History of U.S. Federal Corrections.* Carbondale: Southern Illinois University Press, 1991.

Kim, Scarlet, Taylor Pendergrass, and Helen Zelon. *Boxed In: The True Cost of Extreme Isolation in New York's Prisons.* New York: New York Civil Liberties Union, 2012.

Kim, Victoria, and Kate Mather. "Gov. Jerry Brown Denies Parole for Ex-Mexican Mafia Killer Rene 'Boxer' Enriquez." *Los Angeles Times,* Feb. 20, 2015. www.latimes .com/local/lanow/la-me-ln-rene-enriquez-parole-decision-20150220-story.html.

King, Roy D. "The Effects of Supermax Custody." In *The Effects of Imprisonment,* edited by Alison Liebling and Shadd Maruna, 118–42. London: Willan, 2007.

———. "The Rise and Rise of Supermax: An American Problem in Search of a Solution?" *Punishment and Society* 1, no. 2 (Oct. 1999): 163–86.

Knapp, Kay A., and Denis J. Hauptly. "State and Federal Sentencing Guidelines: Apples and Oranges." *U.C. Davis Law Review* 25 (1991–92): 679–94.

KOAT [Albuquerque]. "Riot Survivors Tour Old Santa Fe Penitentiary." Oct. 25, 2013. www.koat.com/news/new-mexico/riot-survivors-tour-old-santa-fe-penitentiary/-/ 9153762/22645136/-/dsmevi/-/index.html.

Koenig, Alexa. "From Man to Beast: Social Death at Guantánamo." In *Extreme Punishment,* edited by Keramet Reiter and Alexa Koenig, 220–41.

———. "Indefinite Detention/Enduring Freedom: What Former Detainees' Experiences Can Teach Us About Institutional Violence, Resistance, and the Law." Ph.D. diss. University of California, Berkeley, 2013.

Koenig, Alexa K., Eric Stover, and Laurel E. Fletcher. "The Cumulative Effect: A Medico-Legal Approach to United States Torture Law and Policy." *Essex Human Rights Review* 6, no. 1 (Dec. 2009): 146–68.

Kumar, Anita. "Virginia Plans Changes in Prisoner Isolation Process." *Washington Post,* Mar. 30, 2012.

Kupers, Terry. *Prison Madness: The Mental Health Crisis Behind Bars and What We Must Do About It.* San Francisco: Jossey-Bass, 1999.

———. "What to Do with Survivors? Coping with the Long-Term Effects of Isolated Confinement," *Criminal Justice and Behavior* 35, no. 8 (2008): 1005–16.

Kupers, Terry A., Theresa Dronet, Margaret Winter, James Austin, Lawrence Kelly, William Cartier, Timothy J. Morris, et. al. "Beyond Supermax Administrative Segregation: Mississippi's Experience Rethinking Prison Classification and Creating Alternative Mental Health Programs." *Criminal Justice and Behavior* 20, no. 2 (July 2009): 2–14.

Kurfirst, Robert. "Term-Limit Logic: Paradigms and Paradoxes." *Polity* 29 (1996): 119–41.

Kurki, Leena, and Norval Morris. "The Purposes, Practices, and Problems of Supermax Prisons." In *Crime and Justice: A Review of Research*, edited by Michael Tonry, 28:385–424. Chicago: University of Chicago Press, 2001.

Kurshan, Nancy. *Out of Control: A Fifteen-Year Battle Against Control Unit Prisons*. San Francisco: Freedom Archives, 2015.

LaChance, Daniel. *Executing Freedom: The Cultural Life of Capital Punishment in the United States, 1966–Present*. Chicago: University of Chicago Press, 2016.

Lau, Jessie. "Incarceration to Convocation—Life After Solitary Confinement: How Education Paved the Way for Danny Murillo." *Berkeley Daily Californian*, May 10, 2015. www.dailycal.org/2015/05/10/incarceration-to-convocation.

Law, Victoria. "One Month After Historic Hunger Strike Ends, Legislators Hold Hearings About Solitary Confinement." *Truthout*, Oct. 14, 2013. www.truth-out.org/news/item/19359-one-month-after-historic-hunger-strike-ends-legislators-hold-hearings-about-solitary-confinement.

———. "'We Are Not the Worst of the Worst': One Year Later, What's Changed for Pelican Bay's Hunger Strikers?" *Solitary Watch*, July 7, 2014. http://solitarywatch.com/2014/07/07/worst-worst-one-year-later-whats-changed-pelican-bays-hunger-strikers.

Leiderman, Herbert P. "Man Alone: Sensory Deprivation and Behavioral Change." In "The Power to Change Behavior: A Symposium Presented by the United States Bureau of Prisons," *Corrective Psychiatry and Journal of Social Therapy* 8, no. 2 (1962): 64–74.

Levitt, Steven D. "Understanding Why Crime Fell in the 1990s: Four Factors That Explain the Decline and Six That Do Not." *Journal of Economic Perspectives* 18, no. 1 (Winter 2004): 163–90.

Lipson, Albert J., and Mark A. Peterson. *California Justice Under Determinate Sentencing: A Review and Agenda for Research*. Prepared for the State of California, Board of Prison Terms, R-2497-CRB. Santa Monica: Rand, June 1980. www.rand.org/pubs/reports/2005/R2497.pdf.

Lipton, Douglas, Robert Martinson, and Judith Wilks. *Effectiveness of Correctional Treatment: A Survey of Treatment Evaluation Studies*. New York: Praeger, 1975.

Lobel, Jules. "Prolonged Solitary Confinement and the Constitution." *Journal of Constitutional Law* 11 (2008): 115–38.

Los Angeles Times. "California's Hidden Hunger Strike." Editorial. July 20, 2011.

———. "Prison Construction: Yes on 1." May 20, 1982.

Losier, Toussaint. "'. . . For Strictly Religious Reason[s]': *Cooper v. Pate* and the Origins of the Prisoners' Rights Movement." *Souls: A Critical Journal of Black Politics, Culture, and Society* 15, no. 1 (2013): 19–38.

Lovell, David. "Patterns of Disturbed Behavior in a Supermax Population." *Criminal Justice and Behavior* 35, no. 8 (2008): 985–1004.

Lovell, David, L. Clark Johnson, and Kevin C. Cain. "Recidivism of Supermax Prisoners in Washington State." *Crime and Delinquency* 53, no. 4 (2007): 633–56.

Lovett, Ian. "California Inmates Fast to Protest Isolation Cells." *New York Times,* July 8, 2011.

Lowenthal, Gary T. "Mandatory Sentencing Laws: Undermining the Effectiveness of Determinate Sentencing Reform." *California Law Review* 81, no. 1 (Jan. 1993): 61–123.

Lynch, Mona. "Selling 'Securityware': Transformations in Prison Commodities Advertising, 1949–99." *Punishment and Society* 4, no. 3 (2002): 305–19.

———. *Sunbelt Justice: Arizona and the Transformation of American Punishment.* Stanford, Calif.: Stanford University Press, 2010.

———. "Waste Managers? The New Penology, Crime Fighting, and Parole Agent Identity." *Law and Society Review* 32 (1998): 839–70.

Magnani, Laura. *America's First Penitentiary: A 200 Year Old Failure.* San Francisco: American Friends Service Committee, 1990.

Mann, Eric. *Comrade George: An Investigation Into the Life, Political Thought, and Assassination of George Jackson.* New York: Harper & Row, 1974.

Mann, Jim. "High Court Restores Panther's Conviction: 'Harmless' Errors Do Not Void Verdict in San Quentin Escape Case, Justices Rule." *Los Angeles Times,* Dec. 13, 1983.

Marine, Craig. "Exit the Dragon: It's Been 30 Years Since George Jackson Died in a Pool of Blood at San Quentin; His Death Still Reverberates in America." *San Francisco Chronicle,* Aug. 19, 2001. www.sfgate.com/bayarea/article/exit-the-dragon-it-s-been-30-years-since-George-2888071.php.

Mariner, Joanne. *No Escape: Male Rape in U.S. Prisons.* New York: Human Rights Watch, 2001. https://www.hrw.org/reports/2001/prison/report.html.

Marks, Claude, and Isaac Ontiveros. "Pelican Bay Hunger Strike: Four Years and Still Fighting." *CounterPunch,* July 9, 2015. www.counterpunch.org/2015/07/09/pelican-bay-hunger-strike-four-years-and-still-fighting.

Martin, Douglas. "Caleb Foote, Law Professor and Pacifist Organizer, 88, Dies." *New York Times,* Apr. 3, 2006. www.nytimes.com/2006/04/03/us/03foote.html.

Martin, Jonathan. "State Prisons Rethink Solitary Confinement." *Seattle Times,* Jan. 7, 2013. http://seattletimes.com/html/localnews/2020081649_prison08m.html.

Martinson, Robert. "What Works: Questions and Answers About Prison Reform." *Public Interest,* Spring 1974, 22–54.

Mason, Cody. *International Growth Trends in Prison Privatization*. New York: Sentenc-
    ing Project, Aug. 2013. http://sentencingproject.org/doc/publications/inc_Inter
    national%20Growth%20Trends%20in%20Prison%20Privatization.pdf.

Mather, Kate, and Victoria Kim. "Gov. Jerry Brown Weighs Parole for Killer in Contro-
    versial LAPD Lecture." *Los Angeles Times*, Jan. 30, 2015. www.latimes.com/local/
    crime/la-me-killer-meeting-lapd-20150131-story.html.

Mather, Kate, Richard Winton, and Ruben Vives. "LAPD Criticized for Arranging
    Downtown Talk by Mexican Mafia Killer." *Los Angeles Times*, Jan. 29, 2015. www
    .latimes.com/local/crime/la-me-killer-meeting-lapd-20150130-story.html.

Mattera, Phillip, ed. "Public Finance and Public Debt." Corporate research project of
    Good Jobs First, June 2004. Formerly available at www.publicbonds.org/prison
    _fin/prison_fin.htm.

Mauer, Marc. "Addressing Racial Disparities in Incarceration." *Prison Journal* 9, no. 3
    (2011): 87–100.

Maynard, Joyce. "The One Good Man." In *The Moth*, 349–55. New York: Hyperion,
    2013.

Maza, Christine. "LA Prisoner Released After 43 Years in Solitary Confinement; How
    Can He Cope?" *Christian Science Monitor*, June 9, 2015. www.csmonitor.com/USA/
    USA-Update/2015/0609/LA-prisoner-released-after-43-years-in-solitary-confinement
    .-How-can-he-cope-video.

McCarthy, Daniel J. "Response to: A Report of an Audit of Security Measures at Two
    California Prisons." California Department of Corrections, Mar. 1986. California
    State Archives, AN: 2003-029, Joint Committee on Prison Construction and Oper-
    ation Subject Files, Hearing Files 1981–1999, Loc: B4181-2907 (box 1 of 2). Copy on
    file with the author.

McCarty, Heather. "Blood In, Blood Out: The Emergence of California Prison Gangs
    in the 1960s." In *Sunbelt Prisons* (forthcoming; draft on file with the author).

McCoy, Alfred W. "Science in Dachau's Shadow: Hebb, Beecher, and the Development
    of CIA Psychological Torture and Modern Medical Ethics." *Journal of the History of
    the Behavioral Sciences* 43, no. 4 (2007): 401–17.

McKinley, Jesse. "New York Prisons Take an Unsavory Punishment off the Table."
    New York Times, Dec. 17, 2015. www.nytimes.com/2015/12/18/nyregion/new-york
    -prisons-take-an-unsavory-punishment-off-the-table.html.

McLennan, Rebecca. *The Crisis of Imprisonment: Protest, Politics, and the Making of the
    American Penal State, 1776–1941*. New York: Cambridge University Press, 2008.

Mears, Daniel P. *Evaluating the Effectiveness of Supermax Prisons*. Washington, D.C.:
    U.S. Department of Justice, 2006.

Mears, Daniel P., and William D. Bales. "Supermax Incarceration and Recidivism."
    Criminology 47, no. 4 (2009): 1131–65.

Mears, Daniel P., and Michael D. Reisig. "The Theory and Practice of Supermax Pris-
    ons." *Punishment and Society* 8, no. 1 (2006): 33–57.

Meranze, Michael. *Laboratories of Virtue: Punishment, Revolution, and Authority in
    Philadelphia, 1760–1835*. Chapel Hill: University of North Carolina Press, 1996.

Meronek, Toshio. "LSPC Attorney Carol Strickman Speaks Out Against Prison Censorship." *East Bay Express*, June 17, 2014. Available from Legal Services for Prisoners with Children, www.prisonerswithchildren.org/2014/06/lspc-attorney-carol-strickman-speaks-out-against-prison-censorship.

Merton, Robert K. "The Unanticipated Consequences of Purposive Social Action." *American Sociological Review* 1, no. 6 (Dec. 1936): 894–904.

Messinger, Sheldon L., and Phillip D. Johnson. "California's Determinate Sentencing Statute: History and Issues." In *Determinate Sentencing: Reform or Regression*, 13–58. Washington, D.C.: U.S. Department of Justice, 1978. Available at http://scholarship.law.berkeley.edu/facpubs/1886.

Meyer, Bernard S. "Final Report of the Special Attica Investigation" ["Meyer Report"]. Vol. 1. Oct. 27, 1975. www.ag.ny.gov/pdfs/MeyerReportVol1.pdf.

———. "Meyer Report." Vols. 2–3. Released May 21, 2015. www.ag.ny.gov/pdfs/MeyerReportVol2And3.pdf.

Miller, Jerome. "The Debate on Rehabilitating Criminals: Is It True that Nothing Works?" *Washington Post*, Apr. 23, 1989.

Mitford, Jessica. *Kind and Usual Punishment: The Prison Business*. New York: Vintage, 1974.

Mohan, Geoffrey. "From Prison Isolation to a Sense of Doom." *Los Angeles Times*, Nov. 8, 2013. www.latimes.com/science/la-sci-ci-prison-isolation-czifra-20131108-dto-htmlstory.html.

Montgomery, Michael. "Gangster Confidential." American Radioworks. N.d. [2008]. http://americanradioworks.publicradio.org/features/gangster.

———. "Gangster Reveals Mexican Mafia Secrets." NPR, Sept. 6, 2008. www.npr.org/templates/story/story.php?storyId=94333325.

Morain, Dan. "Inmate Convicted in Prison Killing Gets Retrial." *Los Angeles Times*, Sept. 25, 1986.

———. "The Real Story Behind Hunger Strike." *Sacramento Bee*, Aug. 11, 2013.

———. "San Quentin Warden Views Grim Duty with Equanimity." *Los Angeles Times*, Mar. 30, 1990.

Morris, Norval. *The Future of Imprisonment*. Chicago: University of Chicago Press, 1974.

Muhammad, Kahlil Gibran. *The Condemnation of Blackness: Race, Crime, and the Making of Modern Urban America*. Cambridge, Mass.: Harvard University Press, 2011.

Mullane, Nancy. "The Adjustment Center: Where No One Wants to Go." KALW [San Francisco], Oct. 22, 2012. http://kalw.org/post/adjustment-center-where-no-one-wants-go.

Murakawa, Naomi. *The First Civil Right: How Liberals Built Prison America*. New York: Oxford University Press, 2014.

Murray, Stuart J. "The Living from the Dead: Disaffirming Biopolitics." Unpublished manuscript. Copy on file with the author.

Naday, Alexandra, Joshua D. Freilich, and Jeff Mellow. "The Elusive Data on Supermax Confinement." *Prison Journal* 88, no. 1 (2008): 69–92.

Natapoff, Alexandra. *Snitching: Criminal Informants and the Erosion of American Justice*. New York: New York University Press, 2011.

National Institute of Mental Health. "Serious Mental Illness (SMI) Among U.S. Adults." 2014. www.nimh.nih.gov/health/statistics/prevalence/serious-mental-illness-smi-among-us-adults.shtml.

Nellis, Ashley, Judy Greene, and Marc Mauer. *Reducing Racial Disparity in the Criminal Justice System*. Washington, D.C.: Sentencing Project, 2008. www.sentencingproject.org/doc/publications/rd_reducingracialdisparity.pdf.

Nellis, Ashley, and Ryan S. King. *No Exit: The Expanding Use of Life Sentences in America*. Washington, D.C.: Sentencing Project, 2009. http://sentencingproject.org/doc/publications/publications/inc_NoExitSept2009.pdf.

Newcomb, Alyssa. "California Prison Hunger Strike Leader Is Convicted Murderer with Alleged Aryan Brotherhood Ties." ABCNews.com, July 30, 2013. http://abcnews.go.com/US/california-prison-hunger-strike-leader-convicted-murderer-alleged/story?id=19805895.

New York Civil Liberties Union. "NYCLU Lawsuit Secures Historic Reforms to Solitary Confinement." Feb. 19, 2014. www.nyclu.org/news/nyclu-lawsuit-secures-historic-reforms-solitary-confinement.

New York State Special Commission on Attica. *Attica: The Official Report*. New York: Bantam, 1972.

O'Hearn, Denis. "My Friend Todd Ashker, Hunger Striker at Pelican Bay." *Counter-Punch*, Aug. 22, 2013, www.counterpunch.org/2013/08/22/my-friend-todd-ashker-inmate-at-pelican-bay.

O'Keefe, Maureen L., Kelli J. Klebe, Alysha Stucker, Kristin Sturm, and William Leggett. *One Year Longitudinal Study of the Psychological Effects of Administrative Segregation*, Document No. 232973. Washington, D.C.: National Criminal Justice Research Service, National Institute of Justice, 2011. www.ncjrs.gov/pdffiles1/nij/grants/232973.pdf.

Oppel, Richard A., Jr. "Sentencing Shift Gives New Clout to Prosecutors." *New York Times*, Sept. 25, 2011. www.nytimes.com/2011/09/26/us/tough-sentences-help-prosecutors-push-for-plea-bargains.html.

Page, Joshua. *The Toughest Beat: Politics, Punishment, and the Prison Officers' Union in California*. New York: Oxford University Press, 2011.

Pager, Devah. *Marked: Race, Crime, and Finding Work in an Era of Mass Incarceration*. Chicago: The University of Chicago Press, 2007.

Park, James. "Associate Warden's Statement to the Press Concerning the Death of George Jackson." KPFA Radio, Aug. 21, 1971. Pacific Radio Archives No. BC0239.03.

Pass, Michael G. "Race Relations and the Implications of Education Within Prison." *Journal of Offender Counseling Services Rehabilitation* 12, no. 2 (1988): 145–51.

Pearson, Jake. "New York, Prodded by Lawsuit, Becomes Latest State to Reform Solitary Confinement in Prison." Associated Press, Dec. 7, 2015. Available at USNews.com, www.usnews.com/news/us/articles/2015-12-17/new-york-prodded-by-suit-becomes-latest-to-reform-solitary.

Perez, T. E., and D. J. Hickton. Letter to Governor Tom Corbett [of Pennsylvania]. Re: Investigation of the State Correctional Institution at Cresson and notice of expanded investigation. U.S. Department of Justice, May 31, 2013. Copy on file with author.

Perkinson, Robert. *Texas Tough: The Rise of a Prison Empire*. New York: Metropolitan, 2008.

Perlman, Jeffrey. "Issue Second Only to Crime Among County Residents Surveyed." *Los Angeles Times*, Oct. 13, 1982, Orange County ed.

Petersilia, Joan. *When Prisoners Come Home: Parole and Prisoner Re-entry*. New York: Oxford University Press, 2003.

Phelps, Michelle. "Rehabilitation in the Punitive Era: The Gap Between Rhetoric and Reality in U.S. Prison Programs." *Law and Society Review* 45 (2011): 33–68.

Pierson, Paul. "Increasing Returns, Path Dependence, and the Study of Politics." *American Political Science Review* 94, no. 2 (June 2002): 251–67.

Pina, Pablo. "Pelican Bay (shu) Photograph, Canteen List and Menu." Reproduction of letter dated Nov. 14, 2013. *Between the Bars* (blog), https://betweenthebars.org/posts/14975/pelican-bayshu-photograph-canteen-list-and-menu.

Pittendrigh, Nadya. "Making Visible Invisible Suffering: Non-Deliberative Agency and the Bodily Rhetoric of Tamms Supermax Prisoners." In *Extreme Punishment*, edited by Keramet Reiter and Alexa Koenig, 156–76.

Pranis, Kevin. "Doing Borrowed Time: The High Cost of Backdoor Prison Finance." In *Prison Profiteers: Who Makes Money from Mass Incarceration*, edited by Tara Herivel and Paul Wright, 36–51. New York: New Press, 2007.

Prendergast, Alan. "The Caged Life." *Denver Westword News*, Aug. 16, 2007.

Presley, Robert. "Oral History Interview with Honorable Robert Presley, California State Senator, 1974–1994, Agency Secretary, Youth and Adult Correctional Agency, 1999–." By Patrick Ettinger. California State University, Sacramento. California State Archives, State Government Oral History Program, Dec. 18, 2001, Apr. 17, 2002, July 18, 2002, June 5, 2003.

Prisoner Hunger Strike Solidarity. "Prisoners' Demands." Apr. 3, 2011. https://prisoner hungerstrikesolidarity.wordpress.com/the-prisoners-demands-2.

Prison Law Office. "California's Prison Crowding Reduction Plans and Credit Laws." Dec. 12, 2014. Updated Sept. 17, 2015. http://prisonlaw.com/wp-content/uploads/2015/09/pop-reduction-credit-laws-info-letter-September-2015-final.pdf.

Prison Legal News. "Pelican Bay Ruling Issued." Aug. 1995, 3.

Pritchard, Justin. "L.A. Police Spent $22,000 to Get Mexican Mafia Killer Rene 'Boxer' Enriquez to Fancy Dinner." Associated Press, Mar. 20, 2015. Available from the *Orange County Register*, www.ocregister.com/articles/enriquez-654993-police-event.html.

Public Policy Institute of California. "California Poverty Rates by County, 2011–2013." www.ppic.org/main/mapdetail.asp?i=1396.

Quandt, Katie Rose. "Legal Settlement Demands Better Mental Health Care, Less Solitary Confinement in Illinois Prisons." *Solitary Watch*, Jan. 14, 2016. http://sol

itarywatch.com/2016/01/14/legal-settlement-demands-better-mental-health-care
-less-solitary-confinement-in-illinois-prisons.

Quiet Rage: The Stanford Prison Experiment. Directed by Ken Musen, 1992. www.prison
exp.org/quiet-rage.

Raghunath, Raja. "A Promise the Nation Cannot Keep: What Prevents the Application
of the Thirteenth Amendment in Prison?" *William and Mary Bill of Rights Journal* 18
(2009): 395–444.

Rakoff, Jed S. "Why Innocent People Plead Guilty." *New York Review of Books,* Nov. 20,
2014. www.nybooks.com/articles/2014/11/20/why-innocent-people-plead-guilty.

Reiter, Keramet. "Experimentation on Prisoners: Persistent Dilemmas in Rights and
Regulations." *California Law Review* 97, no. 2 (April 2009): 501–66.

———. "The Most Restrictive Alternative: A Litigation History of Solitary Confinement in U.S. Prisons, 1960–2006." *Studies in Law, Politics, and Society* 57 (2012):
71–124.

———. "The Origins of and Need to Control Supermax Prisons." *California Journal
of Politics and Policy* 5, no. 2 (2013): 146–67.

———. "Parole, Snitch, or Die: California's Supermax Prisons and Prisoners, 1987–
2007," *Punishment and Society* 14, no. 5 (Dec. 2012): 530–63.

———. "The Pelican Bay Hunger Strike: Resistance Within the Structural Constraints
of a U.S. Supermax Prison." *South Atlantic Quarterly* 113, no. 3 (Summer 2014):
579–611.

———. "Prisoners' Rights." In *The Social History of Crime and Punishment in America,* edited by Wilbur R. Miller, 1418–22. Thousand Oaks, Calif.: Sage, 2012.

———. "Reclaiming the Power to Punish." *Law and Society Review* 50, no. 2 (2016):
484–518.

———. "Supermax Administration and the Eighth Amendment: Deference, Discretion, and Double Bunking, 1986–2010." *University of California, Irvine Law Review*
5, no. 1 (Apr. 2015): 89–152.

———. "The Supermax Prison: A Blunt Means of Control, or a Subtle Form of Violence?" *Radical Philosophy Review* 17, no. 2 (2014): 457–75.

———. "Transcript: Testimony of U.C. Irvine Professor Keramet Reiter at the joint
legislative hearing on solitary confinement in California–October 9, 2013." Partial
transcript available at What the Folly, Oct. 22, 2013, www.whatthefolly.com/2013/
10/22/transcript-testimony-of-uc-irvine-professor-keramet-reiter-at-the-joint-legis
lative-hearing-on-solitary-confinement-in-california-oct-9-2013/.

———. "(Un)Settling Solitary Confinement in California's Prisons." *Social Justice
Blog,* Sept. 28, 2015. www.socialjusticejournal.org/?p=3214.

Reiter, Keramet, and Thomas Blair. "Punishing Mental Illness: Trans-Institutionalization and Solitary Confinement in the United States." In *Extreme Punishment,*
edited by Keramet Reiter and Alexa Koenig, 177–96.

Reiter, Keramet, and Susan Coutin. "Crossing Borders and Criminalizing Identity:
The Disintegrated Subjects of Administrative Sanctions." Under review at *Law &
Society Review.*

Reiter, Keramet, and Alexa Koenig, eds. *Extreme Punishment: Comparative Studies in Detention, Incarceration, and Solitary Confinement.* New York: Palgrave MacMillan, 2015.

Reiter, Keramet, and Natalie Pifer. "*Brown v. Plata.*" *Oxford Handbooks Online in Criminology and Criminal Justice,* edited by Michael Tonry. New York: Oxford University Press, 2015. doi: 10.1093/oxfordhb/9780199935383.013.113.

Remington, Frank J. "The Decision to Charge, the Decision to Convict on a Plea of Guilty, and the Impact of Sentence Structure on Prosecution Practice." In *Discretion in Criminal Justice: The Tension Between Individualization and Uniformity,* edited by Lloyd E. Ohlin and Frank J. Remington, 73–134. Albany: State University of New York Press, 1993.

Resnik, Judith. "Detention, the War on Terror, and the Federal Courts," *Columbia Law Review* 110 (2010): 579–685.

Reyes, Belinda I., ed. *A Portrait of Race and Ethnicity in California: An Assessment of Social and Economic Well-Being.* San Francisco: Public Policy Institute of California, 2001. www.ppic.org/content/pubs/report/R_201BRR.pdf.

Rhodes, Lorna. "Changing the Subject: Conversation in Supermax." *Cultural Anthropology* 20, no. 3 (2005): 388–411.

———. "Supermax as a Technology of Punishment." *Social Research* 74, no. 2 (Summer 2007): 547–66.

———. *Total Confinement: Madness and Reason in the Maximum Security Prison.* Berkeley: University of California Press, 2004.

Richards, Stephen C., ed. *USP Marion: The First Federal Super-Max Penitentiary.* Carbondale: Southern Illinois University Press, 2013.

Robbins, Tom. "A Brutal Beating Wakes Attica's Ghosts: A Prison, Infamous for Bloodshed, Faces a Reckoning as Guards Go on Trial." *New York Times* (in collaboration with the *Marshall Project*), Mar. 1, 2015.

Robbins, Tom, and Lauren D'Avolio. "No Jail Time for Attica Guards: Brutal Beating Resolved with a Misdemeanor Plea." *Marshall Project,* Mar. 2, 2015. https://www.themarshallproject.org/2015/03/02/no-jail-time-for-attica-guards.

Rodriguez, Dylan. *Forced Passages: Imprisoned Radical Intellectuals and the U.S. Prison Regime.* Minneapolis: University of Minnesota Press, 2005.

Rodriguez, Sal. "How Many People Are in Solitary Confinement in California's Prisons?" *Solitary Watch,* Dec. 4, 2013. http://solitarywatch.com/2013/12/04/many-california-prisoners-solitary-confinement/.

Rosenberg, Carol. "Waste Wars: Captives 'Weaponize' Bodily Fluids." *Miami Herald,* June 18, 2011.

Ross, Richard. *Architecture of Authority.* With an essay by John R. MacArthur. New York: Aperture Foundation, 2007.

Rothman, David. *Conscience and Convenience: The Asylum and Its Alternatives in Progressive America.* Boston: Little, Brown, 1980.

Rubin, Ashley. "A Neo-Institutional Account of Prison Diffusion." *Law and Society Review* 49, no. 2 (2015): 365–99.

Sacramento Bee. "Fixed Prison Terms?" Apr. 16, 1975.

———. "Larson, Carl M., Oct. 25, 1936–Sept. 9, 2013." Sept. 17, 2013. www.legacy
.com/obituaries/sacbee/obituary.aspx?pid=167008350#sthash.qkX8NZ3g.dpu.

San Francisco Chronicle. "Former Inmate at Pelican Bay Wins Judgment Against
State." March 1, 1994.

———. "Pistol and Wig Experiment." Aug. 28, 1971.

Scarborough, Daniel P. *Incident at San Quentin: How a Pistol Was Smuggled into San
Quentin.* Pittsburgh: Dorrance, 2011.

Scharff-Smith, Peter. "The Effects of Solitary Confinement on Prison Inmates: A
Brief History and Review of the Literature." *Crime and Justice* 34 (2006): 441–528.

Schein, Edgar. "Man Against Man: Brainwashing." In "The Power to Change Behavior: A Symposium Presented by the United States Bureau of Prisons," *Corrective
Psychiatry and Journal of Social Therapy* 8, no. 2 (1962): 90–103.

Schept, Judah. *Progressive Punishment: Job Loss, Jail Growth, and the Neoliberal Logic of
Carceral Expansion.* New York: New York University Press, 2015.

Schlanger, Margo. "Inmate Litigation." *Harvard Law Review* 116 (2003): 1555–1706.

———. "No Reason to Blame Liberals (Or, The Unbearable Lightness of Perversity
Arguments)." Review of *The First Civil Right: How Liberals Built Prison America*, by
Naomi Murakawa. *New Rambler.* http://newramblerreview.com/book-reviews/law/
no-reason-to-blame-liberals-or-the-unbearable-lightness-of-perversity-arguments.

———. "Trends in Prisoner Litigation, as the PLRA Enters Adulthood." *University of
California, Irvine Law Review* 15 (2015): 153–78.

Schmitt, Carl. *Political Theology: Four Chapters on the Concept of Sovereignty.* Translated
by George Schwab. Cambridge, Mass.: MIT Press, 1985; orig. pub. 1922.

Schoenfeld, Heather. "Mass Incarceration and the Paradox of Prison Conditions Litigation." *Law and Society Review* 44 (2010): 732–68.

Schwartz, Mark. "The Testimony of Louis E. Tackwood." *Sevendays*, April 19, 1976.
Available from the Harold Weisberg Archive, Hood College, http://jfk.hood.edu/
Collection/White%20Materials/Informers%20And%20Provocateurs/Info-Prov
%20104.pdf.

Scudder, Kenyon J. "The Open Institution." In "Prisons in Transformation," special
issue, *Annals of the American Academy of Political and Social Science* 293 (May 1954):
79–87.

Sentencing Project. "Total Corrections Populations" (interactive map), www.sentenc
ingproject.org/map/map.cfm.

Shalev, Sharon. *Supermax: Controlling Risk Through Solitary Confinement.* Portland,
Ore.: Willan, 2009.

———. "The Power to Classify: Avenues into a Supermax Prison." In *Crime, Social
Control, and Human Rights: From Moral Panics to States of Denial*, edited by David
Downes, Paul Rock, Christine Chinkin, and Conor Gearty, 107–19. Devon, U.K.:
Willan, 2007.

Shames, Alison, Jessa Wilcox, and Ram Subramanian. *Solitary Confinement: Common*

Misconceptions and Emerging Safe Alternatives. New York: Vera Institute of Justice, May 2015. www.vera.org/sites/default/files/resources/downloads/solitary-confine ment-misconceptions-safe-alternatives-report.pdf.

Shane, Scott. "Accused Soldier in Brig as Wikileaks Link Is Sought," *New York Times*, Jan. 13, 2011.

Shapiro, F. *The Yale Book of Quotations*. New Haven, Conn.: Yale University Press, 2006.

Shay, Giovanna. "Ad Law Incarcerated." *Berkeley Journal of Criminal Law* 14 (2010): 329–94.

Simon, Jonathan. "From the Big House to the Warehouse: Rethinking Prisons and State Government in the 20th Century." *Punishment and Society* 2, no. 2 (2000): 213–34.

———. *Governing Through Crime: How the War on Crime Transformed American De- mocracy and Created a Culture of Fear*. New York: Oxford University Press, 2007.

———. *Mass Incarceration on Trial: A Remarkable Court Decision and the Future of Prisons in America*. New York: New Press, 2014.

———. *Poor Discipline: Parole and the Social Control of the Urban Underclass, 1890– 1990*. Chicago: University of Chicago Press, 1993.

Skarbeck, David. *The Social Order of the Underworld: How Prison Gangs Govern the American Penal System*. New York: Oxford University Press, 2014.

Small, Julie. "Under Scrutiny, Pelican Bay Prison Officials Say They Target Only Gang Leaders." KPCC [Pasadena, California], Aug. 23, 2011, www.scpr.org/news/ 2011/08/23/28382/pelican-bay-prison-officials-say-they-lock-gang-bo.

Smith, Philip. *Punishment and Culture*. Chicago: University of Chicago Press, 2008.

Smith, Wendy. "Holding On to Humanity." *Chronicle of Social Change*, May 26, 2015. https://chronicleofsocialchange.org/featured/holding-on-to-humanity/10860.

Spiegelman, Richard. "Review of the *Melancholy History of Soledad Prison*." *Issues in Criminology* 9, no. 2 (Fall 1974): 130–40.

Stanton, Sam, and Denny Walsh. "Was It Suicide? Questions Abound in Death of Pepper-Sprayed Inmate." *Sacramento Bee*, Jan. 21, 2014. www.sacbee.com/news/ investigations/the-public-eye/article2589344.html.

Stein, Mark. "'San Quentin 6' Defendant Spain Will Not Be Retried." *Los Angeles Times*, Apr. 28, 1990.

St. John, Paige. "California Agrees to Move Thousands of Inmates Out of Solitary Confinement." *Los Angeles Times*, Sept. 1, 2015. www.latimes.com/local/lanow/la-me -ln-california-will-move-thousands-of-inmates-out-of-solitary-20150901-story.html.

———. "California Proposes Isolation Units for Mentally Ill Prison Inmates." *Los Angeles Times*, Aug. 29, 2014. www.latimes.com/local/political/la-me-ff-california -prison-system-creates-isolation-cells-for-the-mentally-ill-20140829-story.html.

———. "Hugo Pinell, Infamous 'San Quentin Six' Member, Killed in Prison Riot." *Los Angeles Times*, Aug. 13, 2015. www.latimes.com/local/la-me-ff-inmate-killed-in -california-riot-20150812-story.html.

———. "Prison Hunger Strike Leaders Are in Solitary but Not Alone." *Los Angeles Times,* July 28, 2013. www.latimes.com/news/local/la-me-ff-ashker-20130729,0,1059923.story.

———. "Prison Investigators Name Two Suspects in Killing of Hugo Pinell." *Los Angeles Times,* Oct. 9, 2015. www.latimes.com/local/lanow/la-me-pc-prison-investigators-name-suspects-in-prison-killing-of-hugo-pinell-20151009-story.html.

———. "Slain Inmate Hugo Pinell Was a Target of Prison Gangs, His Lawyer Says." *Los Angeles Times,* Aug. 13, 2015. www.latimes.com/local/political/la-me-slain-prisoner-hugo-pinell-was-a-target-of-prison-gangs-20150813-story.html.

Stuntz, William J. *The Collapse of American Criminal Justice.* Cambridge, Mass.: Harvard University Press, 2011.

———. "The Political Constitution of Criminal Justice." *Harvard Law Review* 119, no. 3 (Jan. 2006): 780–851.

Suarez, Eliana, and Tahany M. Gadalla. "Stop Blaming the Victim: A Meta-Analysis on Rape Myths." *Journal of Interpersonal Violence* 25, no. 11 (Nov. 2010): 2010–35.

Sullivan, Larry E. *Forlorn Hope: The Prison Reform Movement.* New York: Richard Minsky, 2002.

Sullivan, Laura. "Doubts Arise About 1972 Angola Prison Murder." NPR, Oct. 27, 2008. www.npr.org/templates/story/story.php?storyId=96030547.

Sundt, Jody L., Thomas C. Castellano, and Chad S. Briggs. "The Sociopolitical Context of Prison Violence and Its Control: A Case Study of Supermax and Its Effect in Illinois." *Prison Journal* 88, no. 1 (2008): 94–122.

Sykes, Gresham M. *The Society of Captives: A Study of a Maximum Security Prison.* Princeton, N.J.: Princeton University Press, 1958.

Tapley, Lance. "Whistleblower Returns: Maine a Prison-Reform Model." *Portland [Maine] Phoenix,* Mar. 27, 2013. http://portland.thephoenix.com/news/153246-whistleblower-returns-maine-a-prison-reform-model.

Thelton E. Henderson Center for Social Justice, Berkeley Law. "Honorable Thelton E. Henderson." https://www.law.berkeley.edu/research/thelton-e-henderson-center-for-social-justice/about-the-center/hon-thelton-e-henderson.

Thompson, Don. "Parole Recommended for Former Mexican Mafia Chief." *Orange County Register / Associated Press,* Feb. 5, 2016. http://www.ocregister.com/articles/enriquez-703018-year-parole.html.

Thompson, Heather Ann. *Blood in the Water: The Attica Prison Uprising of 1971 and Its Legacy.* New York: Pantheon, 2016.

———. "Lessons from Attica: From Prisoner Rebellion to Mass Incarceration and Back." *Socialism and Democracy* 28, no. 3 (2014): 153–71.

———. "The Lingering Injustice of Attica." *New York Times,* Sept. 8, 2011.

———. "Rethinking Working-Class Struggle Through the Lens of the Carceral State: Toward a Labor History of Inmates and Guards." *Labor: Studies in Working-Class History of the Americas* 8, no. 3 (2011): 15–45.

Thuma, Emily. "Against the 'Prison/Psychiatric State': Anti-Violence Feminisms and the Politics of Confinement in the 1970s." *Feminist Formations* 26, no. 2 (Summer 2014): 26–51.

Time. "The Law: The Longest Trial." July 19, 1976. http://content.time.com/time/magazine/article/0,9171,914334,00.html (subscription required).

Tonry, Michael. *Sentencing Reform Impacts.* Washington, D.C.: National Institute of Justice, 1987.

Toobin, Jeffrey. "Letter from Baltimore: This Is My Jail." *New Yorker,* Apr. 14, 2014. www.newyorker.com/magazine/2014/04/14/this-is-my-jail.

Torrey, E. Fuller. *Care of the Seriously Mentally Ill: A Rating of State Programs.* Washington, D.C.: Public Citizen Health Research Group, 1990.

United Nations. "Solitary Confinement Should Be Banned in Most Cases, UN Expert Says." U.N. News Centre, Oct. 18, 2011. www.un.org/apps/news/story.asp?NewsID=40097.

United Nations General Assembly. *Convention Against Torture, Cruel, Inhuman and Degrading Treatment or Punishment.* Dec. 10, 1984. Entry into force June 26, 1987. United Nations, Treaty Series, 1465:85.

———. *International Covenant on Civil and Political Rights.* Dec. 16, 1966. Entry into force March 23, 1976. United Nations, Treaty Series, 999:171, Article 10. www.unhcr.org/refworld/docid/3ae6b3aao.html.

U.S. Congress. House. Committee on the Judiciary. Hearing before Subcommittee No. 3, *First Session on Corrections, Part II: Prisons, Prison Reform, and Prisoners' Rights: California,* 92nd Cong., Oct. 25, 1971, serial no. 15.

———. "Statement by Henry W. Kerr, Chairman, California Adult Authority." Pages 128–33.

———. "Statement of John Irwin, Associate Professor of Sociology, San Francisco State University, Accompanied by Lewis O. Sawyer and Popeye Jackson." Pages 87–91.

———. "Statement of Raymond K. Procunier, Director, California Department of Corrections." Pages 122–28.

———. "Table—Offense, penal code section—Statutory sentence, months to minimum eligible parole as of January 1,1970—Number and time served in prison before first parole, male felons paroled, 1965 and 1970." Pages 178–83.

U.S. Courts. "Federal Judges." www.uscourts.gov/Common/FAQS.aspx.

———. "Pro Se Law Clerks: A Valuable Resource." *Third Branch,* Apr. 2011. Available at http://content.govdelivery.com/accounts/USFEDCOURTS/bulletins/695a6.

U.S. Department of Justice. Executive Office for United States Attorneys. *United States Attorneys' Annual Statistical Report, Fiscal Year 2002.* Washington, D.C.: Government Printing Office, 2003.

U.S. Department of Justice. Federal Bureau of Prisons. "Merle E. Clutts." https://www.bop.gov/about/history/hero_clutts.jsp.

———. "Robert L. Hoffman." https://www.bop.gov/about/history/hero_hoffmann.jsp.

U.S. Department of Justice. National Institute of Corrections. *Supermax Prisons: Overview and General Considerations,* by Chase Riveland. Washington, D.C.: Government Printing Office, January 1999. www.nicic.org/pubs/1999/014937.pdf.

————. *Supermax Prisons and the Constitution: Liability Concerns in the Extended Control Unit,* by William Collins. Washington, D.C.: Government Printing Office, Nov. 2004.

U.S. Department of Justice. Office of Justice Programs. Bureau of Justice Assistance. *Emerging Issues on Privatized Prisons,* by James Austin and Garry Coventry (National Council on Crime and Delinquency). Monograph NCJ 181249. Washington, D.C.: Government Printing Office, 2001. Available from the National Criminal Justice Reference Service, https://www.ncjrs.gov/pdffiles1/bja/181249.pdf.

————. *National Assessment of Structured Sentencing,* by James Austin, Charles Jones, John Kramer, and Phil Renninger. Washington, D.C.: Government Printing Office, 1996. Available from the National Criminal Justice Reference Service, https://www.ncjrs.gov/pdffiles/strsent.pdf

U.S. Department of Justice. Office of Justice Programs. Bureau of Justice Statistics. *Census of State and Federal Correctional Facilities, 2005.* Washington, D.C.: Government Printing Office, 2010. Available from the Inter-University Consortium for Political and Social Research, https://www.icpsr.umich.edu/icpsrweb/ICPSR/studies/24642.

————. "PREA Data Collection Activities, 2015." NCJ 248824. Washington, D.C.: Government Printing Office, June 2015. www.bjs.gov/content/pub/pdf/pdca15.pdf.

————. *Prison Inmates at Midyear 2008,* by Heather C. West and William J. Sabol. Mar. 2009; revised Apr. 8, 2009. http:/bjs.ojp.usdoj.gov/content/pub/pdf/pim08st.pdf.

————. *Sourcebook of Criminal Justice Statistics Online.* Washington, D.C.: Government Printing Office, 2009. Available from the *Sourcebook of Criminal Justice Statistics,* University of Albany, http://www.albany.edu/sourcebook/pdf/t6802009.pdf.

————. *Use of Restrictive Housing in U.S. Prisons and Jails, 2011–12,* by Alan J. Beck. Washington, D.C.: Government Printing Office, Oct. 2015. www.bjs.gov/content/pub/pdf/urhuspj1112.pdf.

U.S. Department of Justice. Office of Legal Policy. Federal Justice Research Program. *Prison Gangs: Their Extent, Nature, and Impact on Prisons,* by George M. Camp and Camille Graham Camp. Washington, D.C.: Government Printing Office, 1985.

U.S. District Court, Northern District of California. "Senior District Judge Thelton E. Henderson." www.cand.uscourts.gov/teh.

Useem, Bert, and Peter A. Kimball. *States of Siege: Prison Riots, 1971–1986.* New York: Oxford University Press, 1989.

————. "A Theory of Prison Riots." *Theory and Society* 16, no. 1 (Jan. 1987): 87–122.

U.S. Sentencing Commission. "An Overview of the United States Sentencing Commission." June 2009. http://isb.ussc.gov/files/USSC_Overview.pdf.

Van Zuylen-Wood, Simon. "Pelican Bay Redux." *Nation,* Sept. 28, 2011.

Vargas, Dale. "Jury Convicts Folsom Inmate of Prison Murder," *Sacramento Bee*, Apr. 19, 1990.

———. "Stabbed Lawyer Ordered to Keep Defending Inmate," *Sacramento Bee*, Apr. 13, 1990.

Vargas, Dale, and Wayne Wilson. "Defense Lawyer Stabbed by Witness in Inmate's Trial." *Sacramento Bee*, Mar. 29, 1990.

Wacquant, Loïc. "Deadly Symbiosis." *Punishment and Society* 3, no. 1 (2001): 95–134.

———. *The Place of the Prison in the New Government*. Minneapolis: University of Minnesota Press, 2006.

———. *Urban Outcasts: A Comparative Sociology of Advanced Marginality*. Malden, Mass.: Polity, 2008.

Wakefield, Sara, and Christopher Uggen. "Incarceration and Stratification." *Annual Review of Sociology* 36 (2010): 387–406.

Wald, Karen. "The San Quentin Six Case: Perspective and Analysis." *Crime and Social Justice* 6 (Fall–Winter 1976): 58–68.

Walker, Michael L. "Race Making in a Penal Institution." *American Journal of Sociology* 121, no. 4 (2016): 1051–78.

Wallace-Wells, Benjamin. "The Plot from Solitary." *New York Magazine*, Feb. 26, 2014. http://nymag.com/news/features/solitary-secure-housing-units-2014-2.

Ward, David. *Alcatraz: The Gangster Years*. With Gene Kassebaum. Berkeley: University of California Press, 2009.

Ward, David A., and Alan F. Breed. *The United States Penitentiary, Marion, Illinois: A Report to the Judiciary Committee, United States House of Representatives*. Washington, D.C.: U.S. Government Printing Office, October 1984.

Ward, David A., and Thomas G. Werlich. "Alcatraz and Marion: Evaluating Supermaximum Custody." *Punishment and Society* 5, no. 1 (2003): 53–75.

Washington Post. "'Boxcar' Cells Eliminated." Apr. 21, 1978.

———. "Prison: In the Mind." Aug. 22, 1971.

Weidman, Mikel-Meredith. "Comment: The Culture of Judicial Deference and the Problem of Supermax Prisons." *UCLA Law Review* 51 (2004): 1505–53.

Weinrip, Michael, and Michael Schwirz. "Rikers Setting Stricter Limits for Isolation." *New York Times*, Jan. 14, 2015.

Weintraub, Daniel M. "Deukmejian Defends Buildup of Prison System." *Los Angeles Times*, June 15, 1990.

Weisberg, Robert, Debbie Mukamal, and Jordan D. Segall. *Life in Limbo: An Examination of Parole Release for Prisoners Serving Life Sentences with the Possibility of Parole in California*. Stanford, Calif.: Stanford Criminal Justice Center, Stanford Law School, Sept. 2011. www.law.stanford.edu/sites/default/files/child-page/164096/doc/sls public/SCJC_report_Parole_Release_for_Lifers.pdf.

Western, Bruce. *Punishment and Inequality in America*. New York: Sage, 2006.

Whitman, James Q. *Harsh Justice: Criminal Punishment and the Widening Divide Between America and Europe*. New York: Oxford University Press, 2005.

Wicker, Tom. *A Time to Die*. New York: Quadrangle, 1975.

Williams, Michael Vinson. *Medgar Evers: Mississippi Martyr.* Fayetteville: University of Arkansas Press, 2013.

Wilson, James Q., and George L. Kelling. "Broken Windows: The Police and Neighborhood Safety." *Atlantic,* Mar. 1982, 29–38.

Wilson, Wayne. "Prison Killer Gets 21-Years-to-Life Term." *Sacramento Bee,* Apr. 24, 1990.

Wood, Graeme. "How Gangs Took Over Prisons." *Atlantic,* Oct. 2014. www.theatlantic.com/features/archive/2014/09/how-gangs-took-over-prisons/379330.

World Prison Brief. "Highest to Lowest Prison Population Total." www.prisonstudies.org/highest-to-lowest/prison-population-total?field_region_taxonomy_tid=All.

Yale University, Class of 1964. "Class News: Stephen Bingham '64 Interviewed by *Marin Magazine.*" Jan. 2014. http://yale64.org/news/bingham1.htm.

Yee, Min S. *The Melancholy History of Soledad Prison.* New York: Harper's Magazine Press, 1973.

———. "San Quentin Probes Smuggling of Gun." *Washington Post,* Aug. 24, 1971.

Zimbardo, Philip G. *The Lucifer Effect: Understanding How Good People Turn Evil.* New York: Random House, 2007.

———. "The Stanford Prison Experiment: A Simulation Study of the Psychology of Imprisonment Conducted at Stanford University." Stanford Prison Experiment, www.prisonexp.org.

Zimring, Franklin E. *The Great American Crime Decline.* New York: Oxford University Press, 2007.

———. "The Scale of Imprisonment in the United States: Twentieth-Century Patterns and Twenty-First Century Prospects." *Journal of Criminal Law and Criminology* 100, no. 3 (2010): 1225–46.

———. "Sentencing Reform in the States: Sobering Lessons from the 1970s." *Northern Illinois University Law Review* 2, no. 17 (1981–82): 1–18. Reprinted in *Reform and Punishment: Essays on Criminal Sentencing,* edited by Michael Tonry and Franklin E. Zimring. Chicago: University of Chicago Press, 1983.

Zimring, Franklin E., and Richard Frase. *The Criminal Justice System: Materials on the Administration and Reform of the Criminal Law.* Boston: Little, Brown, 1980.

Zimring, Franklin E., and Gordon Hawkins. "The Growth of Imprisonment in California." *British Journal of Criminology* 34 (1994): 83–96.

———. *Prison Population and Criminal Justice Policy in California.* Berkeley, Calif.: Institute of Government Studies Press, 1992.

———. *The Scale of Imprisonment.* Chicago: University of Chicago Press, 1991.

Zimring, Franklin E., Gordon Hawkins, and Sam Kamin. *Punishment and Democracy: Three Strikes and You're Out in California.* New York: Oxford University Press, 2001.

ACKNOWLEDGMENTS

I first crossed the threshold of an American prison at age eighteen, as a college freshman and volunteer tutor. I no longer remember quite what I expected, but it was not what I found: students, mostly older than I was, who were, above all, human beings, with all the uncertainties and kindnesses that condition implies. As I researched this book, prison officials, too, disrupted my expectations. Often, we found common ground in our shared commitments to public service. I am grateful to the prison officials, legal experts, "justice" architects, and others who welcomed me into their offices, shared their personal histories, and helped me understand how hard it is to pinpoint just where our criminal justice system goes wrong.

Many people read this manuscript (several of them more than once) from beginning to end and commented on the writing, structure, and analysis: Melissa Barragan, Eleanor Blume, Dan Berger, Thomas Blair, Susan Coutin, William Frucht, Sam Houshower, Mary Katzenstein, Mona Lynch, Karen Reiter, and Franklin Zimring. Lisa Kerr, Ashley Rubin, and Emily Thuma each provided intensive feedback on a few chapters. These critiques challenged me to be more rigorous. Dan Berger was especially generous in sharing his expertise on George Jackson, the Black Guerrilla Family, and the Black Panthers. Susan Coutin graciously invited me to be her writing partner during the year that I drafted this book. Bill Frucht, who has been fostering this endeavor for more than five years, ultimately did something

I never imagined an editor would do in 2015: he read and commented on every line of this manuscript. Mona Lynch was the first person to read the manuscript from beginning to end, and she provided the same generous and insightful feedback I always treasure from her. Frank Zimring, who chaired my doctoral dissertation committee, has been an intellectual father to me; I aspire to achieve even a fraction of his rigor and relevance.

Countless others have read parts of this manuscript or commented on my research in journals, at conferences, and through lectures. I could not possibly name each of them, but I am especially grateful for ongoing engagement and dialogue with the following: Andrea Armstrong, Hadar Aviram, David Ball, Kitty Calavita, Colin Dayan, Alessandro De Giorgi, Sharon Dolovich, Benjamin Fleury-Steiner, Philip Goodman, Lisa Guenther, Craig Haney, Kelly Hannah-Moffat, Anil Kalhan, Paul Kaplan, Edith Kinney, Johann Koehler, Alexa Koenig, Daniel LaChance, Richard Leo, Chrysanthi Leon, Michael Meranze, Joshua Page, Paul Passavant, Joan Petersilia, Michelle Phelps, Nadya Pittendrigh, Tony Platt, Lorna Rhodes, Austin Sarat, Margo Schlanger, Lori Sexton, Tobias Smith, Jennifer Sumner, and Loïc Wacquant. In addition to this rich community of punishment and society scholars, I have appreciated being part of a community of inspiring writers, dating back to college. Jane Brox taught the first and only creative writing class I ever took. Miranda Mouillot, a friend and classmate whose book preceded mine, has inspired me to write persistently. Leah Spiro, my agent, and Maura Roessner, at the University of California Press, have both believed in this project from the beginning, and have been wonderfully encouraging.

I am grateful to the people at the University of California, Berkeley, who supported this project at its initial stages, when I first began to study solitary confinement and supermaxes as a joint J.D.-Ph.D. student in the Department of Jurisprudence and Social Policy. Franklin Zimring, Marianne Constable, Jonathan Simon, and David Sklansky served on my dissertation committee and have remained generous interlocutors for this project long after their obligations as committee members ended. Harry Scheiber was an honorary member of my dissertation committee; he advised on both grant applications and dissertation chapters, encouraged and supported my comparative studies overseas, and welcomed me into the community of American legal historians. In addition to my dissertation committee,

Lauren Edelman, Malcolm Feeley, David Lieberman, Justin McCrary, and Calvin Morrill were always available for critical feedback on chapters and grant applications. Meanwhile, Toni Mendicino worked behind the scenes to make everything tick. At the Institute for the Study of Societal Issues (ISSI), Deborah Lustig, David Minkus, and Christine Trost modeled engaged scholarship and provided years of committed mentorship. My cohort of ISSI fellows—Corey Abramson, Yolanda Anyon, Trevor Gardner, Anne Martin, Sarah Anne Minkin, and Alex Schafran—taught me to thrive on interdisciplinary dialogue. The Center for Race and Gender funded a Criminal Justice Working Group, which provided me with a community of friendly critics, especially Jeremy Bearer-Friend, Trevor Gardner, Nicole Lindahl, Karin Martin, and Sarah Tahamont. At the School of Public Health, Maureen Lahiff patiently oversaw every statistical analysis I conducted, and critically read much of the dissertation with characteristic grace. At the Human Rights Center, Kristin Reed first encouraged me to communicate about my research with the widest possible array of audiences. In addition to generous funding from ISSI, the Center for Race and Gender, and the Human Rights Center, I also received supporting funding while at Berkeley from the Youth Violence Prevention Initiative, the Doctoral Grants Program, the Department of Jurisprudence and Social Policy, the Center for the Study of Law and Society, and the Institute for Legal Research.

At the University of California, Irvine, where I transformed a dissertation into a book, I have been grateful to join a socially engaged and fundamentally interdisciplinary faculty. There, I have especially appreciated ongoing mentorship from Erwin Chemerinsky, Simon Cole, Susan Coutin, Catherine Fisk, Sora Han, Valerie Jenness, Charis Kubrin, Mona Lynch, Cheryl Maxson, Henry Pontell, Carroll Seron, George Tita, and Christopher Tomlins. The Center for Law, Society and Culture and the Socio-Legal Workshops have been especially inspiring sources of interdisciplinary dialogue and feedback. At UC-Irvine, this project received generous support from the Department of Criminology, Law & Society, the School of Social Ecology, and the Hellman Foundation Fellowship.

Outside the University of California, this research was financially supported by the Charlotte W. Newcombe Foundation and the National Science Foundation Division of Law and Social Sciences (Award No. 1061643). I have presented pieces of this book, and received helpful comments, at the following academic associations and conferences: the American Society of Criminology; the Association for the Study of Law, Culture, and Humanities; the American Society for Legal History; the Law and Society Association; the West Coast Law and Society Retreat; and the Western Society of Criminology. In addition, I have appreciated the opportunity to receive feedback at the Prisoners' Rights Round Table (at the University of Michigan and the University of California, Los Angeles), the Drexel Faculty Workshop, and the University of Toronto Penal Boundaries Workshop.

As an interdisciplinary scholar working at the intersection of history and criminology, I have been lucky to have generous friends and mentors in each of these fields. Among historians, I am especially grateful to Glenda Goodman, Patricia Johnston, Rebecca McLennan, Harry Scheiber, and Barbara Welke. Professor Welke, who led the Hurst Institute for legal historians in the summer of 2011, is a model of intellectual engagement and commitment to teaching. I am also grateful to the other 2011 Hurst Fellows, especially Ari Bryen, Mitch Fraas, Alison Lefkovitz, and Kim Welch, and to the Institute for Legal Research at the University of Wisconsin, which funded the institute. This work also benefitted greatly from conversations with Robert Chase, Norwood Andrews, and the other contributors to the *Sunbelt Prisons* anthology, funded by the Center for the American West at the University of Colorado–Boulder and the Clements Center at Southern Methodist University. In the early 2000s, Christopher Sturr and Steve Wasserman first piqued my interest in the history of prisons and American criminal law. Among criminologists, I am especially grateful to Todd Clear and Larry Sullivan for orienting me to the field and encouraging my academic goals.

Still others have been critical to the research process by helping me find obscure documents, connecting me to key informants, and brainstorming new approaches to questions. Jody Lewen, Michael Montgomery, Sara Norman, Donald Specter, Raphael Sperry, and Keith Wattley generously offered their substantial credibility—in prisoners' rights, correctional, and architectural communities alike—as a proxy for my own. Khym Penfil defended my interests as a university researcher against obstacles from the California prison system. Brian Williams, in the University of California, Irvine, library, has convinced me that I only have to imagine the existence of an interesting historical document and he can find it. Christoph Gielen, Denis O'Hearn, Claude Marks, Raphael Sperry, Carole Travis, and Beth Witrogen helped me track down images for the book. David Chernicoff provided technical assistance at several key points. Ted Conover's ongoing correspondence, along with his work, encouraged me at many steps of this process.

Two chapters of this book appeared in substantially different form in earlier publications: "Reclaiming the Power to Punish: Legislating and Administrating the California Supermax, 1982–1989," in the *Law and Society Review* in 2016 (incorporated into Chapter 4), and "Supermax Administration and the Eighth Amendment: Discretion, Deference, and Double-Bunking, 1986–2010," in the *University of California Irvine Law Review* in 2015 (incorporated into Chapter 5).

Willoughby Anderson, Cory Feldman, Jamie Rowen, Lena Salaymeh, and Megan Wachspress (and by association, Nathan Naze, who titled this book), all colleagues during various phases of graduate training, have inspired me as friends and scholars. Among many supportive family members, my parents, Chuck and Karen Reiter; my cousin, John Neffinger; and my grandfather, Bernie Reiter, encouraged me throughout. Bernie died, at ninety-four, as I was writing the last chapter of this book. He was the last survivor of six siblings who emigrated from Russia in the 1920s. His stubborn sense of justice continues to inspire me. My husband, Tom Blair, has been patiently engaging with the details of this project for more than a decade now, encouraging me when I wanted to give up and proofreading at midnight every time I faced a new deadline.

Finally, I am grateful to the people, incarcerated and formerly incarcerated, who inspired me to do this work: first as dedicated students pursuing high school and college degrees, and then as historians of their own traumatic confinement.

INDEX

Page numbers in italics refer to illustrations. Prisons listed are in California unless otherwise noted.

Adjustment Center (AC). *See* San
 Quentin State Prison
Administrative Maximum (ADX)
 federal supermax (Florence, Colo.),
 5, 57, 138, 237–38 n. 67
Adult Authority (parole board), 72–74,
 75–76, 80
Agamben, Giorgio, 223 n.117, 224 n.4
Alcatraz, 34, 88, 180, 237 n.67
Alejandrez, Frank, 177
American Civil Liberties Union
 (ACLU), 61, 74
American Friends Service Committee,
 38, 63–64, 67, 82
Ammiano, Tom, 60
Anderson, Vanita, 46–47
Anti-Terrorism and Effective Death
 Penalty Act (1996), 139
Arendt, Hannah, 5
Arkansas State Penitentiary, 38,
 227 n.49
Arrington Watkins, 105–6, 110, 113
Aryan Brotherhood, 39, 195; Ashker
 and, 6, 11–20, 26, 29, 195; Ernie

and, 184; Johnny and, 153, 154–56,
 161, 206, 209; Murphy and, 13, 15,
 16–17, 19; symbols of, 153, 184, 206
Ashker, Lewis, 11
Ashker, Todd, 10–20, 31, 131, 136; and
 Aryan Brotherhood, 6, 11–20, 26,
 29; and hunger strikes, 30–31, 54,
 60, 158, 185, 195–98; lawsuits filed
 by, 15, 22–23, 25, 32–33, 60, 169,
 196, 197–200, 202, 203; original
 crime of, 11, 12, 169; parole denied,
 19, 29, 169; sentencing of, 214 n.29;
 shot by guard, 22, 134; solitary
 confinement of, 28, 33, 35, 77, 93,
 121, 196, 198
Ashker v. Brown, 197–200, 202, 203
Asimov, Isaac, laws of robotics, 201
Askari, Kijana Tashiri, 182, 183, 199,
 203
Attica Correctional Facility (New York),
 3, 54–56, 58, 59, 67, 194, 203,
 232 n.122
Auburn State Prison (New York), 180
Avenal State Prison, 88

Beard, Jeffrey, 152, 198, 199, 200
Bentham, Jeremy, 108
Bien, Michael, 137
Billingslea, Fred, 43
Bingham, Stephen, 46–48, 50, 51, 91
"birdbaths," 25
Black Guerrilla Family (BGF), 2, 195;
    and Black Panthers, 3, 37, 39, 40;
    Jackson and, 3, 38, 40, 53, 54; W. L.
    Nolen and, 1, 37
Black Hand, The (Blatchford), 90, 91,
    118, 149
Black Panthers, 7, 126; and BGF, 3, 37,
    39, 40; Cleaver and, 45; and con-
    spiracy theories, 49–50, 56; Davis
    and, 44; and prisoner rights, 40–41
Blatchford, Christopher, 90, 149
Blonien, Rodney J., 71, 84
Boyle, Father Greg, 150
brainwashing, 180–81
Broderick, Henry, 125
Brodeur, Steve, 22
Browder, Kalief, 204
Brown, Craig, 102; and bond debt,
    95–98; on design model, 110, 116,
    118, 239 n.96; and lack of oversight,
    99, 194; on officer protection, 52,
    118; and Pelican Bay facility, 118, 141,
    194; on prison sites, 99–100
Brown, Jerry, 75, 76, 77, 88, 94, 151–53,
    169
Brown v. Allen, 218 n.18
burpees, 24, 25, 28

California: crime rate in, 117; munici-
    pal credit rating, 96; Proposition
    13 in, 96–97; Proposition 36 in,
    183–84, 185; sentencing system in,
    247–48 n.11; "three strikes" law, 79,
    183–84, 185, 208, 247–48 n.11
California Association of Judges, 74
California Correctional Institution
    (Tehachapi), 53, 104, 105, 113, 121, 199

California Correctional Peace Officers'
    Association, 74
California Department of Corrections
    (later Department of Corrections and
    Rehabilitation), 86, 150, 215 n.48;
    and construction of new prisons, 87,
    91, 94, 97, 98, 100, 101, 105, 112,
    116, 117–18, 235 n.31; court-ordered
    reforms and, 68, 104, 126; executive-
    branch oversight of, 234 n.18; head-
    quarters jobs, 102; and hunger
    strikes, 61, 195, 198; prisoner control
    methods, 110–12; and research data,
    167–68; and sentencing reforms, 75;
    and SHU population statistics, 32,
    142, 167–68, 170, 172, 252 n.32; and
    60 Minutes TV broadcast, 131; and
    suicide statistics, 163; and Todd
    Ashker case, 13, 16, 22; violent-death
    statistics, 93
California Institute for Men (Chino),
    47, 106
California Prison Focus, 195
California State Prison, Sacramento, 2,
    71, 201
California State Prison, Solano, 95, 99
Cambra, Steve, 21, 52, 83–84, 134
Canales, Dolores, 62–63, 82, 86
Carbone, Charles, 90
Carter, Jimmy, 125
Center for Constitutional Rights, 196,
    199, 200
Central Intelligence Agency (CIA), 180
Christmas, William, 45
civil rights movement, 7, 40, 41, 46,
    124
Clark, Ramsey, 72
Clarke, Harold W., 172
Cleaver, Eldridge, 37, 45
Clements, Tom, 193
Clutchette, John, 43, 48, 68–70
Clutchette case, 68–69, 72
Clutts, Merle, 57, 59

Coleman v. Schwarzenegger, 163
Coleman v. Wilson, 137
Colorado Department of Corrections, 193
Community Mental Health Act (1963), 164
Control and Rehabilitation Effort (CARE), 180–81
Cooper v. Pate, 218–19 n.18
Corcoran State Prison: construction of, 88, 104; gladiator fights in, 21, 31; guard brutality in, 21, 22, 138; paroles from, 168; SHU in, 4, 32, 105, 113, 134, 168, 174, 194
correctional officers. *See* prison guards
Cozens, Philip, 16, 17–18
Crescent City, Calif., 3, 5–6, 20
Criminal Sentences (Frankel), 65
crime rates: California, 117; and sentencing rates, 79, 231 n.119. *See also* tough-on-crime stance
Critical Resistance, 195
Cunningham, Mark, 36
Czifra, Steven, 62–63, 145, 181–82

Davis, Angela, 44, 45
Davis, Gray, 169
De La Beckwith, Byron, 124
Del Norte County, 99–102, 105, 118
Dershowitz, Alan, 229 n.84
determinate sentencing laws (DSL). *See* prison sentences
Deuel Vocational Institution (Tracy), 219 n.21
Deukmejian, George, 88, 94, 95, 99, 116–17
Dewberry, Ronnie Sitawa, 54
Dickens, Charles, 4, 179
District Attorneys Association, 74
Dortch, Vaughn, 21–22, 23, 31, 131, 164–65, 207
Dostoyevsky, Fyodor, 8
Drumgo, Fleeta, 43, 51, 69, 77

Dunne, John, 55
Duran, Joseph, 163

Eastern State Penitentiary (Pennsylvania), 4
Ebel, Evan, 192–93
Edwards, Cleveland, 42, 53
Effectiveness of Correctional Treatment (New York State), 65–66
Eighth Amendment, 23, 137, 140, 197, 218 n.18, 227 n.49
Enriquez, Rene "Boxer," 6, 90–91, 118–19, 121, 143, 145, 146–53, 156, 162, 166
Ernie (prisoner), 184–93, 197, 201, 203, 208
Evers, Medgar, 124
exercise, 12, 24, 26, 30, 59, 60, 69, 130, 132
exercise yards, 4, 19, 21, 27, 104, 106, 130, 139, 149, 156, 196

Fair Sentencing for Youth Act, 157–58
Fama, Steve, 71, 129, 141, 142
Farmer v. Brennan, 140
feces, smearing and throwing, 21–22, 131–32, 135, 158, 164–65, 215 nn.48–49, 246–47 n.48
Federal Bureau of Investigation (FBI): Cointelpro revelations, 50; prisoner informants, 6, 90, 119, 149–50, 152; witness protection program, 151
Folsom State Prison: hearing in (1985), 110–12; and lawsuits, 69, 101; lockdowns in, 53, 71–72, 105, 141; overcrowding in, 84, 103; SHU, 12–18, 23, 59, 104, 121, 158; violent years in, 14, 233 n.133
Foote, Caleb, 224 n.11
Ford, Gerald R., 74–75, 76, 84
Foreman, James L., 226–27 n.48
Fortner, Michael Javen, 83
Foucault, Michel, 6, 50, 109, 216 n.60

Frankel, Marvin, 65
Fromme, Lynette "Squeaky," 75
Fudge, Lewis, 111

Garcia, Jose, 133
"gassing," 215 n.48
Gilligan, James, 164
Gilmore, Ruth, 96–97, 231 n.119
gladiator fights, 21, 22, 23, 31, 35, 156, 166
Gomez, James, 131–32, 141
Gottschalk, Marie, *Caught*, 217 n.83
Grassian, Stuart, 131–32, 142
Grayson, Darryl, 128
Guantánamo Bay, Cuba, 60, 138, 215 n.49
guns, in prison: guards armed with, 19, 113, 118, 239 n.96; in Jackson case, 48, 49, 50–52, 221 n.73; shooting of prisoners, 22, 23, 34–35, 42, 48, 49–50; zip guns, 130, 133, 141

Hancock, Loni, 60–61, 86, 198
Haney, Craig, 66, 110, 142, 163
Harding, Gregory, 84
Hawkins, Gordon, 231 n.119
Hebb, Donald, 180–81
Henderson, Thelton E., 134–44; author's interview with, 143–44; career of, 124–25; and constitutionality of solitary confinement, 23, 123–24, 137–38, 139, 141–42, 197; and hunger strikes, 60, 61; influence of, 5, 6, 23, 128, 137, 139; and investigation of Pelican Bay, 23, 122–30, 132–33, 143–44; and *Madrid v. Gomez* case, 5, 31, 128–30, 132–33, 134–35, 136–44, 197, 202; and Pelican Bay oversight, 5, 6, 23, 136; prisoners' letters to, 4–5, 122–23; and prisoners' mental states, 134–35, 137, 142, 143, 165; and *Soul of Justice*, 128; and Spain's case, 125–27, 141

Herman, Jerry, 127
High Desert State Prison, 153, 154
Ho Chi Minh, 48
Homeboy Industries, 150

In re Medley, 140
Internal Classification Committee (ICC), 14–15
internal gang investigators (IGI), 14–15, 90, 149
Iowa State Penitentiary, 56
Irish Republican Army, 215 n.49
Ironwood State Prison, 152
Irwin, John, 224–25 n.11
isolation. *See* solitary confinement

Jackson, George, 6, 44, 45–52; alleged escape attempt, 2, 3–4, 34–35, 49, 52, 83, 125, 194; books by, 60, 64, 82; denied parole, 2, 37, 38–39, 64, 72–73, 169; discrimination against, 38–39, 65, 83; guards stabbed, 48, 49, 50, 53; initial crime of, 46, 54, 64, 169; killing of, 3, 36, 48–51, 52, 55, 59, 64, 67, 75, 82, 116; legacy of, 3, 52, 53–54, 55, 58, 61, 75, 82, 84, 121, 201, 202, 203, 232 n.122; legal team of, 46–48, 91; letters from, 36–37, 45; permanent isolation of, 53, 68, 72; politics of, 42–43, 44, 50, 54; reforms sought by, 40, 69
Jackson, Jonathan, 44–46
Jenkins, Nikko, 193
JLCPCO (Joint Legislative Committee on Prison Construction and Operations), 93, 94, 98, 100–101, 115, 116–17
Johnny (prisoner), 145–46, 153–62, 166, 183, 197, 203, 206–9
Johnson, David, 51, 69

Karlton, Lawrence, 137
Keene, Barry, 100, 101

Kelly, Warner, 56
Kennedy, Anthony M., 7
Kennedy, John F., 164
Kernan, Scott, 196
Kind and Usual Punishment (Mitford),
    65, 67
King, Martin Luther, Jr., 124
King, Robert, 56
Kirkland, Rich, 114–15, 116, 118
Kitchell Corporation, 105, 112
Kunstler, William, 55
Kupers, Terry, 181

Larson, Carl: author's interview with,
    51, 89–92, 149, 166–67, 196; death
    of, 86; influence of, 61, 62, 63, 86;
    lack of oversight, 194; and Pelican
    Bay, 3, 83, 92, 112–16, 118, 119–20,
    123, 141, 194; and planning for SHU,
    102–6, 110, 118; and prisoners' rights
    movement, 40, 52; on prisoner
    violence, 40, 53; prison jobs of, 47,
    102–3, 106, 113; on prison sentences,
    78, 83; and racial stereotyping, 83
legal endogeneity, 5, 212 n.15
Legal Services for Prisoners with
    Children, 195, 197
"lethal gun coverage," 113
lockdown (procedure): class-action law-
    suits about, 68–72, 138, 141, 233 n.133;
    effects on prisoners, 110–11; long-
    term, 5, 57, 59, 70, 111, 119, 138, 141;
    permanent, 53, 57–58; and restric-
    tions, 41, 47, 71–72; retaliatory, 5, 38,
    57, 138; as standard procedure,
    70–71; as tool of control, 40, 53, 111
lockups (facilities): expanded, 70,
    102–3, 111, 112, 138, 197; investiga-
    tions of, 71–72, 101, 105, 112; and
    reforms, 59, 68, 70, 71, 84–85, 111;
    for short-term isolation, 236 n.47
Los Angeles Police Department, 49,
    151

Louisiana State Penitentiary, Angola,
    56
Lucasville Penitentiary (Ohio), 57
Lynch, Mona, 110

Madrid, Alejandro, 128–29
Madrid v. Gomez, 128–35, 168; case
    closed, 143–44; changes as a result
    of, 5, 31, 136, 139, 145; and constitu-
    tionality of SHUs, 137–38, 139, 141,
    194, 202; judge's opinion in, 135,
    136–39, 141, 197; legal precedents
    for, 140–41; media stories about,
    130–32, 136, 137–38; original com-
    plaint filed in, 128–29; and Pelican
    Bay conditions, 130, 132–33, 134,
    136–39, 145; as precedent, 137, 139;
    and prisoners' mental health,
    143–44, 164; questions omitted in,
    142–43; trial in, 134, 135, 142–43
Magee, Ruchell, 45
Manson, Charles, 75, 229 n 80
Marquez, Robert, 149
Marshall, Charles D., 123, 128, 132, 141,
    194
Martinson, Robert, 65–66, 67, 76, 79,
    81–82, 84
mass incarceration. *See* prison
    population
Max (former prisoner), 20–21, 26, 28
McCarthy, Dan, 105
McClain, James, 43–45
McDonald, Terri, 197
Mendoza, Arturo, 114, 147
Merton, Robert, 7
Mexican Mafia, 6, 39, 90, 146, 148,
    149, 153, 195, 219 n.21
Miller, Alvin, 42, 53
Miller, Brent, 56
Miller, Opie, 42, 43
Miller v. Alabama, 157, 160, 207
Miller v. Overholer, 218 n.18
Mills, John Vincent, 43, 46, 49, 68

Mitford, Jessica, 65, 67, 76, 79
Montgomery, Michael, 148
Morris, James, 17–18, 19
Mule Creek State Prison, 163
murder rates: California, 14; United States, 74–75
Murphy, "Dirty" Dennis, 13–14, 15, 16–17, 18–19, 29

Nejedly, John, 74, 76
New Folsom Prison (later renamed California State Prison, Sacramento), 71, 104
New Mexico, 105, 138, 203; Department of Corrections, 138; Penitentiary of, 57, 138
Newton, Huey, 37, 50
New York, 39, 50, 54, 55, 65, 105, 164, 173, 182, 196, 202; first penitentiary in, 4, 179–80; supermax paroles in, 171
New York Civil Liberties Union, 204
Nixon, Richard M., 75, 84
Nolen, Cornel, 1
Nolen, Steve, 1, 41–42, 201
Nolen, W. L., 1, 37, 41–42, 44, 53, 67, 68, 82, 201
Norfolk State Prison (Massachusetts), 56–57
Nuestra Familia, 39, 195

O'Hearn, Denis, 11
Ohio State Penitentiary, 138
Oswald, Russell, 55

Page, Joshua, 52
panopticon, 108
Park, James (Jim), 47, 49–50, 51, 102, 116
Parnas, Raymond, 74
parole, 36, 72; board's discretion, 37, 64–65, 72–73, 75, 170, 174; gover-
nor's discretion and, 150–52, 169; hearings, 72–73, 150, 209; life without possibility of, 145, 146, 153, 157–58, 160, 209, 247–48 n.11; "parole, snitch, or die" to escape SHU, 15, 145, 162, 167, 170, 194, 195, 198; release directly from SHU, 168–70, 176, 192, 244 n.1, 247 n.6; restrictions on former prisoners, 178, 187; sentencing reforms and, 73, 75, 76–77, 78, 84; violations of, 228 n.69
Pelican Bay State Prison, 19–23; author's search for documents on, 87–89, 167–68; construction of, 60, 87–88, 99–110, 141, 194, 235 n.31; design of, 3, 4, 19, 21–22, 83, 91, 92, 109, 112–20, 123; double-bunked prisoners in, 133–34, 136, 142, 238 n.84; firearms in, 134; gang activities in, 90–91; guard brutality in, 4–5, 20–22, 122; hunger strikes in, 7, 30, 54, 82, 85, 158, 195–98; independent oversight of, 5–6, 23; judge's visits to, 129–30, 132–33, 143–44, 145; lack of oversight of, 92, 99, 130, 143, 194; lawsuits against, 129–30, 136–39; legislative sign-off for, 114–16; life inside, 10, 23–26, 28, 121–22, 176; and Madrid case, 130, 132–33, 134, 136–39, 145; opening of, 2, 3, 87, 88, 117, 121; paroles from, 168, 170, 175–79; prisoners transferred to, 19–21, 164–65; purpose of, 2, 6, 145; SHU, 2, 10, 23–26, 27, 29, 129–35, 136–39, 141, 145, 146, 148, 174–75, 177; unconstitutional procedures in, 23, 137–38, 139–42
Pennsylvania, 138, 172, 204; first prisons in, 4, 179, 204
Peoples, LeRoy, 204

Peoples v. Fischer, 204

Pinell, Hugo "Yogi," 6, 143, 203; death of, 1–2, 201; in San Quentin Six, 2, 51, 69, 121; in solitary confinement, 51, 53, 59, 68, 77, 121, 201

Plata v. Davis, 137, 144

plea bargaining, 80

populism, penal, 3

Portanova, Bill, 13–14, 16

Powell v. Alabama, 126

Powers, Michael, 133

Presley, Robert, 81, 92–93, 94–99, 112, 115–17

Presley Institute of Corrections Research and Training, 112

prisoners: abused by guards, 4–5, 20–22, 35, 43, 48, 55–56, 57, 65, 67, 119, 122, 131, 134–35, 136, 137, 138, 140, 163, 164, 227 n.49, 242–43 n.86; in "administrative segregation," 70, 84, 233 n.133; brainwashing of, 57; civil rights of, 38, 40–41, 64–67, 68, 69–70, 72–73, 76, 83, 90, 123, 126, 133, 139, 196–97, 205, 218–19 n.18, 227 n.49, 232–33 n.128; communication between, 28, 29, 30; death-watch for, 47–48; disciplinary subjects, 216 n.60; fights with other prisoners, 21, 133, 134, 142, 153, 156; habeas corpus petitions by, 139, 141, 218 n.18; hunger strikes by, 7, 30–31, 33, 54, 60, 61, 82, 85, 152, 158, 185, 195–98, 200, 201, 202; letters outside from, 4–5, 14, 119, 121–23, 148, 156–57, 182, 194–95; medical treatment for, 134, 143–44; mental health problems of, 131–32, 134–35, 137, 139, 143–44, 163–65, 202, 204–5; releases of, 83–84, 185–92, 193, 203, 250 n.46; requests and demands from, 55, 60, 73, 122, 157–58, 195, 197–98, 200, 204, 207; suicides of,

163–64, 195–96; trust accounts of, 25, 148; violence between guards and, 5, 24–25, 38, 40–41, 135. *See also* prison sentences

prison gangs, 90–91; and denial of parole, 2, 19, 29, 37, 39; and hunger strikes, 195; and indefinite solitary confinement, 6, 54, 123; internal gang investigators (IGIs) for, 14–15, 90, 149; and Latino heritage, 91; official monitoring of, 37, 39, 53, 195; rival killings, 148; validation procedures, 14–15, 54, 118, 136, 139, 142, 146, 147, 148, 155, 170–71, 184–85, 197, 203, 209, 213 n.19

prison guards: abuse by, 4–5, 20–22, 35, 43, 48, 55–56, 57, 65, 67, 119, 122, 131, 134–35, 136, 137, 138, 140, 163, 164, 227 n.49, 242–43 n.86; armed with guns, 19, 113, 118, 239 n.96; control sought by, 55, 73, 111, 201–2; fights with, 5, 24–25, 38, 40–41, 135; homicides of, 2, 38, 48, 50, 53; prisoners feared by, 55–56, 84, 91, 201, 202; safety, prison design and, 113; shooting of prisoners, 22, 23, 34–35, 42, 48, 49–50; union of, 52, 111, 116, 239 n.96; violence set up by, 21, 22, 41–43, 49, 156

Prison Law Office, 89, 129

Prison Legal News, 136, 137, 138

Prison Litigation Reform Act (1996), 139

prison officials: control exerted by, 5, 6, 23, 53, 64, 76–77, 82, 83–85, 137, 141, 142, 194, 201; discretion of, 14, 63–67, 71, 77, 78, 100–101, 136, 199–202, 212 n.15, 221–22 n.80, 233 n.134; and Jackson's death, 49–51, 52, 82; public relations stories of, 132, 133, 141–42, 194, 199, 202, 203; violence accepted by, 111 prison population: mass incarceration, 3, 7, 30, 81, 137, 219 n.25, 231 n.119, 232 n.122, 232–33 n.128; new prisons built for, 3, 92–93, 95–99; overcrowding, 12, 81–82, 84, 94, 103, 133–34, 136, 142, 234 n.6, 236 n.48, 238 n.84; race and, 39–40, 64–65, 79, 83, 217 n.2, 219 n.25, 232 n.122

prisons: costs of, 117–18, 159, 192; double-celling or double-bunking in, 70, 84, 113, 133–34, 136, 142, 238 n.84; health care in, 60, 134–35, 137; homicides in, 2, 38, 41–45, 48–51, 135; jobs in, 100, 101, 118, 231 n.119; lack of oversight of, 71–72, 92, 136, 202; reforms recommended for, 59–60, 61, 63–64, 67, 69, 77–78, 82, 84–85, 111–12, 199, 201, 202–5; social order in, 40; violence in, 56–58, 93, 94. *See also* lockdown

prison sentences: controlled by state legislature, 78–79; deference to victims in, 153; federal guidelines, 77; fixed or determinate (DSL), 65, 74–81, 83–84, 170, 183, 225 n.16, 229 n.86, 230 n.108, 231 n.119; increasing, 79, 81–82; indeterminate, 36, 37, 38, 41, 65, 67, 72–75, 83–84, 170; life without parole (LWOP), 146, 153, 155, 157; mandatory minimums, 77, 80–81, 231 n.119; plea bargaining, 80; and prisoner classification, 111–12, 145, 155; prosecutorial discretion in, 79–81; purpose of, 76; "three strikes and you're out," 79, 183–84, 185, 208, 247–48 n.11; unconstitutionality of, 157; unintended consequences of new laws, 7, 78–82, 85

Procunier, Raymond, 75–76
prosecutorial discretion, 79–81
psych tech, visits from, 26, 31
Public Interest, 66

Quakers, 38, 63–64, 67, 82

race, 39–41, 43, 45, 53, 54, 64–65, 66, 79, 83, 142, 217 n.2, 219 n.25, 232 n.122
Rashid (prisoner), 212–13 n.3
Ray (prisoner), 173–79, 201
Red Onion State Prison (Virginia), 172
Rikers Island (New York), 204, 246 n.40
Robinson v. California, 218 n.18
Rockefeller, Nelson A., 55
Romero, Gloria, 90
Rowland v. United States Dist. Court for Northern Dist., 227–28 n.55
Rushen, Ruth, 103, 126

Salerno, Michael, 74
Salinas Valley State Prison, 88, 154
San Quentin Six, 2, 51, 52, 67, 69, 121, 125, 126
San Quentin State Prison, 34–36, 58; Adjustment Center (AC), 43, 45, 47, 48, 49, 52, 68, 73, 84, 121, 138; Aryan Brotherhood formed in, 13; and class-action lawsuits, 68–71, 101; death row prisoners in, 35–36; isolation facilities in, 59, 84, 103–4, 121, 141; Larson's job in, 102–3, 106; lockdowns in, 53, 59, 105, 138; long-range plan for, 227 n.55; violence in, 35, 44–45, 125. *See also* Jackson, George
Scarborough, Daniel P., 47, 51
Schein, Edgar, 180
Schmitt, Carl, 223 n.117
Schneider, John Paul, 17
Schneiderman, Eric, 55
Schull, William, 43
Schwarzenegger, Arnold, 54, 169
Scottsboro Boys, 126
Seale, Bobby, 50
sentences. *See* prison sentences
Sentencing Reform Act (1984), 77

SHU (Security Housing Units), 103–4; cycling prisoners in and out of, 167, 171, 175, 199, 200–201, 203, 204, 205; design of, 104, *114;* paroles from, 168–71, 192; reforms to, 202, 209; unconstitutional operation of, 139, 194, 197, 200, 243–44 n.90. *See also* lockdown; supermax prisons
"SHU syndrome," 181
Silverstein, Tommy, 57, 59, 223 n.110
Simon, Jonathan, 137, 231 n.119
Sixth Amendment, 126
60 Minutes, 23, 130–32, 142
snitching, 146, 150–52, 155, 175–76, 245 n.6
Soledad Brother (Jackson), 60, 82
Soledad Brothers, 43, 44–45, 46, 48, 51; lawsuit brought by, 67–72
Soledad State Prison, 1; lawsuit against, 67–72, 69; lockdowns in, 41, 53
solitary confinement, 4–6, 172–73; constitutionality of, 23, 61, 67, 70, 121, 123–24, 137–39, 141–42, 197; indefinite and long-term, 7, 15, 23, 29–31, 53, 54, 63, 68, 70–71, 118, 138, 139, 146, 179–80, 200, 226–27 n.48, 242 n.81; institutional self-reporting of, 216–17 n.80, 242 n.81; investigation of policies, 60–63, 85–86, 197–98; mental deterioration in, 21, 26, 139, 180–81, 201, 215 n.48; numbers in, 29, 32–33; reviews of, 7–8, 198–201
Soul of Justice (film), 128
Souza-Baranowski Correctional Center (Massachusetts), 138
Spain, Johnny, 48, 51, 53, 59, 69, 125–27, 141
Spain v. Procunier, 69, 126–27
Special Management Unit (SMU) supermax prison (Florence, Ariz.), 5, 105–10, *108,* 112–13, 118, 123, 164, 172, 237–38 n.67

Specter, Don, 89, 129, 137
Stanford Prison Experiment (Zimbardo), 63–64, 66–67
Struggle for Justice (American Friends Service Committee), 38, 63–66, 67, 72, 76, 79
suicides, 163–64, 195–96
supermax (super-maximum security) prisons, 2–3; administrative subjects in, 216 n.60; constitutionality of, 137–39, 202; construction of, 60, 95–110, 138; design of, 83, 99, 104, 106–10, *108, 109;* effects of, 193, 194, 200; events leading to, 7, 52, 164, 203; first, 5, 237–38 n.67; funding of, 94–98, 100–101, 113; model for, 102–10; number of prisoners in, 29–30, 32–33; opacity of, 7, 32, 167–68, 200; "parole, snitch, or die" to get out, 15, 29, 145, 150–52; public attention to, 31, 202, 203; qualities needed in, 102–3; reconsidering, 203–5; special exemptions for, 98, 101, 235 n.31, 235–36 n.33; as "state of exception," 223 n.117; women in, 213 n.20. *See also* lockdown
Supreme Court, U.S.: and *Brown,* 218 n.18; and *Cooper,* 218–19 n.18; and *Miller,* 207; and Ohio State Penitentiary, 138; and *Powell,* 126; on solitary confinement, 180; and *Spain,* 126–27; and *Toussaint,* 68–69, 70

Talamantez, Luis, 51, 69
Talley v. Stevens, 227 n.49
Tamms Correctional Center (Illinois), 203–4, 205
Tanner, Robert, 13
Tate, Willie, 51, 69
Tehachapi. *See* California Correctional Institution
television watching, 10, 25, 31, 132, 159, 172

Texas, incarceration rates in, 81
Thornton, Terry, 172, 195, 200
"three strikes and you're out" laws, 79, 183–84, 185, 208, 247–48 n.11
Time-in-Cell report, 216–17 n.80
Tocqueville, Alexis de, 179–80
Toobin, Jeffrey, 54
torture, 4–5, 62, 179, 181–82, 196, 197, 204
tough-on-crime stance ("law and order" proposals), 3, 7, 75, 79, 81, 83, 84, 94, 99
Toussaint cases, 68–72, 89, 140, 141, 226 n.31, 227–28 n.55
Tracy prison. *See* Deuel Vocational Institution
transparency, 8, 62–64, 73, 85–86, 203
Troxell, Danny, 30, 196
Turner, Nat, 232 n.122

United States Penitentiary (Illinois), 57, 180–81, 237 n.67
Urban Street Terrorism, 149

Vera Institute of Justice, 203
Virginia Department of Corrections, 172

Wacquant, Loïc, 231 n.119
Wald, Karen, 50
Wallace, Herman, 56
Wallace, Mike, 131
Walpole, Mass., prisoner takeover, 138
Wattley, Keith, 2
Whitney, Elizabeth, 96
Wicker, Tom, 55
Wilken, Claudia, 197, 199, 200
Williams, Stanley "Tookie," 53–54
Wilson case, 71
Winter, Margaret, 61
Woodfox, Albert, 56
"worst of the worst," 11, 32, 33, 133, 141–43, 159, 169, 199, 203, 217 n.83; and "tougher than tough" guards, 21, 134, 138, 140
Wright v. Enomoto, 69–70, 89

YACA (Youth and Adult Correctional Authority), 99, 234 n.18
Youth for Fair Sentencing, 161

Zimbardo, Philip, 63–64, 66–67
Zimring, Franklin, 231 n.119
Zirpoli, Alfonso, 68–69, 71